ENGLISH COMPOSITION

CUSTOM EDITION

Taken From:
Self to Sources, Essays & Beyond, by Lee Brandon
and
Paragraphs & Essays, Ninth Edition by Lee Brandon

FROM SELF TO SOURCES: ESSAYS AND BEYOND
by Lee Brandon
Copyright © 2003 by Houghton Mifflin Company. All rights reserved.

Editor in Chief: Patricia A. Coryell
Senior Sponsoring Editor: Mary Jo Southern
Development Editor: Kellie Cardone
Editorial Assistant: Peter Mooney
Senior Project Editor: Kathryn Dinovo
Cover Design Manager: Diana Coe
Senior Manufacturing Coordinator: Marie Barnes
Marketing Manager: Annamarie Rice

PARAGRAPHS AND ESSAYS: A WORKTEXT WITH READINGS, NINTH EDITION
by Lee Brandon
Copyright © 2005 by Houghton Mifflin Company. All rights reserved.

Publisher: Patricia A. Coryell
Development Editor: Kellie Cardone
Editorial Assistant: Peter Mooney
Associate Project Editor: Shelley Dickerson
Manufacturing Manager: Florence Cadran
Marketing Manager: Annamarie Rice

Text credits appear on page 431, which constitutes an extension of the copyright page.

Custom Publishing Editor: Peter Nowka
Custom Publishing Production Manager: Tina Kozik
Project Coordinator: Christina Battista

This book contains select works from existing Houghton Mifflin Company resources and was produced by Houghton Mifflin Custom Publishing for collegiate use. As such, those adopting and/or contributing to this work are responsible for editorial content, accuracy, continuity and completeness.

Compilation copyright © 2005 by Houghton Mifflin Company. All rights reserved.

No part of this work may be reproduced or transmitted in any form or by any means, electronic or mechanical, including photocopying and recording, or by any information storage or retrieval system without the prior written permission of Houghton Mifflin Company unless such copying is expressly permitted by federal copyright law. Address inquiries to College Permissions, Houghton Mifflin Company, 222 Berkeley Street, Boston, MA 02116-3764.

Printed in the United States of America.

ISBN: 0-618-69596-6
N-05701

1 2 3 4 5 6 7 8 9 – CCI – 07 06 05

Houghton Mifflin
Custom Publishing

222 Berkeley Street • Boston, MA 02116

Address all correspondence and order information to the above address.

Brief Contents

Student Overview		xxiii
PART I	**The Writing Process**	**1**
Chapter 1	The Essay and Its Parts	2
Chapter 2	The Writing Process: Prewriting	24
Chapter 3	The Writing Process: Writing, Revising, and Editing	42
Chapter 4	Reading-Related Writing	66
PART II	**Writing Essays: Instructions and Reading Selections**	**95**
Chapter 5	Exemplification: Writing with Examples	96
Chapter 6	Definition: Clarifying Terms	124
Chapter 7	Analysis by Division: Examining the Parts	161
Chapter 8	Classification: Establishing Groups	189
Chapter 9	Process Analysis: Writing about Doing	220
Chapter 10	Comparison and Contrast: Showing Similarities and Differences	249
Chapter 11	Cause and Effect: Determining Reasons and Outcomes	284
Chapter 12:	Literary Analysis	318
PART III	**English Usage**	**353**
Chapter 13	Handbook: Writing Effective Sentences	354

Contents

Thematic Contents — xvii
Preface — xix
Student Overview — xxiii
    Practice with Principles   xxiv
    Strategies for Self-Improvement   xxv

PART I   The Writing Process   1

Chapter 1   The Essay and Its Parts   2

The Essay Defined   3
Essays and Documented Essays   3
    Student Essay: Lvette Lohayza, "Tamales, a Family Production"   5
    "Grandma always greets us with a freshly brewed pot of coffee and some dulce. The next eight hours will be a whirlwind of lively talk and cooperative work."

The Parts of an Essay   6
The Thesis Defined   7
Origin of the Thesis   7
Writing the Thesis   7
Forms of Support for the Thesis   11
Special Paragraphs Within the Essay   12
    Introductory Paragraphs   12
    Support Paragraphs   15
    Concluding Paragraphs   16
Basic Paragraph Patterns   19
Writer's Guidelines   22

Chapter 2   The Writing Process: Prewriting   24

The Writing Process Defined   25
The Writing Process Worksheet   25
Prewriting   26
    Freewriting   26
    Brainstorming and Listing   30
    Clustering   33

Composing the Thesis 34
Outlining 35

Writer's Guidelines 40

Chapter 3 The Writing Process: Writing, Revising, and Editing 42

Writing the First Draft 43
The Recursive Factor 44
Your Audience 44
Revising 45
- Coherence 45
- Language 47
- Unity 50
- Emphasis 51
- Support 52
- Sentences 54

Editing 56

Student Essay: Tanya, "Prison as a Community" 57
"Few free world citizens regard the California Institution for Women as a walled city, but that's what it is."

Writer's Guidelines 64

Chapter 4 Reading-Related Writing 66

Reading for Writing 67
- Underlining 67
- Annotating 68

David Orr, "Like, Whatever . . ." 68
"A national epidemic of incoherence is evident in public discourse, street talk, movies, television, and music."

Outlining Source Material 71

Supporting Ideas with Quotations and References 73
Basic Documentation 73
- Informal Documentation 73
- Formal Documentation 74

Documentation in Action 75
Types of Reading-Related Writing 76
- Single-Source Writing (Summary, Paraphrase, Reaction, Two-Part Response) 76
- Multiple-Source Writing (Synthesis) 82

Contents vii

      Student Essay: Lewan Huang, "Using More Than Laws Against Gangs" 84
      "Gang members are primarily males, but females often play the roles of enablers."

Essays and Applications 86

Cell Phones and Pagers—to Ban or Bless? 86

Gail Washburn, "Allow Cell Phones and Pagers in the Classroom" 86

    "In the future, there will be telephones on wristwatches, backpacks, notebooks. Will we ban them?"

Don Mack, "Ban Cell Phones and Pagers in Classrooms" 89

    "By their very nature, these gadgets insist on being the controlling attraction in the classroom."

Journal Writing 91
Career-Related Writing 92
Writer's Guidelines 92

PART II Writing Essays: Instructions and Reading Selections   95

Chapter 5 Exemplification: Writing with Examples   96

Surveying Exposition 97
Writing Essays of Exemplification 97

Characteristics of Good Examples 97
Techniques for Finding Examples: Listing and Clustering 98
Number and Order of Examples 99

Connecting Sources and Writing 99

    Student Essay: April McClure, "Prison Tattoos" 100
    "A woman named Shirley got born again and had a blood-dripping dagger on her arm covered up with Our Lady of Guadalupe."

Practicing Patterns of Exemplification 101

    Student Documented Essay: Jason Alford, "Biting My Tongue—Sometimes" 103
    "Complainers do not get written up in restaurants, but they may get zapped in other ways, ways that are also silent."

    Rebecca Barry, "Lessons from a Control Freak" 106

"*While conventional wisdom says that control freaks are brittle, authoritarian psychos, I think we're just trying to maintain a sense of order in our lives.*"

David Levine, "I'm Outta Here!"   110

"*Think about it. In some ways it seems perfect. Quit school. Just say No—no more pressure, no more stupid rules, no more deadlines, no more uncaring teachers, no more snobby, clique-conscious peers.*"

Kurt Wiesenfeld, "Making the Grade"   115

"*Then the e-mail assault began: 'I'm shy about coming in to talk to you, but I'm not shy about asking for a better grade. Anyway, it's worth a try.'*"

Wil Haygood, "Underground Dads"   118

"*I know of the cold statistics out there. And yet, the mountain of father-son literature does not haunt me. I've known good black men.*"

Topics for Writing Exemplification   120

Writing Process Worksheet   120
Source-Based Topics   121
Career-Related Topics   122
General Topics   122

Writer's Guidelines   123

Chapter 6   Definition: Clarifying Terms   124

Writing Definition   125

Techniques for Writing Simple Definitions   125
Techniques for Writing Extended Definitions   129

Connecting Sources and Writing   131

Student Documented Essay (Single Source): Vincent Sheahan, "My-graines"   131

"*'This is going to be a bad one,' I told myself as I shut off the lights, took my medication, lay down, and prepared for the inevitable—the relentless throbbing in my temple.*"

Practicing Patterns of Definition   133

Student Documented Essay (Multiple Sources): Michelle Proctor, "Perspectives on Motivation"   134

"*Three very good theories . . . give different perspectives on motivation: Darwin's Instinct Theory, Hull's Drive Reduction Theory, and Maslow's Hierarchy of Needs Theory.*"

Paired Sources on Bullying 137

Richard Jerome et al., "Disarming the Rage" 137

"Across the country, thousands of students stay home from school each day, terrified of humiliation or worse at the hands of bullies."

John Leo, "Bully, Bully" 144

"Bullying behavior may be 'verbal (e.g., name-calling, threats), physical (e.g., hitting), or psychological (e.g., rumors, shunning/exclusion.' . . . With a definition like that, the total of children involved in either bullying or being bullied themselves ought to be around 100 percent."

Paired Sources on Bosses and Workers, Good and Bad 147

Paul B. Hertneky, "You and Your Boss" 147

"Despite a tide of management books, seminars, and videotapes, and an invasion of MBAs, bosses will still be bosses."

U.S. News & World Report Staff, "Why Many Good Workers Turn into Bad Bosses" 151

"The empirical evidence shows you can go on for a long time using fear, intimidation and threat to get an awful lot of the behavior that you want."

Topics for Writing Definition 156

Writing Process Worksheet 156
Source-Based Topics 156
Career-Related Topics 158
General Topics 158

Writer's Guidelines 159

Chapter 7 Analysis by Division: Examining the Parts 161

Writing Analysis by Division 162

Organization 163
Sequence of Parts 163

Connecting Sources and Writing 164

Student Essay: Hsiao Chin Yu, "A Chinese New Year's Feast" 164

"In fact, to the delight of us children, my grandmother always hid some coins in the dumplings she gave us."

Student Documented Essay: Emmett Davis, "Elvis Presley: Twentieth-Century Legend" 165

"Dick Clark, producer and host of American Bandstand *for four decades, said that youth 'copied his style. People imitated his gestures, dressed like him, wanted to be him (or his woman).' "*

Practicing Patterns of Analysis by Division 167

David Bodanis, "A Brush with Reality: Surprises in the Tube" 168

"This seaweed ooze spreads in among the chalk, paint, and antifreeze, then stretches itself in all directions to hold the whole mass together."

Michael D. Lemonick, "Designer Babies" 172

"Before the new millennium is many years old, parents may be going to fertility clinics and picking from a list of options the way car buyers order air conditioning and chrome-alloy wheels."

William Helmreich, "Optimism, Tenacity Lead Way Back to Life" 176

"How, after experiencing . . . unspeakable cruelty in the Nazi death camps . . . were the survivors able to learn to live again, trust again, love again, and bring children into a world that had inflicted such pain on them?"

Joy Harjo, "Three Generations of Native American Women's Birth Experience" 179

"I felt as if I'd come full circle, as if I were watching my mother's labor and the struggle of my own birth."

Topics for Writing Analysis by Division 185

Writing Process Worksheet 185
Source-Based Topics 185
Career-Related Topics 186
General Topics 187

Writer's Guidelines 187

Chapter 8 Classification: Establishing Groups 189

Writing Classification 190

Selecting a Subject 190
Using a Principle to Avoid Overlapping 190
Establishing Classes 191
Using Simple and Complex Forms 191

Connecting Sources and Writing 194

Student Essay: Jolene Carter, "Types of Fly Fighters" 194
"I have discovered that there are three kinds of fly fighters: the shooers, the hiders, and the baiters."

Practicing Patterns of Classification 196
Student Documented Essay: Joel Follette, "Community College Pressures" 196
"At all schools, pressures do exist. They may come from different sources and arrive in different degrees, but they're out there."

Erica Manfred, "Coworkers from Hell and How to Cope" 199
"In every workplace, there are congenial, supportive colleagues. . . . and then there are the other kind—the ones you fantasize about while pummeling the punching bag at the gym."

Eve Golden, "Dangerous Curves" 205
"In fact, all of the women you're going to learn to avoid have some very attractive qualities, qualities that many men instinctively fall for. That's what makes it so critical for you to avoid them."

Franklin E. Zimring, "Confessions of a Former Smoker" 211
"It is vital that everyone understand the different emotional states cessation of smoking can cause. . . . [They are] those of the zealot, the evangelist, the elect, and the serene."

Glen Waggoner, "Shaking Hands" 215
"Extending an empty hand to show that you have no weapon, grasping another's hand to signify your human bond—you have to admit the handshake has impeccable symbolic credentials."

Topics for Writing Classification 217
Writing Process Worksheet 217
Source-Based Topics 217
Career-Related Topics 218
General Topics 218

***Writer's Guidelines* 219**

Chapter 9 Process Analysis: Writing about Doing   220
Writing Process Analysis 221

Two Types of Process Analysis: Directive and Informative 221
Working with Stages 221
Basic Forms 222
Combined Forms 223
Useful Prewriting Procedure 223

Connecting Sources and Writing 224

Student Essay: Brian Landry, "Guarding a Wide Receiver" 224

"As a cornerback, I finally discovered an effective process, one that begins with preparation before the game and ends with strategic action on the field during a pass play."

Practicing Patterns of Process Analysis 226

Student Documented Essay: Kay Eckert, "How to Obtain a Real Estate Listing" 227

"Strategically, I will make sure that our tour ends in the kitchen, because most important decisions in families are made at the kitchen table."

Adam Goodheart, "How to Paint a Fresco" 230

"You should already have extensive drawings for your fresco—these will be much sought by scholars and collectors in centuries to come."

Cynthia Joyce, "Six Clicks from Death" 232

"The first thing I did when I returned to work the next morning was search the Web for information on Bell's palsy—beginning a series of self-misdiagnoses that did more lasting damage than the palsy itself."

Garrison Keillor, "Attitude" 239

"Each player is responsible for his or her own attitude. . . . Spit frequently. Spit at all crucial moments. Spit correctly. Spit should be blown, not ptuied weakly with the lips, which often results in dribble."

Usha Lee McFarling, "Stars" 243

"A star starts out life from what seems like nothing at all. Stars are born in huge clouds of gas that are actually far less dense than the space immediately surrounding Earth."

Topics for Writing Process Analysis 245

Writing Process Worksheet 245
Source-Based Topics 245
Career-Related Topics 247
General Topics 247

Writer's Guidelines 248

**Chapter 10 Comparison and Contrast:
Showing Similarities and Differences** 249

    Comparison and Contrast Defined 250

    Generating Topics and Working with the 4 P's 250

        Purpose 250
        Points 251
        Patterns 252
        Presentation 253

    Connecting Sources and Writing 255

        Student Essay: Daphne Lee, "A Fast Food Face-Off" 255
        "Studying Wendy's menu, I found that, although many of the items are similar to those of McDonald's, Wendy's provides a wider selection, including some foods that wouldn't be considered fast."

    Practicing Patterns of Comparison and Contrast 258

        Student Documented Essay: Lydia Hsiao, "Struggling Against Silence" 259
        "In the same way Kingston allowed silence to '[paint] layers of black over [her life]' (254), silence continued to create a thicker darkness in my life. It first embarrassed me; then it soon robbed me of my self-esteem."

        Philip Kotler and Gary Armstrong, "The Baby Boomers and the Generation Xers" 261
        "Although they seek success, the Xers are less materialistic. They want better quality of life and are more interested in job satisfaction than in sacrificing personal happiness and growth for promotion."

        Suzanne Britt, "That Lean and Hungry Look" 265
        "Fat people are heavily into fits of laughter, slapping their thighs and whooping it up, while thin people are still politely waiting for the punch line."

        Mark Twain, "Two Ways of Viewing the River" 268
        "I had made a valuable acquisition. But I had lost something, too.... All the grace, the beauty, the poetry, had gone out of the majestic river!"

        Alice Walker, "Everyday Use" 270
        "[Maggie] thinks her sister has held life always in the palm of one hand, that 'no' is a word the world never learned to say to her."

Topics for Writing Comparison and Contrast 279

Writing Process Worksheet 279
Source-Based Topics 279
Career-Related Topics 281
General Topics 281

Writer's Guidelines 282

Chapter 11 Cause and Effect: Determining Reasons and Outcomes 284

Writing Cause and Effect 285

Exploring and Organizing 285
Composing a Thesis 286
Writing and Outline 286
Considering Kinds of Causes and Effects 286
Evaluating the Importance of Sequence 287
Introducing Ideas and Working with Patterns 288

Connecting Sources and Writing 289

Student Essay: Shandra Morgan (pseudonym) "Kick Me! Kiss Me!" 289

"Naturally I figured out it would be better to be hit with a flying object than to be pounded, so I learned to move toward whatever he threw."

Practicing Patterns of Cause and Effect 291

Student Documented Essay: Max Dunlop, "It's Time to KO Boxing" 293

"Boxing fans . . . say things like, 'That was a beautiful knockout!' They never say, 'That was a beautiful brain concussion.'"

Multiple Sources on Love, Marriage, and Divorce 295

Anne Roiphe, "Why Marriages Fail" 296

"Even though each broken marriage is unique, we can still find the common perils, the common causes for marital despair."

Ian Robertson, "Romantic Love, Courtship, and Marriage" 301

"Despite the cultural emphasis on love as something mysterious and irrational, the selection of marital partners is more orderly and predictable than romantics might like to think."

Lin Rolens, "Female Mea Culpa" 305

"Certainly there are some general things about women that men would do well to know, some things that seem to escape them."

Daniel Goleman, "His Marriage and Hers: Childhood Roots" 308
"Men and women want and expect very different things out of a conversation, with men content to talk about 'things,' while women seek emotional connection."

Topics for Writing Cause and Effect 313

Writing Process Worksheet 313
Source-Based Topics 313
Career-Related Topics 316
General Topics 316

Writer's Guidelines 317

Chapter 12: Literary Analysis 318

Why We Read Stories 319

Interpreting Narrative Literature 319

Writing About Literature 319

Setting 320
Conflict 320
Characters 320
Plot 320
Theme 321
Point of View 321
Analysis 321

Connecting Reading and Writing 322

Professional Writers: Reading Selections on the Theme of Love 322

Robert J. Trotter, "How Do I Love Thee?" 323
Achieving consummate love ... is like trying to lose weight, difficult but not impossible.

Irwin Shaw, "The Girls in Their Summer Dresses" 325
"I want to go out with my husband all day long. I want him to talk only to me and listen only to me."

Kate Chopin, "The Story of an Hour" 331
Knowing that Mrs. Mallard was afflicted with a heart trouble, great care was taken to break to her as gently as possible the news of her husband's death.

Anonymous, "Frankie and Johnny" 334
He was her man, but he was doing her wrong.

Robert Browning, "My Last Duchess" 337
That's my last Duchess painted on the wall, Looking as if she were alive ....

Student Writers   340
  Ajax Mylonas, "More Than Just a House Call" (demonstration with stages)   342
  If the author had written only about it [the event], the account would be no more than a news story.

  Gloria Mendez, "The Use of Self-Analysis"   345
  It is during this phase of the incident that the doctor joins the struggle at her level.

Finding Topics for Literary Analysis   347
Topics for Writing About Stories   348
Writer's Guidelines   351

PART III   English Usage   353

Chapter 13   Handbook: Writing Effective Sentences   354
Identifying Parts of Speech   355
Identifying Subjects and Verbs   363
Writing Different Kinds of Sentences   365
Combining Sentences   368
Correcting Fragments, Comma Splices, and Run-Ons   372
Working with Verb Forms   375
Making Subjects and Verbs Agree   381
Giving Verbs Voice   385
Selecting Pronouns   387
Using Adjectives and Adverbs   391
Balancing Sentence Parts   395
Mastering Punctuation   397
Conquering Capitalization   402
Improving Spelling   408
Correcting ESL Problems   416

Answer Key   421
Text Credits   431
Author and Title Index   433
Subject Index   437

Thematic Contents

The questions accompanying these five thematic groupings will help you understand some of the relationships among the sources and will also help you relate your own insights and experiences to the sources. Moreover, the questions will help you formulate topics for your reading-related writing based on a combination of your views and the ideas in the selections. Your writing may mix patterns of writing or primarily use a single pattern such as narration, cause and effect, or comparison and contrast. Keep in mind that even the most specific uses of single patterns are almost never pure.

Childhood and Growing Up

What in your childhood shaped you, limited you, or strengthened you? What still lives with you as childhood pivotal experiences? What lingers as memories, sweet or sour? How were the following authors affected in childhood? How does time change one's perception of events so that something that was once painful is now humorous or something that seemed slight then is profoundly important now?

"Tamales, a Family Production," Lvette Lohayza   5
"I'm Outta Here," David Levine   110
"Underground Dads," Wil Haygood   118
"Disarming the Rage," Richard Jerome, et al.   137
"Bully, Bully," John Leo   144
"Designer Babies," Michael D. Lemonick   172
"Kick Me! Kiss Me!" Shandra Morgan   289
"His Marriage and Hers: Childhood Roots," Daniel Goleman   308

Struggle with Dignity

Some people deal with adversity better than others. How do individuals in the following sources deal with difficult predicaments, the problems of their everyday lives, and the threat of death? What instances do you find of dignity, heroism, panic, resignation, and struggle? Do you have absolute definitions of *hero* and *dignity,* or do the definitions depend on the circumstances? Which of these sources is the most realistic reaction to a perceived hardship? Which is the most praiseworthy?

"Disarming the Rage," Richard Jerome et al.   137
"Optimism, Tenacity Lead Way Back to Life," William Helmreich   176

"Coworkers from Hell and How to Cope," Erica Manfred   199
"Six Clicks from Death," Cynthia Joyce   232
"Everyday Use," Alice Walker   270

Work

In what ways do work and the workplace define, limit, and change individuals? What can make life at work generally pleasant or unpleasant? Do the following sources remind you of any of your work experiences?

"You and Your Boss," Paul B. Hertneky   147
"Why Many Good Workers Turn into Bad Bosses," *U.S. News & World Report* Staff   151
"Coworkers from Hell and How to Cope," Erica Manfred   199

The Confrontational Society

What behavior or attitudes are obnoxious in society, and how are they related to freedom, respect for others, and responsibility? What is the most constructive way to complain? Or in some cases are the troubling situations mostly hopeless? How have you on specific occasions dealt with irritating situations?

"Allow Cell Phones and Pagers in the Classroom," Gail Washburn   86
"Ban Cell Phones and Pagers in Classrooms," Don Mack   89
"Biting My Tongue—Sometimes," Jason Alford   103
"Confessions of a Former Smoker," Franklin E. Zimring   211

Gender

Judging from the following reading selections, could one argue that a woman's life—social, work, and love—can be, in some ways, more complicated and difficult than a man's? How are men represented in the following sources?

"Three Generations of Native American Women's Birth Experience," Joy Harjo   179
"Dangerous Curves," Eve Golden   199
"Female Mea Culpa," Lin Rolens   305
"His Marriage and Hers: Childhood Roots," Daniel Goleman   308

Preface

Designed for use in either developmental or freshman composition courses, *English Composition* contains comprehensive writing instruction, a basic handbook, and abundant, engaging readings.

Writing Instruction

Writing instruction includes explanations, examples, and exercises at the sentence, paragraph, and essay levels, with concentration on the essay and the documented essay.

Chapters 1 through 3 define the essay and the documented essay, and explain the writing process.

Chapter 4 covers critical reading, summarizing, paraphrasing, and synthesizing. It shows how students can incorporate ideas from single and multiple sources into their essays and how they can critique or merely explain reading selections.

Chapters 5 through 12 present the patterns of writing exemplified by both the undocumented and the documented essay. This arrangement allows instructors, at any point, to choose an assignment with or without documentation, perhaps beginning with the simple personal essay and advancing toward a more complicated essay of documentation. It even permits the instructor teaching students with disparate writing abilities to mix complexities of assignments within a class.

Here is one available option for instructors using *English Composition:*

- Begin with simple undocumented essays that are related to reading selections in this book; the content in those essays should be parallel or clearly tangential.

- Progress to assignments of documented essays with closer textual ties to single sources, including a few references and a quotation or two. Use MLA style or informal acknowledgment of textbook sources.

- Continue with the assignment of documented essays, using thematically grouped reading assignments and perhaps asking students to find other related material in the library or on the Internet. Students would print out or photocopy the outside material and submit it with their assignments.

Topic suggestions at the ends of chapters include reading-related, career-related, and general topics so that instructors can specify one type or can mix types for class assignments.

Chapter 13 is a handbook that includes explanation, examples, and exercises. Answers to half of the exercises appear in the Answer Key, allowing for both classroom work and independent study.

Reading Selections

Selected as exemplary models of writing on stimulating topics, forty-two professional and twenty-three student essays are integrated with writing instruction. Numerous thematically grouped sources with guidelines allow students to consider different perspectives and to develop their own. Each of Chapters 5 through 12 contains both an undocumented and a documented essay by a student writer. The sources are culturally diverse and varied in subject material, so they will appeal to students of different backgrounds—generational, ethnic, gender, and regional—while stressing the commonality of experience. Cartoons by Buddy Hickerson support chapter themes and instruction.

Guide questions following the selections direct students to analyze the readings for form and to react critically to the content. Reading-related writing suggestions direct students to parallel experiences, evaluations, and analyses.

Special Features

- The best integration of reading selections and writing instruction on the market
- Reading-related writing instruction that helps students build confidence and skills with documented writing before working on a research paper
- Practical exercises in organization and revision
- Demonstrations of student essays showing the prewriting and writing stages
- Computer-related writing tips incorporated into the text
- A Writing Process Worksheet suitable for photocopying and intended to provide guidance for students and to save time and effort for instructors
- Extended instruction in writing the summary, paraphrase, and synthesis
- Sentence-writing exercises with material for individual and group work

Support Material for Instructors

The Instructor's Annotated Edition (IAE) contains immediate answers for exercises and activities, along with the following support:

- The Instructor's Guide (all parts included in the IAE)
- Reproducible quizzes for Chapter 13, Handbook, and many professional essays

Software Resources

- Houghton Mifflin Grammar CD-Rom for PC and Macintosh. Teaches and reinforces the basics of grammar, punctuation, and mechanics.
- Expressways, Version 4.0, for PC, Macintosh, and Windows. Guides students as they write and revise paragraphs and essays.

Acknowledgments

I am profoundly indebted to the following instructors who have reviewed this textbook: Dr. Catherine Packard of Southeastern Illinois College; Joanna Tardoni of Western Wyoming Community College; Kathleen Rice of Community College of Indiana; Carol Miter of Riverside Community College; Thomas Beery of Lima Technical College; Janet Cutshall of Sussex County Community College; Jill A. Lahnstein of Cape Fear Community College; Athene W. Sallee of Forsyth Technical Community College; and Julie Nichols of Okaloosa-Walton Community College. Thanks also to the faculty members at Mt. San Antonio College, with special recognition to the Basic Courses Review Committee.

I deeply appreciate the work of freelance editors Ann Marie Radaskewicz and Mary Dalton Hoffman, Nancy Benjamin of Books By Design, as well as my colleagues at Houghton Mifflin: Mary Jo Southern, Kellie Cardone, Anna Rice, Danielle Richardson, Peter Mooney, and Kathryn Dinovo.

I am especially grateful to my family of wife, children and their spouses, and grandchildren for their cheerful, inspiring support: Sharon, Kelly, Erin, Jeanne, Michael, Shane, Lauren, Jarrett, and Matthew.

Lee Brandon

Student Overview

Practice with Principles, p. xxiv

Strategies for Self-Improvement, p. xxv

Writing Process Worksheet, p. xxvii

© Tribune Media Services, Inc. All Rights Reserved. Reprinted with permission.

Practice with Principles

Some will tell you that to become a better writer you should practice. Others will say that to become a better writer you should learn the principles of writing.

Each view is a half-truth. If you practice without knowing what to do, you'll get better only within your own limitations; any bad habits are likely to become more ingrained. If you learn the principles of writing and do not practice them, they will never become a functioning part of your skills. Making that connection of practice and principles is now within your grasp as you gaze at a book with a well-rounded approach to writing. Combining sound techniques and ample writing practice, *English Composition taken From Self to Sources: Essays and Beyond* is designed for use both in class and on your own.

The subtitle might suggest two subjects to you. The word *beyond* refers to documented essays. Actually, essays and documented essays are quite similar. An *essay* is a group of paragraphs, each of which supports a single idea. A *documented essay* is the same, except that it includes some acknowledged content from another source or sources. The borrowed material may be as little as a single idea taken from one source in this textbook, or it may be many ideas pulled together into a research paper.

It is not difficult to incorporate the views of others into your essay. Moreover, the procedure for giving credit to your source or sources is easy. One premise of this book is that as you write some short documented essays during the first part of the course, you will become comfortable with the process. Later in the course, writing a longer documented essay, the research paper, will be merely the next step. The progression will be logical. The step will be easily accessible.

Each chapter in this book begins with a list of chapter topics.

Chapters 1 through 3 discuss the essay, the documented essay, and the writing process, including a detailed student example.

Chapter 4 explains reading-related writing: reading critically, underlining, annotating, outlining, note taking, summarizing, paraphrasing, synthesizing, evaluating, and documenting.

Chapters 5 through 12 focus on forms of discourse, commonly called patterns of development: narration, description, and exposition (explaining), as well as literary analysis. Each chapter includes a student essay and a student documented essay.

Chapter 13, the handbook, offers instruction in fundamentals, sentence writing, spelling, and ESL problems.

Strategies for Self-Improvement

Here are some strategies you can follow to make the best use of this book and to jump-start the improvement in your writing skills.

1. *Be active and systematic in learning.* Take advantage of your instructor's expertise by being an active class member—one who takes notes, asks questions, and contributes to discussion. Become dedicated to systematic learning: Determine your needs, decide what to do, and do it. Make learning a part of your everyday thinking and behavior.

2. *Read widely.* Samuel Johnson, a great English scholar, once said he didn't want to read anything by people who had written more than they had read. William Faulkner, a Nobel Prize winner in literature, said, "Read, read, read. Read everything—trash, classics, good and bad, and see how writers do it." Read to learn technique, to acquire ideas, and to be stimulated to write. Especially read to satisfy your curiosity and to receive pleasure. If reading is a main component of your course, approach it as systematically as you do writing.

3. *Keep a journal.* Keep a journal even though it may not be required in your particular class. It is a good practice to jot down your observations in a notebook. Here are some topics for daily, or almost daily, journal writing:

   - Summarize, evaluate, or react to reading assignments.
   - Summarize, evaluate, or react to what you see on television and in movies, and to what you read in newspapers and in magazines.
   - Describe and narrate situations or events you experience.
   - Write about career-related matters you encounter in other courses or on the job.

   Your journal entries may read like an intellectual diary, a record of what you are thinking about at certain times. Keeping a journal will help you to understand reading material better, to develop more language skills, and to think more clearly—as well as to become more confident and to write more easily so that writing becomes a comfortable, everyday activity. Your entries may also provide subject material for longer, more carefully crafted pieces. The most important thing is to get into the habit of writing something each day.

4. *Use the Writing Process Worksheet.* Record details about each of your assignments, such as the due date, topic, length, and form. The worksheet will also remind you of the stages of the writing process: explore, organize, and write. A blank Writing Process Worksheet for you to photocopy for assignments appears on page xxvii and 27. Discussed in Chapters 2 and 3, it illustrates student work in almost

every chapter. Your instructor may ask you to complete the form and submit it with your assignments.

5. *Take full advantage of technology.* Although using a word processor will not by itself make you a better writer, it will enable you to write and revise more swiftly as you move, alter, and delete material with a few keystrokes. Devices such as the thesaurus, spell checker, grammar checker, and style checker will help you revise and edit. Many colleges have writing labs with good instruction and facilities for networking and researching complicated topics. The Internet, used wisely, can provide resource materials for compositions.

6. *Be positive.* To improve your English skills, write with freedom, but revise and edit with rigor. Work with your instructor to set attainable goals, and proceed at a reasonable pace. Soon, seeing what you have mastered and checked off your list will give you a sense of accomplishment.

While you progress in your English course, notice how you are getting better at content, organization, and mechanics as you read, think, and write.

Consequently, you can expect writing to become a highly satisfying pleasure. After all, once you learn to write well, writing can be just as enjoyable as talking.

Finally, don't compare yourself with others. Compare yourself with yourself and, as you improve, consider yourself what you are—a student on the path toward more effective writing, a student on the path toward success.

Writing Process Worksheet

TITLE _____

NAME _____ **DUE DATE** _____

ASSIGNMENT In the space below, write whatever you need to know about your assignment, including information about the topic, audience, pattern of writing, length, whether to include a rough draft or revised drafts, and whether your paper must be typed.

PREWRITING STAGE ONE **Explore** Freewrite, brainstorm (list), cluster, or gather information as directed by your instructor. Use the back of this page or separate paper if you need more space.

PREWRITING STAGE TWO **Organize** Write a topic sentence or thesis; label the subject and the treatment parts.

Write an outline or an outline alternative.

WRITING STAGE THREE **Write** On separate paper, write and then revise your paper as many times as necessary for coherence, language (usage, tone, and diction), unity, emphasis, support, and sentences (CLUESS). Read your paper aloud to hear and correct any grammatical errors or awkward-sounding sentences.

Edit any problems in fundamentals, such as capitalization, omissions, punctuation, and spelling (COPS).

Part I

The Writing Process

1

The Essay and Its Parts

The Essay Defined, p. 3
Essays and Documented Essays, p. 3
  Student Essay: "Tamales, a Family Production," p. 5
The Parts of an Essay, p. 6
The Thesis Defined, p. 7
Origin of the Thesis, p. 7
Writing the Thesis, p. 7
Forms of Support for the Thesis, p. 11
Special Paragraphs Within the Essay, p. 12
  Introductory Paragraphs, p. 12
  Support Paragraphs, p. 15
  Concluding Paragraphs, p. 16
Basic Paragraph Patterns, p. 19
Writer's Guidelines, p. 22

THE QUIGMANS by Buddy Hickerson

TONIGHT BEGINS A 13-PART SERIES BASED ON A NOVELIZATION OF A MINI-SERIES BASED ON A PILOT FOR A MID-SEASON REPLACEMENT BASED ON AN IN-DEPTH EXPOSÉ ON REDUNDANCY!

© Tribune Media Services, Inc. All Rights Reserved. Reprinted with permission.

his book begins with the assumption that you have these questions about writing an essay:

- What do you mean by *essay?*
- How do I write an essay?
- How do I use sources in writing essays?

These questions are answered directly in the first four chapters. Chapter 1 defines the word *essay,* examines its parts, and provides an example. Chapters 2 and 3 discuss a system called the writing process. Chapter 4 addresses the use of sources in writing, with an emphasis on connecting reading and writing. All of this instruction is accompanied by exercises that will engage you in the most important part of learning to write well: writing itself.

The Essay Defined

Writing an essay is remarkably similar to other writing you have done. Whether you are composing a friendly e-mail, a job application, a customer complaint, an accident report, or a college essay, you are likely to follow a similar pattern. In some way, you will probably introduce your subject, discuss it, and end on a note of finality.

An essay is a group of paragraphs, each of which supports a controlling idea called a thesis. The length of an essay varies, but in college writing the number of paragraphs in a short essay is likely to be between three and nine. Many short essays are about five paragraphs long, often because of the nature of the assignment and time limitations, but there is no special significance in the number five.

Figure 1.1 shows the essay in its simplest form.

Essays and Documented Essays

You are probably most familiar with the simple personal essay, a relatively independent piece of writing derived from reflection or experience—for example, how you have been influenced by one individual or what you learned from a part-time job. Because it is based on your perceptions and contains no references to sources, it is called an undocumented essay or, simply, an essay.

However, as you move deeper into your college program, you increasingly will be expected to support your ideas by referring to sources, especially reading material. The result will be a documented essay or a research paper. That work will be either informally or formally

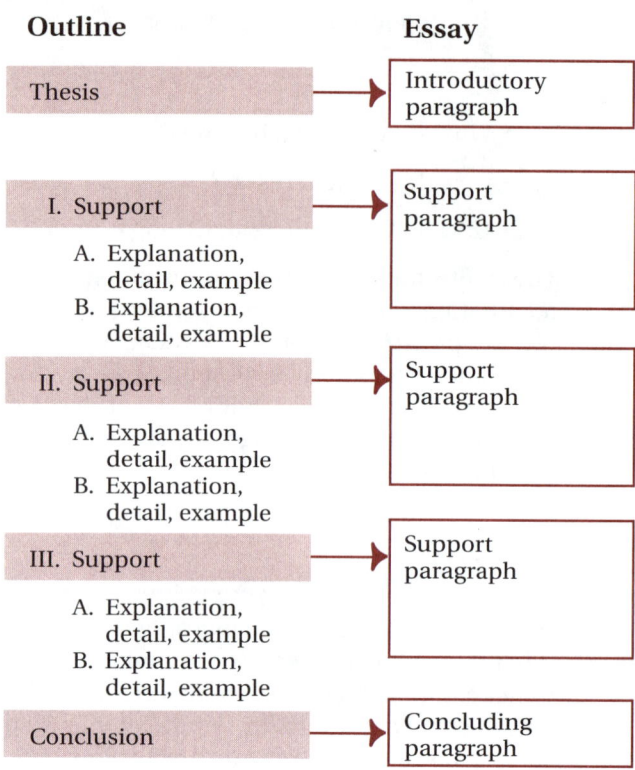

Figure 1.1
Essay Pattern

documented, meaning that you will indicate, in some way, where you found the ideas you borrowed.

The basic form of documented or undocumented essays is about the same, and is similar to that in the following example, although the number of support paragraphs may vary.

Student Essay

Student Lvette Lohayza wrote her simple personal essay in response to this assignment:

> Write an essay about how to do something or about how something was done. For example, you might write about how your family cooks and serves a special holiday meal. Placed within a cultural framework, it could interestingly provide information about both the process and the culture, blending the two.

The parts of the essay are marked to show the structure of both the essay and the supporting paragraphs.

Tamales, a Family Production

Lvette Lohayza

Thesis — Christmas Eve at Grandma's house is a joyous time, especially for the females of my family. <u>That is the time when we assist Grandma in making her wonderfully palatable tamales.</u> Beginning at daybreak and ending after darkness, it is an occasion of bonding and reunion. Grandma always greets us with a freshly brewed pot of coffee and some *dulce.* The next eight hours will be a whirlwind of lively talk and cooperative work.

Topic sentence — <u>Soon after our coffee, we drive off to a special market called the *mercado,* where Grandma leads us in shopping for the items we need.</u> First, we visit the butcher, whose name is Pepé. He is awaiting Grandma's arrival, as he does every year. He has put aside his freshest beefsteaks just for her. She carefully chooses the reddest and the most visibly fat-free meat available. According to Grandma, the meat must be bright red because that is a clear indication of its freshness, and freshness is especially what her tamales depend on. Next, we follow Grandma to an aisle where she examines piles of *ojas,* or corn husks, which are used for wrapping and cooking the tamales. We help her select and count out an equal number of large and medium husks. Then we stop at the canned-food section for what is known as *chili de las palmas,* a hot and spicy red sauce. Finally, we reach the section of the market that prepares and sells *masa,* a cornmeal substance for encasing the meat in the tamales. Shopping as a group has brought us closer together and reminded us of the complete annual event, which will now include the cooking and later will end at the dinner table.

Topic sentence — <u>As soon as we return, at nearly eight in the morning, Grandma, like a colonel, delegates duties for the first stage of our work.</u> A veteran crew boils the meat in black cast-iron pots, each large piece with a clove of garlic embedded in it for flavor. Several older women sort out the corn husks, large from medium, as the younger girls wash them and put them in separate stacks to dry on a six-foot table. By the time the husks have dried, the boiled meat is ready for shredding. With Grandma watching over our shoulders, the room is full of laughter and talk and enjoyable industry. Grandma herself sets two twenty-five-gallon shining steel pots onto burners and pours in about four inches of water. Then she drops in racks that will be used for steaming the tamales. Meanwhile, as the spicy aroma fills the kitchen, and the ambiance becomes ever more cheerful, we all gather around the table and shred the meat with our bare hands.

Topic sentence — <u>After the meat has been shredded, we mix it with chili sauce and olives and begin forming the tamales on the large table, where the dry corn husks lie in stacks of medium and large.</u> The first step is to use a butter knife to spread *masa* on a large corn husk. Next, **Support paragraph** we fork a couple of heaps of meat onto the *masa*. Then we add another generous layer of *masa* and cap it with a medium corn husk. Carefully, we roll the edges of the larger leaf over the edges of the medium leaf to seal the tamale, so that no meat or *masa* leaks out while cooking. This continual spreading, stuffing, and rolling of the tamales will go on for the next two to three hours.

Topic sentence — <u>Once all of the tamales have been rolled, they are carefully stacked in the large cooking pots and a wet hand towel is placed on</u> **Support paragraph** <u>top of the tamales to trap the steam while they are cooking.</u> Four to six hours of steam-cooking pass before the tamales are ready for consumption.

Concluding paragraph — By this time, we all have insatiable appetites and are ready for this well-deserved meal. Smiling broadly and listening to compliments as she takes orders, meaning requests, Grandma is the main server. The children, who have been peeking into the kitchen and begging for bites, are served at their own table. Standing in line with plates, the men are calling out the numbers of tamales they need to satisfy their prodigious appetites. The young men, who are, in their own way, part of the group effort because they provided valet parking as families arrived, follow their fathers and uncles in line. We females, independent as some of us may be most of the year, are fortunate in that we get to enjoy the whole process as team members with Grandma and family, and for that experience, the eating of the Christmas tamales is all the better.

The Parts of an Essay

The main components in an essay are the introduction, support paragraphs, transitions, and the conclusion.

- The *introduction* is usually only one paragraph that includes the thesis, which states the controlling idea.
- *Support paragraphs,* sometimes called the body, offer evidence and reasoning.
- *Transition paragraphs* are single, brief paragraphs that point out divisions of the essay. (They are seldom used in the short essay.)
- The *conclusion* provides an appropriate ending—often a restatement of or a reflection on the thesis.

The Thesis Defined

The six most important words this book can offer you are *State your thesis and support it*. It is not surprising, therefore, that the thesis is an essential part of your introduction and probably the most important sentence in your essay.

Origin of the Thesis

The thesis of an essay can come from different sources. You may generate it early on through prewriting, you may develop it from something you have read, or you may be assigned a topic. In any case, you need to work on your thesis statement—just that one sentence—until you have developed an interesting subject and a well-focused treatment. Your working thesis may differ from the one you finally use in your essay, but it can easily be reworded once you begin writing and revising.

Writing the Thesis

An effective thesis is one that can be developed with supporting information. *It has both a subject* **and** *a treatment.* The **subject** *is what you intend to write about.* The **treatment** *is what you intend to do with your subject.*

Example: <u>Glendora High School</u>   <u>offers a well-balanced</u>
           subject   **treatment**
<u>academic program.</u>

In some instances the subject will follow the treatment:

<u>The time has come for a national law legalizing</u>
            treatment
<u>physician-assisted suicide for the terminally ill.</u>
            subject

In other instances the subject will divide the treatment:

<u>Four factors establish</u> <u>Elvis Presley</u> <u>as the greatest</u>
   treatment   **subject**   **treatment**
<u>entertainer of the twentieth century: appearance,
singing ability, style, and influence.</u>

An ineffective thesis usually presents a treatment that is vague, too broad, or too narrow. It may also have a subject that is too general or too broad.

8 CHAPTER 1

Vague: The Santa Anita Mall is great. (The word *great* is
              ⎯⎯⎯⎯⎯⎯⎯⎯⎯⎯⎯ ⎯⎯⎯⎯⎯⎯⎯
                 subject   treatment
              imprecise.)

Better: The Santa Anita Mall allows me to purchase all of my
             ⎯⎯⎯⎯⎯⎯⎯⎯⎯⎯⎯ ⎯⎯⎯⎯⎯⎯⎯⎯⎯⎯⎯⎯⎯⎯⎯⎯⎯⎯⎯⎯⎯⎯
                subject   treatment
             clothing needs in one location. (The treatment specifies
             ⎯⎯⎯⎯⎯⎯⎯⎯⎯⎯⎯⎯⎯⎯⎯⎯⎯⎯⎯⎯⎯⎯⎯⎯
             something that can be developed.)

Too broad: Shopping malls have caused trouble. (The phrase
               ⎯⎯⎯⎯⎯⎯⎯⎯⎯⎯ ⎯⎯⎯⎯⎯⎯⎯⎯⎯⎯⎯⎯⎯⎯
                  subject   treatment
               shopping malls is general, meaning all malls, and the
               treatment is imprecise.)

Better: The development of the Santa Anita Mall contributed
             ⎯⎯⎯⎯⎯⎯⎯⎯⎯⎯⎯⎯⎯⎯⎯⎯⎯⎯⎯⎯⎯⎯⎯⎯⎯⎯⎯⎯ ⎯⎯⎯⎯⎯⎯⎯⎯⎯
                          subject   treatment
             to the decline of several nearby downtown retail centers.
             ⎯⎯
             (The subject has been restricted from all malls to one mall,
             and the concern is now specified as *development;* the
             treatment, *have caused trouble,* is made more specific.)

Too narrow: The Santa Anita Mall is located in Arcadia,
                ⎯⎯⎯⎯⎯⎯⎯⎯⎯⎯⎯ ⎯⎯⎯⎯⎯⎯⎯⎯⎯⎯⎯⎯⎯
                   subject   treatment
                California. (This is only a fact, something that can be
                ⎯⎯⎯⎯⎯⎯⎯⎯
                verified but not developed.)

Better: The Santa Anita Mall was built at a location
             ⎯⎯⎯⎯⎯⎯⎯⎯⎯⎯⎯ ⎯⎯⎯⎯⎯⎯⎯⎯⎯⎯⎯⎯⎯⎯⎯
                subject   treatment
             highly accessible to urban shoppers. (This adjustment
             ⎯⎯⎯⎯⎯⎯⎯⎯⎯⎯⎯⎯⎯⎯⎯⎯⎯⎯⎯⎯⎯⎯⎯⎯⎯⎯
             indicates that the location is highly important to urban
             shoppers, an idea that can be developed.)

Exercise 1 EVALUATING THESES

In the following theses, underline and label the subjects (S) and treatments (T). Also judge each one as effective (E) or ineffective (I).

Example:

___I___ *Moby Dick* is an interesting book.
          ⎯⎯⎯⎯⎯⎯⎯ ⎯⎯⎯⎯⎯⎯⎯⎯⎯⎯⎯⎯⎯⎯⎯⎯⎯⎯
             S   T

_____ 1. Pop music is a reflection of contemporary values.
                 ⎯⎯⎯⎯⎯⎯⎯⎯ ⎯⎯⎯⎯⎯⎯⎯⎯⎯⎯⎯⎯⎯⎯⎯⎯⎯⎯⎯⎯⎯⎯⎯⎯⎯⎯
                    S   T

_____ 2. William Faulkner was born in Mississippi.
                 ⎯⎯⎯⎯⎯⎯⎯⎯⎯⎯⎯⎯⎯⎯ ⎯⎯⎯⎯⎯⎯⎯⎯⎯⎯⎯⎯⎯⎯⎯⎯⎯⎯⎯⎯
                        S   T

_____ 3. Education has value beyond money.
         S   T

_____ 4. Hope is not the same as expectation.
         S   T

_____ 5. Individuals do not have the right to select the laws they
            S   T
         will obey.

_____ 6. I was born in Brooklyn.
         S   T

_____ 7. Greece has a long history.
         S   T

_____ 8. Sacramento is the capital of California.
         S   T

_____ 9. Knowledge is not the same as wisdom.
         S   T

_____ 10. The history of organically grown foods is fascinating.
              S   T

Exercise 2 — EVALUATING THESES

Complete the following entries to make each one an effective thesis.

1. Puppy love is based on _____

2. Sports at the professional level are becoming _____

3. Tattoos are more expensive to remove *and are often times very painful*

4. Heredity and environment are both important in _____

5. Exercise can become *a daily part of our lives*

6. Toxic waste occurs in _____

7. Television commercials are often *aimed at young children*

8. People who grow up economically deprived _____

9. My unreasonable boss gave me _____

10. My part-time job has taught me _____

Exercise 3 — WRITING THESES

For each subject, add a treatment to create an effective thesis. You may also restrict or alter the subject by making it more specific. The subject need not be the first word in your thesis.

1. Cell phones _are the_ _____

2. Skateboards _can cause numerous_ _____

3. SUVs _____

4. Madonna _____

5. Elvis _____

6. Human clones _____

7. Textbooks _____

8. Truthfulness _____

9. Humor _____

10. Divorce _____

Forms of Support for the Thesis

Some essay assignments benefit from a rich combination of supporting forms for the organization of content. Others require an emphasis on a particular form, as instructors ask students to discuss causes, to show effects, to argue a position, to examine parts of a whole unit, to define concepts, to explain a process, to compare ideas, and so on. Those particular forms will be our main concern in this book. The following basic outlines show some of the most common ways for dividing and organizing ideas. Keep in mind that these are only frameworks for essays and that, in writing, forms will overlap in varying degrees. For instance, you might be comparing and contrasting ideas, but you could still use examples, description, and definitions for further support. In the outlines, each Roman numeral heading represents one or more paragraphs of support. Although the outlines are, by their nature, mechanical, the well-written finished essay submerges the form in flowing content.

- *Narration:* division of time or incident to tell a story
    I. Situation
    II. Conflict
    III. Struggle
    IV. Outcome
    V. Meaning

- *Exemplification:* division into several examples or sets of examples
    I. First example (or a set of examples)
    II. Second example (or a set of examples)
    III. Third example (or a set of examples)

- *Process analysis:* division into steps, telling how something is done (the form used in the student essay on pp. 5–6)
    I. Preparation
    II. Steps
        A. Step 1
        B. Step 2
        C. Step 3

- *Analysis by division:* division of a unit into parts (for example, an essay has an introduction, development of a thesis, and a conclusion).
    I. First part
    II. Second part
    III. Third part

- *Causes and effects:* division into causes or effects
    I. Cause (or effect) one
    II. Cause (or effect) two
    III. Cause (or effect) three

These forms, as well as description, classification, comparison and contrast, definition, and argument are the subjects of individual chapters in this book.

Special Paragraphs Within the Essay

Understanding the function and structure of the three main components of an essay—paragraphs of introduction, support, and conclusion—will help you in both planning and writing your assignments.

Introductory Paragraphs

A good introductory paragraph does many things. It attracts the reader's interest, states or points toward the thesis, and moves the reader smoothly into the support, or developmental, paragraphs. Introductory methods include

- a direct statement of the thesis
- background
- definition of term(s)
- quotation(s)
- a shocking statement
- question(s)
- a combination of two or more methods in this list

You should not decide that some of the methods are good and some are bad. Indeed, all are valid, and the most common one is the last, the combination. Use the approach that best fits each essay. Resist the temptation to use the same kind of introduction in every essay you write.

Each of the following statements is an introductory paragraph. The thesis is the same in all of them, yet each uses a different introductory method. Notice the great variety here.

Direct Statement of the Thesis:

Anyone on the road in any city near midnight on Friday and Saturday is among dangerous people. They're not the product of the witching hour; they're the product of the "happy hour."

The Essay and Its Parts

Subject
Treatment

They're called drunk drivers. <u>These threats to our lives and limbs need to be controlled by federal laws with strong provisions.</u>

Background:

In one four-year period in California (1995–1998), 15,363 people were injured and 5,954 were killed by drunk drivers. Each year, the same kinds of figures come in from all our states. The state laws vary. The federal government does virtually nothing. Drunk driving has reached the point of being a national problem of huge proportions. <u>This slaughter of innocent citizens should be stopped by following the lead of many other nations and passing federal legislation with strong provisions.</u>

Subject
Treatment

Definition of Terms:

Here's a recipe. Take two thousand pounds of plastic, rubber, and steel, pour in ten gallons of gas, and start the engine. Then take one human being of two hundred pounds of flesh, blood, and bones, pour in two glasses of beer in one hour, and put him or her behind the wheel. Mix the two together, and the result may be a drunken driver ready to cause death and destruction. <u>This problem of drunk driving can and should be controlled by federal legislation with strong provisions.</u>

Subject
Treatment

Quotation:

The National Highway Traffic Safety Administration has stated that 50 percent of all fatal accidents involve intoxicated drivers and that "75 percent of those drivers have a blood alcohol content of .10 percent or greater." That kind of information is widely known, yet the carnage on the highways continues. <u>This problem of drunk driving should be addressed by a federal law with strict provisions.</u>

Subject
Treatment

Shocking Statement and Questions:

Almost 60,000 Americans were killed in the Vietnam War. What other war kills more than that number every four years? Give up? It's the war with drunk drivers. The war in Vietnam ended about three decades ago, but our DUI war goes on, and the drunks are winning. <u>This deadly conflict should be controlled by a federal law with strong provisions.</u>

Subject
Treatment

Questions and a Definition:

What is a drunk driver? In California it's a person with a blood alcohol content of .08 percent or more who is operating a motor vehicle. What do those drivers do? Some of them kill. Every year more than 16,000 people nationwide die. Those are easy ques-

Subject Treatment

tions. The difficult one is, What can be done? One answer is clear: <u>Drunk drivers</u> <u>should be controlled by federal laws with strong provisions.</u>

All these introductory methods are effective. Some others, however, are ineffective because they are too vague to carry the thesis or because they carry the thesis in a mechanical way. The mechanical approach may be direct and explicit, but it usually numbs the reader's imagination and interest.

Avoid: The purpose of this essay is to write about the need for strong national laws against drunk driving.

Avoid: I will now write a paper about the need for strong national laws against drunk driving.

The length of an introduction can vary, but the typical length for the introductory paragraph of a student essay is three to five sentences. If your introduction is shorter than three sentences, be certain that it conveys all that you want to say. If it is longer than five, be certain that it only introduces and does not try to expand on ideas. That function is reserved for the developmental paragraphs; a long and complicated introduction may make your essay top-heavy.

Exercise 4 — WRITING AN INTRODUCTION

Pick one of the following theses (altering it a bit to suit your own ideas, if you like) and write at least two introductions for it, using a different method for each one. Underline the thesis in each paragraph, and label the subject and treatment parts.

1. Owning a home makes more sense than renting an apartment.
2. The extent of student cheating is unknown by most instructors.
3. Much sexual harassment goes unreported for understandable reasons.
4. Hunting is not regarded as a sport by animals in the wild.
5. Balancing parts of one's life is a major problem for most students I know.
6. Fanatics are troubled people, even if they are engaged in worthwhile concerns.
7. Heroes exist in everyday life.
8. The ethnic makeup of my neighborhood has changed in the last ten years.

9. Getting a job at _____ is a matter of following certain guidelines.

10. A career choice should be based on factors other than money.

Support Paragraphs

Support paragraphs, also called developmental paragraphs, form the body of an essay and provide information and reasoning that justify the thesis contained in the paragraph of introduction.

The following paragraph is both a definition and an example of the developmental paragraph:

Topic sentence

Support
Support

Support

<u>The developmental paragraph contains three parts: the subject, the topic sentence, and the support.</u> The *subject* is what you will write about. It is likely to be broad and must be focused or qualified for specific treatment. The *topic sentence* contains both the subject and the treatment—what you will do with the subject. It carries the central idea to which everything else in the paragraph is subordinated. For example, the first sentence of this paragraph is a topic sentence. Even when not stated, the topic sentence as an underlying idea unifies the paragraph. The *support* is the evidence or reasoning by which a topic sentence is developed. It comes in several basic patterns and serves any of

the four forms of expression: narration, description, exposition, and argumentation. These forms, which are usually combined in writing, will be presented with both student and professional examples in the following chapters. <u>The developmental paragraph, therefore, is a group of sentences, each with the function of supporting a controlling idea called the topic sentence.</u>

Concluding sentence [margin note]

Concluding Paragraphs

Your concluding paragraph should give the reader the feeling that you have said all you want to say about your subject. Like introductory paragraphs, concluding paragraphs are of various types. Here are some effective ways of concluding an essay:

- Conclude with a final paragraph or sentence that is a logical part of the body of the essay; that is, it functions as part of the support. In the following example, there is no formal conclusion. This form is more common in the published essay than in the student essay.

    One day he hit me. He said he was sorry and even cried, but I could not forgive him. We got a divorce. It took me a while before I could look back and see what the causes really were, but by then it was too late to make any changes.

Maria Campos, "A Divorce with Reasons" [margin note]

- Conclude with a restatement of the thesis in slightly different words, perhaps pointing out its significance and/or making applications.

    Don't blame it on the referee. Don't even blame it on the fight managers. Put the blame where it belongs—on the prevailing mores that regard prize fighting as a perfectly proper enterprise and vehicle of entertainment. No one doubts that many people enjoy prize fighting and will miss it if it should be thrown out. And that is precisely the point.

Norman Cousins, "Who Killed Benny Paret?" [margin note]

- Conclude with a review of the main points of the discussion—a kind of summary. This is appropriate only if the complexity of the essay makes a summary necessary.

    As we have been made all too aware lately in this country, the more energy we conserve now, the more we'll have for the future. The same holds true for skiing. So take the Soft Path of energy conservation as you ski. You'll not only be able to make longer nonstop runs, but you'll have more energy to burn on the dance floor.

Carl Wingus, "Conserving Energy as You Ski" [margin note]

- Conclude with an anecdote related to the thesis.

    Over the harsh traffic sounds of motors and horns and blaring radios came the faint whang-whang of a would-be musician with a beat-up guitar and a money-drop hat turned up at his feet. It all reminded me of when I had first experienced the conglomeration of things that now assailed my senses. This jumbled mixture of things both human and nonhuman was, in fact, the reason I had come to live here. Then it was different and exciting. Later it was the reason I was leaving.

Brian Maxwell, "Leaving Los Angeles"

- Conclude with a quotation related to the thesis.

More than half the fatal traffic accidents involve intoxicated drivers, according to the National Highway Traffic Safety Administration. Cavenaugh and Associates, research specialists, say that drunk drivers killed 47,000 people in California in the five-year period from 1993 through 1997. They go on to say that intoxicated drivers cost us somewhere between eleven billion and twenty-four billion dollars each year. It is time to give drunk drivers a message: "Stay off the road. You are costing us pain, injury, and death, and no one has the right to do that."

Daniel Humphries, "Get Them Off the Road"

There are also many ineffective ways of concluding an essay. Do not conclude with the following:

- a summary when a summary is unnecessary.
- a complaint about the assignment or an apology about the quality of the work.
- an afterthought—that is, something you forgot to discuss in the body of the paper.
- a tagged conclusion—that is, a sentence beginning with such phrases as *In conclusion, To conclude,* or *I would like to conclude this discussion,* or *Last but not least.*
- a conclusion that raises additional problems that should have been settled during the discussion.

The conclusion is an integral part of the essay and is often a reflection of the introduction. If you have trouble with the conclusion, reread your introduction. Then work for a roundness or completeness in the whole paper.

Exercise 5 WRITING A CONCLUDING PARAGRAPH

For Exercise 4, you wrote two introductions. Select the better one, consider the basic information you would probably use for support (jotting down a few ideas if you like), and then write a simple conclusion of three to five sentences. This is an exercise to demonstrate that the conclusion connects with the introduction, is a consequence of the development of the essay, and ends on a note of finality. Of course, in your regular assignments, you will not write your conclusion until after you have written the other paragraphs.

Exercise 6 EVALUATING AN ESSAY

Mark the following essay in this way:
- *Circle the introductory paragraph.*
- *Enclose the concluding paragraph in a rectangle.*
- *Double underline the thesis.*
- *Underline the topic sentence for each support paragraph.*

She Came a Long Way
Shontel Jasper

Eyelids closed, she lay in the white hospital bed in the intensive care ward, her lungs filling with water and collapsing. In three days she would be dead, but she wouldn't go easily. She would go out as she had lived, for she had no choice.

She could have been an aged poster child for emphysema and lung cancer. Her face was drawn around her skull, her head was hairless from chemotherapy, the lines around her eyes revealed years of squinting through tobacco smoke, and her lips were dry and flaky like scales of a dead fish lying in the sun. A thin plastic belt hung loosely under her slack jowls like a necklace and the pendant was a clear plastic plug with a hole in it. The plug had been inserted into an incision in the woman's throat to aid her in breathing, and the air now whistled in and out irregularly. At the head of her bed stood an oxygen bottle like a cold and impersonal sentinel.

The nurse had just checked off items on the chart and left the room. Slowly, warily, the patient opened her eyes, and seeing no one in the room, immediately began her caper. Because of her shallow, rapid breathing, she was a study in slow movement. First there was a faint stirring under the sheet and then the sound of crackling cellophane. Then her hands emerged, holding a crumpled pack of Camels, from which she took a crooked cigarette before putting the remainder back under the covers. Next she removed the thin book of matches from her pillowcase. With the cigarette and matches clutched in her right hand, she fingered the control button to raise the head of her bed to almost ninety degrees. Laboriously, she swung her legs over the edge of the mattress, and choked back a fit of wheezy coughing that made the plug sound like a toddler playing a penny whistle.

Heading for the rest room, she knew exactly what she would do, because she had done it before. After closing the door behind herself, she turned on the exhaust fan. She then popped the insert from the plug and licked the paper at the end of her cigarette. When she raised her chin, the raw flesh showed through the transparent plastic, looking like a gill slit, into which she placed her cigarette and pinched the plastic around the part she had just licked. With trembling hands she scratched a match to flame and raised it awkwardly toward the cigarette. Instinctively, she looked above the commode for a mirror, but there was none. The hospital doesn't want patients in this ward to see their own images.

At last the moment of enjoyment had arrived. After taking a deep drag and removing the cigarette, she coughed, and the smoke streamed out of the hole and billowed. It looked white and vaporous as if she were an internal-combustion engine with a blown head gasket. She held her chin high, and lined up the hole carefully to receive the treat once more.

Basic Paragraph Patterns

Two effective patterns of conventional paragraph structure are shown in Figure 1.2. Pattern A merely states the controlling idea, the topic sentence, and develops it; Pattern B adds a concluding sentence following the topic development. Two other forms of paragraph structure—the paragraph with an unstated but implied topic sentence and the paragraph with the topic sentence at the end of the paragraph—are used less frequently in college writing.

Figure 1.2
Paragraph Patterns

Example of Pattern A:

Pity, Anger, and Achievement Performance

Topic sentence
Support

It is generally thought that pity and sympathy are "good" emotions and that anger is a "bad" emotion. However, attribution theorists have pointed out that the consequences of these emotional expressions are complex. In one investigation, Graham (1984) gave subjects (twelve-year-old children) false failure feedback during an achievement task. For some children, this was accompanied by the remark: "I feel sorry for you" as well as body postures and facial gestures that accompany sympathy (head down, hands folded, etc.). To other students, the experimenter said: "I am angry with you." Students receiving the pity feedback tended to blame the failure on themselves (low ability) and their performance declined. On the other hand, students receiving anger feedback attributed their failure to lack of effort and their performance subsequently increased. This is not to advocate that sympathy is always detrimental and anger always facilitative. Rather, the consequences of feedback depend on how that feedback is construed and what it means to the recipient of the communication. Other kinds of feedback, such as praise for success at an easy task and excessive and unsolicited helping, also tend to convey that the student is "unable" and therefore have some negative consequences.

Support

Seymour Feshbach and Bernard Weiner, *Personality*

The Essay and Its Parts

Example of Pattern B:

Primitive Methods of Lie Detection

Topic sentence — Throughout history there have been efforts to distinguish the guilty from the innocent and to tell the liars from the truthful. **Support** — For example, a method of lie detection practiced in Asia involved giving those suspected of a crime a handful of raw rice to chew. After chewing for some time, the persons were instructed to spit out the rice. The innocent person was anticipated to do this easily, whereas the guilty party was expected to have grains of rice sticking to the roof of the mouth and tongue. This technique relied on the increased sympathetic nervous system activity in the presumably fearful and guilty person. This activity would result in the drying up of saliva that, in turn, would cause grains of rice to stick in the mouth. **Support** — A similar but more frightening technique involved placing a heated knife blade briefly against the tongue, another method used for criminal detection. An innocent person would not be burned while the guilty party would immediately feel pain, again because of the relative dryness of the mouth. **Concluding sentence** — Many of these methods relied (unknowingly) on the basic physiological principles that also guided the creation of the polygraph.

Seymour Feshbach and Bernard Weiner, *Personality*

Exercise 7 ANALYZING A PARAGRAPH

1. Is the following paragraph developed in Pattern A (topic sentence/development) or Pattern B (topic sentence/development/concluding sentence)?

2. Identify the parts of the paragraph pattern by underlining the topic sentence and the concluding sentence, if any, and annotating the support in the left margin. Use the two example paragraphs as models.

But now I can say that I am a Japanese-American. It means I have a place here in this country, too. I have a place here on the East Coast, where our neighbor is so much a part of our family that my mother never passes her house at night without glancing at the lights to see if she is home and safe; where my parents have hauled hundreds of pounds of rocks from fields and arduously planted Christmas trees and blueberries, lilacs, asparagus, and crab apples, where my father still dreams of angling a stream to a new bed so that he can dig a pond in the field and fill it with water and fish. "The neighbors already came for their Christmas tree?" he asks in December. "Did they like it? Did they like it?"

Kesaya E. Noda, "Growing Up Asian in America"

Exercise 8   ANALYZING A PARAGRAPH

1. Is the following paragraph developed in Pattern A (topic sentence/development) or Pattern B (topic sentence/development/concluding sentence)?

2. Identify the parts of the paragraph pattern by underlining the topic sentence and the concluding sentence, if any, and annotating the support in the left margin. Use the two example paragraphs as models.

    I can see myself today as a person historically defined by law and custom as being forever alien. Being neither "free white," nor "African," our people in California were deemed "aliens, ineligible for citizenship," no matter how long they intended to stay here. Aliens ineligible for citizenship were prohibited from owning, buying, or leasing land. They did not and could not belong here. The voice in me remembers that I am always a *Japanese*-American in the eyes of many. A third-generation German-American is an American. A third-generation Japanese-American is a Japanese-American. Being Japanese means being a danger to the country during the war and knowing how to use chopsticks. I wear this history on my face.

Kesaya E. Noda,
"Growing Up Asian in America"

Writer's Guidelines: The Essay and Its Parts

1. An essay is a group of paragraphs, each of which supports a controlling statement called a thesis.

2. Each paragraph in an essay is almost always one of three types: introductory, support, or concluding.

3. An effective thesis has both a subject and a treatment. The subject is what you intend to write about. The treatment is what you intend to do with your subject.

    Example: <u>Bidwell Elementary School</u> <u>is too crowded.</u>
                            subject   **treatment**

4. An effective thesis presents a treatment that can be developed with supporting information.

5. An ineffective thesis is vague, too broad, or too narrow.

6. Supporting information is often presented in patterns, such as narration, exemplification, process analysis, analysis by division, and cause and effect.

7. A good introductory paragraph attracts the reader's interest, states or points toward the thesis, and moves the reader smoothly into the support, or developmental, paragraphs.

8. Introductory methods include a direct statement of the thesis, background, definition of term(s), quotation(s), a shocking statement, question(s), and a combination of two or more methods in this list.

9. Your concluding paragraph should give the reader the feeling that you have said all you want to say about your subject.

10. Some effective methods of concluding are a restatement of the thesis in slightly different words, perhaps pointing out its significance or making applications of it; a review of the main points; an anecdote related to the thesis; and a quotation.

2

The Writing Process: Prewriting

The Writing Process Defined, p. 25

The Writing Process Worksheet, p. 25

Prewriting, p. 26
 Freewriting, p. 26
 Brainstorming and Listing, p. 30
 Clustering, p. 33
 Composing the Thesis, p. 34
 Outlining, p. 35

Writer's Guidelines, p. 40

THE QUIGMANS   by Buddy Hickerson

Camping with a hack writer.

© Tribune Media Services, Inc. All Rights Reserved. Reprinted with permission.

Chapter 1 focused on the parts of an essay. However, it stopped short of presenting an overall plan for completing a specific writing assignment. The reason for that omission is simple. Each assignment has its own guidelines that vary according to the topic, the source of ideas, the time permitted, the conditions for writing, and the purpose. Any writing system must be flexible, because a technique that is an asset for one assignment may be a burden for another. Therefore, a good writer should know numerous techniques, treating each as a tool to be used when needed. All of these tools are in the same box, one labeled "The Writing Process."

The Writing Process Defined

The writing process consists of strategies that can help you proceed from your purpose or initial idea to a final developed essay. Those strategies can be divided into prewriting techniques and writing stages. Using prewriting techniques, you explore, experiment, gather information, formulate your thesis, and develop and organize your support. In the writing stages, you write a first draft, revise your draft as many times as necessary, and edit your writing. For the typical college writing assignment, the writing process looks like this:

1. Prewriting
   - Exploring, experimenting, and gathering information
   - Writing the thesis and organizing and developing support (especially by outline)
2. Writing
   - Drafting, revising, and editing

The process of writing is *recursive,* which means "going back and forth." If, for example, you have begun your essay only to discover that your subject is too broadly considered, you may decide to back up and narrow your thesis and adjust your outline.

Prewriting is discussed in this chapter; writing is discussed in Chapter 3. The writing process is demonstrated in "Prison as a Community" by Tanya. She wrote the essay while she was enrolled in a small, low-cost college program at the California Institution for Women, where she was incarcerated. Her name has been changed to protect her privacy, but the prison she wrote about so colorfully is very real.

The Writing Process Worksheet

A copy of Tanya's essay is presented according to the Writing Process Worksheet, a form providing space to record important information and guidance for you in prewriting and writing. For your instructor, it is a record of the progress of your work. A blank worksheet is provided on page 27, for enlargement and duplication for those who wish to use it. Figure 2.1 shows a reduced image of the worksheet.

These are the main features highlighted in the form:

1. *Assignment:* Record the particulars of the assignment, all too frequently the most neglected aspect of a writing project. If you do not know, or later cannot recall, specifically what you are supposed to write and when you are to submit it, you cannot do satisfactory work. An otherwise excellent composition on a misunderstood assignment may get you a failing grade, a regrettable situation for both you and your instructor.

2. *Prewriting:* On this form, prewriting is divided into two stages.
   - Stage One: Record the appropriate strategies as you explore, experiment, and gather information. This part may take the form of freewriting, brainstorming, clustering, note taking, or a combination of these strategies, depending on your assignment.
   - Stage Two: Write your thesis and an outline or an outline alternative such as a cluster or a list.

3. *Writing:* This portion of the worksheet encompasses writing from the first to the final draft, including all revision and editing.
   - Stage Three: By providing two easily remembered acronyms, the Writing Process Worksheet reminds you of necessary skills of revision—<u>c</u>oherence, <u>l</u>anguage, <u>u</u>nity, <u>e</u>mphasis, <u>s</u>upport, and <u>s</u>entences (CLUESS)—and of editing—<u>c</u>apitalization, <u>o</u>missions, <u>p</u>unctuation, and <u>s</u>pelling (COPS).

Prewriting

Certain strategies commonly grouped under the heading *prewriting* can help you get started, define your topic, and develop your ideas. These strategies—freewriting, brainstorming, clustering, gathering information, writing the thesis, and outlining—are very much a part of writing. The understandable desire to skip to the finished statement is what causes the most common student-writer grief: that of not filling the blank sheet or of filling it but not significantly improving on the blankness. The prewriting strategies described in this section will help you attack the blank sheet constructively with imaginative thought, analysis, and experimentation. They can lead to clear, effective communication. Gathering information is taken up separately in detail in Chapter 4.

Freewriting

Freewriting is a prewriting strategy that its originator, Peter Elbow, has called "babbling in print." In freewriting, you write without stopping, letting your ideas tumble forth. You do not concern yourself with the

Writing Process Worksheet

TITLE _____

NAME _____ DUE DATE _____

ASSIGNMENT   In the space below, write whatever you need to know about your assignment, including information about the topic, audience, pattern of writing, length, whether to include a rough draft or revised drafts, and whether your paper must be typed.

PREWRITING STAGE ONE   **Explore**   Freewrite, brainstorm (list), cluster, or gather information as directed by your instructor. Use the back of this page or separate paper if you need more space.

PREWRITING STAGE TWO   **Organize**   Write a topic sentence or thesis; label the subject and the treatment parts.

Write an outline or an outline alternative.

WRITING STAGE THREE   **Write**   On separate paper, write and then revise your paper as many times as necessary for coherence, language (usage, tone, and diction), unity, emphasis, support, and sentences (CLUESS). Read your paper aloud to hear and correct any grammatical errors or awkward-sounding sentences. Edit any problems in fundamentals, such as capitalization, omissions, punctuation, and spelling (COPS).

Figure 2.1
Writing Process Worksheet

fundamentals of writing, such as punctuation and spelling. Freewriting is an adventure into your memory and imagination. It is discovery, invention, and exploration. If you are at a loss for words on your subject, write down a comment such as "I don't know what is coming next" or "blah, blah, blah," and continue when relevant words come. It is important to keep writing. Freewriting immediately eliminates the blank page and thereby helps you break through an emotional barrier, but that is not the only benefit. The words that you sort through in that idea kit will include some you can use. You can then underline or circle those words and even add notes on the side so that the freewriting continues to grow even after its initial, spontaneous expression.

The way you proceed depends on the type of assignment. You might

- work with a topic of your choice.
- work from a restricted list of topics.
- work with a prescribed topic.

Working with the *topic of your choice* gives you the greatest freedom of exploration. You would probably select a subject that interests you and freewrite about it, allowing your mind to wander among its many parts, perhaps mixing fact and fantasy, direct experience, and hearsay. Freewriting about music might uncover areas of special interest and knowledge, such as jazz or folk rock, that you would want to pursue further in freewriting or other prewriting strategies.

Working from a *restricted list of topics* requires a more focused kind of freewriting. With the list, you can, of course, experiment with several topics to discover which is most suitable for you. If, for example, "career choice," "career preparation," "career guidance," and "career prospects" are on the restricted list, you would probably select one and freewrite about that. If it works well for you, you would probably proceed with the next step of your prewriting. If you are not satisfied with what you uncover in freewriting, you would explore another item from the restricted list.

Working with a *prescribed topic,* you focus on a particular topic and try to restrict your freewriting to its boundaries. If your topic specifies a division of a subject area such as "political involvement of your generation," then you would tie those key words to your own information, critical thinking, and imaginative responses. If the topic is restricted to a particular reading selection such as your reactions to a poem, then that poem would give you a framework for freewriting about your own experiences, creations, and opinions. An analysis of the piece would probably include underlining pertinent ideas, annotating it (writing in the margins), and even taking notes on it.

Freewriting can help you get words on paper to generate topics, develop new insights, and explore ideas. Freewriting can lead to other stages of prewriting and writing, and it can also provide content for details and insights as you develop your topic.

Tanya had received this assignment from her freshman composition instructor:

The Writing Process: Prewriting **29**

Write an essay of 500 to 800 words on a specific group of people who function as a unit, such as a family, a work team, a sports team, a committee, an organization, or some kind of community. Consider social units you have studied or are studying in history, sociology, and psychology courses. Submit the Writing Process Worksheet and at least one preliminary draft with your final typed draft. List any sources you have used.

Tanya's freewriting (a partial example) explains how she settled on her topic and, in this case, provides the reader with perspective for her work.

Unit

Walls and fences

Town

Walling in
Parts

Writing about a group of people gives me a lot of things to think about from where I am in my situation here in prison. I could write about gangs and there are plenty of them around and I could write about prison families and lots of different work stations all over the grounds and I could even write about the guards or correctional officers as they like to be called. And I could find a lot in my other classes that would give me information or at least some definitions and frameworks to work from. One thing I read about in my history book last week made me think even before this assignment. And that was <u>the walled cities</u> that sprung up in Europe more than a thousand years ago. They were little <u>communities. All inside walls.</u> Just <u>like the place where I live now.</u> When I came to prison I'd never been locked up before and I didn't know about prison and I guess I just thought of prison as a place where a bunch of people are locked up and sort of herded around. Then I came here and discovered that <u>prison is like</u> a <u>little town</u> in some ways and it has walls or fences just like the walled city I read about in my history book. Its just that <u>some one of them walled people out</u> and <u>one of them walls people in.</u> Reading the book made me think about my place here and how you've got most <u>everything here that you'll find in a regular city.</u> You've got <u>government, schools, churches,</u> a <u>post office,</u> a <u>hospital, rec space,</u> and <u>citizens</u> and a lot more. The place is called <u>the California Institution</u> for Women, but until about a year ago it had its own name, Frontera, with a separate zip code.

After her freewriting session, Tanya examined what she had written for possible ideas to develop for a writing assignment. As she recognized those ideas, she underlined key words and phrases and made a few notes in the margins. By reading only the underlined words in her freewrite, you can understand what is important to Tanya; it was not necessary for her to underline whole sentences.

In addition to putting words on that dreaded blank sheet of paper, Tanya discovered that she had quite a lot to say about the prison and that she had selected a favorable topic to develop. The entire freewriting process took no more than five minutes. Had she found only a few ideas or no promising ideas at all, she might have freewritten on another topic. In going back over her work, she saw some errors, especially in wording and sentence structure, but she did not correct them because the purpose of freewriting is discovery, not revising or correcting grammar, punctuation, and spelling. Tanya was confident that she could continue with the process of writing a paper.

Exercise 1 FREEWRITING

Try freewriting on a broad topic such as one of the following:

an event that was important to you in your youth
a concert, a movie, or a television program
the ways you use your computer
drugs—causes, effects, a friend with a problem
gangs—causes, effects, an experience
the benefits of using a word processor
ways of disciplining children
why a person is a hero or role model to you
a great or terrible party
a bad or good day at school
why a college education is important

Following the example in Tanya's freewriting, underline and annotate the phrases that may lead to ideas you could explore further.

Brainstorming and Listing

Brainstorming is a strategy for coming up with fresh, new ideas in a hurry. What key words and phrases pop into your mind when you think about your topic? One effective way to get started brainstorming is to ask the big-six questions about your subject area: Who? What? Where? When? Why? and How? Then let your mind run free as you jot down answers in single entries or lists. Using the big-six questions also helps you begin to organize ideas for your writing. Some of the questions may not fit, and some may be more important than others, depending on the purpose of your writing. For example, if you were writing about the causes of an accident, the Why? question could be more important than the others. If you were concerned with how to succeed in college, the How? question would predominate. If you were writing in response to a reading selection, you would confine your thinking to questions related to the content of the reading selection.

Whatever the focus of the six questions, the result is likely to be numerous ideas that will provide information for continued exploration and development of your topic. Thus your pool of information for writing widens and deepens.

An alternative to the big-six-questions approach is simply to make a list of words and phrases related to your subject area or specific topic.

Tanya continued with the subject of the prison, and her topic tightened to focus on particular areas. Although she could have listed the annotations and the words she underlined in her freewriting, she instead used the big-six questions for her framework.

Who?	People at the California Institution for Women
What?	A community with parts: government, education, religion, services, business, citizens, housing
Where?	Inside the fence
When?	All the time
Why?	Because the people make up a unit, a community
How?	As each part of the prison relates to other parts

Notice that each question is answered in this example, but with some topics some questions may not fit. As Tanya addressed the What? question, her brainstorming produced a long list, suggesting an area with strong possibilities for the focus of her paper.

Listing is another effective way to brainstorm, especially if you have a defined topic and a storehouse of information. Skip the big-six-questions approach and simply make a list of words and phrases related to your topic. This strategy is favored by many writers.

Thinking from the outset that she was concerned mainly with prison as a community, Tanya might have gone directly to making a list indicating the components and their relationships.

(churches)
(schools)
(government)
cops
post office
hospital
cafeteria
laundry
(service providers)
(citizens)

recreation

housing

(industry)

stores

maintenance

Exercise 2 BRAINSTORMING

Further explore the topic you worked with in Exercise 1 by first answering the big-six questions and then by making a list.

Big-Six Questions

Who? _____

What? _____

Where? _____

When? _____

Why? _____

How? _____

List

_____
_____
_____
_____
_____
_____
_____
_____

Clustering

Clustering is another prewriting technique. Start by double-bubbling your topic; that is, write it down in the middle of the page and draw a double circle around it, like the hub of a wheel. Then respond to the question What comes to mind? Draw a single bubble around other ideas on spokes radiating from the hub. Any bubble can lead to another bubble or to numerous bubbles in the same way. This strategy is sometimes used instead of an outline or it is used before making an outline to organize and develop ideas.

The more specific the topic inside the double bubble, the fewer the number of spokes that will radiate from it. For example, a topic such as "high school dropouts" would have more spokes than "reasons for dropping out of high school."

Here is Tanya's cluster on the subject of prison as a community. She has drawn dotted lines around subclusters that seem to relate to a workable, unified topic.

Exercise 3   CLUSTERING

Continuing with your topic, develop a cluster of related ideas. Draw dotted lines around subclusters that have potential for focus and more development.

Composing the Thesis

Your thesis can come from any of several places. You may be able to generate it in your initial freewriting, brainstorming, clustering, or information gathering, or you may be given an assigned topic. In any case, your procedure is the same at this point. You need to work on your thesis—just that one sentence—until you have developed an interesting subject and a well-focused treatment. That statement may be a bit more mechanical than the one you actually use in your essay, but it can easily be reworded once you are engaged in writing, revising, and editing.

The controlling idea will probably not pop into your head full-blown. It is more likely to be the result of repeated revisions. Even when you are revising a paper you have written, you may go back and rephrase your topic sentence or thesis. That is part of the back-and-forth (recursive) nature of the writing process.

Note how Tanya reworks her thesis several times before she settles on a well-focused statement capable of being developed.

This prison is a complete community.

Except for freedom, this prison is a microcosm of American society.

Except for freedom, <u>this prison</u> <u>has all the components of a typical community outside the fence.</u>

subject appears above "this prison"; *treatment* appears above "has all the components of a typical community outside the fence."

Exercise 4   COMPOSING A THESIS

After consulting your freewriting, brainstorming or listing, and clustering, write a thesis. Label the subject and treatment parts. Refer to Chapter 1, page 7, if you need more guidance.

Outlining

Outlining is the tool that most people think of in connection with organizing an essay. *Outlining* divides the controlling idea into sections of support material, divides those sections further, and establishes sequence.

An outline is a kind of framework that can be used in two ways: It can indicate the plan for an essay you intend to write, and it can show the organization of a passage you are reading. The outline of a reading passage and the outline as a plan for writing are identical in form. If you intend to write a summary of a reading selection, then a single outline might be used for both purposes.

The two main outline forms are the *sentence outline* (each entry is a complete sentence) and the *topic outline* (each entry is a key word or phrase). The topic outline is more common in writing essays.

In the following topic outline, notice first how the parts are arranged on the page: the indentations, the number and letter sequences, the punctuation, and the placement of words. Then read the outline and see how the ideas relate to one another.

Main idea (usually the thesis for an essay)

    I. Major support

        A. Minor support

           1. Explanation, detail, example

           2. Explanation, detail, example

B. Minor support
      1. Explanation, detail, example
      2. Explanation, detail, example
II. Major support
   A. Minor support
      1. Explanation, detail, example
      2. Explanation, detail, example
   B. Minor support
      1. Explanation, detail, example
      2. Explanation, detail, example

Tanya's next task was to organize her material. For this strategy, she went back to her bubble cluster, which she had divided into eight major parts. She had already decided she wanted to work with the idea of prison as a community and explain it from her perspective. Therefore, she focused on only one part of the cluster—the part indicated by the broken boundary line to enclose "neighborhoods," "commerce," "services," "education," "government," and "religion."

With her divisions selected, Tanya might have started to write a first draft at this point, but instead she decided she wanted to recall and organize more detail, so she began an outline. She used her own memory and private reference sources for information. In her second draft of her outline, she combined "commerce" and "services." If she had been working on a source-based topic, she would have gone back to the reading. If she had been working on a topic requiring research, she would have consulted library and Internet sources.

                          subject   *treatment*

Thesis: Except for freedom, <u>this prison</u> <u>has all the components of a typical community outside the fence.</u>

   I. Government as laws
      A. Administration
      B. Correctional officers
      C. Convicts
  II. Housing
      A. Assignments
         1. Based on behavior
         2. Based on age
         3. Based on health
      B. Special units

III. Commerce and services
    A. Regular jobs
        1. Industry
            a. Free enterprise
            b. Prison products
        2. Prison operation
    B. Underground services
        1. Hustles
        2. Extent

IV. Religion
    A. Larger groups
        1. Protestant
        2. Catholic
        3. Jewish
    B. Others in smaller numbers
        1. Sweat lodge folks
        2. Muslims
        3. Inmate preacher
        4. Voodoo practitioner

V. Education
    A. Formal
        1. Literacy
        2. Vocational
        3. College
    B. Informal
        1. Survival
        2. Life improvement

Exercise 5   COMPLETING OUTLINES

Fill in the missing parts of the following outline. Consider whether you are dealing with time, examples, causes, effects, parts, or steps.

1. Too many of us are preoccupied with material things.
    I. Clothing
    II. Cars
    III. _____

2. Television sitcoms may vary, but every successful show has certain components.
   I. Good acting
   II. _____
   III. Good situations
   IV. _____

3. A person who is trying to discourage unwanted sexual advances should take several measures.
   I. _____
   II. Set clear boundaries
   III. Avoid compromising situations

4. Concentrating during reading involves various techniques.
   I. Preview material
   II. Pose questions
   III. _____

5. Crime has some bad effects on a nearby neighborhood.
   I. People fearful
      A. Don't go out at night
      B. _____
   II. People without love for neighborhood
      A. _____
      B. Put houses up for sale
   III. People as victims
      A. Loss of possessions
      B. _____

6. Exercising can improve a person's life.
   I. Looks better
      A. Skin
      B. _____
   II. Feels better
      A. _____
      B. Body
   III. Performs better
      A. Work
      B. _____

7. Shoppers in department stores can be grouped according to needs.
   I. _____
   II. Specific needs
   III. Bargain hunters

8. There are different kinds of intelligence based on situations.
   I. Street-smart
   II. Common sense
   III. _____

9. Smoking should be discouraged.
   I. Harm to smokers
      A. _____
      B. Cancer risk
   II. Harm to those around smokers
      A. _____
      B. Fellow workers
   III. Cost
      A. Industry—production and absenteeism
      B. _____

10. An excellent police officer must have six qualities.
    I. _____
    II. Knowledge of law
    III. _____
    IV. Emotional soundness
    V. Skill in using weapons
    VI. _____

Exercise 6 — WRITING AN OUTLINE

Working with the thesis you developed in Exercise 4, write an outline. The thesis may suggest a particular pattern of development. Following the lead of that thesis, the Roman numeral headings will often indicate divisions of time or place, steps, causes, effects, or parts of a unit. For example, if you have selected your favorite retail store for your subject and your reasons for choosing it as the treatment, then those reasons would be indicated with Roman numeral headings.

Writer's Guidelines: The Writing Process—Prewriting

1. The writing process consists of strategies that can help you produce a polished essay. *Prewriting* includes exploring, experimenting, gathering information, writing the thesis, and organizing and developing support. *Writing* includes drafting, revising, and editing.

2. Prewriting includes one or more of the following strategies:

    Freewriting: writing without stopping so that you can explore, experiment, and invent

    Brainstorming and listing: responding to *Who? What? Where? When? Why? How?* questions or making lists on likely divisions of your subject

Clustering: showing related ideas by double-bubbling a subject and then connecting single bubbles of related ideas on spokes radiating out and branching from the hub

Gathering information: underlining, annotating, and note taking. (These techniques are explored in Chapter 4.)

Composing the thesis: writing a sentence that has two parts—the subject (what you are writing about) and the treatment (what you will do with the subject)

Outlining: dividing the controlling idea into sections of support material, dividing those sections further, and establishing a workable sequence

3

The Writing Process: Writing, Revising, and Editing

Writing the First Draft, p. 43
The Recursive Factor, p. 44
Your Audience, p. 44
Revising, p. 45
  Coherence, p. 45
  Language, p. 47
  Unity, p. 50
  Emphasis, p. 51
  Support, p. 52
  Sentences, p. 54
Editing, p. 56
  "Prison as a Community," p. 57
***Writer's Guidelines*, p. 64**

Writing the First Draft

Once you have developed your thesis and your outline (or list), you are ready to begin writing your essay. The initial writing is called the first, or rough, draft. Your thesis statement is likely to be at or near the beginning of your essay and will be followed by your support as ordered by your outline. As you write, refer to your thesis often and write a clear topic sentence for each paragraph.

Following your outline for basic organization, you should proceed without worrying about the refinements of writing. This is not the time to concern yourself with perfect spelling, grammar, or punctuation. After you have finished that first draft, read it carefully. If your thesis is sound and your outline has served you well, you now have a basic discussion. You have made a statement and supported it.

Don't be embarrassed by the roughness of your work. You should be embarrassed only if you leave it that way. You are seeing the reason why a first draft is called "rough." Famous authors have said publicly that they wouldn't show their rough drafts even to their closest, most forgiving friends.

Whether you write in longhand or on a computer depends on what works best for you. Some writers prefer to do a first draft by hand, mark it up, and then go to the computer. Computers save you time in all aspects of your writing, especially revision.

The following paragraphs from Tanya's essay show how she wrote her first draft. Notice how the paragraphs follow the order of topics in her outline; they also include some new ideas. The excerpt includes paragraph 2 and part of paragraph 3.

It all begins with rules. n

CIW has a goverment, one that is totalitarian not democratic.

prison
The constitution is a set of laws passed by the state of California.

associates
I. Government as laws — The warden and her ~~deputies~~ administer the law with wisdom. The
   A. Administration
                                                            with grace
   B. Correctional correctional officers enforce the laws fairly. The convicts obey ~~without~~
      officers
                                       acquaintances with bunco experience
   C. Convicts ~~complaining~~. If you believe all of that, I have some ~~friends~~ around here
II. Housing
   A. Assignments   a bundle of
      1. Based on who just found ~~some~~ cash and would like to share it with you.
         behavior
      2. Based on age   where we live
      3. Based on These laws also govern ~~housing~~ in the prison. It is said that the
         health

two most important things in prison are where one lives and where

one works. An inmate's address at prison can be determined by

B. Special units — several factors: ~~such as~~ behavior, reputation, age, and health; Therefore, one can be assigned to a cell block with designations such as ordinary (general dorm, room, or cell), honors, geriatrics, *solitary,* convalescent, protective custody, or psychiatric. At times special living units are formed. Once there was a living unit at CIW called the AIDS ward, for convicts who were HIV positive. ~~A strange procedure developed.~~ If somebody approached these women as they were . . .

The Recursive Factor

The process of writing can be called *recursive,* which means "going back and forth." In this respect, writing is like reading. If you do not understand what you have read, you back up and read it again. After you have read an entire passage, you may need to read it again selectively. The same can be said of writing. If, for example, after having developed an outline and started writing your first draft, you discover that your subject is too broad, you will have to back up, narrow your thesis, and then adjust your outline. You may even want to return to an early cluster of ideas to see how you can use a smaller grouping of them. Revision is usually the most recursive of all parts of the writing process. You will go over your material again and again until you are satisfied that you have expressed yourself as well as you possibly can.

Your Audience

When you speak to a person, you routinely adjust what you say and how you say it. You should do the same for your audience when you write. To the extent that you can, consider the needs, interests, knowledge, and abilities of your intended readers and appropriately adjust your subject, explanations, style, and word choice.

Exercise 1 — WRITING YOUR ROUGH DRAFT

Using the thesis you developed in Chapter 2, write a rough draft of an essay as directed by your instructor.

Revising

The term *first draft* suggests quite accurately that there will be other drafts, or versions, of your writing. Only in the most dire situations, such as an in-class examination when you have time for only one draft, should you be satisfied with a single effort.

What you do beyond the first draft is revision and editing. Revision includes organization, content, and language effectiveness. Editing (discussed later in this chapter) involves a final correction of simple mistakes and fundamentals such as spelling, punctuation, and capitalization. In practice, editing and revising are not always separate activities, although writers usually wait until the next-to-the-last draft to edit minor details and attend to other small points that can be easily overlooked.

Successful revision almost always involves intense, systematic rewriting. You should learn to look for certain aspects of skillful writing as you enrich and repair your first draft. To help you recall these aspects so that you can keep them in mind and examine your material in a comprehensive fashion, this textbook offers a memory device—an acronym in which each letter suggests an important feature of good writing and revision. This device enables you to memorize the features of good writing quickly. Soon you will be able to recall and refer to them automatically. These features need not be attended to individually when you revise your writing, although they may be, and they need not be attended to in the order presented here. The acronym is CLUESS (pronounced "clues"), which provides this guide:

<u>C</u>oherence

<u>L</u>anguage

<u>U</u>nity

<u>E</u>mphasis

<u>S</u>upport

<u>S</u>entences

Each of these features of good writing can be approached with a set of techniques you can apply easily to your first draft. They are presented here with some details, examples, and supporting exercises. The Writer's Guidelines at the end of this chapter provide a concise list of these features and a set of questions you can apply to your own writing and to peer editing.

Coherence

Coherence is the orderly relationship of ideas, each leading smoothly and logically to the next. You must weave your ideas together so skillfully that the reader can easily see how one idea connects to another and to the central thought. This central thought, of course, is expressed in the topic sentence for a paragraph and in the thesis for an essay. You can achieve coherence efficiently by using the following:

overall pattern

transitional terms

repetition of key words and ideas

pronouns

consistent point of view

Overall Pattern

Several chapters in this book discuss strategies for an overall pattern of organization or order. Three basic patterns prevail: *time* (chronology), *space* (spatial arrangement), and *emphasis* (stress on ideas). Sometimes you will combine patterns. The coherence of each can be strengthened by using transitional words such as the following:

Time: *first, then, soon, later, following, after, at that point*

Space: *up, down, right, left, beyond, behind, above, below*

Emphasis: *first, second, third, most, more*

Transitional Terms

By using transitional terms, you can help your readers move easily from one idea to another. Each of the following sentences has one of these terms.

First, I realized I had to get a job to stay in school.

At the same time, my track coach wanted the team to spend more hours working out.

We were, *after all,* the defending champions.

Finally, I dropped one of my courses.

Repetition of Key Words and Ideas

Repeat key words and phrases to keep the main subject in the reader's mind and to maintain the continuity necessary for a smooth flow of logical thought. (See the section on Emphasis on page 51.)

Pronouns

Pronouns, such as *he, her, them,* and *it,* provide natural connecting links in your writing. Why? Every pronoun refers to an earlier noun (called the *antecedent* of the pronoun) and thus carries the reader back to that earlier thought. Here are some examples.

> I tried to buy *tickets* for the concert, but *they* were all sold.

> Assertive *people* tend to make decisions quickly. However, *they* may not make the wisest decisions.

> *Roger* painted a picture of *his* father's pickup truck. *It* was so good that *his* professor asked *him* to enter *it* in an art show.

Consistent Point of View

Point of view shows the writer's relationship to the material, the subject, and it usually does not change within a passage.

If you are conveying personal experience, the point of view will be *first person,* or *I,* which can be either involved (a participant) or detached (an observer).

The second person, *you* and *your,* is usually reserved for how-to writing in college assignments.

If you are presenting something from a distance, geographical or historical (for example, telling a story about George Washington), the point of view will be *third person,* and the participants will be referred to as *he, she,* and *they.*

Along with the consistency of perspective, you should avoid shifts in number (*she* to *they*) and verb tense (*is* to *was*).

Being consistent in these matters will promote coherence.

Language

In the revision process, the word *language* takes on a special meaning, referring to usage, tone, and diction. If you are writing with a computer, consider using the thesaurus feature, but keep in mind that no two words share precisely the same meaning.

Usage

Usage is the kind or general style of language we use. All or almost all of us operate on the principle of appropriateness. If I used *ain't* as part of my explanations in this textbook, you would be surprised and probably disappointed; you would think about my word choice rather than what I have to say. Why would you be surprised? Because *ain't* is not appropriate for my audience in this situation. If you write an essay containing slang, you will probably be understood, but if the slang is not appropriate, you will draw unfavorable attention to your message. That does not mean that slang does not have its place—it does. It can be imaginative and colorful. Often, though, it is only a weak substitute for a more precise vocabulary.

Usage is an important part of writing and revising. Judge what is appropriate for your audience and your purpose. What kind of language is expected? What kind of language is best suited for accomplishing your purpose?

Most of the material in Chapter 13, Handbook: Writing Effective Sentences, is grammatical explanation of standard, mainly formal, English. Using standard verb tenses and pronoun cases will help you to write effectively. Chapter offers clear explanations and examples. It also provides exercises supported by answers in the Answer Key. As you practice the principles of standard English in your writing and revising, you will master them.

Tone

Have you ever heard someone say, "Don't talk to me in that tone of voice" or "I accepted what she was saying, but I didn't like the tone she used when she told me"? *Tone* in these contexts means that the sound of the speaker's voice and maybe the language choices conveyed disrespect to the listener. The tone could have represented any number of feelings about the subject matter and the audience. Tone can have as many variations as you can have feelings: It can, for example, be sarcastic, humorous, serious, cautionary, objective, groveling, angry, bitter, sentimental, enthusiastic, somber, outraged, or loving.

Let's say you are getting a haircut. Looking in those panoramic mirrors bordered with pictures of people with different styles of haircuts, you see that the hair stylist is cutting off too much hair. You could use different tones in giving him or her some timely how-to instructions.

Objective: "If you don't mind, what I meant to say was that I would like a haircut proportioned similar to that one there in the picture of Tom Cruise from *Jerry Maguire*."

Humorous: "I hesitate to make suggestions to someone who is standing at my back and holding a sharp instrument near my throat, but I'm letting my hair grow out a bit. I don't want you to take off a lot in the back and on the sides."

Angry and sarcastic: "Look man, when I sat down, I said I wanted my hair cut in the design of Tom Cruise in *Jerry Maguire*. The way you're hacking at it, you must've thought I said *Top Gun*."

Servile: "I really like the way you cut my hair, and I can see that you are proportioning it with great care, but I would like my hair to be a bit longer than the style that I think you're working on. Do you remember how I used to get my hair cut about a year ago, a little longer on the sides and more bushy on top? You came up with a great style that everyone liked. Could you give me one similar to that?"

Overbearing: "Damn it, buddy. Will you watch what you're doing! I asked for a haircut, not a shave. If God had wanted me to have bare skin above my shoulders, he would've put the hair on my feet."

In speech, feelings and attitudes are represented by inflection, loudness, word choice, and language patterns. In writing, tone is conveyed mainly by word choice and order; it is closely related to style—the variations in the way you write, depending on your purpose. Your purpose is simply to present a particular idea in a particular context. The context implies the audience; it is important to use the tone appropriate to your audience.

Usually your tone will be consistent throughout your presentation, although for the informal essay often assigned in college, you may choose to begin in a lighthearted, amusing tone before switching to a more serious, objective mode.

Diction

Diction is word choice. If you use good diction, you are finding the best words for a particular purpose in addressing a certain audience. There is some overlap, therefore, between usage and diction. I may look at an area in the subway and present my reaction in the following way:

Poor Diction:

This part of the subway is really a mess. Everywhere I look I can see things people have thrown away, which have fallen through the grates above. Along with the solid items are liquids. On the walls are a hodgepodge of posters and writing. The whole area is very dirty and very unpleasant.

Note how the scene comes to life with better word choice:

Good Diction:

[Before me I saw] an unspeakable mass of congealed oil, puddles of dubious liquid, and a mishmash of old cigarette packets, mutilated and filthy newspapers, and the debris that filtered down from the street above. [The walls were a display of posters]—here a text from the Bible, there a half-naked girl, here a pair of girl's legs walking up the keys of a cash register—all scribbled over with unknown names and well-known obscenities. . . .

Gilbert Highet, "Subway Station"

The difference between these two passages is obvious. The first is general. Terms such as "very dirty" and "very unpleasant" carry little meaning. The author has not made us see. The word *very* is an empty modifier. The second passage is specific. You can visualize what the writer is saying through the specific diction, the detail. The first is general and, for content, hardly goes beyond a single phrase—mess in the subway.

The following chart shows the difference between general and specific words.

General	Specific	More Specific
food	fruit	juicy, ripe peach
mess	litter	candy wrappers; empty cans
drink	soda	Diet Pepsi
odor	kitchen smell	aroma of coffee brewing

Another aspect of diction is freshness and originality of expression. To achieve those distinctions, avoid clichés, which are trite, familiar phrases. Consider this sentence:

> When the Prince married Cinderella, her sisters went <u>green with envy</u> because she was now <u>on easy street,</u> leaving them <u>out in the cold.</u>

Those words were written by a person who doesn't care about communicating in a clear and interesting manner. It would be far better to say:

> When the Prince married Cinderella, her sisters were envious because they had no suitors.

This list shows some clichés to avoid:

young at heart	quick as a flash
rotten to the core	slow but sure
uphill battle	other side of the coin
more than meets the eye	breathless silence
bitter end	acid test
as luck would have it	better late than never
last but not least	six of one, half dozen of the other

These are ready-made expressions. A cliché master manipulates language as if it were a prefabricated building going up, not bothering to use any imagination and leaving little opportunity for his or her audience to use theirs. Good diction, however, reflects the writer as an individual and is fresh, original, and clear.

Unity

A controlling idea, stated or implied, unifies every piece of good writing. It is the central point around which the supporting material revolves. For a paragraph, the elements are the topic sentence and the supporting sentences. For an essay, the elements are the thesis and the supporting developmental paragraphs. All the supporting material should be related to the topic sentence or thesis, and it should all be subordinate to the topic sentence or thesis. Unity can be strengthened and made more apparent if you restate the topic sentence or thesis at the end of the unit and if you repeat key words and phrases from time to time. A good check on unity is to ask yourself if everything in your paragraph or essay is subordinate to and derived from the controlling idea.

Don't confuse unity and coherence. Whereas coherence involves the clear movement of thought from sentence to sentence or paragraph to paragraph, unity means staying on the topic. A unified and coherent outline would become incoherent if the parts were scrambled, but the outline technically would still be unified. These qualities of writing go together. You should stay on the topic and make clear connections.

Emphasis

Emphasis, a feature of most good writing, helps the reader focus on the main ideas. It can be achieved in several ways but mainly through placement of key ideas and through repetition.

Placement of Ideas

The most emphatic part of any passage, whether a sentence or a book, is the last part, because we usually remember most easily what we read last. The second most emphatic part of a passage is the beginning, because our mind is relatively uncluttered when we read it. For these reasons, among others, the topic sentence or thesis is usually at the beginning of a piece, and it is often restated at the end in an echoing statement.

Repetition of Key Words and Ideas

Repetition is one of the simplest devices in your writer's toolbox. The words repeated may be single words, phrases, slightly altered sentences, or synonyms. Repetition keeps the dominant subject in the reader's mind and maintains the continuity necessary for a smooth flow of logical thought.

You can use this valuable technique easily. If, as is done in the following example, you are discussing the effects of the school dropout problem, then the words *effect(s),* along with synonyms such as *result(s)* or *consequence(s),* and *school dropout(s)* are likely to be repeated several times. Moreover, phrases giving insight into the issue may be repeated, perhaps with slight variation.

The causes of the school <u>dropout</u> problem have received much attention recently, but the <u>effects</u> are just as important. One obvious <u>result</u> is that of unemployment or low-paying employment. The student who <u>drops out</u> of school is likely to be <u>dropping</u> into poverty, perhaps even into a lifelong condition. Another <u>effect</u> is juvenile crime. The young person who has no prospects for a good job and no hope all too frequently turns to illegal activities. A third <u>result</u> concerns the psychological well-being of the <u>dropout</u>. Although <u>withdrawing</u> from school seems to offer a quick, viable solution to perceived problems, it almost immediately has <u>consequences</u> for the <u>dropout</u>'s self-esteem. Of course, these <u>effects</u> may also be tied to causes, such as drugs, poverty, crime, or psychological problems, but devastating <u>repercussions</u> are there at the far end of the causes-and-effects continuum, and youngsters who are contemplating <u>dropping out</u> should consider them with care.

The effective use of word and phrase repetition should not be confused with an irritating misuse of word repetition. We all at times get hung up on certain words, and the result is a negative response from our audience. Consider this awkward use of repetition:

> She looked at him and frowned. He returned the look and then looked away at a stranger looking for his lost keys.

That's too many *look*'s. Consider this version:

> She looked at him [*or, even better,* She frowned at him]. He glared back and then glanced away at a stranger searching for his lost keys.

The second version preserves the idea of people "looking" by using synonyms. It is more precise, and does not grate on the reader's mind as the first does.

Support

How much support does a piece of writing need? A good developmental paragraph fulfills its function by developing the topic sentence. An essay is complete when it fulfills its function of developing a thesis. Obviously, you will have to judge what is complete. With some subjects, you will need little supporting and explanatory material. With others, you will need much more. Incompleteness, not overdevelopment, is more common among beginning writers. Besides having enough support, be sure that the points of support are presented in the best possible sequence.

Consider the following paragraph. Is it complete? Does the writer make the main idea clear and provide adequate support for it? Are the ideas in the right order?

> A cat's tail is a good barometer of its intentions. By various movements of its tail a cat will signal many of its wants. Other

movements indicate its attitudes. An excited or aggressively aroused cat will whip its entire tail back and forth.

At first glance, this paragraph seems complete. It begins with a concise topic sentence telling us that a cat's tail is a good barometer of its intentions. It adds information of a general nature in the following two sentences. Then it presents a supporting example about the aggressively aroused cat. But the paragraph is not explicit; there is insufficient supporting material for the opening generalization. The paragraph leaves the reader with too much information to fill in. What are some other ways that cats communicate their intentions with their tails? How do they communicate specific wishes or desires? Is their communication effective? If the passage is to answer these questions that may come into the reader's mind, it must present more material to support the beginning generalization. The original paragraph that follows begins with a concise topic sentence that is then supported with details.

Michael W. Fox, "What Is Your Pet Trying to Tell You?"

A cat's tail is a good barometer of its intentions. An excited or aggressively aroused cat will whip its entire tail back and forth. When I talk to Sam, he holds up his end of the conversation by occasionally flicking the tip of his tail. Mother cats move their tails back and forth to invite their kittens to play. A kitten raises its tail perpendicularly to beg for attention; older cats may do so to beg for food. When your cat holds its tail aloft while crisscrossing in front of you, it is trying to say, "Follow me"—usually to the kitchen, or more precisely, to the refrigerator. Unfortunately, many cats have lost their tails in refrigerator doors as a consequence.

We can strengthen our understanding of good support by analyzing the structure of the model paragraph, putting to use the information we have assimilated to this point in the discussion. The paragraph begins with the highest generalization (the main idea in the topic sentence): "A cat's tail is a good barometer of its intentions." It follows immediately with six supporting statements and ends with a final sentence to add humor to the writing. If we place this material in outline form, we can easily see the recurrent pattern in the flow of thought from general to particular.

Topic sentence (highest generalization)   A cat's tail is a good barometer of its intentions.

Major support   A. An excited or aggressively aroused cat will whip its entire tail back and forth.

Major support   B. When I talk to Sam, he holds up his end of the conversation by occasionally flicking the tip of his tail.

Major support   C. Mother cats move their tails back and forth to invite their kittens to play.

Major support   D. A kitten raises its tail perpendicularly to beg for attention;

Major support	E. older cats may do so to beg for food.
Major support	F. When your cat holds its tail aloft while crisscrossing in front of you, it is trying to say, "Follow me"—usually to the kitchen, or more precisely, to the refrigerator.
Added for humor	Unfortunately, many cats have lost their tails in refrigerator doors as a consequence.

Sentences

In the revision process, the term *sentences* pertains to the variety of sentence patterns and the correctness of sentence structure.

Variety of Sentences

A passage that offers a variety of simple and complicated sentences satisfies the reader, just as a combination of simple and complicated foods go together in a good meal. The writer can introduce variety by including both short and long sentences, by using different sentence patterns, and by beginning sentences in different ways.

Length

In revising, examine your writing to make sure that sentences vary in length. A series of short sentences is likely to make the flow seem choppy and the thoughts disconnected. However, single short sentences often work very well. Because they are uncluttered with supporting points and qualifications, they are often direct and forceful. Consider using short sentences to emphasize points and to introduce ideas. Use longer sentences to provide details or show how ideas are related.

Variety of Sentence Patterns

Good writing includes a variety of sentence patterns. Although there is no limit to the number of sentences you can write, you may be pleased to discover that the conventional English sentence appears in only four basic patterns.

Simple:	She did the work well.
Compound:	She did the work well, and she was well paid.
Complex:	Because she did the work well, she was well paid.
Compound-complex:	Because she did the work well, she was well paid, and she was satisfied

An analysis of these patterns with suggestions and exercises for combining sentences is given in Chapter 13.

Each of the four sentence patterns listed has its own purposes and strengths. The simple sentence conveys a single idea. The compound sentence shows, by its structure, that two somewhat equal ideas are connected. The complex sentence shows that one idea is less important than another; that is, it is dependent on, or subordinate to, the idea in the main clause. The compound-complex sentence has the scope of both the compound sentence and the complex sentence.

Variety of Sentence Beginnings

Another way to provide sentence variety is to use different kinds of beginnings. A new beginning may or may not be accompanied by a changed sentence pattern. Among the most common beginnings, other than starting with the subject of the main clause, are those using a prepositional phrase, a dependent clause, or a conjunctive adverb such as *therefore, however,* or *in fact.*

- Prepositional phrase

    In your fantasy, you are the star.

    Like casino owners, game show hosts want you to be cheery.

- Dependent clause

    When the nighttime "Wheel of Fortune" debuted, the slot was occupied by magazine shows.

    As Pat Sajak noted, viewers often solve the puzzle before the contestants do.

- Conjunctive adverb

    Now you know.

    Therefore, you feel happy, excited, and a bit superior.

Problems with Sentences

A complete sentence must generally include an independent clause, which is a group of words that contains a subject and a verb and can stand alone. Some groups of words may sound interesting, but they are not really sentences. Three common problem groupings are the fragment, the comma splice, and the run-on.

- *Fragment:* A word grouping that is structurally incomplete is only a fragment of a sentence.

    Because he left. (This is a dependent clause, not a complete sentence.)

Went to the library. (This has no subject.)

She being the only person there. (This has no verb.)

Waiting there for help. (This phrase has neither subject nor verb.)

In the back seat under a book. (This contains two phrases but no subject or verb.)

- *Comma splice:* The comma splice consists of two independent clauses with only a comma between them.

    The weather was bad, we canceled the picnic. (A comma by itself cannot join two independent clauses.)

- *Run-on:* The run-on differs from the comma splice in only one way: It has no comma between the independent clauses.

    The weather was bad we canceled the picnic.

Fragments, comma splices, and run-ons can easily be fixed (see Chapter 13) during the revising and editing stages of your writing. A computerized grammar checker may help you find these problems.

If you frequently have problems with sentence structure and awkwardness of phrasing, be especially suspicious of long sentences. Test each sentence of fifteen or more words for flaws. Try writing shorter, more direct sentences until you gain confidence and competency. Then work with sophisticated patterns.

See the Writer's Guidelines at the end of this chapter for a concise summary of the strategies for effective revision.

Editing

Editing, the final stage of the writing process, involves a careful examination of your work. Look for problems with capitalization, omissions, punctuation, and spelling (COPS).

Because you can find spelling errors in writing by others more easily than you can in your own, try to have someone you know read your draft and help you locate misspellings. Also, a computerized spell checker is quite useful. However, it will not detect wrong words that are correctly spelled, so you should always proofread. It is often helpful to leave the piece for a few hours or a day, then reread it as if it were someone else's work.

Before you submit your writing to your instructor, do what almost all professional writers do before sending their material along: Read it aloud, to yourself or to a willing audience. Reading material aloud will help you catch any awkwardness of expression, omission and misplacement of words, and other problems that are easily overlooked by an author.

As you can see, writing is a process and is not a matter of just sitting down and banging out a statement. The parts of the process from prewriting to revising to editing are connected, and your movement is ultimately forward, but this process allows you to go back and forth in the recursive manner discussed earlier in this chapter. If your outline is not working, perhaps the flaw is in your thesis. You may need to go back and fix it. If one section of your essay is skimpy, perhaps you will have to go back and reconsider the pertinent material in your outline or clustering. There you might find more details or alter a statement so that you can move into more fertile areas of thought.

The following is her first *draft* that shows Tanya's revision process. The draft also includes some editing (COPS).

Prison as a Community

Few free world citizens ~~look at~~ regard the California Institution for

Women as a walled city but that's what it is. Before I was sent here,

I ~~thought of~~ imagined prison as a bunch of scared and scary people in a fenced pen. Then I

became a resident and discovered that, except for freedom, this

place has all the parts of a community outside the fence. ~~It was an important discovery.~~

It all begins with rules. n
CIW has a goverment, one that is totalitarian not democratic.

prison
The constitution is a set of laws passed by the state of California.

associates
The warden and her ~~deputies~~ administer the laws ~~with wisdom~~. The

correctional officers enforce the laws ~~fairly~~. The convicts obey

with grace   acquaintances with bunco experience
~~without complaining~~. If you believe all of that, I have some ~~friends~~

a bundle of
around here who just found ~~some~~ cash and would like to share it

with you.

where we live
These laws also govern ~~housing~~ in the prison. It is said that the

two most important things in prison are where one lives and where

one works. An inmate's address at prison can be determined by several factors: behavior, reputation, age, and health. Therefore, one can be assigned to a cell block with designations such as ordinary (general dorm, room, or cell), honors, geriatrics, solitary, convalescent, protective custody, or psychiatric. At times special living units are formed. Once there was a living unit at CIW called the AIDS ward, for convicts who were HIV positive. If somebody approached these women as they were being escorted across the yard, a correctional officer would blow a whistle and shout, "Stay away! These inmates have AIDS! These inmates have AIDS!" The HIV positive women now live in housing for the general population, and staff is more enlightened.

The other part of the saying "where you work" is tied in with both free world industry and the operation of the prison. For years CIW has produced clothing for the California Transportation Agency (CalTrans), made mostly of heavy orange fabric. We have also manufactured jeans and underwear for California prisons for men. Most jobs relate to food, laundry, maintenance, and clerical services, such as. All able-bodied women, even those in educational programs, must work. Some jobs provide compensation, the so-called "pay slots," but prison work is almost never connected with vocational training or with post-parole jobs. The money, usually about fifteen to thirty dollars a month, is placed in a trust fund and can be used in the prison store for treats, smokes, hygiene items, health aids, or the like.

Another part of "work" at the prison relates to the underground activities and economy.

~~actions.~~ The hustles include tattooing, gambling, drugs, food running, laundry service, strong-arming, body guarding, and hootch making (a homemade alcohol product). That list tells you more about prison than does the official line offered to the public.

In addition to the commonplace housing and the above and below ground work, CIW also offers religion a la carte. ~~Religion is really important.~~ Convicts have three full-time chaplains. Anyone can attend a Jewish Seder, a Catholic mass, or a protestant spectacular. Last Sunday, I attended a foot-stomping, woman-wailing Gospel Bonanza put on by outside evangelists, the men in spandex and the women with big hair. The program rivaled any free world revival in a three-post tent. Also available are sweat lodge rituals for the Native Americans and services for Muslims.

Like the commercial and service areas, religion also has its underground activities. ~~There are several examples.~~ Currently an inmate, who was an ordained minister on the streets, has been baptizing women in the shower (total immersion, she argues); marrying lesbians, and performing exorcisms (including one on a schizoid yard cat named Blue Eyes). Equally well known, a voodooist has recently constructed personalized images for putting a hex on those she believes have offended her, leading a number of terrified women to dispose of hair and other byproducts of personal hygiene only by the toilet flushing technique.

Another component of the community ~~Then there~~ is school. It may be on an academically low level, such as literacy, or somewhat advanced, such as the GED program.

> Small college programs, such as the one I am now enrolled in, depend on state funding, which in our case will be withdrawn next year.

At the practical level, in recent years, several vocational programs have been offered and then discontinued: plumbing, graphic arts, and hair styling.

Naturally, the other side of formal education at CIW is informal education. No one leaves the same as she was upon entering. Each inmate will learn from the prison and become ^either better or worse. I wish I could say that life improvement usually wins out over other forces. It does sometimes happen in this best of all criminal schools. ^For myself, against odds, I intend to make it so.

Yes, CIW is more than a holding pen for criminal types. It really is a community/ ^B ut being a social unit does not make it a nice place to live. The average person stays here for three to five years and moves on, ~~which is~~ about the average for movement on the street.

And not all is bad. Some of us convicts do save ourselves. We occasionally get some help. ^For most, the help is not enough.

After two more revisions with editing, Tanya typed this *final draft*, proofread it once again, read it aloud, and, satisfied, submitted it to her instructor.

Prison as a Community
Tanya

Few free world citizens regard the California Institution for Women as a walled city, but that's what it is. Before I was sent here, I imagined prison as a bunch of scared and scary people in a fenced pen. Then I became a resident and discovered that, except for freedom, this place has all the parts of a community outside the fence.

It all begins with rules. CIW has a government, one that is totalitarian, not democratic. The constitution is a set of laws passed by the state of California. The warden and her associates administer the laws. The correctional officers enforce the laws. The convicts obey—or else.

These laws also govern where we live in the prison. It is said that the two most important things in prison are where one lives and where one works. An inmate's address at prison can be determined by several factors: behavior, reputation, age, and health. Therefore, one can be assigned to a cell block with designations such as ordinary (general dorm, room, or cell), honors, geriatrics, solitary, convalescent, protective custody, or psychiatric. At times special living units are formed. Once there was a living unit at CIW called the AIDS ward, for convicts who were HIV positive. If somebody approached these women as they were being escorted across the yard, a correctional officer would blow a whistle and shout, "Stay away! These inmates have AIDS! These inmates have AIDS!" The HIV positive women now live in housing for the general population, and staff is more enlightened.

The other part of the saying, "where you work," is tied in with both free world industry and the operation of the prison. For years CIW has produced clothing for the California Transportation Agency (CalTrans), made mostly of heavy orange fabric. We have also manufactured Levis and underwear for California prisons for men. Most jobs relate to services, such as food, laundry, maintenance, and clerical. All able-bodied women, even those in educational programs, must work. Some jobs provide compensation, the so-called "pay slots," but prison work is almost never connected with vocational training or with post-parole jobs. The money, usually about fifteen to thirty dollars a month, is placed in a trust fund and can be used in the prison store for treats, smokes, health aids, hygiene items, or the like.

Another part of "work" at the prison relates to the underground activities and economy. The hustles include tattooing, gambling, drugs, food running, laundry service, strong-arming, body guarding, and hootch (a homemade alcohol product) making. That list tells you more about prison than does the official line offered to the public.

In addition to the commonplace housing and the above and below ground work, CIW offers religion a la carte. Convicts have three full-time chaplains. Anyone can attend a Jewish Seder, a Catholic mass, or a protestant spectacular. Last Sunday, I attended a foot-stomping, woman-wailing Gospel Bonanza put on by outside evangelists, the men in spandex and the women with big hair. The program rivaled any free world revival in a three-post tent. Also available are sweat lodge rituals for the Native Americans and services for Muslims.

Like the commercial and service areas, religion has its underground activities. Currently an inmate, who was an ordained minister on the streets, has been baptizing women in the shower (total immersion, she argues), marrying lesbians, and performing exorcisms (including one on a schizoid yard cat* named Blue Eyes). Equally well known, a voodooist has recently constructed personalized images for putting a hex on those she believes have offended her, leading a number of terrified women to dispose of hair and other byproducts of personal hygiene only by the toilet-flushing technique.

Another component of the community is school. It may be on an academically low level, such as literacy, or somewhat advanced, such as the GED program. At the practical level, in recent years, several vocational programs have been offered and then discontinued: plumbing, graphic arts, and hair styling. Small college programs, such as the one I am now enrolled in, depend on state funding, which in our case will be withdrawn next year.

Naturally, the other side of formal education at CIW is informal education. No one leaves the same as she was upon entering. Each inmate will learn from the prison and become either better or worse. I wish I could say that life improvement usually wins out over other forces. It does sometimes happen in this best of all criminal schools. For myself, against odds, I intend to make it so.

Yes, CIW is more than a holding pen for criminal types. It really is a community. But being a social unit does not make it a nice place to live. The average person stays here for three to five years and moves on, about the average for movement on the street. And not all is bad. Some of us convicts do save ourselves. We occasionally get some help. For most, the help is not enough.

| Exercise 2 | **REVISING AND EDITING A FIRST DRAFT** |

Revise the following student first draft according to CLUESS (coherence, language, unity, emphasis, support, and sentences). Then edit for COPS (capitalization, omissions, punctuation, and spelling). Space is provided for you to add, delete, move, and correct material. Divide the paragraph into a brief three-paragraph essay by placing an "X" after the introductory paragraph and another after the support, or body, paragraph.

*A yard cat is an unowned cat that runs free on the prison grounds.

Feng Shui
James Chow

When my real estate client, Mrs. Wong, asked me, "Do you know about Feng Shui?" I smiled and said, "Sure enough." Without that knowlege I could not do my deals. It is the name for Chinese superstitions. Especially those regarding the interrelationships of a person's birth chart and the home where they live. Describing an ideal house to a client may be a more a matter of describing what it should not have rather than what it should have. These are a few of the downers other than those associated with personal charts. At the entrance heading into the front door there should be no tree, but for it may mean you'll croak or split the blanket. The front door itself should not face the stairwell because all good fortune may roll right out of the house. The back door should also not face the front door such an arrangement may allow the dough that comes in the front door to go out the back. The house itself should sit on a lot that is square or rectangular, sharp angels will bring you down. The land itself should be higher along the fence behind the house to hold in prosperity. The house must face the right direction according to your birthday. This placement can affect a person's future. The number of the house may be more easily understood in Chinese, the number 4 means you're a goner. These and many, many more rules, along with common-sense requirements such as a bright and cheerful feeling and a fine layout are points Mrs. Wong will consider. Because trying to follow all the rules may hold up people from finding a happy pad, I often advise clients not to take them too seriously lest they make life a downer.

Exercise 3   REVISING AND EDITING YOUR PAPER

Revise and edit the rough draft you wrote for Exercise 1.

Writer's Guidelines: Writing, Revising, and Editing

1. Writing

    Write your first draft, paying close attention to your outline, list, or cluster. Do not concern yourself with perfect spelling, grammar, or punctuation.

2. Revising

    Revise your draft, using CLUESS.

    Coherence

    - Are the ideas clearly related, each one to the others and to the central idea?
    - Is there a clear pattern of organization (time, space, or emphasis)?
    - Is the pattern supported by words that suggest the basis of that organization (time: *now, then, later;* space: *above, below, up, down;* emphasis: *first, second, last*)?
    - Is coherence enhanced by the use of transitional terms, pronouns, repetition, and a consistent point of view?

    Language

    - Is the general style of language *usage* appropriate (properly standard and formal or informal) for the purpose of the piece and the intended audience?
    - Is the *tone* (language use showing attitude toward material and audience) appropriate?
    - Is the *diction* (word choice) effective? Are the words precise in conveying meaning? Are they fresh and original?

Unity
- Are the thesis and every topic sentence clear and well stated? Do they indicate both subject and treatment?
- Are all points of support clearly related to and subordinate to the topic sentence of each paragraph and to the thesis of the essay?

Emphasis
- Are ideas properly placed (especially near the beginning and end) for emphasis?
- Are important words and phrases repeated for emphasis?

Support
- Is there adequate material—such as examples, details, quotations, and explanations—to support each topic sentence and thesis?
- Are the points of support placed in the best possible order?

Sentences
- Are the sentences varied in length and beginnings?
- Are the sentences varied in pattern (simple, compound, complex, and compound-complex)?
- Are all problems with sentence structure (fragments, comma splices, run-ons) corrected?

3. Editing
    - Edit your draft for COPS. Are all problems in such areas as capitalization, omissions, punctuation, and spelling corrected?

4
Reading-Related Writing

Reading for Writing, p.67
  Underlining, p. 67
  Annotating, p. 68
  "Like, Whatever . . ." p. 68
  Outlining Source Material, p. 71

Supporting Ideas with Quotations and References, p. 73

Basic Documentation, p. 73
  Informal Documentation, p. 73
  Formal Documentation, p. 74

Documentation in Action, p. 75

Types of Reading-Related Writing, p. 76
  Single-Source Writing, p. 76
  Multiple-Source Writing, p. 82
  Student Essay: "Using More Than Laws Against Gangs," p. 84

Essays and Applications, p. 86
  Cell Phones and Pagers—to Ban or Bless?, p. 86
  "Allow Cell Phones and Pagers in the Classroom," p. 86
  "Ban Cell Phones and Pagers in Classrooms," p. 89

Journal Writing, p. 91

Career-Related Writing, p. 92

Writer's Guidelines, p. 92

THE QUIGMANS   by Buddy Hickerson

© Tribune Media Services, Inc. All Rights Reserved. Reprinted with permission.

Reading for Writing

Because most college writing assignments are connected with reading, it is worthwhile to consider how to focus thoughtful attention on the written word. Of course, if you know about writing assignments or tests beforehand, your reading can be more concentrated. You should always begin a reading assignment by asking yourself why you are reading that particular material and how it relates to your course work and interests. For example, most selections in this book are presented as ideas to stimulate thought and invite reflective comparisons, to provide material for analysis and evaluation, and to show how a pattern or process of writing can be done effectively. The discussion and critical-thinking questions and activities that follow the selections arise from these purposes. Other questions raised by your instructor or on your own can also direct you in purposeful reading. Consider such questions and activities at the outset. Then, as you read, use strategies that are appropriate for the kind of assignment you are working on. Among the most common strategies are underlining, annotating, and outlining. Used correctly, they will help you attain a critical, receptive, and focused state of mind as you prepare for writing assignments.

Underlining

Imagine you are reading a chapter of several pages, and you decide to underline and write in the margins. Immediately, the underlining takes you out of the passive, television-watching frame of mind. You are involved. You are participating. It is now necessary for you to discriminate, to distinguish more important from less important ideas. Perhaps you have thought of underlining as a method designed only to help you with reviewing. That is, when you study the material the next time, you won't have to reread all of it; instead, you can focus on the most important underlined parts. While you are underlining, you are benefiting from an imposed concentration, because this procedure forces you to think, to focus. Consider the following suggestions for underlining:

1. Underline the main ideas in paragraphs. The most important statement, the topic sentence, is likely to be at the beginning of the paragraph.

2. Underline the support for those main ideas.

3. Underline answers to questions that you bring to the reading assignment. These questions may have come from the end of the chapter, from subheadings that you turn into questions, or from your independent concerns about the topic.

4. Underline only the key words. You would seldom underline all the words in a sentence and almost never a whole paragraph.

Does that fit your approach to underlining? Possibly not. Most students, in their enthusiasm to do a good job, overdo underlining.

The trick is to figure out what to underline. You would seldom underline more than about 30 percent of a passage, although the amount would depend on your purpose and the nature of the material. Following the preceding four suggestions will be useful. Learning more about the principles of sentence, paragraph, and essay organization will also be helpful.

Annotating

Annotating, writing notes in the margins, is a practice related to underlining. You can do it independently, although it usually appears in conjunction with underlining to signal your understanding and to extend your involvement in your reading.

Writing in the margins represents intense involvement because it turns a reader into a writer. If you read material and write something in the margin as a reaction to it, then in a way you have had a conversation with the author. The author has made a statement and you have responded. In fact, you may have added something to the text; therefore, for your purposes you have become a co-author or collaborator. The comments you make in the margin are of your own choosing, according to your interests and the purpose you bring to the reading assignment. Your response in the margin may merely echo the author's ideas, it may question them critically, it may relate them to something else, or it may add to them.

The comments and marks in Section 1 of the following essay will help you understand the connection between writing and reading. Both techniques—underlining to indicate main and supporting ideas and annotating to indicate their importance and relevance to the task at hand—will enhance thinking, reading, and writing.

Like, Whatever . . .
An epidemic of inarticulacy could, uh, well, suck

David Orr

Section 1: Problem and Causes [Editor's subtitle]

Bright student

1 He entered my office as a freshman advisee sporting nearly perfect SAT scores and an impeccable academic record—a young man of considerable promise. During a 20-minute conversation,

	however, he displayed a vocabulary that consisted mostly of two words: *cool* and *really*. Almost 800 SAT points hitched to each word. He is no aberration, but an example of diminished literacy in a culture that often fails to use words carefully.
Self-restricted vocabulary **How typical?**	
Source indicating vocabulary decline?	In the past 50 years, by one reckoning, the working vocabulary of the average 14-year-old has declined from 25,000 words to 10,000. This is a decline not merely in words, but also in the capacity to think. We are losing the capacity to say what we mean, and ultimately to think about what we mean, about the things that matter most.
3 **Evidence?**	The problem is not confined to teenagers and young adults. A national epidemic of incoherence is evident in public discourse, street talk, movies, television, and music. Nor is the problem new. As H.L. Mencken, William Safire, and other commentators have noted, language is always coming undone. Why? First, those who intend to control others seize the words and metaphors by which people describe their world; in our time, the attackers are trying to sell one kind of quackery or another: economic, political, religious, or technological. The clarity and felicity of language—as distinct from its quantity—is devalued in an industrial-technological society. In fact, clear, artful language threatens that society.
Causes **First Cause—the controllers**	
4 **Second cause— specialized vocabulary** **Good and bad**	Second, language is in decline because it is being balkanized by specialized vocabularies. The highly technical language of the expert is, of course, both bane and blessing. It is useful for describing fragments of the world, but not for describing how they fit into a coherent whole. The language of molecular biology can describe genetic engineering, but interpreting the act of re-arranging life's genetic fabric requires an altogether different language, and a mind-set that seeks to discover larger patterns.
5 **Third cause—lack of direct experience** **Has virtual experience no value?**	Third, language reflects the range and depth of our experience. But our experience is being impoverished to the extent that it is rendered artificial and prepackaged. Most of us no longer experience skilled physical work on farms or in forests. Consequently, words and metaphors based on intimate knowledge of soils, plants, trees, animals, landscapes, and rivers have all but vanished. Recreation and software industries are engineering and shrink-wrapping our experience of an increasingly uniform and ugly world, and peddling it back to us as "fun" or "information."
6 **Fourth cause—no common literature**	Fourth, we are no longer held together by reading a common literature or listening to the same stories. Allusions to the Bible and great literature no longer resonate because those works are unfamiliar to a growing number of people.
7	Of the roughly 6,000 languages now spoken, linguists predict that less than half are expected to survive to the year 2050. Lan-

Language goes global and gets trimmed

-guage is being whittled down to the dimensions of the global economy and homogenized to accord with the "information age." This represents a loss of cultural information, a blurring of our capacity to understand the world and our place in it, and a losing bet that people armed with the words, metaphors, and mind-set of industry and technology can, in fact, manage the earth.

8

In management age, language gets managed

Language, George Orwell once wrote, "becomes ugly and inaccurate because our thoughts are foolish, but the slovenliness of our language makes it easier for us to have foolish thoughts." The new class of corporate chiefs, global managers, genetic engineers, and money speculators will reduce language to the level of utility, function, and management. Evil begins not only with words used with malice, but also with words that diminish people, land, and life. The prospects for evil grow as those for language decline.

9

Language and humanity
Lincoln
Churchill

Our affinity for language makes us human. We are never better than when we use words clearly eloquently, and civilly. Language can elevate thought and ennoble behavior. Abraham Lincoln's words at Gettysburg in 1863 gave meaning to the terrible sacrifices of the Civil War. Winston Churchill's words inspired a nation in the dark hours of 1940. If we intend to protect and enhance our humanity, we must first protect and enhance language and fight anything that undermines and cheapens it.

Section 2: Solutions [Editor's subtitle]

10

First solution— direct communication

But how to deal with mass population?

What does this mean? First, we must restore the habit of talking directly to each other—whatever the loss in economic efficiency. I propose that we smash every communication device used in place of a real person, beginning with answering machines.

11

Second, we can restore the habit of public reading. One of my distinctive childhood memories is attending a public reading of Shakespeare by the British actor Charles Laughton. With no prop other than a book, he read with energy and passion for two hours, keeping a large audience—including at least one 8-year-old boy—enthralled. No movie was ever as memorable. Further, I propose that adults turn off the television, unplug the computer, and read good books to their children. I know of no better or more pleasurable way to stimulate thinking, encourage love of language, and facilitate a child's ability to form images.

12

Third solution— language accountability

Third, we ought to hold those who corrupt language accountable, beginning with the advertising industry, which spends hundreds of billions of dollars each year to sell us an unconscionable amount of often useless, environmentally destructive, and un-

Methods? **Laws?**	healthy stuff. We should insist that they abide by community standards of truthfulness, including full disclosure of what products do to the environment and to those who buy them.
13	
Fourth solution—protect local culture	Fourth, we need to protect local culture from domination by national media, markets, and power. Language grows from the outside in, from periphery to center. It is renewed in the vernacular, where human intentions intersect places and circumstances, and by everyday acts of authentic living and speaking. It is corrupted by contrivance, pretense, and fakery. We need to protect the independence of local newspapers and local radio stations, as well as those parts of our culture where memory, tradition, and devotion to place still exist.
Protect by law? by education?	
14	
Role of teachers	<u>Finally,</u> since language is the currency of truth, we <u>should defend</u> the <u>integrity and clarity of language</u> as the <u>highest priority</u> for <u>schools, colleges,</u> and <u>universities.</u> As teachers, we should insist on good writing, assign readings that are well written, and restore rhetoric—the ability to speak clearly and well—to the liberal arts curriculum. And we, too, should be held accountable for what we say.
15	
Threat of propaganda and advertising	In terms of volume, this is surely an information age. But in terms of understanding, wisdom, spiritual clarity, and civility, we have entered a darker age. We are committing what C.S. Lewis once called "verbicide." The volume of words is inversely related to our capacity to use them well, and to think clearly about what they mean. <u>It</u> is <u>no wonder</u> that <u>in</u> a <u>dreary century</u> of gulags, genocide, global wars, and nuclear weapons, our use of language has been dominated by propaganda and advertising. And what will be said in the 21st century, as the stark realities of biotic impoverishment become apparent? Can we summon the clarity of mind to speak the necessary words?

Outlining Source Material

After reading, underlining, and annotating the piece, the next step could be to outline it. If the piece is well organized, you should be able to reduce it to a simple outline so that you can, at a glance, see the relationship of ideas (sequence, relative importance, and interdependence). Outlining is explained on pages 35–39.

Here is an outline of Section 1 of "Like, Whatever . . ."

I. National problem with language decline
   A. Among the young
   B. Among society generally

II. Causes
   A. Word controllers
      1. Methods
      2. Agendas
   B. Specialized vocabularies
      1. Good effects
      2. Bad effects
   C. Lack of direct experience
      1. Cultural changes
      2. Engineered activities
   D. No common literature
III. Global language
   A. Homogenized process
   B. Earth managed
   C. Dehumanization

Exercise 1   UNDERLINING, ANNOTATING, AND OUTLINING

Complete the underlining and annotation in Section 2 of "Like, Whatever...". Then complete the following outline that covers the same passage.

IV. Solutions
   A. Restore direct communication
      1. _____
      2. Smash answering machines
   B. Restore public reading
      1. Turn off _____
      2. Read _____
   C. Make violators _____
      1. Impose _____
      2. Require disclosure
   D. Protect _____
      1. Oppose _____
      2. Cherish local expression
   E. Educate
      1. Defend _____
      2. Require high standards in _____
      3. Hold teachers _____

V. The challenge
   A. Language dominated by _____ and _____
   B. Uncertain response

Supporting Ideas with Quotations and References

In your reading-related writing assignments, you are likely to use three methods in developing your ideas: explanation, direct reference to the reading selection, and quotation from the reading. The explanations can take different forms, such as causes or effects, comparison, definition, or exemplification. These forms are explored later in this book. The references point the reader directly toward the reading selection. The more specific the reference—including even the page number—the more helpful it is to your readers. As for quotations, remember that the words are borrowed. They can be very effective as support, but you must give credit to the original writer.

The use of quoted material is justified if it cannot be easily restated or if it carries weight because of its eloquence or origin. Usually, you should paraphrase or summarize rather than quote material to maintain the smooth flow of your thoughts. When quotation is called for, most writers use short quotations (just a few words) and blend them with paraphrase or summary; this compromise preserves the flavor and force of the original without creating an unevenness of presentation.

Basic Documentation

Borrowing words or ideas without giving credit to the source is called *plagiarism*. At best, plagiarism is sloppy scholarship; at worst, it is intellectual thievery. Therefore, your instructor will ask you to document or, in some way, to acknowledge original material in your source-based writing. Your method may be either informal or formal.

Informal Documentation

If you are writing in response to a single source—for example, from your textbook—your instructor may not ask you to indicate by page number where you found each borrowed idea. However, you will be expected to make clear, by use of quotation marks and names of authors, that you *have* borrowed ideas. If you are writing from an assigned reading selection, your references would not list your textbook as a source or use page number references unless your instructor directs you to do so. Simply writing something such as "I agree with Suzanne Britt when she says that thin people are unpleasant" would suffice.

Formal Documentation

If you are using material from sources other than your textbook, your instructor will probably ask you to use formal documentation, which includes citations and the listing of works that are cited.

Citations are acknowledgments of borrowed material. One documentation method is Modern Language Association (MLA) style. Here are some of the most common principles that can be used for textbook or other restricted sources, with some examples.

- If you use material from a source you have read, identify that source so the reader will recognize it or be able to find it.
- Document any original idea borrowed, whether it is quoted, paraphrased (written in your words but not shorter), or summarized (written in your words and shorter). Basic situations include the following:

> Normally, you need give only the author's name and a page number enclosed in parentheses: (Rivera 45).

> If you state the author's name in introducing the quotation or idea, then usually give only the page number in parentheses: (45).

> If the author has written more than one piece in the book, then a title or shortened form of the title is also required: (Rivera, *The Land* 45).

Here is an example of documenting a quotation by an author represented only once in a textbook, using the author's name to introduce:

> Suzanne Britt says that thin people have "speedy little metabolisms that cause them to bustle briskly" (265).

Following is an example of documenting an idea borrowed from an author but not quoted, using the author's name to introduce:

> Suzanne Britt believes that thin people are weak in character (267).

Here is an example of documenting an idea borrowed from another source but not using the author's name to introduce:

> Music often helps Alzheimer's patients think more clearly (Weiss 112).

MLA style also provides guidance for the listing of sources, called *Works Cited.* Here are three examples of commonly used materials.

Article in a Monthly or Bimonthly Magazine
Fallows, James. "Why Americans Hate the Media." *Atlantic Monthly* Feb. 1996: 45–64.

Newspaper Article
Gregory, Tina. "When All Else Fails." *Philadelphia Inquirer* 2 Apr. 1990: C12.

A Work in an Anthology (or in a textbook, other than by the author of that textbook)
Brock, Elizabeth. "A Bee in My Bonnet." *Paragraphs and Essays.* Ed. Lee Brandon. Boston: Houghton Mifflin Company, 2001. 106–107.

Documentation in Action

Your essay may include ideas from newspapers, magazines, or books. To make life simpler for you, most of the reading-related assignments in this book are based on selections included in this book. When you are writing about some thing you have read, just write as you usually would, but bring in ideas and quotations from that source. You may also want to refer to more than one source. You may even use ideas from other sources to contrast with your own. For example, you may say, "Unlike Fred M. Hechlinger in 'The First Step in Improving Sex Education: Remove the Hellfire' (351), I believe that public schools should not offer sex education." Do not feel that each point you make must be directly related to sources.

Here is a paragraph by student Jackie Malone illustrating how to incorporate ideas and document them:

Sexist men are victims of their own bias against females. Because they cannot accept women as full human beings, they themselves are smaller in dimension. In Irwin Shaw's "The Girls in Their Summer Dresses," Michael looks at his wife, but he doesn't see a full human being; he just sees a sexual object: "what a pretty girl, what nice legs" (314). Because he sees her and other women that way, he cannot ever have the relationship with her that she deserves and that he would find fulfilling. Of course, thinking of women as just soft and cuddly has its effects on men in other ways. The man as father who thinks that way may very well regard his own daughter as one limited in her ranges of activities and limited in her potential. He may be one of those fathers who immediately stereotype their daughters as headed for a "life of the affections," not like a son's, "earning a living" (Lurie 249). Unfortunately, these men cannot accept females as their equals in any important respect, and, in doing so, they deprive themselves, as well as others.

Types of Reading-Related Writing

Many college assignments will require you to use source material, rather than write only about personal experience. The extent to which you write from sources will depend on your purpose in fulfilling assignments. Some assignments will be very precise, asking you to paraphrase, summarize, explain, or evaluate specific reading material. Others will ask you to relate a source or part of a source to your experiences.

These reading-related assignments will be based on single or multiple sources. All of them will require a careful reading of a source or sources. As you concentrate on your purpose, your skills in underlining, annotating, and outlining will help you to interpret material and locate useful ideas that can be borrowed for your writing.

Single-Source Writing

Writing from a single source will take one or more of the following forms:

- a *summary* (material in your own words; only main ideas)
- a *paraphrase* (material in your own words; more than main ideas)
- a *reaction* (usually ideas on how the reading relates specifically to you, your experiences, and your attitudes; it also is often a critique of the worth and logic of the reading)
- a *two-part response* (includes both a summary and a reaction, but they are separate)

Summary

A *summary* is a rewritten, shortened version of a piece of writing in which you use your own wording to express the main ideas. Learning to summarize effectively will help you in many ways. Summary writing reinforces comprehension skills in reading. It requires you to discriminate among the ideas in the reading passage. Summaries are usually written in the form of a well-designed paragraph or a cluster of brief paragraphs and are frequently used in essays and research papers.

The following rules will guide you in writing effective summaries.

1. Cite the author and title of the text.
2. Keep the length shorter than the original by about two-thirds (although the exact reduction will vary depending on the content of the original).
3. Include the main ideas. (Include details only infrequently.)
4. Change the original wording without changing the idea.

5. Do not evaluate the content or give an opinion (even if you see an error in logic or fact).
6. Do not add ideas (even if you have an abundance of related information).
7. Do not include any personal comments (do not use *I,* referring to self).
8. Use quotations sparingly. (If you do quote directly from the source, enclose the quoted material in quotation marks.)
9. Use author tags ("says York," "according to York," or "the author explains") to remind the reader(s) that you are summarizing the material of another author.

Paraphrase

A *paraphrase* is similar to a summary in that both are a recasting of a reading passage into your own words. It is different, however, in that the summary includes only main ideas, whereas the paraphrase can include the rewording of any statement. The summary is shorter than the original; the paraphrase can be longer, shorter, or about the same length. However, both forms are reworded products. Except for the rules about a summary being shorter and concentrating on main ideas, the same rules apply to writing a paraphrase.

Exercise 2　EVALUATING A SUMMARY

Apply the rules of summary writing to the following summary of Section 1 of "Like, Whatever..." (p. 68). Use rule numbers (pp. 76–77) to annotate the faulty parts of the summary.

"Like, Whatever..."

The author says "a national epidemic of incoherence is evident in public discourse, street talk, movies, television, and music." His main example is a 14-year-old with high SAT scores and mainly a two-word vocabulary. It seems to me that he had to have a big vocabulary to achieve high SAT scores. The author goes on to explain that four causes are evident. One, the controllers—economic, political, religious, or technological—have imposed their own words to characterize their main concerns, thereby controlling the way people think about certain things, such as abortion, industrial safety, and unemployment. Two, language has developed in certain areas to pertain only to those areas and not to relate to other concerns, thus setting up communication barriers. The author could have and should have focused more here. Three, our direct experience with our physical world in nature has diminished, and with that loss goes the use of language pertaining to our direct experience. I think he means we do not go camping or practice farming very much anymore. Four, we are no longer held together by reading a common literature or listening to the same stories. Moreover, the problem of language decline is global. Languages are disappearing, and international business leaders are imposing their words and thought patterns on the world population. Humanity depends on us to make language strong and to fight anything that undermines and cheapens it.

Following is an example of an effective summary of the Section 1 of "Like, Whatever . . .".

A Summary of "Like, Whatever . . ." by David Orr

In "Like, Whatever . . ." David Orr says the decline of language usage is a national problem that threatens our ability to think effectively. He explains that four causes are evident. One, the controllers—"economic, political, religious, or technological"—have imposed their own words to characterize their main concerns, thereby controlling the way people think about certain things. Two, language has developed in certain areas to pertain to those areas and not to relate to other concerns, thus setting up communication barriers. Three, our direct experience with our physical world in nature has diminished, and with that loss goes the use of language relating to our direct experience. Virtual experience and commercially packaged encounters do not lead to language invention. Four, we do not share a literature derived from common reading and listening experiences. Moreover, the problem of language decline is global. Languages are disappearing, and international business leaders are imposing their words and thought patterns on the world population. Humanity depends on our maintaining and improving our language skills.

Reaction

As with all reading-related assignments, after clarifying exactly what you are setting out to do in writing your reaction, you read, underline, and annotate your subject passage. You may even outline or summarize the material before you proceed to writing your response. At this time, you know the author's purpose, the main points, and the reasoning and supporting information. The focus of your reaction will depend on the author's purpose in writing the passage. All reactions will include some summary and paraphrase. Following are some of the approaches you may take:

- *Agreement or disagreement:* You may agree or disagree with the author's ideas and present your views on a point-by-point basis, typically discussing each point in a paragraph composed of a summary, probably some quotation, and your response. Or you may select only a few points for your treatment. Whatever your range, your position will be supported by your own reasoning and by your own evidence, such as examples.
- *Critique, or evaluation:* This approach usually has a broader scope than the reaction of agreement or disagreement. It emphasizes critical thinking and reveals the worth, logic, and overall effectiveness of the piece.
- *Parallel experience (sometimes called a* spin-off*):* You may concentrate on your own experience or experiences as related to one or more ideas in the passage. For example, if your subject reading selection is about a struggle over a career choice and you have had a similar struggle, you may decide to use the framework of the reading passage to guide you in discussing your struggle. You would refer specifically to the subject passage, perhaps use some quotation, and point out similarities and dissimilarities between the reading selection and your experience. Your reader would recognize your grasp of the original piece and appreciate the skill with which you relate it to your experience. This approach may use only a part of the subject work, a substantial portion, or all the major points.

The following paragraph is a reaction in which the student writer agrees with one aspect of Section 1 of "Like, Whatever . . .".

Response to "Like, Whatever . . ." by David Orr

In "Like, Whatever . . ." David Orr makes a strong case for his thesis that language usage is declining worldwide. Language is part of society and reflects all its changes and values. As the economy becomes global, so does language. As international companies advertise and use public relations techniques, everyone is exposed over and over to phrases that are carefully crafted by individuals with agendas, such as CEOs, politicians, preachers, and ad-persons. He says they want to control how we think. Orr's examples of language decline easily bring to mind other examples that bombard us daily. We are more likely to buy a car that is "preowned" than one that is "used." We would rather live in the "inner city" than a "slum" or "ghetto." It is easier for a company to "downsize" than to "fire people." It is better for a gas stove to "puff-back" than to "explode." We can hardly avoid using certain words that bother us, such as "pro-life" or "pro-choice." And we vaguely realize that as we accept words adopted and adapted by others to characterize their positions, our thoughts are being controlled. Yet we do not look around for words to fit our situations. Instead, we are provided with virtual experiences, complete with words. As with a song video, we are given the words, and we are given the pictures so we do not have to use our imagination. Almost every phase of life is becoming a video. David Orr is saying we should sing more of our own songs and write them with care.

Student author's reactions, agreeing with the subject piece and providing new examples

Two-Part Response

As you have seen, the reaction includes a partial summary or is written with the assumption that readers have read the original piece. However, your instructor may prefer that you separate each form— for example, by presenting a clear, concise summary followed by a reaction to the passage. This format is especially useful for critical examination of a text or for problem-solving assignments, because it requires you to understand and repeat another's views or experiences before responding. The two-part approach also helps you avoid the common problem of writing only a summary of the text when your instructor wants you to both summarize and evaluate or otherwise react. Before writing a summary and a reaction, ask your instructor if you should separate your summary from your response.

Following is a two-part response to Section 2 of "Like, Whatever . . .". The first paragraph is a summary of the passage, and the second is the reader's reaction to it.

Two-Part Response to Section 2 of "Like Whatever . . ."
by David Orr

Summary

In "Like, Whatever . . ." David Orr does not just describe the problem of language decline; he also offers five clear solutions. The first solution is to restore direct communication by "talking directly to each other" and forsaking electronic substitutes. The second is to bring back public reading after disconnecting such instruments as television sets and computers. The third is to make those who debase the language accountable by requiring full explanations of the harmful effects of advertised products. The fourth is to protect local customs and cultures by promoting local rather than national media. The fifth is to make effective language the primary concern in all educational institutions. Teachers themselves should require high standards in reading and writing. Orr says that our "language has been dominated by propaganda and advertising." He says we have the answers to the problem of language decline, and now he wonders if we have the strength to respond.

Reaction

> **Student's experience that illustrates one of Orr's basic ideas**

In his essay "Like, Whatever . . ." David Orr details the problem of language decline and offers five solutions. One solution struck a familiar chord in my experience, that of our need to communicate directly with others and to turn off electronic devices such as the television set. When I was in the fifth grade, my school promoted an experiment. We students were asked to persuade our families to unplug our television sets for one month. It was not an easy argument to make in my household, but my family finally did agree. The result was pretty remarkable. Instead of watching reruns of "Star Trek" during dinner, we talked. At first we did not have much to say, and once my mother made out a list of topics. But soon we were talking straight through the meals, and not just during television commercials. I learned family folklore that I never would have heard about, and I still remember some of it. At times I contributed by talking more about school and what I was doing than I ever had. After dinner we played games and engaged in a lot of banter. Before bedtime, my parents and I read stories to my two younger siblings. The experiment lasted for just that one month. At the end of that one experimental month, my family talked about never plugging in the television set. Then came the professional football playoff games. My youngest sister confessed that she had been sort of cheating all along by visiting with friends to watch television. She said she had needed to watch so she would not feel like a nerd with her friends. Then I was sick for a couple of weeks. Television helped me pass the time. Soon we were a television family again. We kids were being told to hush up during the mealtime news programs. During "Wheel of Fortune," we could speak up with answers. As

David Orr says, we were listening to speech "dominated by propaganda and advertising." For the most part, we had made the choice. Unfortunately and regrettably, we liked it.

Multiple-Source Writing

Synthesis

A *synthesis* is the blending of two or more sources with your own commentary. The extent to which the sources are used varies. You may be writing about a controversial issue and need some expert insights or observations. You would naturally read several sources. You may even summarize some of them as you identify main ideas. In your search you may discover that one reading selection yields a single answer while another yields a different answer. A third has perhaps two solutions. From your perspective all four of the ideas are sound and you decide to show how they can work together to solve the problem.

The procedure is simple.

- Make notes from the sources. If the sources are not in your textbook, you may want to use a standard note-card form, which includes the relationship of the idea to your topic, identification of your source, location of the material within the work, and the idea as quoted or paraphrased, as shown in the following student example.

Editorial note — **Topic division** — **Author's name** — **Page location**

Entertainment   Carpenter 60

Text
Quote — "Citizens of more than one city [see Los Angeles] have strenuously battled their zoos when officials tried to get rid of lions or bears to make room for less romantic but more endangered species." Citizens usually win.

Summary — Relevance: shows influence of zoo goers on policy.

As material relates to paper

- If the sources are in your textbook, underline and mark material for use—or, even better, copy the passage you intend to quote or paraphrase—and key it to your outline by using symbols or by copying it onto your outline.

- As you present the ideas, identify them by source information in citations and discuss their relationship.

The result of this procedure may be a paragraph, with the ideas blended, or it may be an essay. The essay form might include an introduction defining the issue, a separate paragraph for each author's view, a paragraph or so for explaining precisely how the borrowed ideas relate, and then the conclusion.

Whether the blending of two or more sources occurs within a sentence, a paragraph, or an essay, it is still synthesis. The ideas are always presented in a relationship that builds an idea, discusses an idea from a different perspective, or even opposes an idea.

A synthesis can relate to the summary and the paraphrase. The summary identifies main ideas in sources. The synthesis will use one or more of those ideas to compare and contrast with other ideas from sources. The ideas themselves may be used as quotations, but they are more likely to be restated, or paraphrased.

Demonstration of Synthesis

Following is a demonstration of synthesis as it occurs in a short essay. To save space, only excerpts from three key sources are included here. The borrowed quotations are underlined and annotated. Note that each source is concerned with how to deal with youth gangs, but each has a different solution. Student Lewan Huang sees merit in all views and creates a simple synthesis. The citations, as they occur in parentheses in her essay on page 84, might not be required by some instructors if the sources are all from the same book.

Gangs and gang violence have become subjects of great interest and concern for all of Southern California. Law-enforcement agencies are expending enormous resources in their fight against gang-related crime. But, for the mothers of the targets of this law-enforcement effort, the problem is far more immediate than newspaper headlines and stories on TV news. The problem is family. . . .

Community involvement as one solution

Capt. Jack <u>Blair</u> of the <u>Pomona Police Department</u> <u>leads weekly gang-truce meetings</u> attended by <u>parents,</u> <u>gang members</u> and <u>local clergy.</u> In the course of his year-long involvement with the Pomona program, he has become convinced that "parents are the key to [solving] the whole problem." At his meetings, and at other meetings of parents around the county, Blair believes that parents have begun to make a difference. <u>"Once the parents unite and form groups, talking to each other and sharing information, that is threatening to the gang members.</u> They want anonymity. They don't want their tactics or activities talked about with parents of rival gangs. When the moms are

84 CHAPTER 4

Sue Horton, "Mothers, Sons, and the Gangs"

saying 'Hey, don't go over to this neighborhood,' or 'I know that you went over to that neighborhood,' there is a certain amount of sport removed." **230**

But in those days, most *vatos* became *veteranos* by their 20s and outgrew the crazy life. Some led a dual life, going to school or work during the week and hanging out in the neighborhood on weekends. Guns were a rare commodity and drive-bys were just beginning to be used as a gang tactic. Most *veteranos* made the transition to the work force as semiskilled and skilled laborers and as professionals. . . . Guys working for a living as did their fathers and grandfathers before them.

Economic cause

Carlos A. Chavez and Antonio H. Rodriguez, "*La Vida Loca: Crazy Life, Crazy Death*"

The loss of blue-collar jobs, combined with the curtailment of social spending, has eroded employment and educational opportunities for our children to the point that they are extremely marginalized. In the process, the adolescent lifestyle for many of them appears to have become a life sentence. **C3**

Hundreds of young women and girls have hooked up with the Bloods and Crips in Portland, giving their boyfriends safe haven and sometimes joining them in the violence of gang culture.

Police say the future of gangs may hinge on these young women, who dress their children—especially little boys—in gang colors, teach them hand signs and nurture an allegiance to vendettas.

Enablers

"If we could get the girls to stop associating with the male gang members, we wouldn't have any gangs," policewoman Dorothy Elmore says bluntly.

"Girls are the backbone of gangs," say Elmore, who works with the Portland Police Bureau's Gang Enforcement Team.

Holly Gilbert, "Girls Form Backbone of Gangs"

"Girls give the males a place to lay their heads. Girls shelter them. Girls feed them. They protect them. They nurture them. Girls carry their guns and their dope. They are the key. **A3**

Student Essay

Using More Than Laws Against Gangs

Lewan Huang

One of the most difficult crimes to combat is youth crime, specifically that perpetrated by gangs. If gangs could be eradicated or even if their criminal activities could be curtailed, the crime rate would drop dramatically. Incarceration is always available as a solution, but it does not get at the causes or treat the gang problems within their own communities. Broader-based solutions pertain to drug culture, families, education, and the economy.

Gang members are primarily males, but females often play the roles of enablers. Holly Gilbert says in "Girls Form Backbone of Gangs" that females are the key to gang survival. These females support their male companions, help them in crime, conceal their drugs and weapons, and bear their children. Then they dress the children in gang clothing and pass along gang behavior, traditions, and hand signs. Gilbert quotes Portland, Oregon, policewoman Dorothy Elmore as saying, "'If we could get the girls to stop associating with the male gang members, we wouldn't have any gangs'" (A3). Getting these girls to recognize how they are being used and abused would be an important step in combatting gang activity.

Another solution lies with the actual families of gang members. Gang members themselves often come from troubled families but not always. And well-meaning family members can help if they are given the opportunity through some kind of organized structure. Sue Horton, in "Mothers, Sons, and the Gangs," writes about one such program in Pomona, California. There the local police department brings together the gang members, their parents, and the clergy to discuss neighborhood problems. Captain Jack Blair says, "'Once the parents unite and form groups, talking to each other and sharing information, that is threatening to gang members'" (230). There the parents have become part of the solution.

One of the most significant causes of gang formation is economic. Carlos A. Chavez and Antonio H. Rodriguez say that gangs have long existed in Los Angeles, but now the underlying conditions have changed. In previous times, the gang members would go through a brief period of rebellion; then they would mature and join the job market for skilled and unskilled workers in factories. But those jobs are no longer available. According to Chavez and Rodriguez, "The loss of blue-collar jobs, combined with the curtailment of social spending," has reduced work and school opportunities, and gang life now extends well into maturity (C3).

These three solutions came from three different articles, but taken together they offer the multidirectional approach that is necessary. We need to educate the girlfriend enablers and to work with the family members. Beyond that, we as a society should provide educational and job opportunities. As for the gang members and their personal responsibility, they need to be receptive and adaptive. Of course, if they are not law abiding, the police should lock them up.

Works Cited

Chavez, Carlos A., and Antonio H. Rodriguez. "*La Vida Loca:* Crazy Life, Crazy Death." *Los Angeles Times* 17 Aug. 1995: C3.

Gilbert, Holly, "Girls Form Backbone of Gangs." *The Oregonian* 30 Sept. 1990: A3.

Horton, Sue. "Mothers, Sons, and the Gangs." *Celebrating Diversity.* Ed. Lee Brandon. Lexington, Mass.: D.C. Heath, 1995, 229–239.

Essays and Applications

The following paired essays demonstrate many of the elements of good writing that we have been exploring. To help you evaluate and write in response to those selections, each essay is accompanied first by a set of discussion and critical thinking questions and then by several reading-related writing suggestions. As you read, underline and annotate the material.

Cell Phones and Pagers—to Ban or Bless?

Both students and instructors are likely to react to allowing cell phones and pagers in the classroom with rapture or rage. Good representations of the opposing views on this issue, these paired informal essays by teachers Gail Washburn and Don Mack appeared on the same page of *NEA Today,* March 2001.

Allow Cell Phones and Pagers in the Classroom

Gail Washburn

Gail Washburn teaches art at Rangeland Elementary School in Louisville, Kentucky. A 21-year teaching veteran, she recently served on a National Board for Professional Teaching Standards committee, writing elementary art standards.

1. "Mom's working late tonight, son. Please wait for me by the front door of your school immediately after basketball practice.

2. "Don't play around in the gym, because I have another Association meeting this evening and your dad is working second shift."

3. If only I could give this message to my son!

4. I was always taught to be the most I could be. Get involved in your job and community, volunteer, give back. I have taught my students and children to have that same work ethic and attitude. How disconnected I feel when I can't reach my son at school to tell him of a change of plans.

5. If only I could talk to him now.

6. How many times have I left messages with an already overworked office secretary? And how often have I left notes in my school mailbox, unread for days?

7. I am a teacher, and I believe disruptive beeps and rings should be turned off and the phone set to vibrate mode during class. But in this great age of E-technology, I should be able to reach my son.

8. There are more single parents, divorced custodial parents, and workaholic parents than ever. More moms are choosing careers over staying at home. More dads are choosing to commute out-of-town for better jobs.

9. All this is juggled with after-school classes, sports, clubs, detention—what are parents to do?

10. We now have daycares at the workplace. Personal Internet camera surveillance at child-care facilities seems to improve employee morale and attendance.

11. Let's face it—parents work better when they know their kids are okay. We, as educators, want them to be more involved with their kids. And cell phones are one way to accomplish that.

12. But there's more than the parents' dilemma. Let's look at the bigger picture. Times are changing. E-commerce is on the rise. In the future, there will be telephones on wristwatches, backpacks, notebooks. Will we ban them?

13. I remember grounding my son once and telling him he couldn't use the telephone. Hearing laughter and talking coming from his room, I tiptoed up the steps and quickly opened the door. To my surprise, he was on his computer, talking to his friends face to face, voice to voice.

14. The future is now. Computers are cell phones and pagers. Students will find a way to use them, just as our generation used the once-prohibited calculators and tape recorders.

15. Finally, we say we should teach by example. Can we as teachers live without our cell phones and pagers?

16   How many times has our school telephone system blacked out because of heavy rains and strong winds (better known as long-winded teachers on the only available phone line)?

17   In case of emergencies, cell phones can be the only lifeline out of the school facility. Remember Columbine?

18   Not all cellular technology interferes with learning. With the newest technology, students can use their cell phones to connect to the Internet.

19   Let's find ways like these to incorporate cellular technology into our classroom curriculum.

Exercise 3 DISCUSSION AND CRITICAL THINKING

Purpose
1. What is Washburn's position?

2. Does she allow for any exceptions to her position?

Support
3. What are Washburn's main points of support?

Organization and Special Techniques
4. How convincing are Washburn's examples, both real and hypothetical?

5. What comparison does she use? How apt is it?

6. How effective is Washburn's placement of her main idea toward the middle of the essay?

Personal Reaction
7. Are you persuaded by her argument? Why or why not? Has she overlooked any good points on her side?

Ban Cell Phones and Pagers in Classrooms

Don Mack

Don Mack is a computer lab facilitator and chair of the learning media services department at Laramie High School in Wyoming. He has taught for 23 years. He edits the Albany County Education Association newsletter and is Wyoming's representative to the NEA Resolutions Committee.

1. Increasingly, authorities have outlawed the use of cell phones by motorists because of the risk of accidents. In a school classroom, we don't typically have students driving automobiles, but we conduct a wide variety of activities that require every bit as much attention from the student as traffic would from a motorist.

2. Schools are islands of learning where a teacher and a group of students are provided the opportunity to interact, interrupted only by the passing bell.

3. Educational professionals have campaigned long and hard to eliminate the incessant intercom and paper barrage that accosts the classroom. In many places, we have been successful, and interruptions from secretaries, counselors, and administrators have been cut to a bare minimum.

4. The incursion of cell phones and beepers could deal a severe setback to any progress that's been made to bar interruptions.

5. Early this year, a colleague's presentation was disrupted when a student's cell phone, carried into the classroom in a backpack, began ringing. Initially, both the teacher and students attempted to ignore the distraction and continued working. But after several rings, the owner of the cell phone apologized and answered the call.

6. The call was of a social nature and the student hung up as quickly as possible. But the flow of instruction was disrupted, and valuable learning time was lost. This isn't an isolated occurrence.

7. Setting the phone to vibrate instead of ring is not enough. Whether the phone beeps, squawks, belts out an N'Sync tune, or simply vibrates, the pesky little device will continue to demand attention. Very few adults will let a call go unanswered. And my observations of my own children and students indicate than an unanswered phone call drives them up a wall.

8. If the phone is answered, all learning comes to a screeching halt while a classroom full of ears listens to one side of a conversa-

tion and imagines the dialogue that must be coming from the invisible intruder.

9 By their very nature, these gadgets insist on being the controlling attraction in the classroom. For some students, the distraction comes because they don't have a cell phone or pager and wish they did. These items are also attractive to the thieves who may inhabit our hallways and prey on the unsuspecting.

10 School curriculums are created to provide the best possible education for the students. When a phone call interrupts the classroom regimen, it destroys the planning and instruction that have been carefully crafted by the educator, be it lecture, group work, test taking, or silent seat work.

11 Policies and procedures have been adopted and office personnel have been well trained in the answering of school phones and the delivery of messages. There's little in the way of emergency or critical information that can't get from a school secretary to a student in a matter of seconds, should the need arise. In our school, there is a pay phone for students who must place a call.

12 Cell phones and pagers have no place among the possessions that a student brings to school.

Exercise 4   DISCUSSION AND CRITICAL THINKING

Purpose
1. Which sentence most clearly states Mack's thesis?

2. Does he allow any exceptions or make any concessions?

Support
3. What are Mack's main points of support?

Organization and Special Techniques
4. Mack begins with a comparison to stress the importance of his position. Is the comparison of driving an automobile and sitting in a classroom valid?

5. Does the example in paragraph 5 work well? Explain.

6. In paragraph 11, Mack offers a refutation to those who say that students and parents need to be able to communicate effectively. In his refutation, Mack argues that such communication occurs now without use of cell phones or pagers. Is his reasoning persuasive?

Personal Reaction
7. Relying on your experience and reasoning, evaluate Mack's argument.

Exercise 5   SUGGESTIONS FOR READING-RELATED WRITING

Complete one of the following reading-related responses.

1. Write a summary of one of the essays.
2. Write a reaction response to one of the essays. Be sure to incorporate your own views and discuss your experiences with cell phones and pagers.
3. Write a two-part response composed of labeled summary and reaction parts.
4. Write a synthesis on one of the following points. Refer to both sources to some extent and include citations.
    a. the use of cell phones in restaurants and movie theaters or the use of cell phones by automobile drivers (not based mainly on the two essays but sharing some points of concern)
    b. your own view on whether to allow cell phones and pagers in classrooms, perhaps including some examples from your experience

Journal Writing

Your journal entries are likely to be concerned primarily with the relationship between the reading material and you—your life experiences, your views, your imagination. The reading material will give you something of substance to write about, but you will be writing especially for yourself, developing confidence and ease in writing, so that writing becomes a comfortable part of your everyday activities, as speaking already is.

These journal entries will be part of your intellectual diary, recording what you are thinking about a certain issue. They will be of use in helping you understand the reading material, in helping you develop your writing skills, in uncovering ideas that can be used on other assignments, and in helping you think more clearly and imaginatively. Because these entries are of a more spontaneous nature than the more structured writing assignments, organization and editing are likely to be of less concern.

Each journal entry should be clearly dated and, if reading related, should specify the title and author of the original piece.

Even if your instructor wants you to concentrate on what you read for your journal writing, he or she might not want you to be restricted to the material in this text. Fortunately, you are surrounded by reading material in newspapers, magazines, and, of course, textbooks from other courses. These topics can serve you well, especially if you want to begin your journal writing now.

Career-Related Writing

This textbook includes career-related writing topics at the end of Chapters 5 through 12. They are a special feature designed to offer options to students who would like to write about jobs they currently hold, major areas of study, and intended careers. Because students are often studying materials in other classes and have access to other published sources, career-related writing may include ideas from reading material. Those ideas can be documented with a listing of the source, which usually includes the name of the author, title of the work, place of publication, publisher, date, and page numbers. The citations for quotations or specific references can be made in the same fashion as the ones for textbook sources.

Writer's Guidelines: Reading-Related Writing

1. Underlining helps you to read with discrimination.
   - Underline the main ideas in paragraphs.
   - Underline the support for those ideas.
   - Underline answers to questions you bring to the reading assignment.
   - Underline only the key words.
2. Annotating enables you to actively engage the reading material.
   - Number parts if appropriate.
   - Make comments according to your interests and needs.
3. Outlining the passages you read sheds light on the relationship of ideas, including the major divisions of the passage and their relative importance.

4. Summarizing helps you concentrate on main ideas.
   - Cite the author and title of the text.
   - Keep the length shorter than the original by about two-thirds (although the exact reduction will vary depending on the content of the original).
   - Include the main ideas. (Include details only infrequently.)
   - Change the original wording without changing the idea.
   - Do not evaluate the content or give an opinion in any way (even if you see an error in logic or fact).
   - Do not add ideas (even if you have an abundance of related information).
   - Do not include any personal comments (Do not use *I*, referring to self.).
   - Use quotations sparingly. (If you do quote directly from the source, enclose the quoted material in quotation marks.)
   - Use author tags ("says York," "according to York," or "the author explains") to remind the reader(s) that you are summarizing the material of another author.

5. Three other types of reading-related writing are
   - the *reaction*—a discussion of how the reading relates to you, your experiences, and your attitudes; also, often your critique of the worth and logic of the piece.
   - the *two-part response*—a summary and a reaction, usually presented in separate paragraphs.
   - the *synthesis*—a blending of ideas from two or more sources.

6. Most ideas in reading-related papers are developed using one or more of these ways: explanation, direct references, and quotations.

7. Documenting is giving credit to borrowed ideas and words.

Part II

Writing Essays:
Instructions and Reading Selections

5
Exemplification: Writing with Examples

Surveying Exposition, p. 97

Writing Essays of Exemplification, p. 97
   Characteristics of Good Examples, p. 97
   Techniques for Finding Examples: Listing and Clustering, p. 98
   Number and Order of Examples, p. 99

Connecting Sources and Writing, p. 99
   Student Essay: "Prison Tattoos," p. 100
   Practicing Patterns of Exemplification, p. 101
   Student Documented Essay: "Biting My Tongue—Sometimes," p. 103
   "Lessons from a Control Freak," p. 106
   "I'm Outta Here!" p. 110
   "Making the Grade, p. 115
   "Underground Dads," p. 118

Topics for Writing Exemplification, p. 120
   Writing Process Worksheet, p. 120
   Source-Based Topics, p. 121
   Career-Related Topics, p. 122
   General Topics, p. 122

Writer's Guidelines, p. 123

THE QUIGMANS by Buddy Hickerson

"So what do you have that's fresh?"

© Tribune Media Services, Inc. All Rights Reserved. Reprinted with permission.

Surveying Exposition

With this chapter on exemplification, we turn to *exposition*, a form of writing whose main purpose is to explain. This and the following six chapters will explore these questions:

Exemplification	Can you give me an example or examples of what you mean?
Analysis by Division	How do the parts work together?
Classification	What types of things are these?
Process Analysis	How do I do it? How is it done?
Comparison and Contrast	How are these similar and dissimilar?
Cause and Effect	What is the reason for this? What is the outcome?
Definition	What does this term mean?

In most informative writing, these various methods of organizing and developing thought are used in combination, with one method dominating according to the writer's purpose for explaining. The other forms of discourse can be used in combination with these. You have already learned that narration and description are frequently used for expository purposes.

Writing Essays of Exemplification

Exemplification means using examples to explain, convince, or amuse. Lending interest and information to writing, exemplification is one of the most common and effective ways of developing ideas. Examples may be developed in a sentence or more, or they may be only phrases or even single words, as in the following sentence: "Children like packaged breakfast foods, such as *Wheaties, Cheerios,* and *Rice Krispies.*"

Characteristics of Good Examples

As supporting information, the best examples are specific, vivid, and representative. These three qualities are closely linked; collectively, they must support the topic sentence of a paragraph and the thesis of an essay.

You use examples to inform or convince your reader. Of course, an example by itself does not necessarily prove anything. We know that examples can be found on either side of an argument, even at the extreme edges. Therefore, in addition to providing specific examples so that your reader can follow you precisely and vivid ones so that your reader will be interested, you should choose examples that are representative. Representative examples are examples that your reader can consider, accept as appropriate, and even match with examples of his or her own. If you are writing about cheating and you give one specific, vivid, and representative example, your reader should be able to say, "That's exactly what happens. I can imagine just how the incident occurred, and I could give some examples that are similar."

Techniques for Finding Examples: Listing and Clustering

Writing a good essay of exemplification begins, as always, with prewriting. The techniques you use will depend on what you are writing about. If you were writing about cheating at school, you might work effectively with a list, perhaps including a few insights into your topic if you have not already formulated your controlling statement. The following is one such list compiled by student Lara Olivas. This is her controlling statement: Cheating students often put themselves under more stress than honest students. She has circled items she thinks she can use.

Student Cheating

When I copied homework
Looking at a friend's test answers
A student with hand signals
Jake and his electronic system
Time for planned cheating
Those who got caught
(A person who bought a research paper)
Jess, who copied from me
The Internet "Cheaters" source
The two students who exchanged identities
(More work than it's worth)
(More stress than it's worth)
The teacher's assistant and his friends
(The girl from the biology class)

If you are pretty well settled on your subject and you expect to use several different kinds of examples, clustering may work very well for you. Student Garabed Yegavian first used clustering to explore and then transferred much of his information to an outline. Yegavian's cluster is shown on page 99.

Cultural Diversity in My Life cluster:
- TV: Spanish, Armenian, English
- food: sushi bar, bagel, Zancou's Chicken—Armenian, Perrier water, Turkish coffee
- car: Japanese, Korean mechanic (oil—USA), tires (Kelly—USA)
- home
- clothes: socks—Mexico, shoes—Italy, shirt (cloth from India, made in USA)

Number and Order of Examples

After you have explored your topic and collected information, you must decide whether to use only one example with a detailed explanation, a few examples with a bit less information, or a cluster of examples. A well-stated topic sentence or thesis will guide you in making this decision. When you are writing about a personal topic, you will probably have far more examples than you can use.

If your example is an incident or a series of incidents, you will probably use time order, reinforcing that arrangement with terms such as *next, then, soon, later, last*, and *finally*. If your examples exist in space (maybe in different parts of a room), then you would use space references (*up, down, left, right, east, west, north*, and *south*). Arranging examples by emphasis means going from the most important example to the least important or from the least to the most important.

Connecting Sources and Writing

Student Essay

April McClure became a full-time college student after she was paroled from the California Institution for Women near Chino, California. As she examined a list of prompts for her college writing assignment, one caught her eye:

> Write about an article of clothing, an accessory, or an expression of body art that you have seen change in

acceptance or popularity from one time to another or from one place to another. Use specific examples.

Prison Tattoos
April McClure

Imagine my surprise when I was paroled and discovered that, in the free world, tattoos were cool! Of course, I had watched television and seen a few movies. I knew NBA players wore tattoos. I knew rock stars flaunted them. But I did not know the extent to which even the goody-two-shoes were getting inked up. My God, I was in style. And I had come from a place where tattoos were just like articles of clothing, except we could not take them off so easily. The upshot of it all is that now when people find out I have done time, they look at my butterfly and bird illustrations and ask how tattooing fits in with prison life.

For one thing, tattooing is a trade on the yard. A person with a bit of talent in basic art finds clients waiting. All that person needs is a tattoo gun, some ink, and a pattern book. An electric tattoo gun can be made out of a motor from an electric shaver, a barrel from a ball point pen, a spoon, a guitar cord, and some tape. My friend Frisco is the best in the business. She made a gun, got some ditto masters for designs, and burned black dominos and styrofoam for ink. In two years she became the main tattooist on the yard.

The kinds of tattoos convicts get are as varied as are the convicts, which is quite varied. Some want humor. I knew this woman named Dawson who had fleas tattooed along her hairline. They looked real. She also had "sweet" and "sour" over her breasts, and a little man with a lawnmower headed down her stomach. Then an inmate called Sunshine had a list of men's names tattooed on her arm, seven at last count. All but the last one was crossed out. She said he was about ready to go; then she would cross his name off and find another guy.

Many tattoos are about love—family, boyfriend, or girlfriend. They're likely to come with hearts or flowers. One inmate I knew named Paula paid Frisco to tattoo a heart with "I love you, Maria" inside it. Then a guard saw the tattoo when it was half finished, and he wrote her up. She was told that if the tattoo was finished, she would get extra time. For two years she carried around the image of a heart with "I lo" inside. Her prison nickname became *Ilo,* and it still was when I left.

Some prison women get religion. Then they want to get rid of devil, monster, and dragon tattoos. A woman named Shirley got born again and had a blood-dripping dagger on her arm covered up with Our Lady of Guadalupe. The funny thing was that there was a tiger under Our Lady's feet. Shirley liked to play the piano, and when she did, her muscles rippled and Our Lady seemed to be dancing on the tiger's back.

For every woman who sincerely gets religion, several make connections with the prison crime scene. Their tattoos are likely to be about dope, gangs, and rebellion. Of course, it is stupid for a person who is going to break the law to get any tattoo, because tattoos are identifiable marks and, therefore, useful to all law enforcement. Once a convict named Ruby Red talked her way out of the San Bernardino County Jail and escaped. Soon she was caught after someone recognized her by the pistol tattooed on her ankle.

I am glad some people in the free world like tattoos. That makes it easier for folks like me to walk the streets. But still in the general public, tattoos are a liability. Tattooed people may get some favorable glances, but mainly, from what I can see, they still get glares and stares, and they lose out on a lot of good jobs. Pinto, my last roommate, is back there in prison with tattoos all over her arms. When she returned last time, she told me her mother had made her wear long-sleeved shirts around the house. What her mother does not know is that her daughter now has tattoos on her hands. I guess Pinto will have to wear gloves.

Exercise 1   **DISCUSSION AND CRITICAL THINKING**

1. Circle the thesis.
2. Underline topic sentences.
3. Identify each specific example by writing the word *example* in the margin beside each one.

Practicing Patterns of Exemplification

The simple patterns in Exercise 2, based on "Prison Tattoos," will help you see the relationship between purpose and example(s).

Exercise 2   COMPLETING PATTERNS OF EXEMPLIFICATION

Clustering is a helpful strategy for developing ideas by exemplification. Fill in the empty bubbles.

Clustering in Stage One of your writing will help you recall examples and decide on headings for your outline. You will probably cluster more examples than you will need in your final essay. Fill in the blanks in this outline. If necessary, refer back to "Prison Tattoos."

Thesis: When people discover that I have done time, they ask me about tattooing and prison life.

   I. Tattooing as a trade in prison

      A. Necessary equipment and supplies

         1. Tattoo gun

         2. _____

         3. _____

      B. Frisco, an example of a prison tattoist

  II. Kinds of prison tattoos

      A. Humorous

         1. Dawson's tattoos

         2. _____

B. Love tattoos, with example

C. _____ tattoos, with example

D. _____ tattoos, with example

Student Documented Essay

Jason Alford considered a list of subjects for his essay with information from one or more sources. The idea of apathy appealed to him, and then his instructor suggested that he read a well-known essay titled "Why Don't We Complain?" by William F. Buckley, Jr.

After photocopying the essay, he underlined and annotated it; then he reflected on Buckley's ideas. He was surprised to discover that one of the reasons people do not complain more was not discussed by Buckley. He had his topic: He would summarize Buckley's essay and add to its insights, with examples from his own experience.

Biting My Tongue—Sometimes

Jason Alford

Complainers, as I use the word, are not whiners, wailers, or whimperers—people who harp about weather, sore feet, rock music, and other people's tattoos. They are people who do not like what is happening; they are concerned with things they think should be changed, usually of a personal nature. Unlike whining, complaining can be a good thing. But, as William Buckley, Jr., points out in his essay "Why Don't We Complain?", we all too frequently don't complain. He has some good explanations for our hesitancy, but I think he misses one of the main reasons.

From his experience, Buckley offers several examples of situations worthy of complaint. Once he was on a train that was 85 degrees in the passenger car; no one complained about the heat. He was in the movie theater and the picture was out of focus; no one complained. He was served his milk late after having asked for it repeatedly in the restaurant; he did not complain. He was on the airplane and an attendant was not responsive to his needs; he did not complain (62–64). They did not complain because they thought someone else would, because they were apathetic, because they were shy, because they did not want to make a scene. But Buckley overlooks one reason for not complaining: possible retaliation.

Retaliation can take two forms in school: open and silent. We all know the danger of complaining about a bully. My brother was bullied on campus in junior high school. When my parents learned about it, they went to the principal. The bullying stopped on campus, but it was taken off campus and became worse, even after my parents talked to the bullies' parents. Although one has to complain in that situation, retaliation may be the only result if one is dealing with irrational people, or the complaint is not handled in just the right way.

The silent retaliation is worse. In elementary school all my teachers but one were good. She was overbearing and impatient, and she brought religion into every subject with values. My parents complained to her, then to the principal. Although I had done well in other classes, I did not get picked for awards in her class, I was not tested for the advanced program, although others with similar qualifications were. (I was tested the next year and was accepted.) Years later a law was passed that parents could review the cumulative files kept by teachers. Out of curiosity, my parents reviewed mine and found that the teacher had inserted a number of negative comments about both me and my interfering parents. Those were comments that were available to all my teachers for the next nine years. Some parents, having decided that one teacher would not spoil their child's education, would not have complained.

Complainers do not get written up in restaurants, but they may get zapped in other ways, ways that are also silent. While I was still in high school, I worked as a busboy in a restaurant. I remember that it was not uncommon for a table server to punish a complainer by substituting regular coffee for decaffeinated, which would make a grouchy customer even grouchier, but only after he or she left the building. Everyone has heard about servers or cooks spitting in the food. I saw it happen only once. It is more likely that a server will be "slow" in delivering food, the check, or change to a complainer. Now, most of these complainers were well justified in their grievances, but some were complaining to the wrong people, in the wrong way, or at the wrong time. Mostly, if retaliation occurred, it was in response to the way they complained. But a lot of the complainers got punished. Not all of them knew just how.

The same thing can happen to people living in apartment buildings. There are so many things to complain about: the heavy feet above, the loud music, the loud talking, the pets, the kids, the trash, the unruly pool parties, the parking, and a few more. If one needs to complain, complaints should be phrased with care. I recall one instance in an apartment building when a tenant complained about a barking dog (dogs were not permitted) to the owner. After that complaint was rebuffed, the complainer went to the landlord. The landlord had the dog removed. The dog owner retaliated by harassing the complainer with late-night phone calls and finally vandalism of his car. Nothing could be proved. The complainer relocated.

Buckley is right in saying we should complain when something is wrong. He even offers some good insights into why we often don't complain. But he overlooks the retaliation point. Caution should not make us into cowards, yet caution should lead us to making deliberate choices of occasion, language, and demeanor. After all, among the good people out there are the tired, the irrational, the vindictive, and, yes, in varying degrees, even the lunatics.

Work Cited

Buckley, William F. Jr. "Why Don't We Complain?" *Patterns of Exposition*. Ed. Robert A. Schwegler. Boston: Longman, 2000. 61–69.

Example 3 — DISCUSSION AND CRITICAL THINKING

1. Circle the thesis.
2. Underline the topic sentences.
3. Annotate Alford's examples by writing the word *example* in the margin beside each one.
4. What does Alford apparently mean by his title "Biting My Tongue—Sometimes"?
5. How do your experiences in places such as school, restaurants, work, and apartments compare with those of Alford?

Lessons from a Control Freak

Rebecca Barry

In this defense of control freaks, Rebecca Barry offers lessons on how to accept and appreciate what people like her do for and to others. At once a confession and an appeal by a power mom, this essay first appeared in *Redbook*.

1. I'm a control freak. I know this because it's come up in therapy and my friend Lisa often reminds me. "Remember how you bossed everyone around at your last party?" Well, boss is a little strong. I simply found a nice man standing alone by the vegetable dip and suggested that he dance with my neighbor, Mrs. Howland. (Okay, so I gave him a little push in her direction, but it was gentle, more like a friendly tap.) "And what about that time at Laura's dinner party when you took over the stereo?" Yeah. So? People danced, didn't they?

2. While conventional wisdom says that control freaks are brittle, authoritarian psychos, I think we're just trying to maintain a sense of order in our lives. We can't help that we're good at it. Sure, some of us go too far—refusing to work with people who don't keep their pencils as sharp as ours, or following our daughters around on their dates—when they're 30. In moderation, however, a few controlling tendencies can do a body good.

Ruling the Work Scene

3. A wicked (okay, obsessive) eye for detail has paid off for Paula Currie, 42, executive director of Catholic Charities in Cortland, New York. "In everything—managing my staff, writing proposals and grants—detail is very important. For example, when the instructions for a grant proposal say, 'Leave a one-inch margin on the right side,' that's the kind of thing I notice, and need to notice," she says. (And she's never had a proposal kicked back for messy margins.) A control freak like me may brood for days about a single sentence, and I may call my editor back three times to discuss it, but in the end I know the story will be better for it. (You're enjoying this one, aren't you?)

4. The business world smiles on this kind of dedication. It's unlikely that a control freak will ever skip a step, miss a deadline, or be late for lunch (we check traffic reports). A manager's delight, a control freak always looks professional and seems meeting-

ready. She consistently generates coffee stain-free work and is sure not to say inappropriate things about the company in front of clients. "I do things so carefully that I know I won't be wrong," says Courtney Adams, 30, manager of human resources at a consulting firm in San Francisco. "If I send something out and someone questions me about it, I will have my research on hand to back myself up. I even spell-check my e-mails to friends." In the boss's chair, control freaks can make you want to please them and inspire you to develop skills you didn't even know you had.

Tackling Domestic Challenges

5   As for husbands and boyfriends . . . well, they're another story. A marriage is a partnership, and many control freaks, driven by the belief that their way is the best and only way, might secretly (or blatantly) prefer a dictatorship. (Is that so wrong?) "My husband recently said that being married to me is like being in the driver's seat but never quite being able to reach the steering wheel," says Marya Montoya, 32, a software salesperson in Denver.

Raising Very Well-Behaved Guests and Children

6   There are, however, many benefits to having a control freak under your roof. We anticipate problems, and we get things done. We make sure the plumber shows up—and stays until he fixes the leak. We steer the finances clear of debt territory. ("I have never bounced a check," Currie says with pride.) The car won't fall apart because no one changed the oil, the housework and bills will never be an issue because the control freak takes care of them.

7   And let's be honest. Control freaks can be downright charming. Our parties, planned down to the last dance, are beautiful and fun. We won't shrink into the background. In love, we are very good at asking for what we want. It doesn't matter if I'm from Saturn and he's from France, my mate won't be wandering around in a hazy fog, trying to figure out why he wasn't greeted at the door with a full-blown kiss. "I'll make my husband a list if he wants to know what to change," says Montoya.

8   Rules and structure, two things at which a control freak is very good, are also essential to child rearing. In Montoya's experience, children respond remarkably well to order. "We've instituted an allowance policy where he has something to work for," she says of her 12-year-old stepson. "He gets a certain amount for each chore he does, and I think it makes him feel good to know that if he wants to buy something, he can because he's earned it." Most control freaks pass a strong work ethic along to their kids. "I taught my children that if they didn't do a chore right the first time they'd have to

go back and do it again," says Currie. "When my son went to sleep-away camp, he wrote us a letter saying he hated the food, but that he was the only one who didn't have to clean the latrine twice."

9   Kids feel safe knowing that their mothers are in charge. "I don't want to be that mom who doesn't show up on parent/teacher visiting day," says Marjorie Cohn, a senior vice president at Nickelodeon in New York. To prevent her worst fears from coming to life, she tacks a two-week calendar on the fridge where she writes down every important event in her child's schedule.

10 And since control freaks are master planners, our kids are rarely bored. "I try not to sit him in front of the TV set," says Adams of her 3-year-old son. "I take him to museum exhibits, I read to him, I encourage him to color. I think it will make him a brighter, happier

---

Here's how to deal with your anal-retentive loved ones:

- *Understand the nature of the beast.* Control is about comfort, says Monica Basco, Ph.D., author of *Never Good Enough: Freeing Yourself from the Chains of Perfectionism.* "People get angry and assume the controlling person is being mean, but she's really trying to reduce her own anxieties."

- *Choose your battles.* "If you can live with letting them have their way in a situation, do it," suggests Deborah Luepnitz, Ph.D., a psychotherapist in Philadelphia. Sit quietly when your boss notes that there are no Os in Bermuda after you turn in your vacation memo (as long as she still okays your days off).

- *Develop a thick skin.* "If you share close quarters with a control freak, you can't be on the defensive all the time," says Dan Neuharth, Ph.D., author of *If You Had Controlling Parents.* . . . It will help if you realize that she has a lot on her shoulders—making sure her checkbook is balanced down to the penny, and her kids have dirt-free sneakers. If she's mad, it's probably not at you, but at the dust on that shelf in the bathroom.

- *Celebrate his or her successes.* "A control freak spends lots of energy trying to avoid criticism from others, or always feeling like the ax is going to fall when there is no ax," says Dr. Basco. The result is that while a control freak may appear confident, she may never quite fully give herself the credit she deserves.

- *Urge the control freak to let go now and then.* Wresting your beloved's power away may seem daunting, but it's good practice for both of you. As Dr. Neuharth says, "A relationship is a dance. If one person is always leading, it gets really boring."

person." (Of course it will—as long as he learns to color within the lines.)

You Know You're Too Controlling When

your family salutes when you come into the room.

your children call you their "smother."

you stay late at the office Friday to proofread your husband's chore list for Saturday.

you close most of your staff meetings with, "Never mind, I'll do it myself."

you redo your children's homework so often that their teacher mistakes your handwriting for theirs.

the last time you were wrong was 1976, and even then it was due to a misprint in *Consumer Reports*.

the phrase "remote control" makes you nervous.

Exercise 4

DISCUSSION AND CRITICAL THINKING

1. What is Rebecca Barry's main point?

2. How does Barry define *control freak?*

3. According to Barry, how does conventional wisdom define *control freak?*

4. Name the individuals who are used in examples to support the idea that control freaks have some good effects on others.

5. Are control freaks in moderation really control freaks? Why or why not?

6. Do you see this essay as an explanation or a rationalization?

7. If you take each example and push it beyond moderation, what do you have?

Paula Currie:

Courtney Adams:

Marya Montoya:

Marjorie Cohn:

8. How might this essay by a confessed control freak be perceived as an attempt to control?

I'm Outta Here!

David Levine

Every day, three thousand students give up on high school—for good. They push open the doors and walk out. Turn their backs on it. Drop out. Now what? Using colorful examples, freelance author David Levine provides some of the answers.

1   Think about it. In some ways it seems perfect. Quit school. Just say No—no more pressure, no more stupid rules, no more deadlines, no more uncaring teachers, no more snobby, clique-conscious peers. Nearly every high school student has imagined what it would be like.

2   Beth Kierny* did more than imagine. A few months into her senior year at Columbia High School, in East Greenbush, New York, she dropped out of school.

3   Beth is a shy eighteen-year-old with dark, curly hair who hated getting up early for classes. She was spending most of her time "gypping," leaving the building (or never showing up) and hanging out with her friends instead. Her parents didn't know; she was having problems with them and had moved in with her boyfriend, Dave, who had dropped out a few years earlier. When Beth found out she had missed so many days that she couldn't take her exams, she figured: Why not just leave?

4   She thought it would be great. She'd just get a job like Dave, sleep in later, work at some cool place instead of sitting in boring classes, and lead an easier, more interesting life.

5   But without a diploma, Beth found it difficult to get a job. She had to finally settle for one at the Hessmart gas station a few miles down Route 20. Being the youngest and newest employee, she got stuck working the worst shifts. Often she had to get up even earlier than she had to for school—sometimes she had to be *at work* by 7:00 A.M. Or she'd have to work the midnight shift, which was scary because you never knew if the place might get held up. Or she'd have to work weekends, when her friends were all out partying.

6   The money was terrible—at minimum wage she cleared maybe $90 a week—and she couldn't afford a car, so she had to take cabs to and from work, which cost almost ten bucks a day. That didn't leave much for her share of the $425 a month in rent on their small apartment behind the Burger King.

7   And if Dave, a part-time carpenter, found himself out of work, things were really tight. They were weeks and weeks late with the rent and got letters from the landlord threatening eviction (they'd already been thrown out of another place only a few months earlier). The bills wouldn't stop coming. The electricity was turned off. The telephone was disconnected. She and Dave fought all the time, mostly about money, sometimes about stupid things.

8   Then spring came, and her friends still in school were talking about the prom and the parties, and she found herself left out. Then came graduation, with its class rings and college plans and yearbooks, and Beth felt like a total outsider. She was more depressed than she'd ever been in her life.

9   Like many students, Beth thought that school was hard and the world outside of school would be easier. Instead, she found that the world outside of school was hard, too.

10   Everyone knows kids like Beth, who for one reason or another believe they can't handle school and decide to quit. What you might not realize is that all those kids add up to a dropout epidemic. Every day, up to three thousand kids leave school—that's between thirty and sixty busloads of students. Although the estimates vary, about half a million leave each year. The national graduation rate, which has been dropping for years, is now 71 percent, meaning nearly one in three students don't finish school. In some urban areas, the dropout rate can be over 50 percent. While the majority of high school dropouts—60 percent—are white and do not live in cities, minorities as a group are hardest hit: Hispanic students, for example, have a dropout rate more than twice the national average. One recent study found that one in four black guys will drop out, while one in five black girls will. One study found that 62 percent of Hispanic students dropped out, along with 53 percent of black students and 42 percent of Native American students. Overall, boys are only slightly more likely to drop out than girls.

11   Within this larger puzzle are the individual pieces—the reasons why kids quit school. According to the Department of Education, there are six things that put students at higher risk. They include having a dropout sibling, coming from a single-parent

*Names with asterisks have been changed.

family, coming from a household with an income below $15,000, being home alone more than three hours a day, not speaking English well, and having parents who didn't finish high school. What makes any student actually quit is harder to assess. Caroline Abbott, sixteen, who lives in Charlotte, North Carolina, never stopped going to school entirely, she just missed a lot of days. "I'd sit home, go to a friend's house," she says. "A good friend of mine dropped out, and I wanted to, too. I just wanted to be with her."

12 "Poor attendance is a symptom, not the disease," says Joseph Markham, director of pupil personnel services for the Albany City School District, in New York. And these days there are many diseases.

13 A student's initial trouble may come from parents' marital problems, domestic violence, drug or alcohol use, or physical abuse. For Darrell Maynard,* now a tenth grader in Columbia, South Carolina, it was moving when he was in the eighth grade. "I didn't know no one," he says. So he started to hang out, and soon after that he began to sell drugs. He says he didn't like doing it. "It was kind of scary, really," Darrell says. "Other students looked at us as gangsters, and the teachers were afraid to get involved." But he felt as if he had nothing else in his life. "My mom keeps foster kids," he says. "She wasn't paying attention to me. My dad was away all week working." Eventually, he was caught with a machete in school and got kicked out. "When my dad found out, he said I had to go to work every day with him. I didn't want that."

14 Curt Niedrach, seventeen, is a junior at Jackson Alternative School, in Jackson Township, New Jersey. All of his closest friends have dropped out. "They didn't think about how it was really going to be outside of school," he says. "They want to be free, but they don't think about what they're losing. Mostly, they don't want to be organized or deal with other people's deadlines, like showing up for class. Also, no one wants to get hassled if they don't follow every little rule." Edwin Soto, a sophomore at Bayard Ruskin High School, in New York City, has a lot of friends who've dropped out, too. "A typical day in their lives is getting up about 10:00 A.M., then finding each other and all the other guys from around the way," he says. "They try to gather as much money as possible to buy weed and go to the park to hang out. Later on, they head to pick up their girlfriends at school. After that, they go back to the park to hang out some more."

15 Some students leave school because they feel as if nobody cares. "Classes were too big, with thirty-five or more students in them," says Heather Murphy, seventeen, from Miami, who dropped out when she was fourteen. "I wasn't getting anything

from my school in return for going. Teachers didn't have time for me, so why should I go?" Given the size and impersonal nature of some public high schools, finding help can be hard. Forty percent of the girls who drop out every year leave because they're pregnant. Other students quit because they feel it's a way of sparing themselves the failure.

16 Take Caroline. In eighth grade everything was great: honor roll, cheerleading. She loved school, had lots of friends. Everyone told her that high school would be great, too. But it wasn't. "I hated it," she says. "They weren't friendly people. I wasn't interested in the classes." Caroline's ex-boyfriend—who had left the state—came back to the town. She couldn't keep her mind on school.

17 Still, she was trying, really trying. But when she failed algebra, something in her snapped. "You think, I'm trying so hard, I must be doing well, then one thing turns it all around. So I thought, Well, forget it. Why try so hard and accomplish nothing? I thought I was just dumb. So I just stopped trying. I gave up."

18 "To think that all dropouts or potential dropouts leave school because they aren't smart enough to hack it is to miss the point," says John K. Dougherty, Ph.D., president of alternative education for the state of New Jersey. Many kids lack motivation, and they aren't getting enough support at home to overcome that. Absenteeism pushes them further behind, so they can't perform well when they do show up at school. The discouragement spirals.

19 Some of the blame for the high dropout rate must fall on the schools themselves. Unfortunately, much of traditional education is uninspiring, and some experts believe it's simply obsolete. Teachers aren't paid well, and budget and staff cuts have left them unsupported. Classes are regularly overcrowded, and, too often, quiet or uninvolved kids are overlooked.

20 Schools are trying to adapt and respond to the crisis. Cities In Schools, Inc. (CIS), a national organization designed to get dropout-prone students into personalized programs that address their problems, believes that schools have to do more than educate. CIS president Bill Milliken says that what's needed is a sense of community, a sense that adults really care. He says schools should abandon the system of churning out graduates on an assembly line and bring the resources to the kids. "You have to build the community," he says. "If they don't have positive relationships at home and have negative ones on the street, then we have to build positive ones for them at school."

21 There's no denying that a high school diploma opens doors; staying in school and graduating extends the range of options of what you can do with your life. It's also a fact that the conse-

quences of dropping out are severe and the prospects for dropouts are bleak. According to the National Dropout Prevention Center, less than 50 percent of dropouts find jobs when they leave school. When they do, they earn 60 percent less than high school graduates (over a lifetime, that adds up to $250,000). They are not accepted into military service and are 50 percent more likely to be on welfare. Eighty-eight percent of female dropouts under age thirty who head households live in poverty.

22   More than half of Curt Niedrach's friends are now enrolled in a GED (general equivalency diploma) program. Beth Kierny is also going for her GED, but she's afraid that even this might not be good enough. "A lot of jobs want a diploma, not a GED," she says. Things are better with her parents—they're talking again, at least—but the pressures of her life still don't let up. She and Dave are looking for their third place to live in eighteen months. "It's hard, because a lot of places don't want to rent to kids," she says.

23   Because she's taking classes again, Beth has had to quit her job at the Hessmart and support herself with baby-sitting jobs. She's making even less money than she was before. Dave has decided to join the army. Beth, because she doesn't yet have a GED, can't.

24   There just aren't many options. "You have to finish school to get a decent job and to afford a car. You can't make it on minimum wages, working at gas stations or restaurants on weekends," she says. "You just can't."

Exercise 5   **DISCUSSION AND CRITICAL THINKING**

1. Circle the sentence that most clearly indicates the student view that Levine will explore.

2. Is this essay concerned mainly with cause or effects, or a combination?

3. Are most of the examples used to show causes or effects?

4. Is Levine's purpose to inform or to persuade, or both?

5. Annotate Levine's examples by writing the word *example* in the margin beside each one.

6. Is the order of presentation more that of time or space?

Making the Grade

Kurt Wiesenfeld

Grading for academic performance, a concept taken for granted for most, is disregarded by about 10 percent of Kurt Wiesenfeld's physics students at Georgia Tech. These students are more concerned with negotiating and bargaining. This essay was first published in *Newsweek*.

1 It was a rookie error. After 10 years I should have known better, but I went to my office the day after final grades were posted. There was a tentative knock on the door. "Professor Wiesenfeld? I took your Physics 2121 class? I flunked it? I wonder if there's anything I can do to improve my grade?" I thought: "Why are you asking me? Isn't it too late to worry about it? Do you dislike making declarative statements?"

2 After the student gave his tale of woe and left, the phone rang. "I got a D in your class. Is there any way you can change it to 'Incomplete'?" Then the e-mail assault began: "I'm shy about coming in to talk to you, but I'm not shy about asking for a better grade. Anyway, it's worth a try." The next day I had three phone messages from students asking *me* to call *them*. I didn't.

3 Time was, when you received a grade, that was it. You might groan and moan, but you accepted it as the outcome of your efforts or lack thereof (and, yes, sometimes a tough grader). In the last few years, however, some students have developed a disgruntled-consumer approach. If they don't like their grade, they go to the "return" counter to trade it in for something better.

4 What alarms me is their indifference toward grades as an indication of personal effort and performance. Many, when pressed about why they think they deserve a better grade, admit they don't deserve one but would like one anyway. Having been raised on gold stars for effort and smiley faces for self-esteem, they've learned that they can get by without hard work and real talent if they can talk the professor into giving them a break. This attitude is beyond cynicism. There's a weird innocence to the assumption that one expects (even deserves) a better grade simply by begging for it. With that outlook, I guess I shouldn't be as flabbergasted as I

was that 12 students asked me to change their grades *after* final grades were posted.

5   That's 10 percent of my class who let three months of midterms, quizzes and lab reports slide until long past remedy. My graduate student calls it hyperrational thinking: if effort and intelligence don't matter, why should deadlines? What matters is getting a better grade through an unearned bonus, the academic equivalent of a freebie T shirt or toaster giveaway. Rewards are disconnected from the quality of one's work. An act and its consequences are unrelated, random events.

6   Their arguments for wheedling better grades often ignore academic performance. Perhaps they feel it's not relevant. "If my grade isn't raised to a D I'll lose my scholarship." "If you don't give me a C, I'll flunk out." One sincerely overwrought student pleaded, "If I don't pass, my life is over." This is tough stuff to deal with. Apparently, I'm responsible for someone's losing a scholarship, flunking out or deciding whether life has meaning. Perhaps these students see me as a commodities broker with something they want—a grade. Though intrinsically worthless, grades, if properly manipulated, can be traded for what has value: a degree, which means a job, which means money. The one thing college actually offers—a chance to learn—is considered irrelevant, even less than worthless, because of the long hours and hard work required.

7   In a society saturated with surface values, love of knowledge for its own sake does sound eccentric. The benefits of fame and wealth are more obvious. So is it right to blame students for reflecting the superficial values saturating our society?

8   Yes, of course it's right. These guys had better take themselves seriously now, because our country will be forced to take them seriously later, when the stakes are much higher. They must recognize that their attitude is not only self-destructive, but socially destructive. The erosion of quality control—giving appropriate grades for actual accomplishments—is a major concern in my department. One colleague noted that a physics major could obtain a degree without ever answering a written exam question completely. How? By pulling in enough partial credit and extra credit. And by getting breaks on grades.

9   But what happens once she or he graduates and gets a job? That's when the misfortunes of eroding academic standards multiply. We lament that schoolchildren get "kicked upstairs" until they graduate from high school despite being illiterate and mathematically inept, but we seem unconcerned with college gradu-

ates whose less blatant deficiencies are far more harmful if their accreditation exceeds their qualifications.

10   Most of my students are science and engineering majors. If they're good at getting partial credit but not at getting the answer right, then the new bridge breaks or the new drug doesn't work. One finds examples here in Atlanta. Last year a light tower in the Olympic Stadium collapsed, killing a worker. It collapsed because an engineer miscalculated how much weight it could hold. A new 12-story dormitory could develop dangerous cracks due to a foundation that's uneven by more than six inches. The error resulted from incorrect data being fed into a computer. I drive past that dorm daily on my way to work, wondering if a foundation crushed under kilotons of weight is repairable or if this structure will have to be demolished. Two 10,000-pound steel beams at the new natatorium collapsed in March, crashing into the student athletic complex. (Should we give partial credit since no one was hurt?) Those are real-world consequences of errors and lack of expertise.

11   But the lesson is lost on the grade-grousing 10 percent. Say that you won't (not can't, but won't) change the grade they deserve to what they want, and they're frequently bewildered or angry. They don't think it's fair that they're judged according to their performance, not their desires or "potential." They don't think it's fair that they should jeopardize their scholarships or be in danger of flunking out simply because they could not or did not do their work. But it's more than fair; it's necessary to help preserve a minimum standard of quality that our society needs to maintain safety and integrity. I don't know if the 13th-hour students will learn that lesson, but I've learned mine. From now on, after final grades are posted, I'll lie low until the next quarter starts.

Exercise 6   VOCABULARY HIGHLIGHTS

Write a short definition of each word as it is used in the essay. (Paragraph numbers are given in parentheses.) Be prepared to use the words in your own sentences.

tentative (1)

cynicism (4)

intrinsically (6)

saturated (7)

eccentric (7)

eroding (9)

blatant (9)

accreditation (9)

jeopardize (11)

integrity (11)

118 CHAPTER 5

| Exercise 7 | DISCUSSION AND CRITICAL THINKING |

1. Circle the thesis.

2. Is this essay concerned with mainly causes, effects, or both?

3. Annotate Wiesenfeld's examples by writing the word *example* in the margins beside each one.

4. What does Wiesenfeld think grades should represent?

5. What does Wiesenfeld believe grades represent to the wheedling 10 percent of his students?

6. Which paragraph contains examples that suggest the possible consequences of lowered academic standards?

7. Does Wiesenfeld have a solution to the problem? Explain.

8. Do you have a solution?

9. Can one make an argument for extra credit, special testing, and selective (your definition) generosity?

Underground Dads
Wil Haygood

As a child, Wil Haygood did not have an actual dad around the house. But he was fortunate. He had men around who gave him the love and guidance he needed. Three men in particular were his surrogate fathers, and he learned important lessons from each. This essay was first published in the *New York Times Magazine*.

1   For years, while growing up, I shamelessly told my playmates that I didn't have a father. In my neighborhood, where men went to work with lunch pails, my friends thought there was a gaping hole in my household. My father never came to the park with me to toss a softball, never came to see me in any of my school plays. I'd explain to friends, with the simplicity of explaining to someone that there are, in some woods, no deer, that I just had no father.

My friends looked at me and squinted. My mother and father had divorced shortly after my birth. As the years rolled by, however, I did not have the chance to turn into the pitiful little black boy who had been abandoned by his father. There was a reason: other men showed up. They were warm, honest (at least as far as my eyes could see) and big-hearted. They were the good black men in the shadows, the men who taught me right from wrong, who taught me how to behave, who told me, by their very actions, that they expected me to do good things in life.

2   There are heartbreaking statistics tossed about regarding single-parent black households these days, about children growing up fatherless. Those statistics must be considered. But how do you count the other men, the ones who show up—with perfect timing, with a kind of soft-stepping loveliness—to give a hand, to take a boy to watch airplanes lift off, to show a young boy the beauty of planting tomatoes in the ground and to tell a child that all of life is not misery?

3   In my life, there was Jerry, who hauled junk. He had a lean body and a sweet smile. He walked like a cowboy, all bowlegged, swinging his shoulders. It was almost a strut. The sound of his pickup truck rumbling down our alley in Columbus, Ohio, could raise me from sleep.

4   When he wasn't hauling junk, Jerry fixed things. More than once, he fixed my red bicycle. The gears were always slipping; the chain could turn into a tangled mess. Hearing pain in my voice, Jerry would instruct me to leave my bike on our front porch. In our neighborhood, in the 60's, no one would steal your bike from your porch. Jerry promised me he'd pick it up, and he always did. He never lied to me, and he cautioned me not to tell lies. He was, off and on, my mother's boyfriend. At raucous family gatherings, he'd pull me aside and explain to me the importance of honesty, of doing what one promised to do.

5   And there was Jimmy, my grandfather, who all his life paid his bills the day they arrived: that was a mighty lesson in itself—it taught me a work ethic. He held two jobs, and there were times when he allowed me to accompany him on his night job, when he cleaned a Greek restaurant on the north side of Columbus. Often he'd mop the place twice, as if trying to win some award. He frightened me too. It was not because he was mean. It was because he had exacting standards, and there were times when I didn't measure up to those standards. He didn't like shortcutters. His instructions, on anything, were to be carried out to the letter. He believed in independence, doing as much for yourself as you possibly could. It should not have surprised me when, one morn-

ing while having stomach pains, he chose not to wait for a taxi and instead walked the mile to the local hospital, where he died a week later of stomach cancer.

6   My uncles provided plenty of good background music when I was coming of age. Uncle Henry took me fishing. He'd phone the night before. "Be ready. Seven o'clock." I'd trail him through woods—as a son does a father—until we found our fishing hole. We'd sit for hours. He taught me a patience and an appreciation of the outdoors, of nature. He talked, incessantly, of family—his family, my family, the family of friends. The man had a reverence for family. I knew to listen.

7   I think these underground fathers simply appear, decade to decade, flowing through the generations. Hardly everywhere, and hardly, to be sure, in enough places, but there. As mystical, sometimes, as fate when fate is sweet.

8   Sometimes I think that all these men who have swept in and out of my life still couldn't replace a good, warm father. But inasmuch as I've never known a good, warm father, the men who entered my life, who taught me right from wrong, who did things they were not asked to do, have become unforgettable. I know of the cold statistics out there. And yet, the mountain of father-son literature does not haunt me. I've known good black men.

Exercise 8 — DISCUSSION AND CRITICAL THINKING

1. Copy here the sentence that focuses on the main idea of the essay.

2. Paraphrase the thesis.

3. Name the three examples used to support Haygood's main idea.

4. What did Haygood learn from each man?

5. How does Haygood relate his experiences shown in the examples to statistics?

✎ Topics for Writing Exemplification

Writing Process Worksheet

You will find a Writing Process Worksheet on page 27. It can be photocopied and enlarged, filled in, and submitted with each assignment if your instructor directs you to do so.

Source-Based Topics

Each essay developed from these suggested source-based topics should include at least one reference to the reading selection by the author's name and the title. Quotations should be enclosed in quotation marks. Follow your instructor's directions in documenting the ideas you borrow. Whether you use informal or formal documentation, the form is not complicated, and you will soon learn to use it for these essays without checking each time. See pages 73 and 74 for a discussion of MLA style and informal documentation.

Underlining and annotating reading selections will help you in finding support material. In prewriting brief essays, consider marking your outline to indicate where you will use quotations or other borrowed ideas. If the quotations or reworded statements are short and few, you could even insert them inside parentheses or circles in your outline; if you do, also include the author's last name and the page number. A sound system, consistently used, will save you time and ensure technically strong papers.

"Prison Tattoos"

1. Write an essay about people you know who have tattoos. Use specific examples. Unify the essay around a specific idea, such as one of the following: Tattoos are more easily acquired than removed. Tattoos help people define themselves for others. We need stricter laws to protect juveniles from tattooists.

"Biting My Tongue—Sometimes"

2. Write about the effectiveness of complaining, if the process is handled thoughtfully. Provide three or more examples.

3. Using this essay as a model, discuss the problems that can sometimes occur as the result of complaining, especially if the complaining is not handled well. Use your own examples. Refer directly to Alford's essay, and consider referring to Buckley's ideas as noted by Alford.

"Lessons from a Control Freak"

4. Rebecca Barry says that controlling in moderation is beneficial. Write an essay in which you argue that controlling is inherently bad. Use quotations from Barry's essay and examples from your own experience. Consider these questions: Have you ever been controlled? Have you observed someone who has been controlled for a long period of time? Have you ever tried to control others?

5. Write an essay in which you agree with Barry's thesis. Quote her and use your own examples.

"I'm Outta Here!"

6. Write an essay in which you make the same argument as Levine. Give Levine credit for the ideas you borrow and provide your own examples.

"Making the Grade"

7. Write an essay in which you side with Wiesenfeld. Provide your own examples.

8. Write an essay in which you question whether most grading is truly based on academic achievement. To what extent are Wiesenfeld's standards typical? Refer to courses you have taken, experiences you have had, and stories you have heard. Discuss important knowledge or skills you have acquired that were never tested properly. Refer to extra-credit projects, if any.

"Underground Dads"

9. Write about mother or father figures who influenced you in special ways as you grew up. Who were they? Exactly how did they help? Might a mother or father have provided what they did?

Career-Related Topics

10. Use specific examples to support one of the following statements as applied to business or work.

    It's not what you know, it's who you know.

    Don't burn your bridges.

    Like Legos, business is a matter of connections.

    Tact is the lubricant that oils the wheels of industry.

    The customer is always right.

    If you take care of the pennies, the dollars will take care of themselves.

    A kind word turns away wrath.

11. Use another common saying or invent one of your own and illustrate it with an example or examples.

12. Discuss how a specific service or product can benefit its users. Use an example or examples.

General Topics

13. Choose one of the following statements as a thesis for an essay. Support the statement with specific examples.

    Television commercials are often amusing [misleading, irritating, sexist, racist, useless, fascinating].

Rap music often carries important messages [makes me sick, brings out the best in people, brings out the worst in people, degrades women, promotes violence, presents reality, appeals to our better instincts, tells funny stories].

Rock groups don't have to be sensational in presentation and appearance to be popular.

A person can be an environmentalist in everyday life.

Many people who consider themselves law-abiding citizens break laws on a selective basis.

Television news is full of stories of violence, but we can also find acts of kindness in everyday life.

Car salespeople behave differently depending on the kind of car they are selling and the kind of customer they have.

The kinds of toys people buy for their children tell us much about their social values.

People who do not have a satisfying family life will find a family substitute.

One painful experience reminded me of the importance of human rights [student rights, worker rights, gender rights].

Drug abuse, including alcohol abuse, may be a problem even with people who seem to be functioning well.

Country music appeals to some of our most basic concerns.

Writer's Guidelines: Exemplification

1. Use examples to explain, convince, or amuse.
2. Use examples that are vivid, specific, and representative.
    - Vivid examples attract attention.
    - Specific examples are identifiable.
    - Representative examples are typical and therefore the basis for generalization.
3. Tie your examples clearly to your thesis.
4. Draw your examples from what you have read, heard, and experienced.
5. Brainstorm a list or cluster of possible examples before you write.
6. The order and number of your examples will depend on the purpose stated in your thesis.

6

Definition: Clarifying Terms

Writing Definition, p. 125
  Techniques for Writing Simple Definitions, p. 125
  Techniques for Writing Extended Definitions, p. 129

Connecting Sources and Writing, p. 131
  Student Documented Essay (Single Source): "My-graines," p. 131
  Practicing Patterns of Definition, p. 133
  Student Documented Essay (Multiple Sources): "Perspectives on Motivation," p. 134
  Paired Sources on Bullying, p. 137
    "Disarming the Rage," p. 137
    "Bully, Bully," p. 144
  Paired Sources on Bosses and Workers, Good and Bad, p. 147
    "You and Your Boss," p. 147
    "Why Many Good Workers Turn Into Bad Bosses," p. 151

Topics for Writing Definition, p. 156
  Writing Process Worksheet, p. 156
  Source-Based Topics, p. 156
  Career-Related Topics, p. 158
  General Topics, p. 158

Writer's Guidelines, p. 159

THE QUIGMANS   by Buddy Hickerson

"I don't care if all my friends say you're primitive, Sven. I love you from your sloping, suborbital-ridge forehead to your hairy, prehensile toes."

© Tribune Media Services, Inc. All Rights Reserved. Reprinted with permission.

Writing Definition

Most definitions are short; they consist of a *synonym* (a word or phrase that has about the same meaning as the term to be defined), a phrase, or a sentence. For example, we might say that a hypocrite is a person "professing beliefs or virtues he or she does not possess." Terms can also be defined by *etymology,* or word history. *Hypocrite* once meant "actor" (*hypocrites*) in Greek because an actor was pretending to be someone else. We may find this information interesting and revealing, but the history of a word may be of little or no use because the meaning has changed drastically over the years. Definitions can occupy an entire essay. The short definition is called a *simple definition;* the longer one is known as an *extended definition.*

Techniques for Writing Simple Definitions

If you want to define a term without being abrupt and mechanical, you have several alternatives. All of the following techniques allow you to blend the definition into your developing thought.

- *Basic dictionary meaning.* You can quote the dictionary's definition, but if you do, you are obliged to indicate your source, which you should do directly and explicitly. Always give the complete title of the dictionary, such as "*The American Heritage Dictionary* says," not simply "Webster says." Dozens of dictionaries use the "Webster" designation.
- *Synonyms.* Although no two words have exactly the same meaning, synonyms often follow as if in parentheses.

    Example: He was guilty of the ancient sin of *hubris,* of excessive pride.

- *Direct explanation.* You can state the definition.

    Example: This spontaneous and loyal support of our preconception—this process of finding "good" reasons to justify our routine beliefs—is known to modern psychologists as *rationalizing*—clearly a new name for a very ancient thing.

    James Harvey Robinson, "On Various Kinds of Thinking"

- *Indirect explanation.* You can imply the definition.

    Example: Trance is a similar abnormality in our society. Even a mild mystic is *aberrant* in Western civilization.

    Ruth Benedict, *Patterns of Culture*

- *Analytical or formal definition.* In using this method, you define by placing the term (the subject) in a class (genus) and then identifying it with characteristics that show how it differs from other members of the same class, as the following examples show:

CHAPTER 6

Subject	Class	Characteristics
A democracy	is a form of government	in which voters elect representatives to manage society.
A wolf	is a dog-like mammal	that is large and carnivorous, with coarse fur, erect, pointed ears, and a bushy tail.
Jazz	is a style of music	that features improvisation and performance.

Exercise 1 WRITING SIMPLE DEFINITIONS

Complete the following formal definitions.

Subject	Class	Characteristics
1. A workaholic	is a person	
2. Dreadlocks	is a natural hairstyle	
3. A hawk		that has a short, hooked bill and strong claws.
4. Hay fever		affecting the mucous membranes of the upper respiratory tract and the eyes, causing sneezing, runny nose, and itchy, watery eyes.
5. A muumuu	is a dress	
6. Bongos	are two connected drums	
7. A patriot		
8. A desert	is a large land area	
9. Jealousy	is a state of mind	
10. Sociology		

Dictionary Entries—Which One to Use

Suppose that you do not know the meaning of the term in italics in the following sentence:

>That kind of cactus is *indigenous* to the Mojave Desert.

As you consider the term in context, you look at the dictionary definitions.

American Heritage Dictionary of the English Language

>in•dig•e•nous (ĭn-dĭj´ə-nəs) *adj.* **1.** Originating and living or occurring naturally in an area or environment. See synonyms at native **2.** Intrinsic; innate. [From Latin *indigena,* a native. See INDIGEN.]

The first definition seems to fit the context of *indigenous.* It is followed by a reference: See synonyms at **native.** Then you look at the second set of definitions: "Intrinsic, innate." The words are synonyms. You can see that only *native* fits. To provide more information for the reader, the dictionary also presents *native* with a special treatment of synonyms as indicated by the reference.

Looking under the word *native,* you find this definition:

>***Synonyms*** native, indigenous, endemic, autochthonous, aboriginal These adjectives mean of, belonging to, or connected with a specific place or country by virtue of birth or origin. *Native* implies birth or origin in the specified place: *a native New Yorker; the native North American sugar maple. Indigenous* specifies that something or someone is native rather than coming or being brought in from elsewhere: *an indigenous crop; the Ainu, a people indigenous to the northernmost islands of Japan.* Something *endemic* is prevalent in or peculiar to a particular locality or people: *endemic disease. Autochthonous* applies to what is native and unchanged by outside sources: *autochthonous folk melodies. Aboriginal* describes what has existed from the beginning; it is often applied to the earliest known inhabitants of a place: *the aboriginal population; aboriginal nature.* See also synonyms at **crude.**
>
>*Usage Note* When used in reference to a member of an indigenous people, the noun *native,* like its synonym *aborigine,* can evoke unwelcome stereotypes of primitiveness or cultural backwardness that many people now seek to avoid. As is often the case with words that categorize people, the use of the noun is more problematic than the use of the corresponding adjective. Thus a phrase such as *the peoples native to northern Europe* or *the aboriginal inhabitants of the South Pacific* is generally much preferable to *the natives of northern Europe* or *the aborigines of the South Pacific.* • Despite its potentially negative connotations, *native* is enjoying increasing popularity in ethnonyms such as *native Australian* and *Alaska Native,* perhaps due to the

wide acceptance of *Native American* as a term of ethnic pride and respect. These compounds have the further benefit of being equally acceptable when used alone as nouns (*a native Australian*) or in an adjectival construction (*a member of a native Australian people*). Of terms formed on this model, those referring to peoples indigenous to the United States generally capitalize *native*, as in *Alaska Native* (or the less common *Native Alaskan*) and *Native Hawaiian*, while others usually style it lowercase.

American Heritage Dictionary of the English Language

In the synonyms at the close of the entry, did you observe the various shades of meaning, especially the meaning of *indigenous* and *native?* A dictionary is an invaluable aid to definition, but it must be used with care if you want to express yourself clearly and precisely. No two words have exactly the same meaning, and a word may have many meanings, some that extend to very different concepts.

Avoiding Common Problems

- Do not use the expression *is where* or *is when* in beginning the main part of the definition. The verb *is* (a linking verb) should be followed by a noun, a pronoun, or an adjective.

  Weak: A stadium is where they hold sports spectaculars.

  Better A stadium is a structure in which sports spectaculars are held.

  Weak: Socialism is when the ownership and operation of the means of production and distribution are vested in the community as a whole.

  Better: Socialism is a theory or system of community organization that advocates that the ownership and control of the means of production, capital, land, and so forth, be vested in the community as a whole.

- Do not use the *circular definition,* a practice of defining a term with the term itself.

  Circular: An aristocracy is a form of government based on rule by the aristocrats.

  Direct: An aristocracy is a form of government in which the power resides in the hands of the best individuals or a small privileged class.

- Do not define the subject in more complicated language than the original.

  Murky: *Surreptitious* means "clandestine."

  Clear: *Surreptitious* means "secret."

- Do not substitute the example for the definition; the example may be excellent for clarification, but it does not completely define.

Weak: Political conservatives are people like William F. Buckley, Jr., and Pat Robertson.

Better: Political conservatives are people who are dedicated to preserving existing conditions. Examples of conservatives are William F. Buckley, Jr., and Pat Robertson.

Techniques for Writing Extended Definitions

Essays of definition can take many forms. Among the more common techniques for writing a short essay of definition are the patterns we have worked with in previous chapters. Consider each of those patterns when you need to write an extended definition. For a particular term, some forms will be more useful than others; use the pattern or patterns that best fulfill your purpose.

Each of the following questions takes a pattern of writing and directs it toward definition.

- *Narration:* Can I tell an anecdote or story to define this subject (such as *jerk, humanitarian,* or *citizen*)? This form may overlap with description and exemplification.

- *Description:* Can I describe this subject (such as *a whale* or *the moon*)?

- *Exemplification:* Can I give examples of this subject (such as naming individuals, to provide examples of *actors, diplomats,* or *satirists*)?

- *Analysis by Division:* Can I divide this subject into parts (for example, the parts of a *heart, cell,* or *carburetor*)?

- *Process Analysis:* Can I define this subject (such as *lasagna, tornado, hurricane, blood pressure,* or any number of scientific processes) by describing how to make it or how it occurs? (Common to the methodology of communicating in science, this approach is sometimes called the "operational definition.")

- *Cause and Effect:* Can I define this subject (such as *a flood, a drought, a riot,* or *a cancer*) by its causes and effects?

- *Classification:* Can I group this subject (such as kinds of *families, cultures, religions,* or *governments*) into classes?

Subject	Class	Characteristics
A republic	is a form of government	in which power resides in the people (the electorate).

- *Comparison and Contrast.* Can I define this subject (such as *extremist* or *patriot*) by explaining what it is similar to and different from?

If you are defining *orangutan* to a person who has never heard of one but is familiar with the gorilla, then you could make comparison-and-contrast statements. If you want to define *patriot,* then you might want to stress what it is not (the contrast) before you explain what it is: a patriot is not a one-dimensional flag waver, not someone who hates "foreigners" because America is always right and always best.

When you use prewriting strategies to develop ideas for a definition, you can effectively consider all the patterns you have learned by using a modified clustering form (Figure 6.1). Put a double bubble around the subject to be defined. Then put a single bubble around each pattern and add appropriate words, extending from that pattern. If a pattern is not

Figure 6.1
Bubble cluster showing how a term could be defined using different essay patterns.

relevant to what you are defining, leave it blank. If you want to expand your range of information, you could add a bubble for a simple dictionary definition and another for an etymological definition.

Order

The organization of your extended definition is likely to be one of emphasis, but it may be space or time, depending on the subject material. You may use just one pattern of development, such as narration or analysis by division, for the overall sequence. If so, you would use the principles of organization discussed in previous chapters.

Introduction and Development

Consider these ways of introducing a definition: with a question, with a statement of what it is not, with a statement of what it originally meant, or with a discussion of why a clear definition is important. You may use a combination of these ways or all of them before you continue with your definition.

Development is likely to represent one or more of the patterns of narration, description, exposition (with its own subdivisions), and argumentation.

Whether you personalize a definition depends on your purpose and your audience. Your instructor may ask you to write about a word from a subjective or objective viewpoint.

Connecting Sources and Writing

Student Documented Essay (Single Source)

The assignment was to read several essays related to health and write a documented essay of extended definition about one health condition as it related to the student's experience. The final product would include at least two quotations and several paraphrases from the source, each to be formally identified. The source would be listed at the end, according to MLA form for an article in an anthology. (Your instructor may not ask you to formally document an essay based on a single textbook source.)

My-graines

Vincent Sheahan

The aura set in like a suffocating stillness before a tropical storm. "This is going to be a bad one," I told myself as I shut off the lights, took my medication, lay down, and prepared for the inevitable—the relentless throbbing in my temple. About three hours of incapacitating agony later, I recovered, feeling strangely drained, and skimmed through my reading assignment for my college English class. What a coincidence! It included "In Bed," an essay about migraines by Joan Didion. Because I had only recently been diagnosed with migraines (although I had long suffered), I naturally had enormous curiosity about the subject, and now homework coincided with my private need for information. By closely comparing my family history, my triggers for attacks, and my personality with Joan Didion's, perhaps I could find some informed answers to my questions and be able to define *migraines* more precisely.

A year ago when I decided to seek medical help, the matter of family history was of immediate concern. At my first appointment, my neurologist informed me that, although no one knows why, migraines tend to run in families. I said the only person in my family who has migraines is my Uncle Joe, my father's brother. For Didion, the family connection is more apparent and pervasive: Both of her grandmothers, her father, and her mother all suffer from migraine headaches. But she does go on to explain, "One inherits, of course, only the predisposition" (59). Therefore, it is possible that everyone on my father's side has carried the gene for migraines, but only Uncle Joe has ever actually developed the headaches.

After the doctor asked his questions, I had one of my own: What actually causes migraine headaches? I was fearful that my job as an emergency medical technician (E.M.T.), with its debilitating stress and irregular hours, was the main reason. He explained that the exact causes are not completely understood and that my fatigue and irregular sleep patterns are not the causes of my migraines, because there are plenty of E.M.T.s who have the same sleep patterns as I do yet do not have migraines. Nevertheless, the fatigue and irregular sleep may trigger migraine headaches. For Didion, the triggers are varied. She says, "Almost anything can trigger a specific attack of migraine: stress, allergy, fatigue, an abrupt change in barometric pressure, a contretemps over a parking ticket. A flashing light. A fire drill" (60). Yet she explains that her headaches are not triggered at times when she needs to be alert and thinking clearly, such as an emergency situation, but instead, they are triggered when she is feeling overwhelmed or extremely stressed (60).

In addition to the exposure to these triggers, a migraine sufferer like me usually has what is called a "migraine personality." Didion offers a good definition of that term, saying that she is typical, a perfectionist who is "ambitious, inward, intolerant of error, rather rigidly organized" (60). But she points out that not all perfectionists have migraines and not all people with migraines are perfectionists. She says that she is a perfectionist about writing, not housekeeping (60). And, as for me, I try—probably harder than most—to be organized when it comes to my education, work, and personal life.

Like Joan Didion, I am intensely interested in migraines, and I am learning about them. We migraine sufferers have much in common, though each of us has his or her own family history of migraines, triggers, and migraine personality. Knowing that others go through what I do and having more information about my condition make it easier for me to deal with the pain of my migraines. I will continue to do the same thing Joan Didion does when she has an aura: I won't try to fight it. I will lie down and endure. When it's finally over, I will count my blessings.

Work Cited

Didion, Joan. "In Bed." *Health Views*. Ed. Marjorie Ford and Jon Ford. Boston: Houghton Mifflin, 1998. 58–61.

Exercise 2   DISCUSSION AND CRITICAL THINKING

1. Circle the thesis and underline the topic sentences in the support paragraphs.

2. Forms of writing other than definition are often used to define. Which form provides structure for this extended definition?

3. How is Sheahan's introduction connected to his conclusion?

4. How do you explain Sheahan's change of verb tenses?

Practicing Patterns of Definition

Doing the following exercise will help you remember the patterns of writing used in extended definitions.

Exercise 3   COMPLETING PATTERNS OF DEFINITION

Fill in the double bubble with a term to be defined. You might want to define culturally diverse society, educated person, leader, role model, friend, infatuation, true love, success, *or* intelligence. *Then complete a bubble on the right for each paragraph or essay pattern. If the pattern does not apply (that is, if it would not provide useful information for your definition), mark it NA ("not applicable). If you were actually writing an essay on the topic you selected, you would use ideas from your cluster to form points in an outline.*

- narration
- description
- exemplification
- analysis by division
- process analysis
- cause and effect
- classification
- comparison and contrast

Student Documented Essay (Multiple Sources)

The assignment was to write an extended definition of an abstract term used in a college subject other than English. Proctor, a current student in Psychology 3, selected *motivation*. She was expected to use at least three sources from which she would quote and paraphrase. Her English instructor pointed out that she could include discussion of more than one definition, an approach that fit her term.

Perspectives on Motivation
Michelle Proctor

What is *motivation?* It is basically defined as any action or behavior that drives people to satisfy their biological or psychological needs. There are three very good theories that give different perspectives on motivation: Darwin's Instinct Theory, Hull's Drive Reduction Theory, and Maslow's Hierarchy of Needs Theory.

Charles Darwin's Instinct Theory explains that our basic instincts are what motivate us. The salmon's basic instincts tell it when to swim a thousand miles across an ocean to a river and up into the gravel bed where it was spawned years before and where it will spawn now. Instinct theorists regard motivation in several ways. They believe our curiosity drives us to learn and acquire more. Our jealousy of others and yet our fearfulness of being alone motivates us to behave, while our needs of sociability lead us to do many things in order to be accepted. This theory seems to be good for defining much biological motivation, but it does not explain much of behavior. Douglas A. Bernstein points out that theorists have "named more than 10,000 instincts" and that instincts have "become meaningless labels describing behavior without explaining it" (259).

The Drive Reduction Theory was brought forth in 1943 by Clark Hull. He believed motivation came from primary drives and secondary or acquired drives. Primary drives are the need for sleep, food, water, and other basic needs. Secondary needs would be our affiliation with others and our contact with them. If a person were dying of thirst and came to a town where he could find water, then the primary need would be to get water while his secondary need would be to socialize with the townspeople. The fault in Drive Reduction Theory is that after our primary needs have been filled, our behavior does not stop. Our relationship with our environment is a good example of this. In earlier years we were motivated by a need to survive in our environment. Now that that need has been met, we still want to master our environment to the point that we may pollute it until no one will survive. Connecting with our everyday experience, Rod Plotnik says that "drive-reduction theory has difficulty explaining why, after we satisfy our hunger need with a complete meal, and say we are full, we then eat a dessert" (330).

The third theory on motivation came from Abraham Maslow in 1970. Maslow's Hierarchy of Needs is explained in a pyramid of five steps, starting from the lowest need, the biological, to the highest need, self-actualization. Each step may be reached only by the completion of the previous step. In Maslow's pyramid the first need that must be met is biological. This contains our basic needs of food, water, and sleep. After that has been fulfilled, then safety must be met. We must be physically and psychologically secure in our environment and our surroundings to reach the next stage of love and belongingness. Here we must be able to love someone or something to receive love in return. This is where step four, self-esteem, comes into play, and self-esteem must be very high for us to reach the final step, self-actualization. Of course, not all people do that. In *Theories and Systems of Psychology,* Robert Lundin says, "Maslow allows that only a small percentage (perhaps 10 percent) of people really become self-actualized, or 'fully human'" (373). Maslow himself says, "There are no perfect human beings" (Lundin 374). But to some extent, we can all accept our environment and work to help others learn and survive in their surroundings.

The first two theories define *motivation* primarily on the basis of our biological needs. Both contributed valuable insights into our understanding of why we behave as we do. Maslow was able to build on the ideas the other social scientists had developed. His Hierarchy of Needs is more comprehensive, offering a combination of biological and psychological needs. It represents the best definition we now have.

Works Cited

Bernstein, Douglas A., and Peggy W. Nash. *Essentials of Psychology.* 2nd ed. Boston: Houghton Mifflin, 2002.

Lundin, Robert W. *Theories and Systems of Psychology.* 5th ed. Lexington, Mass.: D.C. Heath, 1996.

Plotnik, Rod. *Introduction to Psychology.* 5th ed. Belmont, Calif.: Wadsworth, 1999.

Exercise 4 **DISCUSSION AND CRITICAL THINKING**

1. Is the purpose mainly to persuade or to inform?

2. Underline definitions in the second, third, and fourth paragraphs.

Definition: Clarifying Terms **137**

3. In the left margin, annotate the text by indicating the form(s) of discourse used for defining: example, analysis by division, comparison and contrast, cause and effect.

4. If Proctor uses one form more than others, list it here.

5. Circle the sentence that best defines *motivation*.

Paired Sources on Bullying

Few people go through school without being bullied. The victims may also at times be the perpetrators. Bullies come in different guises and in different sexes. Their destructive work takes different forms. In "Disarming the Rage," the team of reporters says, "Children all over the country are feeling fear, hopelessness and rage, emotions that turn some of them into bullies and others into their victims." In the companion essay, "Bully, Bully," John Leo acknowledges a severe problem but sees part of the current concern over bullying to be an overreaction. He says that some of us have been "taking a lot of harmless and minor things ordinary children do and turning them into examples of bullying." The difference between the views of these two essays must begin with definitions. What is a bully? What is bullying?

Disarming the Rage

Richard Jerome, Ron Arias, Mary Boone, Lauren Comander, Joanne Fowler, Maureen Marrington, Ellen Mazo, Jamie Reno, Don Sider, Gail Cameron Wescott

This team of *People* magazine writers reports on efforts in the United States to curb bullying in schools in response to school shootings. In brief case studies, they explain how acts of violent reprisals are linked to bullying and define *bullying, bullies,* and *victims.*

1   Across the country, thousands of students stay home from school each day, terrified of humiliation or worse at the hands of bullies. In the wake of school shootings—most recently in

California and Pennsylvania—parents, teachers and lawmakers are demanding quick action.

2   In the rigid social system of Bethel Regional High School in Bethel, a remote town in the tundra of southwest Alaska, Evan Ramsey was an outcast, a status earned by his slight frame, shy manner, poor grades and broken family. "Everybody had given me a nickname: Screech, the nerdy character on *Saved by the Bell*," he recalls. "I got stuff thrown at me, I got spit on, I got beat up. Sometimes I fought back, but I wasn't that good at fighting." Taunted throughout his years in school, he reported the incidents to his teachers, and at first his tormentors were punished. "After a while [the principal] told me to just start ignoring everybody. But then you can't take it anymore."

3   On the morning of Feb. 19, 1997, Ramsey, then 16, went to school with a 12-gauge shotgun, walked to a crowded common area and opened fire. As schoolmates fled screaming, he roamed the halls shooting randomly—mostly into the air. Ramsey would finally surrender to police, but not before killing basketball star Josh Palacios, 16, with a blast to the stomach, and principal Ron Edwards, 50, who was shot in the back. Tried as an adult for murder, Ramsey was sentenced to 210 years in prison after a jury rejected a defense contention that he had been attempting "suicide by cop," hoping to be gunned down but not intending to kill anyone. Still, Ramsey now admits in his cell at Spring Creek Correctional Center in Seward, Alaska, "I felt a sense of power with a gun. It was the only way to get rid of the anger."

4   Unfortunately Ramsey is not alone. Children all over the country are feeling fear, hopelessness and rage, emotions that turn some of them into bullies and others into their victims. Some say that is how it has always been and always will be—that bullying, like other adolescent ills, is something to be endured and to grow out of. But that view is changing. At a time when many parents are afraid to send their children to school, the wake-up call sounded by the 13 killings and 2 suicides at Columbine High School in Colorado two years ago still reverberates. It is now clear that Columbine shooters Dylan Klebold and Eric Harris felt bullied and alienated, and in their minds it was payback time.

5   In recent months there have been two other horrifying shooting incidents resulting, at least in part, from bullying. On March 5, 15-year-old Charles "Andy" Williams brought a .22-cal. pistol to Santana High School in Santee, Calif., and shot 15 students and adults, killing 2. He was recently certified to stand trial for murder as an adult. His apparent motive? Lethal revenge for the torment

he had known at the hands of local kids. "We abused him pretty much, I mean verbally," concedes one of them. "I called him a skinny faggot one time."

6   Two days after the Williams shooting, Elizabeth Bush, 14, an eighth grader from Williamsport, Pa., who said she was often called "idiot, stupid, fat, ugly," brought her father's .22-cal. pistol to school and shot 13-year-old Kimberly Marchese, wounding her in the shoulder. Kimberly, one of her few friends, had earned Elizabeth's ire by allegedly turning on her and joining in with the taunters. Bush admitted her guilt and offered apologies. A ward of the court until after she turns 21, she is now in a juvenile psychiatric facility. Kimberly, meanwhile, still has bullet fragments in her shoulder and is undergoing physical therapy.

7   As school enrollment rises and youths cope with the mounting pressures of today's competitive and status-conscious culture, the numbers of bullied children have grown as rapidly as the consequences. According to the National Education Association, 160,000 children skip school each day because of intimidation by their peers. The U.S. Department of Education reports that 77 percent of middle and high school students in small midwestern towns have been bullied. And a National Institutes of Health study newly released in the *Journal of the American Medical Association* reveals that almost a third of 6th to 10th graders—5.7 million children nationwide—have experienced some kind of bullying. "We are talking about a significant problem," says Deborah Prothrow-Stith, professor of public health practice at Harvard, who cites emotional alienation at home as another factor in creating bullies. "A lot of kids have grief, loss, pain, and it's unresolved."

8   Some experts see bullying as an inevitable consequence of a culture that rewards perceived strength and dominance. "The concept of power we admire is power over someone else," says Jackson Katz, 41, whose Long Beach, Calif., consulting firm counsels schools and the military on violence prevention. "In corporate culture, in sports culture, in the media, we honor those who win at all costs. The bully is a kind of hero in our society." Perhaps not surprisingly, most bullies are male. "Our culture defines masculinity as connected to power, control and dominance," notes Katz, whose work was inspired in part by the shame he felt in high school when he once stood idly by while a bully beat up a smaller student.

9   As for the targets of bullying, alienation runs like a stitch through most of their lives. A study last fall by the U.S. Secret Service found that in two-thirds of the 37 school shootings since 1974, the attackers felt "persecuted, bullied, threatened, attacked or injured." In

more than three-quarters of the cases, the attacker told a peer of his violent intentions. William Pollack, a clinical psychologist and author of *Real Boys' Voices,* who contributed to the Secret Service study, said that several boys from Columbine described bullying as part of the school fabric. Two admitted to mocking Klebold and Harris. "Why don't people get it that it drives you over the edge?" they told Pollack. "It isn't just Columbine. It is everywhere."

10   That sad fact is beginning to sink in, as the spate of disturbing incidents in recent years has set off desperate searches for answers. In response, parents have begun crusades to warn and educate other families, courts have seen drawn-out legal battles that try to determine who is ultimately responsible, and lawmakers in several states—including Texas, New York and Massachusetts—have struggled to shape anti-bullying legislation that would offer remedies ranging from early intervention and counseling to the automatic expulsion of offenders.

11   One of the most shocking cases of victimization by bullies took place near Atlanta on March 28, 1994. That day, 15-year-old Brian Head, a heavyset sophomore at suburban Etowah High School, walked into economics class, pulled out his father's 9-mm handgun and pressed it to his temple. "I can't take this anymore," he said. Then he squeezed the trigger. Brian had been teased for years about his weight. "A lot of times the more popular or athletic kids would make him a target," his mother, Rita, 43, says of her only child, a sensitive boy with a gift for poetry. "They would slap Brian in the back of the head or push him into a locker. It just broke him." Not a single student was disciplined in connection with his death. After his suicide, Rita, a magazine copy editor, and her husband, Bill, 47, counseled other parents and produced a video for elementary school students titled *But Names Will Never Hurt Me* about an overweight girl who suffers relentless teasing.

12   Georgia residents were stunned by a second child's death on Nov. 2, 1998. After stepping off a school bus, 13-year-old Josh Belluardo was fatally punched by his neighbor Jonathan Miller, 15, who had been suspended in the past for bullying and other infractions. In that tragedy's wake Georgia Gov. Roy Barnes in 1999 signed an anti-bullying law that allows schools to expel any student three times disciplined for picking on others.

13   On the other side of the continent, Washington Gov. Gary Locke is pressing for anti-bullying training in schools, following two high-profile cases there. Jenny Wieland of Seattle still cannot talk of her only child, Amy Ragan, shot dead at age 17 more than eight years ago, without tearing up. A soccer player and equestrian in her senior year at Marysville-Pilchuck High School, Amy was heading

to the mall on the night of Nov. 20, 1992, when she stopped at a friend's apartment. There, three schoolmates had gathered by the time Trevor Oscar Turner showed up. Then 19, Turner was showing off a .38-cal. revolver, holding it to kids' heads, and when he got to Amy, the weapon went off. Turner pleaded guilty to first-degree manslaughter and served 27 months of a 41-month sentence.

14 "I can't help but wonder what Amy's life would be like if she was still alive," says Wieland today. "I wonder about her career and if she'd be in love or have a baby." Wieland turned her grief into action. In 1994 she helped start Mothers Against Violence in America (MAVIA), an activist group patterned after Mothers Against Drunk Driving. She left her insurance job to become the program's director and speaks annually at 50 schools. In 1998 she became the first director of SAVE (Students Against Violence Everywhere), which continues to grow, now boasting 126 student chapters nationwide that offer schools anti-harassment and conflict-resolution programs. "People ask how I can stand to tell her story over and over," she says. "If I can save just one child, it's well worth the pain."

15 Not long after Amy Ragan's death, another bullying scenario unfolded 50 miles away in Stanwood, Wash. Confined to a wheelchair by cerebral palsy, Calcutta-born Taya Haugstad was a fifth grader in 1993, when a boy began calling her "bitch" and "retard." The daily verbal abuse led to terrible nightmares. By middle school, according to a lawsuit Taya later filed, her tormentor—a popular athlete—got physical, pushing her wheelchair into the wall and holding it while his friends kicked the wheels. Eventually Taya was diagnosed with posttraumatic stress disorder. "Imagine that you can't run away or scream," says her psychologist, Judith McCarthy. "Not only was she traumatized, she's handicapped. She felt terribly unsafe in the world." Her adoptive parents, Karrie and Ken Haugstad, 48 and 55, complained to school authorities and went to court to get a restraining order against the bully, but it was never issued. Taya sued the school district and the boy in 1999. The judge awarded her $300,000 last year, ruling that the school was negligent in its supervision, thus inflicting emotional distress. (The ruling is under appeal.) Taya, now 19 and a high school junior, hopes to study writing in college. She says she holds no grudge against her nemesis, who received undisclosed punishment from the school. "I don't think about him," she says.

16 But Josh Sneed may never forgive the boys he refers to as the Skaters. It was in 1996, late in his freshman year at Powell High School in Powell, Tenn., when, he says, a group of skateboarders began to terrorize him. With chains clinking and baseball bats

pounding the pavement, he claims, they chased him and threatened to beat him to death. Why Josh? He was small and "a country boy," says his homemaker mother, Karen Grady, 41. "They made fun of him for that. They told him he was poor and made fun of him for that."

17   Then on Oct. 17, 1996, "I just snapped," her son says. As Jason Pratt, known as one of the Skaters, passed him in the cafeteria, Sneed whacked him on the head with a tray. "I figured if I got lucky and took him out, all the other nonsense would stop." But after a few punches, Josh slipped on a scrap of food, hit his head on the floor and lost consciousness as Pratt kneed him in the head several times. Finally a football player leapt over two tables and dragged Sneed away, likely saving his life. Four titanium plates were needed to secure his shattered skull, and he was so gravely injured that he had to relearn how to walk and talk. Home-schooled, Sneed eventually earned his GED, but he hasn't regained his short-term memory. Assault charges against both him and Pratt were dismissed, but Pratt (who declined to comment) was suspended from school for 133 days.

18   Grady sued the county, claiming that because the school knew Josh was being terrorized but never disciplined the tormentors, they effectively sanctioned the conditions that led to the fight. Her attorney, James A.H. Bell, hopes the suit will have national implications. "We tried to make a statement, holding the school system accountable for its failure to protect," he says. In February Sneed and Grady were awarded $49,807 by a judge who found the county partly at fault. A tractor buff who once aspired to own a John Deere shop, Josh now lives on his grandfather's farm, passing his days with cartoons, video games and light chores. "Everybody's hollering that they need to get rid of guns, but it's not that," he says. "You need to find out what's going on in school."

19   Around the country, officials are attempting to do precisely that, as many states now require a safe-school plan that specifically addresses bullying. Most experts agree that metal detectors and zero-tolerance expulsions ignore the root of the problem. Counseling and fostering teamwork seem most effective, as evidenced by successful programs in the Cherry Creek, Colo., school district and DeKalb County, Ga. "We create an atmosphere of caring—it's harder to be a bully when you care about someone," says John Monferdini, head counselor at the DeKalb Alternative School, which serves 400 county students, most of whom have been expelled for bullying and violent behavior. Apart from academics, the school offers conflict-resolution courses and team-oriented outdoor activ-

ities that demand cooperation, "Yeah, I'm a bully," says Chris Jones, 15. "If I'm with friends and we see someone coming along we can jump on, we do it. It's like, you know, an adrenaline rush." But a stint in DeKalb is having a transformative effect. "When I came here, it was because we beat up a kid so badly—sticking his head in the bleachers—and the only thing I wished was that we'd had a chance to hurt him worse before we got caught. That's not the way I am now."

One wonders if intervention might have restrained the bullies who tormented Evan Ramsey. Ineligible for parole until 2066, when he'll be 86, Ramsey, now 20, spends most days working out, playing cards, reading Stephen King novels and studying for his high school diploma. He also has plenty of time to reflect on the horrible error in judgment he made. "The worst thing is to resort to violence," he says. "I'd like to get letters from kids who are getting problems like I went through. I could write back and help them." His advice: "If they're being messed with, they have to tell someone. If nothing's done, then they have to go [to] higher and higher [authority] until it stops. If they don't get help, that's when they'll lose it and maybe do something bad—really bad. And the pain of doing that never really stops."

Exercise 5

DISCUSSION AND CRITICAL THINKING

1. Which two of the many forms used in defining terms—example, cause and effect, description, narration, and so on—do these authors use most extensively?

2. Annotate the essay for the use of cause and effect, example, description, and narration. Note that some of the forms overlap.

3. Bullying is shown to be the immediate cause of many of the acts of violence discussed by the team of writers. What factors are suggested as two of the causes of the bullying? (See paragraph 7.)

4. What are some of the feelings of emotional distress that both the bullies and the victims often share? (See paragraphs 4, 7, and 9.)

5. A single definition of bullying is not included. Compose a definition based on the material included in this essay.

6. To what extent can school intervention curb bullying?

7. Do you agree with Jackson Katz's view on the cultural causes of bullying: "The concept of power we admire is power over someone else.... In corporate culture, in sports culture, in the media, we honor those who win at all costs. The bully is a kind of hero in our society"?

Bully, Bully

John Leo

John Leo, staff writer for U.S. News and World Report, *offers his observations on the currently hot-button issue of bullying in the United States. Focusing on definitions in a national study, he argues that rumors and dirty looks and putting up with horrible classmates are all part of growing up and should not be classified as bullying.*

Do Gossip and Rumors Count as Punishable Behavior?

1   Now we have a big national study on bullying, and the problem with it is right there in the first paragraph: Bullying behavior may be "verbal (e.g., name-calling, threats), physical (e.g., hitting), or psychological (e.g., rumors, shunning/exclusion)." Uh-oh. The study may or may not have put bullying on the map as a major national issue. But it rather clearly used a dubious tactic: taking a lot of harmless and minor things ordinary children do and turning them into examples of bullying. Calling somebody a jerk and spreading rumors counted as bullying in the study. Repeated teasing counted too. You achieved bully status if you didn't let the class creep into your game of catch, or if you just stayed away from people you didn't like (shunning, exclusion).

2   With a definition like that, the total of children involved in either bullying or being bullied themselves ought to be around 100 percent. But no, the bullying study says only 29.9 percent of the students studied reported frequent or moderate involvement—and that total was arrived at by lumping bullies and their victims together in the statistics.

3   **Debatable Definitions**   The low numbers and highly debatable definitions undercut the study's conclusion that bullying is "a serious problem for U.S. youth." Of the 29.9 figure, 13.0 percent were bullies, 10.6 percent were targets of bullying, and 6.3 percent were both perpetrators and victims. The study, done by the National Institute of Child Health and Human Development, is based on 15,686 questionnaires filled out by students in grades six through 10 in public and private schools around the country.

4   We have seen this statistical blending of serious and trivial incidents before. The American Association of University Women produced a 1993 report showing that 80 percent of American students have been sexually harassed, including a hard-to-believe 76 percent of all boys. The AAUW got the numbers up that high by including glances, gestures, gossip, and naughty jokes. The elastic definition encouraged schools and courts to view many previously uncontroversial kinds of expression as sexual harassment. Before long, schools were making solemn lists of harassing behaviors that included winking, and calling someone "honey."

5   Another set of broad definitions appeared when zero-tolerance policies descended on the schools. Antidrug rules were extended to cover aspirin. Antiweapons regulations covered a rubber knife used in a school play. Just two months ago, a third grader in Monroe, La., was suspended for drawing a picture of G.I. Joe. Now the antibullying movement is poised to provide a third source of dubious hyperregulation of the young. One antibullying specialist says "hard looks" and "stare downs"—everyday activities for millions of hormone-driven adolescents—should be punishable offenses under student codes.

6   This has all the makings of an antibullying crusade with many of the same wretched excesses of the zero-tolerance and anti-harassment campaigns. Serious bullying can be ugly. Parents and schools should stop it and punish offenders. And schools should do whatever they can to create a culture of civility and tolerance. But rumors and dirty looks and putting up with horrible classmates are a part of growing up. So are the teenage tendencies to form cliques and snub people now and then. Adults shouldn't faint when they see this behavior, or try to turn it into quasi-criminal activity.

7   Another pitfall: In focusing on gossip, rumors, and verbal offenses, the crusade has the obvious potential to infringe on free speech at schools. Will comments like "I think Catholicism is wrong," or "I think homosexuality is a sin," be turned into anti-

bullying offenses? The crusade could also demonize those who bully, instead of helping them change. Some of the antibully literature circulating in Europe is hateful stuff. One screed calls "the serial bully" glib, shallow, evasive, incapable of intimacy, and a practiced liar who "displays a seemingly limitless demonic energy." Yet a lot of the academic literature reports that bullies often aren't very psychologically different from their victims. And the national study says a fifth of bullying victims are bullies themselves.

8   The example of Europe's more advanced antibullying crusade should make Americans cautious. The European campaign has expanded from schools into the adult world and the workplace. Several nations are considering antibullying laws, including Britain. Definitions are expanding too. A proposed antibullying law in Portugal would make it illegal to harass workers by giving them tasks for which they are overqualified. Deliberately giving employees erroneous information would count as bullying too. Ireland's antibullying task force came up with a scarily vague definition of bullying: "repeated inappropriate behavior, direct or indirect," which could "reasonably be regarded as undermining the individual's right to dignity at work." Imagine what the American litigation industry could do with wording like that.

9   It's time to stop and ask: Where is our antibullying campaign going?

Exercise 6 DISCUSSION AND CRITICAL THINKING

1. Circle the thesis sentence.

2. The definition in question defines *bullying* as "verbal, physical, or psychological" behavior directed against the victim. Of those three characteristics, which two does Leo find troublesome?

3. Why does Leo find those two characteristics troublesome?

4. Does he have a good point in criticizing the definition or is he unfairly ridiculing the definition?

5. Does Leo believe there should be no antibullying campaign?

6. What does Leo have to say about bullying?

7. What part of the questioned definition does he say is actually part of growing up? (See paragraph 6.)

8. How does Leo use comparison and contrast to evaluate the definition of *bullying,* according to the national study?

9. Leo does not provide us with his definition of *bullying.* Write a definition for him or explain what kind of regulation he would use to confront bullying.

Paired Sources on Bosses and Workers, Good and Bad

Chances are, if you eavesdrop in a management meeting room, you will hear comments about good and bad workers. Conversely, if you listen in to a group gathering of workers, perspectives on good and bad bosses will be somewhere on the agenda. The paired sources here recognize that special workplace interest. The essay "You and Your Boss" relates directly to the restaurant business, but it has much broader applications. The interview "Why Many Good Workers Turn into Bad Bosses" focuses on roles and relationships.

You and Your Boss

Paul B. Hertneky

Of all businesses the typical person encounters, the food industry is probably the most visible. We watch the workers—the servers, the buspersons, the clerks, and the hosts and hostesses. We may even glimpse the kitchen personnel—the cooks and helpers. We may see less of the individual who oversees the operation, but the service and product we receive will certainly be affected by whether that person, called the boss, is "good" or "bad." This article was originally published in *Restaurant Hospitality*.

1   In the last thirty years, computers have shrunken from humongous to handheld. We can grow vegetables without dirt. We can watch television while getting a root canal. We can have breakfast in London and lunch in New York. But life with a boss has changed more slowly. Dilbert,* instead of Dagwood,† could just as easily be working for Mr. Dithers.‡ And Ebenezer Scrooge§ continues to remind us of bosses we've all known. Despite a tide of management books, seminars, and videotapes, and an invasion of MBAs, bosses will still be bosses.

2   In the restaurant business, managers come and go as independent operators and companies restructure their organizations. Mammoth foodservice firms serve stockholders above all others. Nearly everyone in this business reports to at least one boss. In fact, we have enough bosses, laid shoulder-to-shoulder, to sink Long Island. Vivienne Wildes, who runs The Waiters Association, bristles at the word "boss." She says it carries "negative connotations," preferring "supervisors" or "employers." Okay, enlightened bosses avoid bossing their employees around. They seek consensus and focus more on listening, drawing ideas from employees and developing their skills.

3   But the vast number of restaurants don't glow with enlightened bosses. Owners nicknamed "Vulture" and "Bubblebutt" bark orders, publicly humiliate, and harass their employees. Turnover rates are blamed on everything from low pay to transient workers, but veterans point to nasty, inept bosses.

4   Maryanne, a bartender who chose to remain anonymous, works part-time in four restaurants. Her experience spans a couple of decades and covers every job in the front of the house. She describes one of her bosses as a hands-off owner who pays well for competency; another as a chef for whom cooking and serving is a religion; another is a virginal owner and all-around nice guy; and yet another serves lousy food while tooling around on an ego trip.

5   Foodservice bosses come in more varieties than fried appetizers in a fern bar.¶ But according to their employees, they share one dominant characteristic: a thriving ego. Their restaurants reflect their philosophies and lifestyles. Maryanne says "the best bosses I've had were chef/owners . . . their mission is clear and single-

---

*Dilbert is a contemporary cartoon character.
†Dagwood is a hapless cartoon character of the 1940s and 1950s.
‡Mr. Dithers is the boss who harasses Dagwood.
§Ebenezer Scrooge is the stingy main character who repents in Charles Dickens's *A Christmas Carol.*
¶A fern bar is an upscale social bar.

minded." Acknowledging that most operators fall in-between, Maryanne says the worst bosses allow their egos to "lead them into a lifestyle that undermines the restaurant . . . to lead them to the wrong side of the bar." A training director for a fast-growing chain had worked for too many operators who exhibited "egotism to a fault—out of control—hating to give credit or praise, and, most of all, not listening."

6   Bull-headed operators are a hallmark of this business and they may also be the scourge. Every day, we all face the balance between when to talk and when to listen. Listening comes harder to those who hold themselves and their ideas in high regard. One franchise vice president considers a boss's worst trait "a disregard for other's ideas." Her sentiments match those of a veteran freelance waiter, who blames closed-mindedness for a manager's inability to adapt to situations, new hires, and new systems.

7   An open mind consistently discovers new frontiers, listening offers true leaders perspective and respect—two vision-related qualities that govern how a boss views his or her world and is viewed by it. Scrooge's lifetime of self-centeredness blinded him to the surrounding reality—to Tiny Tim*—and we all cheer as the ghosts[†] open his eyes to the reality of his miserly past, his egocentric present, and his miserable future.

8   Respect is the word most frequently uttered when restaurant workers talk about their bosses. "Once respect goes, it all tumbles down," says Maryanne, who has seen her share of failed restaurants. John, a sous chef, said that "once I realized that I'd lost all respect for a boss I was gone." And a former manager, now a high-profile waiter, insists "if ever there was a cog that makes the machinery of a restaurant run, it's respect—that ability to look at a situation calmly and view staff, suppliers, and customers with respect."

9   But respect can be a slippery idea. We know this: sometimes it must be earned and sometimes it is immediately granted and expected to be maintained; it means seeing the value of others' skills, ideas, the way they do their jobs and live their lives. So, a boss or employee who doesn't listen or show imagination and diligence won't get much respect. Respect also tends to come to those who respect others. One waiter referred to a manager, ten years his junior, who offered no respect and got none. "He wanted to be liked, and he was. But nobody respected him. After a while,

---

*Tiny Tim is an impoverished crippled lad who benefits from Scrooge's change of heart.
[†]The ghosts are the spirits who visit Scrooge to tell him what he was, what he is, and what he will be if he doesn't change.

he calmed down and began to notice and rely on the strength of his staff—now I have a great deal of respect for him."

10   Lack of respect is sad; disrespect is deplorable. "This business is just full of sexual harassment," whispered one franchise executive over the phone. "You know, there's innuendo and all that crap and I know sometimes bosses don't know how inappropriate their actions and words are. I think we overlook it," she said, "because we figure we're just not as professional as other businesses, and that it goes with the territory." She also pointed out that, in an industry scraping for good managers, "you're willing to tolerate more than if you had someone standing at the door waiting for a job."

11   Indeed, stupid bosses exhibit intolerance that keeps career-minded people away. And these bosses haunt all levels of the industry. One female job applicant recalled an interview in which she was quizzed about her sexual fantasies. When she was offered the job, she declined.

12   Good bosses? Great bosses? They know who they are. If you wonder about the qualities most valued in bosses, they are opposite the faults listed above. Their egos fit through doorways. They listen and treat everyone the way they would like to be treated. They extend themselves in an effort to appreciate those who are new and different. They set a good example. They take interest in the lives of their employees. They possess what it took Scrooge a couple of horrifying nights to acquire—eyes that are wide open, and hearts and minds that follow.

Exercise 7 — DISCUSSION AND CRITICAL THINKING

1. Circle the thesis.

2. Underline the first definition of *good bosses*.

3. In paragraph 5, what does Maryanne mean when she says, "The best bosses I've had were chef/owners . . . their mission is clear and single-minded"?

4. Why is a large ego a problem for bosses?

5. How does not listening handicap the boss?

6. What does listening provide for the manager?

7. How is a self-centered boss like Scrooge?

8. In paragraph 8, to what three targets is the idea of respect directed?

9. What is worse than lack of respect?

10. What is the effect of bosses' intolerance?

11. Complete this definition based on Hertneky's essay: A good boss is a human resources manager who is _____, _____. _____, and _____ (opposite of *egocentric, closed minded, disrespectful and unappreciative,* and *intolerant*).

Why Many Good Workers Turn into Bad Bosses

U.S. News & World Report Staff

It is a common assumption that employees, having proved themselves as workers, would naturally transfer their excellence to a management position. Not necessarily so, says noted human resources specialist Charles Dwyer in this interview.

1   **Q** Mr. Dwyer, why are so many people ineffective as bosses?

A For a couple of reasons. One is that people are not consciously sensitive to what is important to other people. But there's a far more subtle reason: My behavior is designed by me, however unconsciously, to take care of my values first. I can say: "I'm the boss, and I can tell him what to do. That feels good." That's one reason quality-control circles have been ineffective in this country. They scare supervisors who want to maintain control over people.

2   **Q** Doesn't that forceful approach often work in managing employees?

A I'll show you S.O.B.s by the legion who get to the top of their organizations through aversive behavior control. It does work. The empirical evidence shows you can go on for a long time using fear, intimidation and threat to get an awful lot of the behavior that you want.

Q What are the dangers in taking that approach?

A It is not a pragmatic way to manage in terms of investment and return of energy. If I threaten you, you don't like it but you do what I want. But you're also looking for a way out. You're pushing back up, like a spring. I have to use more energy to keep you down.

Q What are some of the other results?

A Good people start to leave. Absenteeism goes up. Tardiness starts to increase. You end up with slowdowns, lost paper, sabotage.

If those coping mechanisms don't work, people get sick. It starts to wear on them. That makes them less sharp. There are more accidents, more safety violations, more sick time and more people quitting.

Q Why do managers bother using this approach?

A Because it feels good. You are in control of people even though the system you are using is an inefficient way to be productive and profitable.

Q What would an effective boss do?

A If you want people to behave in certain ways, you appeal to what is important to them. Most people want respect and autonomy. They want to feel they have some control. They want recognition and some status. They want emotional as well as financial security. Some employees will be yours forever if you pat them on the head twice a week—with sincerity, assuming you think they deserve it. Recognition is a very effective device for influencing human behavior.

Q What other motivators work?

A Besides these things, employees want to have fun at work.

Q Did you say "fun"?

A Yes. People like to have fun. You can build fun deliberately into an organization—lay out a whole series of things that say, "We can have fun here as long as we reach production goals." You can have joke boards, candid photographs and all kinds of things.

9   **Q** What does this do for employee performance and morale?

A I've seen people come from dull-as-dust assembly-line jobs who just had a wonderful day. I've seen people come in to work when they were sick and should have stayed home. They wouldn't miss a day of work, not because the work was enjoyable or intrinsically satisfying, but because it was fun to be there.

10   **Q** What else is important in managing subordinates?

A Feedback is very important. People want to know how well they're doing. You can't imagine how many people don't have the vaguest notion of how they are doing until somebody seriously fills out one of those rarely useful performance appraisals.

There are fundamental human values you can appeal to. You can sometimes work wonders with assembly-line workers by unbolting their chairs and bins so that they can put them wherever they want them.

11   **Q** You haven't stressed money as an effective motivator of people—

A It is, sometimes. If used in piecework pay and commissions, money works if you don't violate people's sense of fairness. But most people are paid wages and salaries, so money doesn't motivate them on a daily basis. They know they'll get paid almost no matter what.

Money is very different from status, recognition, security, fun, affiliation, feeling good, respect and autonomy. You want money as a way to have fun, be amused, be secure and feel good about yourself. Even if I gave you those things directly, you still need some money to live in a decent place and to be able to do certain kinds of things. But money is not the only motivator. It is an instrument to all those other things that I may be able to give you directly.

12   **Q** What personal traits does the effective boss have?

A There's flexibility and simplicity. If you look at people who are respected in corporations, you will see they have clarity and breadth of vision. They have their priorities clearly in mind. They use their time effectively. They know when to ignore and neglect things and when to stop hitting their heads against the wall. They have a strong, as opposed to a big, ego. They have a tough skin and confidence in themselves.

13 **Q** Can these traits be learned?

A Yes, but I know many who never learn them. That's part of the current criticism of the training of MBAs in this country: They don't understand the politics of organizations, human behavior or human motivation.

14 **Q** Do some managers lack these traits because they are promoted beyond their ability?

A People can move out of their technical specialties into higher management without learning to deal with planning and coordination and without understanding people. For all their technical knowledge, they find themselves in positions for which they've never been trained. Unfortunately for them, it's impossible to admit this, and equally impossible to take a promotion and then find out it's not for them and move back down.

15 **Q** Which skills are most often lacking?

A In middle to upper management, one mostly notices executives who cannot deal well with people. As one moves up the ladder, what are most often lacking are intellectual or conceptual skills—the breadth of vision, the planning, the ability to see multiple pieces come together.

16 **Q** What kind of questions should one ask in assessing whether he or she will be an effective boss?

A Ask yourself: What is important to me? Is deference important? Is being on top important? Do I have driving ambition? Is visibility important? Is a job well done important?

Try ranking those values. You may begin to see whether or not the position that you're aspiring to is likely to be satisfying. Also, know what is expected of you and what you expect of yourself.

17 **Q** Do you think a boss can change his or her behavior?

A Yes—even an MBA! I've been doing it with people for a long time. While I don't have careful empirical studies, there's a fair mass of anecdotal evidence from people who have said, "Hey, I realize something I never realized before," and they changed their behavior to become more effective.

18 **Q** How does a boss avoid becoming ineffective?

A Our culture seems to place a high value on deference, authority, moving up and status. These things may not breed effective behavior toward others and may even bring on wars within ourselves. But we can make our own choices—what to say through the intercom, how to greet people, how to treat people, when to listen and when to talk.

People should define their own concepts of value and not allow society, a business school or anyone else to do it for them.

Understand yourself, your values, your behavior and its effect on other people—to realize, in other words, what it costs you, in terms of effectiveness, to do and say certain kinds of otherwise satisfying things.

Exercise 8

DISCUSSION AND CRITICAL THINKING

1. According to Charles Dwyer, why are so many people ineffective bosses?

2. What are the main negative results of the forceful approach to managing?

3. What does an effective manager do to give people what they want?

4. Dwyer says that employees want to have fun at work. To what extent is that possible at places where you have worked?

5. Why is money overrated as an effective motivator?

6. What is the difference between a strong ego and a big ego?

7. In Q&A 14, what does the phrase "promoted beyond their ability" mean?

8. What difficulty does the person promoted beyond his or her ability face?

9. Does Dwyer say it is possible for ineffective bosses to become effective? Does your experience confirm that view?

✎ Topics for Writing Definition

Writing Process Worksheet

You will find a Writing Process Worksheet on page 27. It can be photocopied and enlarged, filled in, and submitted with each assignment if your instructor directs you to do so.

Source-Based Topics

Each essay developed from these suggested source-based topics should include at least one reference to the reading selection by the author's name and the title. Quotations should be enclosed in quotation marks. Follow your instructor's directions in documenting the ideas you borrow. Whether you use informal or formal documentation, the form is not complicated, and you will soon learn to use it for these essays without checking each time. See pages 73 and 74 for a discussion of MLA style and informal documentation.

Underlining and annotating reading selections will help you in finding support material. In prewriting brief essays, consider marking your outline to indicate where you will use quotations or other borrowed ideas. If the quotations or reworded statements are short and few, you could even insert them inside parentheses or circles in your outline; if you do, also include the author's last name and the page number. A sound system, consistently used, will save you time and ensure technically strong papers.

"My-Graines"

1. Using this essay as a model, write an essay about anyone you know who suffers from the same condition or any other chronic illness.

2. Use the Internet or another source to investigate a disease and then discuss that disease by referring to your source and by using examples from personal experience or observation.

"Perspectives on Motivation"

3. Select an abstract term (for example, *depression, stress, stroke, enabler, manipulation, controlling personality*) from any field you have studied or are studying and write an extended definition. You may have a

textbook that will give you a basic definition and discussion. Include some examples from your experience to enliven your essay.

"Disarming the Rage"

4. Take the most basic definition you can derive from this essay and a few insights and apply them to situations with which you are familiar. Your examples may come from your childhood experiences.

5. Using the idea about the characteristics shared by bullies and victims, discuss bullies you observed when growing up.

6. If you had enormous power as an educator, what would you do to curtail bullying? Discuss the main characteristics of bullying in relation to your plan. Give credit to this essay or any other sources.

"Bully, Bully"

7. Write an analysis of Leo's essay, and evaluate his ideas. To what extent do you agree with him? Examine the definitions along with him and explain what you think is and is not workable. Ask your instructor if you should separate your main summary from your critical reaction.

8. Discuss Leo's reservations about the definition of *bullying* from the national study as they apply to the examples of bullying and consequent bullying in "Disarming the Rage." Explain how the definition should be narrowed, if at all.

Paired Sources on Bullying

9. Write about the practice of bullying as you have witnessed or experienced it. "Disarming the Rage" accepts the definition developed by the national study, whereas "Bully, Bully" rejects it as being too broad. Give your views on both positions in your essay, as you construct your own definition of the word *bully*.

"You and Your Boss"

10. Use Hertneky's definition of a bad boss (or, by reversing it, the definition of a good boss) and discuss bosses you have had. Instead of observations by his informants—Maryanne, the waiter, and the franchise vice president—use insights from your own informants, along with whatever you have observed or experienced. You may have to modify Hertneky's definition to fit bosses in business other than food service.

11. Using this essay as a model, discuss a good worker. This topic will work best if you can define a good worker in a particular job.

12. Write an essay about someone else that is good, for example, good teachers, good soldiers (person in military service), good preachers, good neighbors, good police officers, or good siblings.

"Why Many Good Workers Turn into Bad Bosses"

13. Using this title as your theme, write about someone you know or know about who has been promoted to a management job and then seemed to change. This will usually be a person who was well liked and respected in a job in which he or she excelled and then became a person disliked or not respected in the management job. In your essay, define *efficient boss* and *efficient worker* and explain why the roles are often not similar.

14. Using Dwyer's definition of an efficient boss, discuss some bosses with whom you are familiar

15. Using the questions from this selection, or modifications of those questions, interview a person or persons in management. Write up the interview in the same form. You may want to include comments on the differences between Dwyer's comments and those of your informant.

Paired Sources on Bosses and Workers, Good and Bad

16. Write an essay about a good or bad boss you have observed. Explain why that boss was promoted to the position he or she holds. What qualities did that boss have as a worker? How have those qualities contributed to the person's strength or weakness as a boss. Refer to both essays in your analysis. Make sure that you include a clear definition of a good boss.

Career-Related Topics

17. Define one of the following terms by using other patterns of development (such as exemplification, cause and effect, narration, comparison and contrast): *total quality management, quality control, business ethics, customer satisfaction, cost effectiveness, Internet, temporary workers, union, outsource,* or *downsize.*

18. Define a term from computer technology, such as *Internet, World Wide Web, search engine,* or *chat room.*

General Topics

Select one of the following topics and write an extended definition of it; most of these topics will also serve well for writing simple definitions.

19. Conservative	30. Educated	41. Chicano
20. Asian American	31. Gang	42. Jock
21. Bonding	32. Freedom	43. Hispanic American
22. Sexist	33. Body language	
23. Cult	34. Hero	44. African American
24. Biker	35. Druggie	45. Macho
25. Liberal	36. Convict	46. Cool
26. Workaholic	37. Teen slang	47. Native American
27. Surfer	38. Psychopath	
28. Personal space	39. School spirit	48. Jerk
29. Clotheshorse	40. Feminist	

Writer's Guidelines: Definition

Simple Definition

1. No two words have exactly the same meaning.
2. Several forms of simple definitions can be blended into your discussion: basic dictionary definitions, synonyms, direct explanations, indirect explanations, and analytical definitions.
3. For a formal or analytical definition, specify the term, class, and characteristic(s).

    Example: <u>Capitalism</u> <u>is an economic system</u> <u>charactierzed by investment of money, private ownership, and free enterprise</u>.

    term — class — characteristics

4. Avoid "is where" and "is when" definitions, circular definitions, and the use of words in the definition that are more difficult than the word being defined.

Extended Definition

1. Use clustering to consider other patterns of development that may be used to define your term.

```
                narration
              description
            exemplification
            analysis by
              division
    ( )
            process
            analysis
            cause and
              effect
          classification
      comparison
      and contrast
```

2. The organization of your extended definition is likely to be one of emphasis, but it may be space or time, depending on the subject material. You may use just one pattern of development for the overall organization.

3. Consider these ways of introducing a definition: with a question, with a statement of what it is not, with a statement of what it originally meant, or with a discussion of why a clear definition is important. You may use a combination of these ways before you continue with your definition.

4. Whether you personalize a definition depends on your purpose and your audience. Your instructor may ask you to write about a word within the context of your own experience or to write about it from a detached, clinical viewpoint.

7

Analysis by Division: Examining the Parts

Writing Analysis by Division, p. 162
   Organization, p. 163
   Sequence of Parts, p. 163

Connecting Sources and Writing, p. 164
   Student Essay: "A Chinese New Year's Feast," p. 164
   Student Documented Essay: "Elvis Presley: Twentieth-Century Legend," p. 165
   Practicing Patterns of Analysis by Division, p. 167
   "A Brush with Reality: Surprises in the Tube," p. 168
   "Designer Babies," p. 172
   "Optimism, Tenacity Lead Way Back to Life," p. 176
   "Three Generations of Native American Women's Birth Experience," p. 179

Topics for Writing Analysis by Division, p. 185
   Writing Process Worksheet, p. 185
   Source-Based Topics, p. 185
   Career-Related Topics, p. 186
   General Topics, p. 187

Writer's Guidelines, p. 187

THE QUIGMANS by Buddy Hickerson

I'm afraid you have a compound, compound, compound, fracture, fracture, fracture, fracture.

© Tribune Media Services, Inc. All Rights Reserved. Reprinted with permission.

Writing Analysis by Division

If you need to explain how something works or exists as a unit, you will write an analysis by division. You will break down a unit (your subject) into its parts and explain how each part functions in relation to the operation or existence of the whole. The most important word here is *unit*. You begin with something that can stand alone or can be regarded separately: a poem, a heart, a painting, a car, a bike, a person, a school, a committee. The following procedure will guide you in writing an analysis by division. Move from subject to principle, to division, to relationship.

Step 1: Select something that is a unit.

Step 2: State one principle by which the unit can function.

Step 3: Divide the unit into parts according to that principle (the perceived purpose or role).

Step 4: Discuss each of the parts in relation to the unit.

Here's how a writer might apply this general procedure to a real object (unit).

Step 1: For the unit, I choose a pencil.

Step 2: For my principle, I see the pencil as a writing instrument.

Step 3: For dividing the unit into parts based on the principle of a pencil as a writing instrument, I divide the pencil into an eraser, an eraser holder, a wooden barrel, and a thin graphite core with a sharpened point.

Step 4: For my discussion of the parts in relation to the unit, I might say: "At the top of the wooden barrel is a strip of metal encircling an eraser and clamping it to the barrel. In the center of the barrel is a core of graphite that can be sharpened to a point at the end and used for writing. The eraser is used to remove marks made by the graphite point. Thus I have a complete writing tool, one that marks and erases marks."

Like many things, a pencil can be regarded in different ways. For example, an artist might *not* consider a pencil mainly as a writing tool. Instead, an artist might look at a pencil and see it as an object of simple functional beauty that could be used as a subject in a still-life painting. Here is how an artist might follow the procedure.

Step 1: For the unit, I choose a pencil.

Step 2: For the principle or way of regarding the unit, I see the pencil as an object of simple functional beauty.

Step 3: For the division into parts based on my principle, I divide the pencil into texture, shape, and color.

Step 4: For the discussion of parts in relation to the unit, I will explain how the textures of the metal, graphite, and wood, along with their shapes and colors, produce a beautiful object.

Either treatment of the same unit, the pencil, is valid, but mixing the treatments by applying more than one principle at a time causes problems. For example, if we were to say that a pencil has an eraser, an eraser holder, a wooden barrel, a graphite core, and a beautiful coat of yellow paint, we would have an illogical analysis by division, because all parts but the "beautiful coat of yellow paint" relate to the pencil as a writing instrument.

Organization

In an essay of analysis by division, the main parts are likely to be the main points of your outline or main extensions of your cluster. If they are anything else, reconsider your organization. For the pencil, your outline might look like this:

I. Eraser

II. Eraser holder

III. Wooden barrel

IV. Graphite core with point at one end

Sequence of Parts

The order in which you discuss the parts will vary according to the nature of the unit and the way in which you view it. Here are some possible sequences for organizing the parts of a unit.

Time: The sequence of the parts in your composition can be mainly chronological, or time-based (if you are writing about something that functions on its own, such as a heart, with the parts presented in relation to stages of the function).

Space: If your unit is a visual object and if, like the pencil, it does nothing by itself, you may discuss the parts in relation to space. In the example about the pencil, the parts of the pencil begin at the top with the eraser and end at the bottom with the graphite point.

Emphasis: Because the most emphatic part of any piece of writing is the end (the second most emphatic part is the beginning), consider placing the most significant idea of the unit at the end. In the example, both space and emphasis govern the placement of the pencil point at the end of the order.

Connecting Sources and Writing

Student Essay

When asked to write an essay about a unit that could be divided into three or more parts for discussion, Hsiao Chin Yu turned to her culture. One special occasion stood out: Chinese New Year. The main feature of the celebration was a family feast. The food was delicious; it was served in courses, and each item was assigned symbolic value.

A Chinese New Year's Feast
Hsiao Chin Yu

Throughout my childhood, the traditional Chinese New Year's Feast was prepared by my grandmother at her house every year. My two aunts and three uncles and their families joined my family for the celebration. By then my grandmother was a widow, who had raised six children by herself since 1943. She was responsible for holding our family close together, and it was the Feast each year that helped connect us to our Chinese culture, because each dish had a symbolic meaning. The grownups already knew the traditions, but we children were learning. The food was served in three courses.

The first course was *chuen hop*, a tray for togetherness that contained eight kinds of sweet meats, each carrying a special meaning. For instance, candied lotus meant that our family would have sons. Candied melon promoted growth and health. Candied coconuts represented togetherness. Watermelon seeds symbolized having plenty. Peanuts promoted giving birth more than once. Thus the generations would keep growing, and our family would be as one.

The second course consisted of a fried fish, a whole boiled chicken (including the head and feet), and roasted pork with its skin attached. A whole pig could be purchased in a local butcher's shop, but most years my grandmother bought only the amount of pork we could eat that day. As we ate it, we were told that pork stood for luck. The fish symbolized the special nature of desire. The chicken symbolized newness. With these foods, we wished each other much extra good luck for a New Year.

These three items would be offered to our ancestors first in a ceremony during which we burned incense and prayed for them. After the ceremony, these dishes were cut and served with other foods at our dining table. The other foods included steamed dumplings (*yuan pao*), which were shaped like coins. In fact, to the delight of us children, my grandmother always hid some coins in the dumplings she gave us.

The third course featured egg rolls, prepared to observe the banishing of the old kitchen god and the welcoming of the new. A sweet rice cake (*nyuen kao*) and sweet fruits (usually tangerines) accompanied the egg rolls. A square red paper, which proclaimed "happiness and luck," decorated the top of the rice cake, which indicated that the New Year would be even better than the last. Then came the noodles, representing a long life.

My grandmother is now with my ancestors, but the knowledge of Chinese culture and our family are still with us. She gave me ideas and inspiration that I will try to pass on to my children.

Exercise 1   **DISCUSSION AND CRITICAL THINKING**

1. Underline the thesis.

2. What terms would you use for the three courses?

3. What terms would you use to generalize the symbols represented in each course?

4. In what way is this meal an educational experience for the children?

Student Documented Essay

Emmett Davis faced an assignment in analysis by division in which he would discuss the qualities that made a person successful. He was expected to refer to at least two sources. Davis turned to the early days of rock and roll, his special interest. Almost every source he skimmed, both on the Internet and in his college library's database, contained discussion of Elvis Presley, who became his subject.

Elvis Presley: Twentieth-Century Legend
Emmett Davis

After having moved a few years into the twenty-first century, we still look back and revise lists of top people of the previous one hundred years. One much-discussed category is the Greatest Performers in Popular Music. Although I have trouble choosing the top person in some areas, in this case I have no problem. Of course, it's

Elvis Presley. Four factors stand out and make my choice easy: he was good looking, he could sing, he had style, and he influenced the main world of popular music, which we call "rock 'n' roll."

As for his looks, he was darkly handsome, some would say even beautiful, with thick, unruly hair and a sneering smile that appealed to the rebellious side of young people. Dick Clark, producer and host of *American Bandstand* for four decades, said that youth "copied his style. People imitated his gestures, dressed like him, wanted to be him (or his woman)" (148). Much has been made of the young Elvis and the old Elvis. The young was the person of slender body in a leather jacket. From that image he soon morphed into his spangled outfit phase, a reflection of his ties with country music entertainers but also becoming the model for the glitter look of numerous rock stars. Unfortunately, toward the end of his life, he put on too much weight and favored white bejeweled jump suits.

As for singing, he had a powerful, deep voice with a wide range similar to the big voices in rhythm and blues and black gospel music he had listened to and loved as he grew up in Mississippi and Tennessee. Early in his career he was sometimes criticized for not sounding more like traditional crooners. Although it was true that he did howl, wail, and shout in certain arrangements, he could sing religious songs and simple love ballads such as "Teddy Bear" and "Love Me Tender" with great clarity and warmth.

When he was on stage, his style was personal, as he shook his hips and belted out songs like "Heartbreak Hotel" and "You Ain't Nothin' But a Hound Dog." While making the guitar respectable, he popularized the driving rhythm of rock. He made music more personal and more aggressive. His body language may look tame today, but in the 1950s, it was revolutionary.

Because he was so different and so good, he influenced and inspired others who would become famous artists of rock 'n' roll. Groups like the Beatles and the Rolling Stones gave him credit for his innovations. His influence even extends to academia. In 1995 the University of Mississippi convened an international conference entitled "In Search of Elvis." Professor Vernon Chadwick, who helped organize the conference, said that Elvis "is better known and in many cases more influential than William Faulkner" (Geier 14). Though Chadwick's statement may have upset some of his colleagues, it is well in line with what many of his fans believe.

Some fanatical fans believe Elvis is off hiding in the witness protection program and shopping at the K-Marts and Wal*Marts of the world, but, to me, he's alive in a more important way: he's a legend—he's the Greatest Performer in Popular Music for the Twentieth Century.

Works Cited

Clark, Dick. "Remembering 'Presleymania.'" *Newsweek* 8 June 98: 148.
Geier, Thom. "Eggheads for Elvis." *U.S. News & World Report* 7 August 1995: 14.

Exercise 2   **DISCUSSION AND CRITICAL THINKING**

1. Circle the thesis.

2. What is the unit being considered?

3. What is the principle for dividing the unit?

4. Underline the topic sentences that indicate the parts of the unit and, in the margin to the left, use single words to annotate those parts.

Practicing Patterns of Analysis by Division

In analysis by division, Roman numeral headings almost always indicate parts of the unit you are discussing as your subject. Learning to divide the unit into parts will help you move through your assignment quickly and efficiently.

Exercise 3   **COMPLETING PATTERNS OF ANALYSIS BY DIVISION**

Fill in the blanks to complete an Outline of Emmett Davis's "Elvis Presley: Twentieth-Century Legend" on page 165.

I. Appearance
   A. _____
   B. Dress
   C. Grooming
II. Singing ability
   A. _____
   B. _____

III. Style

    A. _____

    B. Animal magnetism

IV. _____

    A. Innovative

    B. Inspiring

A Brush with Reality
Surprises in the Tube
David Bodanis

For many years, David Bodanis taught a survey of intellectual history at Oxford University. He is the author of several books, including *The Secret Family* and the bestseller *The Secret House*, from which this excerpt is taken. A native of Chicago, he lives in London, England.

1   Into the bathroom goes our male resident, and after the most pressing need is satisfied it's time to brush the teeth. The tube of toothpaste is squeezed, its pinched metal seams are splayed, pressure waves are generated inside, and the paste begins to flow. But what's in this toothpaste, so carefully being extruded out?

2   Water mostly, 30 to 45 percent in most brands: ordinary, everyday simple tap water. It's there because people like to have a big gob of toothpaste to spread on the brush, and water is the cheapest stuff there is when it comes to making big gobs. Dripping a bit from the tap onto your brush would cost virtually nothing; whipped in with the rest of the toothpaste the manufacturers can sell it at a neat and accountant-pleasing $2 per pound equivalent. Toothpaste manufacture is a very lucrative occupation.

3   Second to water in quantity is chalk: exactly the same material that schoolteachers use to write on blackboards. It is collected from the crushed remains of long-dead ocean creatures. In the Cretaceous seas chalk particles served as part of the wickedly sharp outer skeleton that these creatures had to wrap around themselves to keep from getting chomped by all the slightly larger other ocean creatures they met. Their massed graves are our present chalk deposits.

4   The individual chalk particles—the size of the smallest mud particles in your garden—have kept their toughness over the aeons, and now on the toothbrush they'll need it. The enamel outer coating of the tooth they'll have to face is the hardest substance in the body—tougher than skull, or bone, or nail. Only the chalk particles in toothpaste can successfully grind into the teeth during brushing, ripping off the surface layers like an abrading wheel grinding down a boulder in a quarry.

5   The craters, slashes, and channels that the chalk tears into the teeth will also remove a certain amount of build-up yellow in the carnage, and it is for that polishing function that it's there. A certain amount of unduly enlarged extra-abrasive chalk fragments tear such cavernous pits into the teeth that future decay bacteria will be able to bunker down there and thrive; the quality control people find it almost impossible to screen out these errant super-chalk pieces, and government regulations allow them to stay in.

6   In case even the gouging doesn't get all the yellow off, another substance is worked into the toothpaste cream. This is titanium dioxide. It comes in tiny spheres, and it's the stuff bobbing around in white wall paint to make it come out white. Splashed around onto your teeth during the brushing it coats much of the yellow that remains. Being water soluble it leaks off in the next few hours and is swallowed, but at least for the quick glance up in the mirror after finishing it will make the user think his teeth are truly white. Some manufacturers add optical whitening dyes—the stuff more commonly found in washing machine bleach—to make extra sure that that glance in the mirror shows reassuring white.

7   These ingredients alone would not make a very attractive concoction. They would stick in the tube like a sloppy white plastic lump, hard to squeeze out as well as revolting to the touch. Few consumers would savor rubbing in a mixture of water, ground-up blackboard chalk, and the whitener from latex paint first thing in the morning. To get around that finicky distaste the manufacturers have mixed in a host of other goodies.

8   To keep the glop from drying out, a mixture including glycerine glycol—related to the most common car antifreeze ingredient—is whipped in with the chalk and water, and to give *that* concoction a bit of substance (all we really have so far is wet colored chalk) a large helping is added of gummy molecules from the seaweed *Chondrus Crispus*. This seaweed ooze spreads in among the chalk, paint, and antifreeze, then stretches itself in all directions to hold the whole mass together. A bit of paraffin oil (the fuel that flickers in camping lamps) is pumped in with it to help the moss ooze keep the whole substance smooth.

9   With the glycol, ooze, and paraffin we're almost there. Only two major chemicals are left to make the refreshing, cleansing substance we know as toothpaste. The ingredients so far are fine for cleaning, but they wouldn't make much of the satisfying foam we have come to expect in the morning brushing.

10   To remedy that, every toothpaste on the market has a big dollop of detergent added too. You've seen the suds detergent will make in a washing machine. The same substance added here will duplicate that inside the mouth. It's not particularly necessary, but it sells.

11   The only problem is that by itself this ingredient tastes, well, too like detergent. It's horribly bitter and harsh. The chalk put in toothpaste is pretty foul-tasting too for that matter. It's to get around that gustatory discomfort that the manufacturers put in the ingredient they tout perhaps the most of all. This is the flavoring, and it has to be strong. Double rectified peppermint oil is used—a flavorer so powerful that chemists know better than to sniff it in the raw state in the laboratory. Menthol crystals and saccharin or other sugar simulators are added to complete the camouflage operation.

12   Is that it? Chalk, water, paint, seaweed, antifreeze, paraffin oil, detergent, and peppermint? Not quite. A mix like that would be irresistible to the hundreds of thousands of individual bacteria lying on the surface of even an immaculately cleaned bathroom sink. They would get in, float in the water bubbles, ingest the ooze and paraffin, maybe even spray out enzymes to break down the chalk. The result would be an uninviting mess. The way manufacturers avoid that final obstacle is by putting something in to kill the bacteria. Something good and strong is needed, something that will zap any accidentally intrudant bacteria into oblivion. And that something is formaldehyde—the disinfectant used in anatomy labs.

13   So it's chalk, water, paint, seaweed, antifreeze, paraffin oil, detergent, peppermint, formaldehyde, and fluoride (which can go some way towards preserving children's teeth)—that's the usual mixture raised to the mouth on the toothbrush for a fresh morning's clean. If it sounds too unfortunate, take heart. Studies show that thorough brushing with just plain water will often do as good a job.

Exercise 4   VOCABULARY HIGHLIGHTS

Write a short definition of each word as it is used in the essay. (Paragraph numbers are given in parentheses.) Be prepared to use the words in your own sentences.

splayed (1)

extruded (1)

lucrative (3)

aeons (4)

abrading (4)

carnage (5)

errant (5)

dollop (10)

gustatory (11)

intrudant (12)

Exercise 5   DISCUSSION AND CRITICAL THINKING

1. What is the unit?

2. What is the principle of Bodanis's division?

3. Circle the words indicating the parts of the division as they first appear.

4. Bodanis is discussing a chemical formula. Does he address a general reading audience or a reading audience with a specific knowledge of industrial chemistry?

5. Explain how Bodanis's use of definitions of the ingredients suggests the audience for whom this essay is intended.

6. How would you characterize the *tone* (how the author regards his subject material and his audience) of the article?

7. Give some examples of word choice that contribute to that tone.

8. Why did Bodanis select the humorous tone?

Designer Babies

Michael D. Lemonich

Designer drugs, designer foods, designer music—what's next? Michael D. Lemonich, staff writer for Time, *says it may be babies. Ordinarily, we analyze a person for his or her qualities according to the person's development. Now science has provided us with a way to pick the qualities before birth. The technological decisions may be much easier to make than the ethical ones. This essay was first published in a special January 1999 issue, "The Future of Medicine."*

1. Until just a few years ago, making a baby boy or a baby girl was pretty much a hit-or-miss affair. Not anymore. Parents who have access to the latest genetic testing techniques can now predetermine their baby's sex with great accuracy—as Monique and Scott Collins learned to their delight two years ago, when their long-wished-for daughter Jessica was born after genetic prescreening at a fertility clinic in Fairfax, Va.

2. And baby Jessica is just the beginning. Within a decade or two, it may be possible to screen kids almost before conception for an enormous range of attributes, such as how tall they're likely to be, what body type they will have, their hair and eye color, what sorts of illnesses they will be naturally resistant to, and even, conceivably, their IQ and personality type.

3. In fact if gene therapy lives up to its promise, parents may someday be able to go beyond weeding out undesirable traits and start actually inserting the genes they want—perhaps even genes that have been crafted in a lab. Before the new millennium is many years old, parents may be going to fertility clinics and picking from a list of options the way car buyers order air conditioning and chrome-alloy wheels. "It's the ultimate shopping experience: designing your baby," says biotechnology critic Jeremy Rifkin, who is appalled by the prospect. "In a society used to cosmetic surgery and psychopharmacology, this is not a big step."

4. The prospect of designer babies, like many of the ethical conundrums posed by the genetic revolution, is confronting the world so rapidly that doctors, ethicists, religious leaders and politicians are just starting to grapple with the implications—and trying to decide how they feel about it all.

5. They still have a bit of time. Aside from gender, the only traits that can now be identified at the earliest stages of development are about a dozen of the most serious genetic diseases. Gene ther-

apy in embryos is at least a few years away. And the gene or combination of genes responsible for most of our physical and mental attributes hasn't even been identified yet, making moot the idea of engineering genes in or out of a fetus. Besides, say clinicians, even if the techniques for making designer babies are perfected within the next decade, they should be applied in the service of disease prevention, not improving on nature.

6   But what doctors intend is not necessarily what's going to happen. Indeed, the technology that permitted the Collins family to pick the sex of their child was first used to select for health, not gender per se. Adapting a technique used on livestock, researchers at the Genetics & IVF Institute in Fairfax took advantage of a simple rule of biology: girls have two X chromosomes, while boys have one X and one Y. The mother has only Xs to offer, so the balance of power lies with the father—specifically with his sperm, which brings either an X or a Y to the fertilization party.

7   As it happens, Y chromosomes have slightly less DNA than Xs. So by staining the sperm's DNA with a nontoxic light-sensitive dye, the Virginia scientists were able to sort sperm by gender—with a high rate of success—before using them in artificial insemination. The first couple to use the technique was looking to escape a deadly disease known as X-linked hydrocephalus, or water on the brain, which almost always affects boys.

8   But while the technique is ideal for weeding out this and other X-linked disorders, including hemophilia, Duchenne muscular dystrophy and Fragile X syndrome, most patients treated at Genetics & IVF want to even out their families—a life-style rather than a medical decision. The Fairfax clinic has been willing to help, but such a trend doesn't sit well with some other practitioners. "Our view at the moment," says Dr. Zev Rosenwaks, director of the Center for Reproductive Medicine and Infertility at Cornell Medical Center in New York City, "is that these techniques should be used for medical indications, not family balancing."

9   But now that parents know that the technology is available, and that at least some clinics will let them choose a child's gender for nonmedical reasons, it may be too late to go back. In a relatively short time, suggests Princeton University biologist Lee Silver, whose book *Remaking Eden* addresses precisely these sorts of issues, sex selection may cease to be much of an issue. His model is in vitro fertilization, the technique used to make "test-tube" babies. "When the world first learned about IVF two decades ago," he says, "it was horrifying to most people, and most said that they wouldn't use it even if they were infertile. But growing demand

makes it socially acceptable, and now anybody who's infertile demands IVF."

10   That's not to say in vitro fertilization hasn't created its own set of ethical problems, including custody battles over fertilized embryos that were frozen but never used, questions about what to do with the embryos left over after a successful pregnancy, and the increased health risks posed by multiple births. Yet no one is suggesting the practice be stopped. Infertile couples would never stand for it.

11   Sex selection will undoubtedly raise knotty issues as well. Societies that value boys more highly than girls, including China and India, are already out of balance; this could tip the scales even further. Such an outcome is unlikely in the U.S., where surveys show that equal numbers of parents want girls as boys. But the same polls report that Americans believe an ideal family has a boy as the oldest child. Boys often end up being more assertive and more dominant than girls, as do firstborn children; skewing the population toward doubly dominant firstborns could make it even harder to rid society of gender-role stereotypes.

12   The ethical issues raised by techniques emerging from the genetic labs are likely to be even more complex. What if parents can use preimplantation genetic diagnosis to avoid having kids with attention-deficit disorder, say, or those predestined to be short or dullwitted or predisposed to homosexuality? Will they feel pressure from friends and relations to do so? And will kids who are allowed to be born with these characteristics be made to feel even more like second-class citizens than they do now?

13   Even thornier is the question of what kinds of genetic tinkering parents might be willing to elect to enhance already healthy children. What about using gene therapy to add genes for HIV resistance or longevity or a high IQ? What about enhancements that simply stave off psychological pain—giving a child an attractive face or a pleasing personality? No one is certain when these techniques will be available—and many professionals protest that they're not interested in perfecting them. "Yes, theoretically you could do such things," says Baylor University human-reproduction specialist Larry Lipshultz. "It's doable, but I don't know of anyone doing it."

14   Sooner or later, however, someone will do it. In countries with national health services, such as Canada and Britain, it tends to be easier to dictate what sorts of genetic enhancement will be permitted and what will be forbidden. But in the U.S., despite the

growth of managed care, there will always be people with enough money—or a high enough limit on their credit cards—to pay for what they want. "Typically," says Princeton's Silver, "medical researchers are moved by a desire to cure disease more effectively. Reprogenetics [a term Silver coined] is going to be driven by parents, or prospective parents, who want something for their children. It's the sort of demand that could explode."

15 Silver even contemplates a scenario in which society splits into two camps, the "gen-rich" and the "gen-poor," those with and those without a designer genome. The prospect is disturbing, but trying to stop it might entail even more disturbing choices. "There may be problems," admits James Watson, whose co-discovery of the structure of DNA in 1953 made all this possible. "But I don't believe we can let the government start dictating the decisions people make about what sorts of families they'll have."

Exercise 6

DISCUSSION AND CRITICAL THINKING

1. Apply the following aspects of an analysis by division to paragraph 2. What is the unit?

   What is the principle of dividing the unit into parts?

   What are the main parts of the division?

2. Of the attributes that may be selected for children, which ones do clinicians say should be the only concern for development (paragraph 5)?

3. What does Lemonich say is likely to be in the future of baby designing, regardless of what appears to be the prevailing ethical view?

4. Of the attributes mentioned in paragraphs 2, 12, and 13, which ones should be allowed in designing babies?

5. What controls on baby designing can and should be imposed?

Optimism, Tenacity Lead Way Back to Life

William Helmreich

William Helmreich is Professor of Sociology and Jewish Studies at City University Graduate Center and City College of New York and co-director of the City College Conflict Resolution Center. Author of ten books, Helmreich has written for metropolitan newspapers and numerous scholarly journals. In this article for the Los Angeles Times, *he writes about the traits that enabled Holocaust survivors to function well again in society.*

1. Accounts of tragedy and catastrophe have been much in the news: hurricanes in Florida and Hawaii, famine in Somalia and Sudan. The media focus tends to be on death and destruction and the terrible aftereffects on human beings. This is not surprising, but there are other, more hopeful, lessons to be learned from calamity.

2. I have spent the last six years traveling the United States, from New York to California, from Wisconsin to Mississippi, hearing from hundreds of people who lived through the greatest horror of the 20th Century, the Holocaust.* I was curious as to how the lives of these Jews had turned out and whether they were able to recover from their terrible experiences.

3. The results, when compared with the stereotypical anecdotal accounts of survivors who succumb to depression, anxiety and hopelessness, were highly surprising. While many survivors did have these serious emotional problems, the great majority did not. They led relatively normal lives, holding down jobs, having and raising children and contributing to the communities in which they settled. Some, such as Rep. Tom Lantos (D-Burlingame); Abraham Resnick, former vice mayor of Miami; Maj. Gen. Sidney Shachnow and the director of the Anti-Defamation League, Abraham Foxman, achieved considerable fame in their chosen fields. Others, not so well-known, became musicians, tailors, businessmen, teachers and farmers.

4. Naturally, all of the survivors are still affected, even haunted, by what happened to them. But they also constitute, on the

---

*The Holocaust was an era of persecution of Jews and other minorities that was part of German leader Adolf Hitler's plan to exterminate all Jewish people. Hitler led the Nazi Party.

whole, a community whose members display a zest for life and who have faith in the future.

5   How did they do it, I wondered? How, after experiencing betrayal and unspeakable cruelty in the Nazi death camps and elsewhere in Europe, were the survivors able to learn to live again, trust again, love again, and bring children into a world that had inflicted such pain on them? The answers contain lessons for everyone who goes through crisis and adversity, be it loss of a loved one, crippling illness, natural disaster or even a job reversal.

6   Most of the survivors who succeeded in rebuilding their lives possessed several traits:

7   First was flexibility, a willingness to adapt to new situations, much like what faces the survivors of Hurricanes Andrew and Iniki. In addition, there was a need to be assertive—a recognition that help given by others would be temporary and that ultimately they were on their own. Related to this was tenacity, an approach to life that refused to accept initial setbacks as the status quo.

8   One of the most crucial survivor characteristics was optimism. More than not thinking about the past, it reflected a certain mindset. Alex Gross, a real estate developer who survived Auschwitz and Buchenwald,* later lost his only son, at 14, in a farming accident. When he saw the mangled body, he resolved never to reveal the details of the death to his wife. Alas, that was not the end of Gross's woes. Nine years later his wife was murdered. Despite this double tragedy, Alex Gross has remarried and is active in his community. He is a survivor.

9   Survivors who did well were intelligent. This trait, which includes "street smarts," amounts to an ability to think quickly, analyze a situation and act. Another key feature was distancing ability, the capacity to view the Holocaust as a unique event requiring certain behavior that was appropriate then but not now. This was accompanied by group consciousness, the forging of a common bond with others who shared their tragedy.

10   Related to this was a more subtle trait, assimilation of the knowledge that they survived. This amounted to using the fact that one has prevailed over hardship as a source of strength. Of equal significance was finding meaning in one's life. For some it was their work, for others religion, and for many it was the bonds of love within the family structure.

11   Finally, there was courage. Simply continuing with life was an act of bravery. Specifically, however, it took many forms—fighting

---

*Auschwitz and Buchenwald were the names of two concentration camps.

back from debilitating illness, taking risks in business or standing up to bigotry.

12 Those who have lived through the riots in Los Angeles or the siege in Sarajevo, those who have lived through earthquakes, hurricanes and floods, can draw strength and sustenance from Hitler's survivors. The reason is that the success story of the survivors is not one of remarkable people. Rather, it is one of just how remarkable people can be.

Exercise 7 VOCABULARY HIGHLIGHTS

Write a short definition of each word as it is used in the essay. (Paragraph numbers are given in parentheses.) Be prepared to use the words in your own sentences.

stereotypical (3)

anecdotal (3)

succumb (3)

constitute (4)

inflicted (5)

adversity (5)

assertive (7)

assimilation (10)

debilitating (11)

sustenance (12)

Exercise 8 DISCUSSION AND CRITICAL THINKING

1. What is the unit?

2. What is the principle by which that unit functions; that is, what does the unit do or represent from this perspective? Write the answer here, and circle the passage that states or suggests the principle.

3. What are the ten parts (traits) that make up the unit according to this principle? Underline them in the text, and write them here.

4. Go back to your answer to question 3 and number the traits to indicate your view of the relative importance of each one.

5. What is the order of the parts (time, space, emphasis, or a combination) in Helmreich's essay?

Three Generations of Native American Women's Birth Experience

Joy Harjo

Joy Harjo, a Native American of Creek, Cherokee, and white ancestry, has written screenplays, three books of poetry, and numerous essays, all about her culture. She is a consultant for the National Indian Youth Council and the Native American Broadcasting Consortium, and a professor of creative writing at the University of New Mexico. Here she gives accounts of childbirth experienced by her mother, herself, and her daughter.

1   It was still dark when I awakened in the stuffed back room of my mother-in-law's small rented house with what felt like hard cramps. At 17 years of age I had read everything I could from the Tahlequah Public Library about pregnancy and giving birth. But nothing prepared me for what was coming. I awakened my child's father and then ironed him a shirt before we walked the four blocks to the Indian hospital because we had no car and no money for a taxi. He had been working with another Cherokee artist silk-screening signs for specials at the supermarket and making $5 a day, and had to leave me alone at the hospital because he had to go to work. We didn't awaken his mother. She had to get up soon enough to fix breakfast for her daughter and granddaughter before leaving for her job at the nursing home. I knew my life was balanced at the edge of great, precarious change, and I felt alone and cheated. Where was the circle of women to acknowledge and honor this birth?

2   It was still dark as we walked through the cold morning, under oaks that symbolized the stubbornness and endurance of the Cherokee people who had made Tahlequah their capital in the new lands. I looked for handholds in the misty gray sky, for a voice announcing this impending miracle. I wanted to change everything; I wanted to go back to a place before childhood, before our tribe's removal to Oklahoma. What kind of life was I bringing this child into? I was a poor, mixed-blood woman heavy with a child who would suffer the struggle of poverty, the legacy of loss. For the second time in my life I felt the sharp tug of my own birth cord, still connected to my mother. I believe it never pulls away, until death, and even then it becomes a streak in the sky symbol-

izing that most important warrior road. In my teens I had fought my mother's weaknesses with all my might, and here I was at 17, becoming as my mother, who was in Tulsa, cooking breakfasts and preparing for the lunch shift at a factory cafeteria as I walked to the hospital to give birth. I should be with her; instead, I was far from her house, in the house of a mother-in-law who later would try to use witchcraft to destroy me.

3   After my son's father left me, I was prepped for birth. This meant my pubic area was shaved completely, and then I endured the humiliation of an enema, all at the hands of strangers. I was left alone in a room painted government green. An overwhelming antiseptic smell emphasized the sterility of the hospital, a hospital built because of the U.S. government's treaty and responsibility to provide health care to Indian people.

4   I intellectually understood the stages of labor, the place of transition, of birth—but it was difficult to bear the actuality of it, and to bear it alone. Yet in some ways I wasn't alone, for history surrounded me. It is with the birth of children that history is given form and voice. Birth is one of the most sacred acts we take part in and witness in our lives. But sacredness seemed to be far from my lonely labor room in the Indian hospital. I heard a woman screaming in the next room with her pain, and I wanted to comfort her. The nurse used her as a bad example to the rest of us who were struggling to keep our suffering silent.

5   The doctor was a military man who had signed on this watch not for the love of healing or out of awe at the miracle of birth, but to fulfill a contract for medical school payments. I was another statistic to him; he touched me as if he were moving equipment from one place to another. During my last visit I was given the option of being sterilized. He explained to me that the moment of birth was the best time to do it. I was handed the form but chose not to sign it, and am amazed now that I didn't think too much of it at the time. Later I would learn that many Indian women who weren't fluent in English signed, thinking it was a form giving consent for the doctor to deliver their babies. Others were sterilized without even the formality of signing. My light skin had probably saved me from such a fate. It wouldn't be the first time in my life.

6   When my son was finally born I had been deadened with a needle in my spine. He was shown to me—the incredible miracle nothing prepared me for—then taken from me in the name of medical progress. I fell asleep with the weight of chemicals and awoke yearning for the child I had suffered for, had anticipated in the months proceeding from this unexpected genesis when I was

still 16 and a student at Indian school. I was not allowed to sit up or walk because of the possibility of paralysis (one of the drug's side effects), and when I finally got to hold him, the nurse stood guard as if I would hurt him. I felt enmeshed in a system in which the wisdom that had carried my people from generation to generation was ignored. In that place I felt ashamed I was an Indian woman. But I was also proud of what my body had accomplished despite the rape by the bureaucracy's machinery, and I got us out of there as soon as possible. My son would flourish on beans and fry bread, and on the dreams and stories we fed him.

7   My daughter was born four years later, while I was an art student at the University of New Mexico. Since my son's birth I had waitressed, cleaned hospital rooms, filled cars with gas (while wearing a miniskirt), worked as a nursing assistant, and led dance classes at a health spa. I knew I didn't want to cook and waitress all my life, as my mother had done. I had watched the varicose veins grow branches on her legs, and as they grew, her zest for dancing and sports dissolved into utter tiredness. She had been born with a caul* over her face, the sign of a gifted visionary.

8   My earliest memories are of my mother writing songs on an ancient Underwood typewriter after she had washed and waxed the kitchen floor on her hands and knees. She too had wanted something different for her life. She had left an impoverished existence at age 17, bound for the big city of Tulsa. She was shamed in a time in which to be even part Indian was to be an outcast in the great U.S. system. Half her relatives were Cherokee full-bloods from near Jay, Oklahoma, who for the most part had nothing to do with white people. The other half were musically inclined "white trash" addicted to country-western music and Holy Roller[†] fervor. She thought she could disappear in the city; no one would know her family, where she came from. She had dreams of singing and had once been offered a job singing on the radio but turned it down because she was shy. Later one of her songs would be stolen before she could copyright it and would make someone else rich. She would quit writing songs. She and my father would divorce and she would be forced to work for money to feed and clothe four children, all born within two years of each other.

9   As a child growing up in Oklahoma, I liked to be told the story of my birth. I would beg for it while my mother cleaned and ironed. "You almost killed me," she would say. "We almost died."

---

*A caul is part of the membrane enclosing the fetus.
†Holy Rollers are fundamentalist Christian enthusiasts, who sometimes go into trances and roll on the floor.

That I could kill my mother filled me with remorse and shame. And I imagined the push-pull of my life, which is a legacy I deal with even now when I am twice as old as my mother was at my birth. I loved to hear the story of my warrior fight for my breath. The way it was told, it had been my decision to live. When I got older, I realized we were both nearly casualties of the system, the same system flourishing in the Indian hospital where later my son Phil would be born.

10. My parents felt lucky to have insurance, to be able to have their children in the hospital. My father came from a fairly prominent Muscogee Creek family. *His* mother was a full-blood who in the early 1920s got her degree in art. She was a painter. She gave birth to him in a private hospital in Oklahoma City; at least that's what I think he told me before he died at age 53. It was something of which they were proud.

11. This experience was much different from my mother's own birth. She and five of her six brothers were born at home, with no medical assistance. The only time a doctor was called was when someone was dying. When she was born her mother named her Wynema, a Cherokee name my mother says means beautiful woman, and Jewell, for a can of shortening stored in the room where she was born.

12. I wanted something different for my life, for my son, and for my daughter, who later was born in a university hospital in Albuquerque. It was a bright summer morning when she was ready to begin her journey. I still had no car, but I had enough money saved for a taxi for a ride to the hospital. She was born "naturally," without drugs. I could look out of the hospital window while I was in labor at the bluest sky in the world. Her father was present in the delivery room—though after her birth he disappeared on a drinking binge. I understood his despair, but did not agree with the painful means to describe it. A few days later Rainy Dawn was presented to the sun at her father's pueblo and given a name so that she will always be recognized as a part of the people, as a child of the sun.

13. That's not to say that my experience in the hospital reached perfection. The clang of metal against metal in the delivery room had the effect of a tuning fork reverberating fear in my pelvis. After giving birth, I held my daughter, but they took her from me for "processing." I refused to lie down to be wheeled to my room after giving birth; I wanted to walk out of there to find my daughter. We reached a compromise, and I rode in a wheelchair. When we reached the room, I stood up and walked to the nursery and

demanded my daughter. I knew she needed me. That began my war with the nursery staff, who deemed me unknowledgeable because I was Indian and poor. Once again I felt the brushfire of shame, but I'd learned to put it out much more quickly, and I demanded early release so I could take care of my baby without the judgment of strangers.

14   I wanted something different for Rainy, and as she grew up I worked hard to prove that I could make "something" of my life. I obtained two degrees as a single mother. I wrote poetry, screenplays, became a professor, and tried to live a life that would be a positive influence for both of my children. My work in this life has to do with reclaiming the memory stolen from our peoples when we were dispossessed from our lands east of the Mississippi; it has to do with restoring us. I am proud of our history, a history so powerful that it both destroyed my father and guarded him. It's a history that claims my mother as she lives not far from the place her mother was born, names her as she cooks in the cafeteria of a small college in Oklahoma.

15   When my daughter told me she was pregnant, I wasn't surprised. I had known it before she did, or at least before she would admit it to me. I felt despair, as if nothing had changed or ever would. She had run away from Indian school with her boyfriend and they had been living in the streets of Gallup, a border town notorious for the suicides and deaths of Indian peoples. I brought her and her boyfriend with me because it was the only way I could bring her home. At age 16, she was fighting me just as I had so fiercely fought my mother. She was making the same mistakes. I felt as if everything I had accomplished had been in vain. Yet I felt strangely empowered, too, at this repetition of history, this continuance, by a new possibility of life and love, and I steadfastly stood by my daughter.

16   I had a university job, so I had insurance that covered my daughter. She saw an obstetrician in town who was reputed to be one of the best. She had the choice of a birthing room. She had the finest care. Despite this, I once again battled with a system in which physicians are taught the art of healing by dissecting cadavers. My daughter went into labor a month early. We both knew intuitively the baby was ready, but how to explain that to a system in which numbers and statistics provide the base of understanding? My daughter would have her labor interrupted: her blood pressure would rise because of the drug given to her to stop the labor. She would be given an unneeded amniocentesis and would have her labor induced—after having it artificially

17   My daughter's induced labor was unnatural and difficult, monitored by machines, not by touch. I was shocked. I felt as if I'd come full circle, as if I were watching my mother's labor and the struggle of my own birth. But I was there in the hospital room with her, as neither my mother had been for me, nor her mother for her. My daughter and I went through the labor and birth together.

18   And when Krista Rae was born, she was born to her family. Her father was there for her, as were both her grandmothers and my friend who had flown in to be with us. Her paternal great-grandparents and aunts and uncles had also arrived from the Navajo Reservation to honor her. Something *had* changed.

19   Four days later, I took my granddaughter to the Saguaro forest before dawn and gave her the name I had dreamed for her just before her birth. Her name looks like clouds of mist settling around a sacred mountain as it begins to speak. A female ancestor approaches on a horse. We are all together.

Exercise 9 — DISCUSSION AND CRITICAL THINKING

1. How are the generations of Harjo's family different? On what basis other than time can they be divided?

2. In what way is this essay optimistic?

3. What strains of pessimism do you find in this essay?

4. What does Harjo see as the key to improvement for Native American culture?

5. Argue for or against calling the three generations described here the old, the transitional, and the new.

✎ Topics for Writing Analysis by Division

Writing Process Worksheet

You will find a Writing Process Worksheet on page 27. It can be photocopied and enlarged, filled in, and submitted with each assignment if your instructor directs you to do so.

Source-Based Topics

Each essay developed from these suggested source-based topics should include at least one reference to the reading selection by the author's name and the title. Quotations should be enclosed in quotation marks. Follow your instructor's directions in documenting the ideas you borrow. Whether you use informal or formal documentation, the form is not complicated, and you will soon learn to use it for these essays without checking each time. See pages 73 and 74 for a discussion of MLA style and informal documentation.

Underlining and annotating reading selections will help you in finding support material. In prewriting brief essays, consider marking your outline to indicate where you will use quotations or other borrowed ideas. If the quotations or reworded statements are short and few, you could even insert them inside parentheses or circles in your outline; if you do, also include the author's last name and the page number. A sound system, consistently used, will save you time and ensure technically strong papers.

"A Chinese New Year's Feast"

1. Write about a holiday feast or other cultural event that can be discussed as a unit with parts.

"Elvis Presley: Twentieth-Century Legend"

2. If you are familiar with Elvis, write your own analysis by division, providing your own support.

3. If you disagree with the view of Emmett Davis, summarize his essay and explain why you think he is wrong. Preserve the basic form of unit, principle, parts, and relationship of parts.

4. Write about someone else who you believe has achieved legendary status. Use Davis's essay as a model for organization as you discuss your candidate's qualities for excellence in a particular field such as politics, entertainment, athletics, or art.

"A Brush with Reality: Surprises in the Tube"

5. Using this essay as a model, write about another product with ingredients. Consider makeup, breakfast cereal, bread, soft drinks, beer, perfume, insect repellant, mouthwash, and chewing gum. If you have difficulty in defining some of the terms, consider checking with

your campus experts in departments such as chemistry, biology, and health sciences. Also consult the Internet; try "chewing gum [or any other term] and ingredients." Try to discover how the common ingredients are used in other concoctions.

"Designer Babies"

6. Borrowing the list of attributes in paragraph 2, discuss which ones would and would not be acceptable according to your value system. Explain what kinds of people might favor certain attributes for their babies.

"Optimism, Tenacity Lead Way Back to Life"

7. Using this essay as a model, discuss the traits that were necessary in any significant struggle that you have witnessed or heard about. The significant struggle might be of a large magnitude involving a great number of people or it might pertain to only one individual, perhaps yourself. At the individual level it might involve death, illness, divorce, betrayal, unemployment, or relocation to another country or to a different cultural group.

"Three Generations of Native American Women's Birth Experience"

8. Using this essay as a model, write about three generations of birth experience in a family you are familiar with. Consider discussing your project with family members.

9. Summarize Harjo's essay by using this pattern for organization: unit, principle, parts, relationships of parts. Include comments on the differences in the three generations and point out both progress and lack of progress. Use a combined summary and reaction or a two-part response (summary separated from the reaction, as discussed in Chapter 4).

10. Using this essay as a model, write about three generations of people within a family you are familiar with, focusing on marriage (circumstances, ceremonies, customs, tone), education (opportunities, achievements), independence (circumstances of leaving home as a young person), or work.

Career-Related Topics

11. Explain how the parts of a product function together as a unit.

12. Explain how each of several qualities of a specific person—such as his or her intelligence, sincerity, knowledgeability, ability to communicate, manner, attitude, and appearance—makes that individual an effective salesperson, manager, or employee.

13. Explain how the demands or requirements for a particular job represent a comprehensive picture of that job.

14. Explain how the aspects of a particular service (such as friendly, competent, punctual, confidential) work together in a satisfactory manner.

General Topics

Some of the following topics are too broad for a short writing assignment and should be narrowed. For example, the general "a wedding ceremony" could be narrowed to the particular: "José and María's wedding ceremony." Select a topic from the following list. Narrow the topic, divide it into parts, and analyze it in a short essay.

15. A machine such as an automobile, a computer, a camera

16. A city administration, a governmental agency, a school board, a student council

17. An offensive team in football (any team in any game)

18. A family, a relationship, a gang, a club, a sorority, a fraternity

19. An album, a performance, a song, a singer, an actor, a musical group, a musical instrument

20. A movie, a television program, a video game

21. Any well-known person—athlete, politician, criminal, writer

Writer's Guidelines: Analysis by Division

Almost anything can be analyzed by division—for example, how the parts of the ear work in hearing, how the parts of the eye work in seeing, or how the parts of the heart work in pumping blood throughout the body. Subjects such as these are all approached with the same systematic procedure.

1. This is the procedure.
   - Step 1. Begin with something that is a unit.
   - Step 2. State the principle by which that unit functions.
   - Step 3. Divide the unit into parts according to the principle.
   - Step 4. Discuss each of the parts in relation to the unit.

2. This is the way you might apply that procedure to a good boss.
   - *Unit.* Manager
   - *Principle of function.* Effective as a leader
   - *Parts based on the principle.* Fair, intelligent, stable, competent in field
   - *Discussion:* Consider each part in relation to the person's effectiveness as a manager.

3. This is how a basic outline of analysis by division might look.

   Thesis: To be effective as a leader, a manager needs specific qualities.
   - I. Fair
   - II. Intelligent
   - III. Stable
   - IV. Competent in field

Classification: Establishing Groups

Writing Classification, p. 190
Selecting a Subject, p. 190
Using a Principle to Avoid Overlapping, p. 190
Establishing Classes, p. 191
Using Simple and Complex Forms, p. 191

Connecting Sources and Writing, p. 194
Student Essay: "Types of Fly Fighters," p. 194
Practicing Patterns of Classification, p. 196
Student Documented Essay: "Community College Pressures," p. 196
"Coworkers from Hell and How to Cope," p. 199
"Dangerous Curves," p. 205
"Confessions of a Former Smoker," p. 211
"Shaking Hands," p. 215

Topics for Writing Classification, p. 217
Writing Process Worksheet, p. 217
Source-Based Topics, p. 217
Career-Related Topics, p. 218
General Topics, p. 218
Writer's Guidelines, p. 219

THE QUIGMANS by Buddy Hickerson

"THE MOST UNPLEASANT THING ABOUT BEING THE ONLY STUDENT IN THIS CLASS WILL BE WHEN I ASK YOU TO BREAK UP INTO GROUPS."

© Tribune Media Services, Inc. All Rights Reserved. Reprinted with permission.

Writing Classification

To explain by classification, you put persons, places, things, or ideas into groups or classes based on their characteristics. Whereas analysis by division deals with the characteristics of just one unit, classification deals with more than one unit, so the subject is plural.

To classify efficiently, try following this procedure:

1. Select a plural subject.
2. Decide on a principle for grouping the units of your subject.
3. Establish the groups, or classes.
4. Write about the classes

Selecting a Subject

When you say you have different kinds of neighbors, friends, teachers, bosses, or interests, you are classifying; that is, you are forming groups.

In naming the different kinds of people in your neighborhood, you might think of different groupings of your neighbors, the units. For example, some neighbors are friendly, some are meddlesome, and some are private. Some neighbors have yards like Japanese gardens, some have yards like neat-but-cozy parks, and some have yards like abandoned lots. Some neighbors are affluent, some are comfortable, and some are struggling. Each of these sets is a classification system and could be the focus of one paragraph in your essay.

Using a Principle to Avoid Overlapping

All the sets in the preceding section are sound because each group is based on a single concern: neighborly involvement, appearance of the yard, or wealth. This one concern, or controlling idea, is called the *principle*. For example, the principle of neighborly involvement controls the grouping of neighbors into three classes: friendly, meddlesome, and private.

All the classes in any one group must adhere to the controlling principle for that group. You would not say, for example, that your neighbors can be classified as friendly, meddlesome, private, and affluent, because the first three classes relate to neighborly involvement, but the fourth, relating to wealth, refers to another principle. Any of the first three—the friendly, meddlesome, and private—might also be affluent. The classes should not overlap in this way. Also, every member should fit into one of the available classes.

Establishing Classes

As you name your classes, rule out easy, unimaginative phrasing such as *fast/medium/slow, good/average/bad,* and *beautiful/ordinary/ugly.* Look for creative, original phrases and unusual perspectives.

Subject: neighbors

Principle: neighborhood involvement

Classes: friendly, meddlesome, private

Subject: neighbors

Principle: yard upkeep

Classes: immaculate, neat, messy

Subject: neighbors

Principle: wealth

Classes: affluent, comfortable, struggling

Using Simple and Complex Forms

Classification can take two forms: simple and complex. The simple form does not go beyond main divisions in its groupings.

Subject: Neighbors

Principle: Involvement

Classes: I. Friendly

        II. Meddlesome

        III. Private

Complex classifications are based on one principle and then subgrouped by another related principle. The following example classifies neighbors by their neighborly involvement. It then subgroups the classes on the basis of motive.

  I. Friendly
    A. Civic-minded
    B. Want to be accepted
    C. Gregarious

 II. Meddlesome
    A. Controlling
    B. Emotionally needy
    C. Suspicious of others

III. Private
   A. Shy
   B. Snobbish
   C. Secretive

Here are two examples by professional writers on other topics, one organized as a simple form and the other organized as a complex form.

Simple:

> Listeners can be classified into four groups: (1) Some do not listen; they "tune the speaker out" and think of matters foreign to the speaker's subject. They get little from a speech. (2) Some only half-listen; their spasmodic listening fluctuates all the way from careful attention to no attention. They understand fragments of the speech, but they do not see the idea as a whole. (3) Some listen with passive acceptance; they accept all the speaker says without question. Because of their lack of discrimination, they add little to what the speaker says from their own experiences. (4) Some listen with discrimination; this critical type of listener gets the most from a speech.

Subject
Development of classes
I. Some do not listen.
II. Some only half-listen.
III. Some listen with passive acceptance.
IV. Some listen with discrimination.

Glenn R. Capp, *Listen Up!*

Complex:

Subject
Main class I

> There are two principal types of <u>glaciers;</u> the <u>continental</u> and the <u>valley.</u> The <u>continental glaciers</u> are great sheets of ice, called ice caps, that cover parts of continents. The earth has two continental glaciers at present: one spreads over most of Greenland and one over all of Antarctica save for a small window of rock and the peaks of several ranges. The Greenland ice sheet is over 10,000 ft. thick in the central part and covers an area of about 650,000 sq. miles. The Antarctic sheet has been sounded, in one place at least, to a depth of 14,000 ft., and it spreads over an area of 5,500,000 sq. miles. This is larger than conterminous United States in the proportion of 5½:3. It is calculated to store 7 million cu. miles of ice, which if melted would raise the ocean level 250 ft.

Main class II

Subclass A (conventional)

Subclass B

Subclass C

> <u>Valley glaciers</u> are ice streams that originate in the high snow fields of mountain ranges and flow down valleys to warmer climates, where they melt. <u>Some break up</u> into icebergs and eventually melt in the ocean. In certain places the valley glaciers flow down the mountain valleys to adjacent plains and there spread out as lobate feet. These are called <u>expanded-foot glaciers.</u> Generally the sprawling feet of several valley glaciers coalesce to form one major sheet, and this is called a <u>piedmont glacier.</u>

Notice that the valley glacier is subdivided:

A. J. Eardley, "Glaciers: Types and Subtypes"

```
        Continental ─────────── Valley
                              ┌──────┼──────┐
                         conventional  expanded foot  piedmont
```

As you can see, glaciers are of two types based on their location (with implications for size): (1) the continental glacier, such as the huge one in the Antarctic, and (2) the valley glacier. The valley glacier can be subdivided into the conventional valley glacier, flowing straight; the expanded-foot glacier, which spreads out; and the piedmont glacier, which is made up of several expanded-foot glaciers. This information could be organized in an outline as follows:

I. Continental glacier

II. Valley glacier

    A. Conventional

    B. Expanded-foot

    C. Piedmont

This outline on glaciers could be cut down to just the "valley glacier" part and developed into an essay. Moving in the other direction, we can say that almost all classifications can be part of a higher level of classification. For example, glaciers are one type of earth-altering process. (Others include earthquakes, volcanoes, and wind erosion.)

Most essays of classification will be simple (based on one principle) in concept, informative in purpose, and organized class by class.

Exercise 1 AVOIDING OVERLAPPING CLASSES

Mark each set of classes as OK or OL (overlapping); circle the classes that overlap.

	Subject	Principle	Classes
Example: ___OL___	speech	uses	formal informal (garbled)
_____	1. shoppers	intentions	one item bargains looking aggressive
_____	2. gym members	needs	body building young good health social

_____ 3. fast foods   ownership   franchise
                                           company
                                           individual
                                           popular

_____ 4. local politicians   motives   connections
                                           step to higher office
                                           controversial
                                           community service

_____ 5. graffiti   purposes   artistic
                                           political
                                           gang

Connecting Sources and Writing

Student Essay

In prison, Jolene Carter had become a student of human behavior. Then, given the opportunity to write about such matters, she knew she was surrounded by a wealth of highly original raw material. One of the suggested general topics in her textbook was the classification of people according to how they deal with unwanted and uninvited intruders, such as pesky insects, sneaky rodents, unruly neighborhood pets, rambunctious visiting children, aggressive store salespersons, annoying telemarketers, snoopy neighbors, and zealous religious proselytizers. She did not have to go beyond the first item on the list.

Types of Fly Fighters
Jolene Carter

One of the major annoyances here at the women's prison is flies. Situated as it is in the middle of an agricultural zone where breeding sites for flies abound, the prison attracts them by the millions. Inmates, even those who have seldom dealt with fly infestation, must learn to cope with the problem, especially at eating time, when the flies want to share our meals. In observing what goes on at different tables in the dining hall, I have discovered that there are three kinds of fly fighters: the shooers, the hiders, and the baiters.

The shooers are the most unimaginative. They wave their hands at the flies, shooing them after they have landed, or by constant waving trying to keep them from landing. This technique requires an almost constant movement, one which is contrary to the movements associated with eating and is almost as difficult as patting one's head while rubbing one's stomach. At any time one can look around the dining room and see the women waving their hands and the flies waving their wings as if they are all communicating. If so, the flies have the last word.

The hiders, the second class, practice stealth, figuring that any human being should be intelligent enough to hide food from a small-brained creature like a fly. After using several napkins to enshroud food, the hiders, head bent forward to close space, scoop food from under the covering and "chow down." Unfortunately, the food often saturates the napkin, or flies manage to crawl under the covering. But overall, this technique is fairly successful and is probably the most popular.

The baiters, the third class, while being the most clever, are probably the most cynical. They have concluded that flies will succeed in some fashion. The baiters offer a self-serving compromise to the flies. Upon taking a seat at the table, they will immediately deposit a spoonful of food near the edge of the tray or even on the table itself. The next step is to use the hiders' technique of covering the major portion of food. While flies swarm to the exposed portion—the bait—the baiters, often with a smug look of superiority, eat and then carry the bait away to the dump zone.

Although the baiting method is probably the most successful, it is used the least. Most women shoo flies or hide food as an expression of their good manners and dignity. If you believe that last statement, I have a very entertaining fly farm kit I am selling for only $29.95

Exercise 2   DISCUSSION AND CRITICAL THINKING

1. Circle the subject (what is being classified) the first time it appears in the essay. Write it here.

2. What is the principle of the classification (on what basis is the classifying being done)?

3. Underline the topic sentences that contain the classes.

4. State the thesis (the author's exact words or your own phrasing).

5. Is the main purpose to inform or to persuade?

6. What is the basis of the humor in this piece?

Practicing Patterns of Classification

Because the basic pattern of classification consists of classes, the initial outline is predictable: It uses Roman numeral headings for the classes, although some classes may be longer and more complex than others.

Exercise 3 **COMPLETING PATTERNS OF CLASSIFICATION**

Fill in the blanks in this outline based on "Types of Fly Fighters."

Thesis: I have discovered that there are three types of fly fighters.

    I. _____

        A. Wave their hands

        B. Always in motion

   II. Hiders

        A. _____

        B. Scoop food from under napkins

  III. _____

        A. Hide some food

        B. _____

        C. Let flies eat bait

        D. _____

Student Documented Essay

For an essay assignment in freshman composition, Joel Follette was asked to read the essay "College Pressures" and to apply its basic ideas to his experience at the community college he attended. Initially, he thought he was writing about two opposing worlds, Yale and Mt. San Antonio College, but then he found some similarities.

Community College Pressures
Joel Follette

All college students have pressures. In his essay "College Pressures," William Zinsser describes the "modern undergraduate primarily as a driven creature," who is "fearful of risk" and "goal-obsessed." He says various harmful pressures exist "throughout American education" (78). Although he has some good insights, his focus is on Yale University, not a community college, such as the one I attend. The pressures he writes about—economic, parental, peer, and self-induced—do exist at Mt. San Antonio College in Southern California to some extent, but they take very different forms.

Zinsser says the Yale students feel economic pressure because they are looking for a "passport to security," and only good grades will get that for them (74). They are competing for slots in famous programs in law and medicine, such as the ones at Yale and Harvard. Other economic pressures come from the cost of education. He says some Yale students work part time during the school year and full time during the summer and still get loans. Students I know in the evening program at my school also have economic problems. I have a full-time job the year round in a company that makes cardboard boxes. I work overtime whenever I can get it without missing classes. I have a wife, who works part time, and two children in elementary school. I, too, have loans, but they're for a little house we bought last year and for a car that I first leased and then bought in a foolish transaction. Unlike Yale, my school only costs a few hundred dollars a year for the three classes I take in evening school each semester, but I passed on a job offer with a good salary because the new hours would have interfered with my class schedule.

Zinsser links economic pressure with parental pressure (75). The parents of most Yale students are paying for their education, and those parents expect results. They expect their offspring to do well in class and to major in a field that will pay well. He says the students want "to fulfill their parents' expectations." They often feel guilty if they do not do well and neglect their own preferences in what to study. Although that may exist to a lesser degree at my community college, usually the parents themselves do not have a college degree and now they are not paying all the college costs for their children, although a large percentage of students in day school still live at home. Most evening students work full time, and the family pressure comes from a spouse and maybe children. When I get home on class nights at ten-thirty and see my kids sleeping and my tired wife, I know why I'm going to college, and I feel guilty if I don't do well. And, to some extent like the students at Yale, I'm thinking about security, not so much about being a doctor but about having a better job.

The other two pressures discussed by Zinsser, the peer and self-induced (76), are also linked. Again, there are big differences between the students at Yale and Mt. San Antonio College. Zinsser says that Yale students are very competitive, and they often "do more than they are expected to do" in order to excel (77). He uses the term "grade fever" (77). I have a *B* average and I know I have to make some *A*s to offset some *C*s, but I don't feel I am competing with my peers. We talk about grades, and usually ask each other about grades when we get tests or papers back. But I haven't seen a lot of competition. Of course, we have our pride, and we're embarrassed if we don't do well. Then we feel as if we've let ourselves and others down. According to my friend at UCLA, the students there are so grade conscious they hardly talk about their grades. Last semester one of his peers jumped to his death from a high-rise dorm room after finals. We don't jump here. I did see a guy kick a trash can one day after getting low marks on a research paper.

At all schools, pressures do exist. They may come from different sources and arrive in different degrees, but they're out there. Sometimes we do it to ourselves, and sometimes people do it to us. Pressures are the forces that may get in the way of our getting a good education, because we become too practical. But pressures are also what keep us going when we're dog-tired, sleepy, and cranky. I think Zinsser would say that if we didn't have so many of these pressures that we might just sit down and read a good book—and that just might be the best education of it all.

Work Cited

Zinsser, William. "College Pressures." *Blair & Ketchum's Country Journal* 4 (April 1979): 72–78.

Exercise 4 — DISCUSSION AND CRITICAL THINKING

1. Circle the thesis and underline all topic sentences.

2. What is the main pressure?

3. Which pressure differs to the greatest extent between Yale students and evening division community college students?

4. Is Follette a typical community college student? Discuss.

Coworkers from Hell and How to Cope

Erica Monfred

Not all types of coworkers are classified here by Erica Monfred. Just the ones from hell. Along with her classification, she provides suggestions about how to send those obnoxious people back to their fiery place of origin. This essay was first published in *Cosmopolitan* in 1997.

1   In every workplace, there are congenial, supportive colleagues.... and then there are the other kind—the ones you fantasize about while pummeling the punching bag at the gym. Is there an officemate sabotaging your success? Here is a primer on how to handle the most common culprits.

1. Petty Bureaucrats

2   The petty bureaucrat is either the gatekeeper to someone important or in charge of something everyone desperately needs, like health insurance or paper clips. She doesn't actually have the authority to get things done, but she does have the power to prevent things from getting done.

3   Let's say your department needs another copier. You've noticed that accounting has three machines, one of which is almost never used. The head of that department says it's okay to take her extra copier, but the petty bureaucrat in charge of office equipment demands a long memo explaining in excruciating detail why you need it—with cc's to at least five other people who also have to give their approval, including the CEO, who happens to be in Belgrade for the month and can't be reached due to political upheaval.

4   How to cope? If you wait patiently, you'll be ready for retirement before the order comes through. Getting angry will just make

the petty bureaucrat gloat with satisfaction, because frustrating others' wishes is her game.

5 There's only one way to deal with this type: You must befriend her. Remember: She's insecure, a lonely misfit, desperate for a kind word or smile, shunned because she's so self-important and hateful. If you want that copier, start sucking up. Ask her to lunch. Show an excessive interest in her prize geraniums and philandering husband over your tuna melt and you'll be whizzing through that pile by the end of the day.

2. Credit Grabbers

6 In most cases, the thief is your boss, which puts you in a bind. Psychologist William Knaus, author of *Change Your Life Now,* says this is the problem Lee Iacocca* ran into with Henry Ford. "Iacocca talks about how threatened Ford was when he [Iacocca] started to get a lot of good publicity," Knaus explains. "Iacocca tried to make it work at Ford, but it was a losing proposition, because his credit-grabber boss was the most powerful person in the organization."

7 Eventually, Ford fired Iacocca, which was the best thing that ever happened to him—he went on to great success at Chrysler. "There are some people you simply shouldn't work for," Knaus asserts. "Life is too short to spend month after month, year after year, reporting to a parasitic boss who's going to damage your self-esteem."

8 If the culprit is a peer or subordinate, however, you have more options. The key is to document, document, document. After any meeting with a credit grabber, instantly send a memo to her and a copy to your boss, summarizing whatever ideas you contributed. If you team up on a project, create a computerized system outlining each of your responsibilities under the guise of getting organized. And keep quiet about any terrific ideas until they're documented as belonging to you.

3. Backstabber

9 Many backstabbers are what Michael Zey, M.D., author of *Winning With People,* calls friendly enemies. They're helpful and encouraging when you're down, he says, "but when you finally get that raise or promotion, they subtly start undermining your confidence and questioning your abilities." Even more insidious are those who remain friendly to your face and do their nasty work behind the scenes.

*Lee Iacocca is a former CEO at Chrysler.

10   Rumormongering is their most common and malignant tactic. Rumors can be impossible to counter once they've been spread, but you can insulate yourself against them by developing a network of supportive colleagues who'll report all office gossip to you. If you know who the fiend is, enlist their help to defeat her by confronting her directly, spreading a counter-rumor, or reporting her to management.

4. Nonstop Talkers

11   She plops down in your office, regardless of what you're doing at the moment, and launches into a litany of complaints about how the boss doesn't appreciate her; how she was overcharged when she took her incontinent dog, Spot, to the vet; how unfair it is that international terrorism is forcing her to wait in long lines at the airport. The usual signals, like saying, "I'm on deadline and can't talk now," don't deter her in the least.

12   Courtesy stops most of us from employing the kind of drastic tactics that actually work with this bulldozer. Recognize that divesting yourself of a motormouth may call for behavior your mother wouldn't approve of. First, try the kind of preemptive strike employed by media mogul Ted Turner. Turner tells people at the outset of a conversation how much time he can give them. When the allotted period has elapsed, he'll say something like "Your five minutes are up, and I've gotta go."

13   If that doesn't work, most experts agree that it's okay to employ even more abrupt measures. If she corners you at the water cooler, mumble an apology and take off in the opposite direction. If she has you trapped behind your desk, tell her you have to make a call, then pick up the phone and start talking very loudly. Even the most relentless blatherers will get the message eventually and start approaching colleagues who are nicer than you. You can bet your rude behavior will be at the top of their nonstop complaint list.

5. Alarmists

14   This corporate Chicken Little constantly races into your office with doomsday reports: You're getting a new boss who's so tyrannical he makes Attila the Hun* look like Leo Buscaglia[†]; such radical downsizing is on the way that the cleaning person will be doing your job. You have a panic attack every time you see this squawker coming down the hall.

*Attila the Hun was a violent barbarian of ancient Asia and Europe.
[†]Leo Buscaglia is a contemporary public relations expert.

15 Unfortunately, these days the sky really is falling on so many hardworking women that the office alarmist may be spreading an all too-accurate message. Be smart and use her latest warning as a wake-up call. Think about what you'd do if you did lose your job. Who would hire you? Do you have a network of contacts who'll help you? Talk to a few headhunters* and find out what's out there. Then, when the alarmist comes around, you can greet her latest disaster scenario by saying, "Who cares?"

6. Control Freaks

16 Control freaks are probably the most infuriating and hardest to handle of all difficult coworkers because they're so completely relentless. These obsessive-compulsives don't stop at a hands-on approach; they need to have a stranglehold on everything they touch. Your work is continually met with such comments as "Let's just check those figures one more time" and "I don't think that'll work; why don't we do it my way?" According to psychiatrist John M. Oldham, coauthor of *The New Personality Self Portrait: Why You Think, Work, Love, and Act the Way You Do,* control freaks "are tense, strained, anxious, and overwhelmed by the amount of work they have to do." Yet they're willing to devote so much time and energy to their jobs that they tend to move up in their professions, so chances are, you'll someday run into an overbearing higher-up.

17 According to psychologist Barry Lubetkin, of the Institute for Behavior Therapy in New York, passive resistance is the most effective way of dealing with these types. "Confrontation will only trigger even more controlling behavior," he says, "so avoid arguments and power struggles at all costs." When this coworker obsesses about some insignificant detail, make a neutral comment like "I understand what you're saying," then go about your business. He'll think you agreed with him and feel reassured.

7. Snoops

18 You can't leave a single piece of paper on your desk, because she always manages to read everything, personal and work-related. She grills you about your private life during business discussions, and you've even seen her lurking behind doorways while you chat with your boss.

19 Unlike backstabbers, who accumulate information to use against you, snoops have no ulterior motive; they just love to gossip. They're the kind of people for whom the saying "Get a life" was invented. The solution: Give them something to feed on with-

---

*Headhunters are people who find employees for companies.

out revealing personal secrets—so make stuff up! Leave hot fictional love notes from imaginary boyfriends on your desk. When she inquires about your personal life, tell her a lurid tale of multiple marriages and affairs with celebrities. When other colleagues come back to you asking if these stories are true, laugh and say, "I made all that up to get Mary Jane off my back."

8. Put-down Artist

"It took you a whole month to do this report."

"I can't believe they hired you with only a year's experience."

Verbal zingers act like sandpaper, rubbing slowly across your sense of self, eventually wearing it away. If you work for a put-down artist or with the kind of coworkers who constantly throw barbs your way, you'll soon dread coming into the office.

The first step in self-defense is acknowledging you've been hurt. Then set up a defense. Jennifer James, author of *Defending Yourself Against Criticism,* offers these strategies for countering an attack:

- Agree with everything the sniper says. This works with people who are so dense that nothing else gets to them or who have a sense of humor. For example:

    Put-down: "Are you sure you spoke with the sales department before using these figures? They don't look right to me."

    Defense: "Sales department? Why would I speak to them?"

- Register the hit. Say something like "Ooh, that really hurt," and go on with the conversation. This is a signal that you're not easy prey, and the tactic should stop everyone but the worst offenders.

- Send it back. For example:

    Put-down: "Are you sure you should be eating that doughnut?"

    Defense: "What I eat is a personal matter."

9. Bullies

Most of us adhere to an unspoken social contract that includes a modicum of considerate behavior. Bullies are unaware that such an agreement exists. Their no-holds-barred tactics include public humiliation, making scenes, threatening to get you fired, and generally treating you like an unruly two-year-old instead of an adult.

Why do these outrageous tactics work? In his book *Coping With Difficult People,* psychologist Robert Bramson explains that bullies possess tremendous power because of the typical responses their behavior arouses in their victims: "confusion, mental or physical flight, a sense of helpless frustration that leads to tears or a tantrumlike rage." In other words, they get away with it because we let them.

33. The traditional wisdom about a schoolyard bully applies as well to the corporate type: You have to stand up to her. Bullies will often back down if you show you're willing to fight. Your strategy:

34. • Use positive body language. Don't let your shoulders droop and eyes drop when intimidated. Look her in the eye, and don't retreat.

35. • Give her time to cool down. "Remain in place and wait," recommends Bramson. "When the attack begins to lose momentum, jump in."

36. • Don't become paralyzed by fear. Even if you're so distraught you can't come up with the right retort, say something—anything to counter the onslaught.

37. • Stay rational. Ignore the intimidation, and slowly and reasonably make your case.

Exercise 5 — VOCABULARY HIGHLIGHTS

Write a short definition of each word as it is used in the essay. (Paragraph numbers are given in parentheses.) Be prepared to use the words in your own sentences.

pummeling (1)

excruciating (3)

parasitic (7)

insidious (9)

insulate (10)

litany (11)

divesting (12)

mogul (12)

ulterior (19)

modicum (31)

Exercise 6 — DISCUSSION AND CRITICAL THINKING

1. What is the main subject for the classification?

2. What is the principle, or basis, of the classification?

3. How many classes are there?

4. How would you rank the classes, starting with the most troublesome?

5. Why don't you tell them just to go back where they came from?

6. Which of the classes of coworkers can be identified most easily?

7. Which groups also exist in settings other than work-related on campus?

8. This passage has no conclusion. Should there be one? Explain why this form works or does not work for you.

Dangerous Curves
from Men's Health Magazine

Eve Golden

Freelance author Eve Golden has written mainly about women for a general reading audience, most notably the biographies *Platinum Girl: The Life and Legends of Jean Harlow* and *Vamp: The Rise and Fall of Theda Bara*. Here she addresses men, giving them advice on the kinds of women they should avoid in what she refers to as the "Dating Game from Hell."

1   My girlfriends and I spend an inordinate amount of time grousing about the terrible guys we fall for. So far the winner is Marie, who dated a guy who (1) lived in a trailer park because he liked it; (2) slept with a gun under the pillow; and (3) kept holy water in the freezer to *keep it holy longer.*

2   But—as the guys in my life are constantly making clear to me—men make the exact same mistakes, and fall for just as many of the wrong women. So in an effort to "C'mon, be fair about this, okay?" I've gone in search of *Five Women You Should Never Fall For.* . . . I spoke with Atlanta psychiatrist Frank Pittman, M.D., author of *Man Enough: Fathers, Sons and the Search for Masculinity.* After I described some of the terrible romances the men I know have wound up in, Dr. Pittman, who spends much time counseling couples with dysfunctional relationships, didn't let me

down. "The women you mention are all Incomplete Women," he told me, making me feel nicely superior. "They seem safe to incomplete men," he added, thus explaining my current lack of social life: A complete, dangerous woman, that's me.

3   In fact, all of the women you're going to learn to avoid have some very attractive qualities, qualities that many men instinctively fall for. That's what makes it so critical for you to avoid them. So without further ado, let's meet our contestants in the Dating Game from Hell.

The Damsel in Distress

4   She's the woman you see on those made-for-TV movies starring Barry Bostwick or Stephen Collins, about a good-natured guy who winds up entangled with some woman from the *Twilight Zone* (usually played by Meredith Baxter). She's helpless and heartbroken and just waiting for a big, strong man like you to come and sweep her off her feet. Does that sound a little anti-feminist, coming from a card-carrying NOW member? Remember, these women do exist. And they should all come equipped with big signs reading "Dangerous Curves Ahead."

5   "She is a disaster for everybody," Dr. Pittman states flat out. "Damsels in distress are never capable of knowing who is St. George and who is the dragon. If she is being abused by everyone in her life and you try to rescue her, I promise you it will only be a matter of time before you're seen as the next abuser."

6   My friend Rick agrees, having been the Stephen Collins character in one of those relationships. He tells me a sob story about his personal Damsel. "Ultimately, I stayed with her because she needed rescuing. I stuck around for a year and a half and never did rescue her. I learned from her, though: If there's a problem, get out early before it starts to affect your psyche."

7   How can you recognize the Damsel type? Dr. Pittman referees a lot of these relationships. "Any woman who falls in love with you too quickly, too desperately, too completely, must be nuts." Gee, there goes the plot of every movie made between 1929 and 1950. If you're married, you'll be able to spot her easily—she's the one making eyes at you from across the room. "These women are the sort of people who fall into affairs with married men," Dr. Pittman says. "Normal women don't do that." What makes a guy dumb enough to fall back? "A victim—a woman with more problems than you've got—will distract you from your problems. Briefly. Men are all too eager to believe that they're heroes, and that someone has finally noticed it." The lesson: Don't think too highly

of yourself, and don't think too highly of anyone who thinks too highly of you.

The (S)motherer

8   You know how sometimes a man and a woman will have the exact same cold, yet the woman's up making hot tea and the man's in bed moaning, "Call a priest"? Some men just invite mothering, and some women (not me, not on your life) love playing Mama. Maybe 100 years ago, when women didn't have actual lives, that was a good way to vent emotional and physical energy. But nowadays, any woman who puts 100 percent of her hopes, dreams, fears and desires on her man's life rather than her own is not someone you need.

9   Dr. Pittman, of course, agrees. "A motherer doesn't require that you give anything back. She's so constantly giving that you end up feeling like a child." Surprisingly, this kind of woman still exists in the 1990s. I have to admit, I couldn't find any Big Mamas or their admirers around my New York digs, so I called my friend Norman, whose Deep-South sister is June Cleaver II. "Oh, she bought a vacuum cleaner for one boyfriend," says Norman. "She made payments on his truck, she did his laundry. He just ate it up."

10 You can see how this kind of relationship can be wonderful for a guy, at least for a while. But it can't be permanent. Eventually, you'll want to give something back, and she won't want what you have to offer. All she wants, Dr. Pittman says, is to live vicariously through you, and living two people's lives is a little bit more of a burden than most anyone would want to tackle. What ever happened to Norman's sister's boyfriend? "He got some other girl pregnant and married her," Norman says. "The guys who are attracted to my sister tend to be young and immature." Which reinforces my belief: that guys who fall for motherly types are entirely too much in touch with their inner child. Do us all a favor, will you, and get in touch with your inner adult?

The Chameleon

11 You know the type: Suddenly she has a Boston accent, and suddenly she loves touch football, just because she's dating a Kennedy. "She's never an equal partner," Dr. Pittman says of this clinging vine, "because she gets her identity from adapting to the guy."

12 Oh, and I do know one or two chameleons. Very nice gals, but not with the best of self-images. Blanche was understandably defensive when I approached her on the topic, though she happily

admitted that she indeed fit the bill. "I dress like my boyfriend. I think it's good," she says philosophically. "We can share clothes." Blanche went on to try and explain herself. "Guys' opinions and ways of doing things just rub off from being around them. It's an ego thing for them." But doesn't it show kind of a lack of ego on Blanche's part? So far, Blanche and her boyfriend seem happy, though she is starting to look more and more like him every day and everyone's pretty much hoping he doesn't start sporting a mustache.

13 Yet this type of one-sided relationship will eventually drag a man under. "The guy finds it flattering for a while, but neither the man nor the woman has the possibility of give-and-take, of being able to adapt to the other," Dr. Pittman says. "They naturally begin to feel something's missing." I talked to one of Blanche's ex-boyfriends, Max. Why did they break up? "We were just bored," he said. "We fell into a rut. Doing the same thing"—his thing, I might add—"night after night." Didn't the fact that Blanche brought nothing to the ball game have something to do with this? Max claimed not to know what I was talking about. "Well, yeah, we had a lot of the same interests, that's why we had such a great time together, isn't it?" I've known Blanche for years, I told him, and she was never the slightest bit interested in basketball, Van Damme films or Japanese food before they met. "Yeah?" His eyes light up; he's obviously delighted. "Well, I guess she got a few things out of the relationship, then, right?"

The Uptown Girl

14 You know her, or at least you've seen her: She's Sharon Stone, Geena Davis, whoever's on the cover of *Sports Illustrated* this year. Happily, most men don't go around shooting U.S. presidents to impress her. But it's hard not to fall for a woman who's just—let's face it—out of your league.

15 The most insidious thing about this unattainable glamour girl is that she thinks she's Just Folks. I tried to reach Sharon Stone, Drew Barrymore and Kelly Lynch for their opinions on the topic, but they proved to be, well, unattainable. I did, however, get my friend Lauren, a successful film producer, to comment. Lauren has natural red hair, looks like a more glamorous Jodie Foster, as sweet as you'd wish. But she started back in horror when I described her as Unattainable. "But I'm not!" she squealed, as a male friend rolled his eyes helplessly behind her. "I mean, I'm not gorgeous or anything like that!" She does admit that men seem afraid to approach her, but puts that down to shyness. She's

utterly wrong. My not-too-terribly-shy friend Rick admits even he's intimidated by women like Lauren. "I just gaze at them with sheep eyes."

16 "There are women who just don't notice the guys who are pursuing them: that's what makes them unattainable," Dr. Pittman says. The men who pursue these glamorous ghosts "don't really want a woman. They're like dogs chasing cars. It's great exercise, as long as you know you'll never catch one. This is the perfect set-up for the guy who wants to be in love without all the problems of having a relationship. It's safe. Plus, he gets an identity from feeling the love he holds for her."

17 On the other hand, if you have normal, mutual relationships with other women, there's nothing wrong with having a crush on someone now and then. Dr. Pittman sheepishly admits that "I have that relationship with Susan Sarandon—whom I've never met, of course."

The Cruise Director

18 Okay, I have a confession. When my editor described this kind of Woman to Avoid, I thought he was being sarcastic and describing me: opinionated, always in control, bossy, having to make all the plans and double-check them afterward. This type of woman may be nerve-racking, but I hasten to add she always gets her stories in on deadline.

19 "She sounds real nice," agrees Dr. Pittman. "I have entirely too many pleasures in life to waste time running my life. I prefer having someone else do it for me. A Cruise Director can be someone who frees you up to be successful, to be creative."

20 That's fine as long as you're happy to leave your social life up to someone else's whims, and as long as she's willing to play cruise director for an extended tour. But it doesn't always work out that way. My friend Walter refused to talk about his ex-wife, but his new wife, Carol, was delighted to help. "Oh, she was such a pushy type," Carol enthused. "She ran everything, which was fun for both of them, at least for a while. But then the challenge was over, and she and Walter split up." Dr. Pittman says there can indeed be downsides to dating a Cruise Director. "If you're scared of women and you've got one who runs your life, you're going to feel controlled, that your autonomy is impinged upon, like an adolescent. She's for a guy who's got something to do that's more important

than proving that women can't tell him what to do. But for the guy who's scared of female control, she'd be a disaster."

21 So maybe you're smart enough to avoid the above bachelorettes. Or maybe you're the type who clings to one after the other like Tarzan swinging through the vines. What's Dr. Pittman's advice for guys who keep falling for the wrong woman? "Get into a permanent, full-time committed relationship with someone with whom you don't get along terribly well and are basically incompatible." Yikes! He continues: "That puts you in the position of having to constantly examine yourself, develop new skills, learn to see the world from another perspective—it's a great maturing process." So is running away to join the circus, but I wouldn't recommend it for everyone.

22 "Seriously," Dr. Pittman explains, "you need incompatibility in a relationship. Of course, you need compatibility, too—to make you feel comfortable, safe, understood. But compatibility is never complete, and never permanent. It takes a certain amount of conflict to give a relationship life."

23 If that's the hard way, here's the easy one: Guys, if you want to have a relationship in the worst way, take it from me, you will. There's this odd notion today that if you're not involved in a romantic/sexual relationship, you're somehow half a person and cannot possibly be happy.

24 Bull. How many hours have you spent on the phone with friends, moaning to your barkeep or to your therapist about how unhappy you are in one relationship or another? Take my advice and think long and hard next time you fall. As my wise old Aunt Ida once told me, "It's better to be alone than to wish you were."

("Dangerous Curves" by Eve Golden from *Men's Health Magazine.* Reprinted by permission of *Men's Health Magazine.* Copyright 1994 Rodale, Inc. All rights reserved. For subscription information, call 1-800-666-2303.)

Exercise 7   **DISCUSSION AND CRITICAL THINKING**

1. What is being classified?

2. What are Golden's main sources of support?

3. From what field does Golden draw her examples and why?

4. What do all her types have in common?

5. After men remove these types from their prospective dating pool, about how many are left (in a percentage figure)?

6. Golden refers to these women as types. Discuss the possibility that some of these women are only posing as these types as a technique for attracting men and then reverting to what they really are. If that occurs, is it all bad?

7. Do some men project the need for some of the types of women discussed here? Explain.

8. What are the qualities a stable, normal man should look for in a woman?

Confessions of a Former Smoker

Franklin E. Zimring

Distinguished author and professor of law Franklin E. Zimring has written about a variety of social ills. Here he reflects on his own personal experience to explain and classify the different kinds of ex-smokers. His books include *Capital Punishment and the American Agenda* (1986) and *American Youth Violence* (1998). This essay first appeared in *Newsweek*.

1   Americans can be divided into three groups—smokers, nonsmokers, and that expanding pack of us who have quit. Those who have never smoked don't know what they're missing, but former smokers, ex-smokers, reformed smokers can never forget. We are veterans of a personal war, linked by that watershed experience of ceasing to smoke and by the temptation to have just one more cigarette. For almost all of us ex-smokers, smoking continues to play an important part in our lives. And now that it is being restricted in restaurants around the country . . . , it is vital that everyone understand the different emotional states cessation of smoking can cause. I have observed four of them; and in the interest of science I have classified them as those of the zealot, the

evangelist, the elect, and the serene. Each day, each category gains new recruits.

2   Not all antitobacco zealots are former smokers, but a substantial number of fire-and-brimstone opponents do come from the ranks of the reformed. Zealots believe that those who continue to smoke are degenerates who deserve scorn, not pity, and the penalties that will deter offensive behavior in public as well. Relations between these people and those who continue to smoke are strained.

3   One explanation for the zealot's fervor in seeking to outlaw tobacco consumption is his own tenuous hold on abstaining from smoking. But I think part of the emotional force arises from sheer envy as he watches and identifies with each lung-filling puff. By making smoking in public a crime, the zealot seeks reassurance that he will not revert to bad habits; give him strong social penalties and he won't become a recidivist.

4   No systematic survey has been done yet, but anecdotal evidence suggests that a disproportionate number of doctors who have quit smoking can be found among the fanatics. Just as the most enthusiastic revolutionary tends to make the most enthusiastic counterrevolutionary, many of today's vitriolic zealots include those who had been deeply committed to tobacco habits.

5   By contrast, the antismoking evangelist does not condemn smokers. Unlike the zealot, he regards smoking as an easily curable condition, as a social disease, and not a sin. The evangelist spends an enormous amount of time seeking and preaching to the unconverted. He argues that kicking the habit is not *that* difficult. After all, *he* did it; moreover, as he describes it, the benefits of quitting are beyond measure and the disadvantages are nil.

6   The hallmark of the evangelist is his insistence that he never misses tobacco. Though he is less hostile to smokers than the zealot, he is resented more. Friends and loved ones who have been the targets of his preachments frequently greet the resumption of smoking by the evangelist as an occasion for unmitigated glee.

7   Among former smokers, the distinctions between the evangelist and the elect are much the same as the differences between proselytizing and nonproselytizing religious sects. While the evangelists preach the ease and desirability of abstinence, the elect do not attempt to convert their friends. They think that virtue is its own reward and subscribe to the Puritan* theory of predestina-

---

*The Puritans were an early American religious group.

tion. Since they have proved themselves capable of abstaining from tobacco, they are therefore different from friends and relatives who continue to smoke. They feel superior, secure that their salvation was foreordained. These ex-smokers rarely give personal testimony on their conversion. They rarely speak about their tobacco habits, while evangelists talk about little else. Of course, active smokers find such bluenosed behavior far less offensive than that of the evangelist or the zealot, yet they resent the elect simply because they are smug. Their air of self-satisfaction rarely escapes the notice of those lighting up. For active smokers, life with a member of the ex-smoking elect is less stormy than with a zealot or evangelist, but it is subtly oppressive nonetheless.

8   I have labeled my final category of former smokers the serene. This classification is meant to encourage those who find the other psychic styles of ex-smokers disagreeable. Serenity is quieter than zealotry and evangelism, and those who qualify are not as self-righteous as the elect. The serene ex-smoker accepts himself and also accepts those around him who continue to smoke. This kind of serenity does not come easily, nor does it seem to be an immediate option for those who have stopped. Rather it is a goal, an end stage in a process of development during which some former smokers progress through one or more of the less-than-positive psychological points en route. For former smokers, serenity is thus a positive possibility that exists at the end of the rainbow. But all former smokers cannot reach that promised land.

9   What is it that permits some former smokers to become serene? I think the key is self-acceptance and gratitude. The fully mature former smoker knows he has the soul of an addict and is grateful for the knowledge. . . . He doesn't regret that he quit smoking, nor any of his previous adventures with tobacco. As a former smoker, he is grateful for the experience and memory of craving a cigarette.

10 Serenity comes from accepting the lessons of one's life. And ex-smokers who have reached this point in their worldview have much to be grateful for. They have learned about the potential and limits of change. In becoming the right kind of former smoker, they developed a healthy sense of self. This former smoker, for one, believes that it is better to crave (one hopes only

occasionally) and not to smoke than never to have craved at all. And by accepting that fact, the reformed smoker does not need to excoriate, envy, or disassociate himself from those who continue to smoke.

Exercise 8 — VOCABULARY HIGHLIGHTS

Write a short definition of each word as it is used in the essay. (Paragraph numbers are given in parentheses.) Be prepared to use the words in your own sentences.

zealot (1)

tenuous (3)

recidivist (3)

anecdotal (4)

vitriolic (4)

unmitigated (6)

proselytizing (7)

predestination (7)

foreordained (7)

excoriate (10)

Exercise 9 — DISCUSSION AND CRITICAL THINKING

1. What are the division and subdivision of classification that Zimring uses in the first paragraph?

2. On what basis does Zimring divide the ex-smokers in his classification?

3. With which classes do you associate the following words?
   arrogance:
   acceptance:
   preachy:
   hostility:

4. What are some other categories of ex-smokers?

5. How would you compare ex-smokers with ex-drinkers, ex-meat eaters, and ex-couch potatoes?

Shaking Hands

Glen Waggoner

Shaking hands is a necessary part of many of our greetings. In this brief essay, former Esquire *senior writer Glen Waggoner explains that different people have different styles and that most of the styles are wrong. This essay was first published in* Esquire.

1. A handshake tells you a lot about a man. For one thing, it tells you that he's probably an American. Europeans hug when they greet each other, the English nod, the Japanese bow, but Americans shake hands. And that's the way it is.

2. Extending an empty hand to show that you have no weapon, grasping another's hand to signify your human bond—you have to admit the handshake has impeccable symbolic credentials. Too bad that it has become so commonplace as to have lost much of its original meaning. Anyway, it's our way of saying hello, so we might as well get straight once and for all the main kinds of handshake; especially the only one that is correct.

The Politician's Pump

3. A familiar face with a toothy grin that materializes out of a crowd as its owner grabs your right hand in a firm grip, while simultaneously seizing your right forearm in his left hand. Two short, strong shakes and you find yourself being moved sideways as Teeth swivels to mug the next voter. (Also known as the Receiving-Line Two-Hand when practiced by college presidents.)

The Preemptive Squeeze

4. All fingers and thumb. Your extended hand is caught just short of its target by a set of pincers that encloses your four fingers at the second knuckle and leaves your thumb pointing west. No palm contact whatsoever. One quick squeeze, a side-to-side waggle, and your hand is unceremoniously dropped, leaving it utterly frustrated.

The Limp Fish

5. The most hated of all. Someone puts his fingers in your hand and leaves them there. Excusable in foreigners, who are still grappling with a language where *gh* and *f* sound alike (as in "tough fish"). For others, unacceptable.

The Macho Man

6. The old bone-crusher, the familiar signature of the emotionally insecure but physically strong. If you're alert, you can see this one coming in time to take countermeasures. The best defense is a good offense: grab his hand toward the base of the palm, cutting down on his fingers' leverage, and start your grip before he starts his. Of course, if he's strong enough and macho enough, it won't work, and he'll bond your individual digits into a single flipper for trying to thwart him.

The Preacher's Clasp

7. As your right hands join, his left folds over the top and immobilizes them both (okay, all three, but who's counting?). Always accompanied by steady eye contact (no way you won't be the first to blink), and usually by a monologue delivered two inches closer to your face than is really necessary. Once the exclusive province of Presbyterian ministers, the Clasp is now practiced by a broad spectrum of the relentlessly sincere, including motivational speakers and honors graduates of weekend-therapy marathons. The worst thing about it is that it makes your hand sweat.

The Right Way

8. A firm, full-handed grip, a steady squeeze, and a definite but understated downward snap (but no up-and-down pumping, unless you're contemplating a disabling karate move), followed at once by a decisive release accompanied by eye contact and performed only if both parties are standing (the ritual implies mutual respect and equality, after all). Sounds easy enough, but how frequently do you encounter a really good one?

Footnote: Shaking Hands with Women

9. No difference in grip (the Right Way is always right), but convention has it that you should wait for her to extend her hand first. These days, chances are good she will.

Exercise 10   **DISCUSSION AND CRITICAL THINKING**

1. Underline the thesis.

2. On what principle is the classification based?

3. On what other principles might a classification of handshaking be based?

4. This article was written for *Esquire*, so the audience was mainly men. Is the footnote pertaining to shaking hands with women enough?

✎ Topics for Writing Classification

Writing Process Worksheet

You will find a Writing Process Worksheet on page 27. It can be photocopied and enlarged, filled in, and submitted with each assignment if your instructor directs you to do so.

Source-Based Topics

Each essay developed from these suggested source-based topics should include at least one reference to the reading selection by the author's name and the title. Quotations should be enclosed in quotation marks. Follow your instructor's directions in documenting the ideas you borrow. Whether you use informal or formal documentation, the form is not complicated, and you will soon learn to use it for these essays without checking each time. See pages 73 and 74 for a discussion of MLA style and informal documentation.

Underlining and annotating reading selections will help you in finding support material. In prewriting brief essays, consider marking your outline to indicate where you will use quotations or other borrowed ideas. If the quotations or reworded statements are short and few, you could even insert them inside parentheses or circles in your outline; if you do, also include the author's last name and the page number. A sound system, consistently used, will save you time and ensure technically strong papers.

"Types of Fly Fighters"

1. Use this essay as a model for the same prompt that Carter used: Write a classification of people according to how they deal with unwanted and uninvited intruders, such as pesky insects, sneaky rodents, unruly nei ghborhood pets, rambunctious visiting children, aggressive store salespersons, annoying telemarketers, snoopy neighbors, and zealous religious proselytizers.

"Community College Pressures"

2. Using Follette's basic framework, write about your own college pressures.

"Coworkers from Hell and How to Cope"

3. Select one of the classes and subdivide it for your own essay of classification.

4. Using the relevant classes from Monfred's essay, discuss the coworkers from hell whom you encountered at a particular job. Use specific examples.

"Dangerous Curves"

5. Write an essay of classification in which you warn women about how to identify certain types of men, thereby avoiding dysfunctional relationships. Following Golden's lead, use examples of well-known people from popular culture (movie stars, other entertainers, politicians) to illustrate your classes.

"Confessions of a Former Smoker"

6. Using Zimring's categories as a model, discuss the behavior of people who were formerly heavy drinkers, meat eaters, nonexercisers, or frequent television viewers, and are now teetotalers, vegetarians, exercise buffs, or television abstainers.

"Shaking Hands"

7. Using Waggoner's classification as a model, write about different ways of hugging, waving, kissing, or saying goodbye.

Career-Related Topics

8. Discuss different types of managers you have encountered (democratic, authoritative, autocratic, buddy, aloof).

9. Discuss different types of customers with whom you have dealt (perhaps according to their purpose for seeking your services or products).

10. Discuss different types of employees you have observed.

11. Discuss different qualities of products or services available in a particular field.

12. Discuss different kinds of chat rooms on the Internet.

General Topics

Write an essay using one of the topics listed here. Divide your topic into groups according to a single principle.

13. Intelligence
14. Waitresses
15. Dates
16. Smokers
17. Smiles
18. Liars
19. Gossips
20. TV watchers
21. Styles in clothing
22. Sports
23. Dopers
24. Sports fans
25. Churchgoers
26. Laughs
27. Bus drivers
28. Riders on buses or airplanes
29. Junk food
30. Graffiti
31. Home computers
32. Mothers or fathers
33. Rock music
34. Talkers on the telephone
35. Pick-up lines (as in a bar)
36. Chicken eaters
37. Surfers (Internet or ocean)
38. Beards
39. Pet owners

Writer's Guidelines: Classification

1. Follow this procedure for writing essays of classification:
   - Select a plural subject.
   - Decide on a principle for grouping the units of your subject.
   - Establish the groups, or classes.
   - Write about the classes.

2. Avoid uninteresting phrases for your classes, such as *good/average/bad, fast/medium/slow,* and *beautiful/ordinary/ugly.*

3. Avoid overlapping classes.

4. The Roman numeral parts of your outline will probably indicate your classes.

   I. Class one

   II. Class two

   III. Class three

5. If you use subclasses, clearly indicate the different levels.

6. Following your outline alternative, give somewhat equal (however much is appropriate) space to each class.

9

Process Analysis: Writing about Doing

Writing Process Analysis, p. 221
Two Types of Process Analysis: Directive and Informative, p. 221
Working with Stages, p. 221
Basic Forms, p. 222
Combined Forms, p. 223
Useful Prewriting Procedure, p. 223

Connecting Sources and Writing, p. 224
Student Essay: "Guarding a Wide Receiver," p. 224
Practicing Patterns of Process Analysis, p. 226
Student Documented Essay: "How to Obtain a Real Estate Listing," p. 227
"How to Paint a Fresco," p. 230
"Six Clicks from Death," p. 232
"Attitude," p. 239
"Stars," p. 243

Topics for Writing Process Analysis, p. 245
Writing Process Worksheet, p. 245
Source-Based Topics, p. 245
Career-Related Topics, p. 247
General Topics, p. 247

Writer's Guidelines, p. 248

THE QUIGMANS by Buddy Hickerson

"Hey, hey, hey! How am I supposed to kiss you if you keep holdin' your nose?"

© Tribune Media Services, Inc. All Rights Reserved. Reprinted with permission.

Writing Process Analysis

If you have any doubt about how frequently we use process analysis, just think about how many times you have heard people say, "How do you do it?" or "How is [was] it done?" Even when you are not hearing those questions, you are posing them yourself when you need to make something, cook a meal, assemble an item, take some medicine, repair something, or figure out what happened. In your college classes, you may have to discover how osmosis occurs, how a rock changes form, how a mountain was formed, how a battle was won, or how a bill goes through the legislature.

If you need to explain how to do something or how something was (is) done, you will engage in *process analysis*. You will break down your topic into stages, explaining each so that your reader can duplicate or understand the process.

Two Types of Process Analysis: Directive and Informative

The questions How do I do it? and How is (was) it done? will lead you into two different types of process analysis—directive and informative.

Directive process analysis explains how to do something. As the name suggests, it gives directions for the reader to follow. It says, for example, "Read me, and you can bake a pie [tune up your car, read a book critically, write an essay, take some medicine]." Because it is presented directly to the reader, it usually addresses the reader as "you," or it implies the "you" by saying something such as "First [you] purchase a large pumpkin, and then [you].. . ." In the same way, this textbook addresses you or implies "you" because it is a long how-to-do-it (directive process analysis) statement.

Informative process analysis explains how something was (is) done by giving data (information). Whereas the directive process analysis tells you what to do in the future, the informative process analysis tells you what has occurred or what is occurring. If it is something in nature, such as the formation of a mountain, you can read and understand the process by which it emerged. In this type of process analysis, you do not tell the reader what to do; therefore, you will seldom use the words *you* or *your*.

Working with Stages

Preparation or Background

In the first stage of the directive type of process analysis, list the materials or equipment needed for the process and discuss the necessary setup arrangements. For some topics, this stage will also provide technical terms and definitions. The degree to which this stage is detailed will depend on both the subject itself and the expected knowledge and experience of the projected audience.

The informative type of process analysis may begin with background or context rather than with preparation. For example, a statement explaining how mountains form might begin with a description of a flat portion of the earth made up of plates that are arranged like a jigsaw puzzle.

Steps or Sequence

The actual process will be presented here. Each step or sequence must be explained clearly and directly, and phrased to accommodate the audience. The language, especially in directive process analysis, is likely to be simple and concise; however, avoid dropping words such as *and, a, an, the,* and *of,* and thereby lapsing into "recipe language." The steps may be accompanied by explanations about why certain procedures are necessary and how not following directions carefully can lead to trouble.

Order

The order will usually be chronological (time based) in some sense. Certain transitional words are commonly used to promote coherence: *first, second, third, then, soon, now, next, finally, at last, therefore, consequently,* and—especially for informative process analysis—words used to show the passage of time such as hours, days of the week, and so on.

Basic Forms

Consider using this form for the directive process (with topics such as how to cook something or how to fix something).

How to Prepare Spring Rolls

  I. Preparation
      A. Suitable cooking area
      B. Utensils, equipment
      C. Spring roll wrappers
      D. Vegetables, sauce
  II. Steps
      A. Season vegetables
      B. Wrap vegetables
      C. Fold wrappers
      D. Deep fry rolls
      E. Serve rolls with sauce

Consider using this form for the informative process (with topics such as how a volcano functions or how a battle was won).

How Coal Is Formed

I. Background or context
   A. Accumulation of land plants
   B. Bacterial action
   C. Muck formation
II. Sequence
   A. Lignite from pressure
   B. Bituminous from deep burial and heat
   C. Anthracite from metamorphic conditions

Combined Forms

Combination process analysis occurs when directive process analysis and informative process analysis are blended, usually when the writer personalizes the account. For example, if I tell you from a detached view how to write a research paper, my writing is directive process analysis, but if I tell you how I once wrote a research paper and give you the details in an informative account, then you may very well learn enough so that you can duplicate what I did. Thus, you would be both informed and instructed. Often the personalized account is more interesting to the general reader, but if you need to assemble a toy the night before your child's birthday, for example, you just want directions.

Many assignments are done as a personalized account. A paper about planting radish seeds may be informative, but it would probably be uninspiring. However, a paper about the time you helped your grandpa plant his spring garden (giving all the details) may be informative, directive, and entertaining. It is often the cultural framework provided by personal experience that transforms an ordinary directive account into something memorable. That's why some instructors ask their students to explain how to do something within the context of experience.

Useful Prewriting Procedure

All the strategies of freewriting, brainstorming, and clustering can be useful in writing a process analysis. However, if you already know your subject well, you can simply make two lists, one headed *Preparation* or *Background* and the other *Steps* or *Sequence*. Then jot down ideas for each. After you have finished with your listing, you can delete parts, combine parts, and rearrange parts for better order. That editing of your lists will lead directly to a formal outline you can use in Stage Two of the writing process. Following is an example of listing for the topic of how to prepare spring rolls.

Preparation (Background)	Steps
stainless steel bowl	slice and mix vegetables
deep-fry pan	add sauce to vegetables
spoon	beat eggs
damp cloth	place wrappers on damp cloth
spring roll wrappers	add 2 to 3 tablespoons of vegetables per wrapper
eggs	
sauce	fold and seal wrapper with egg
cabbage	freeze for later or deep fry immediately
celery	serve with sweet and sour sauce
carrots	
bean sprouts	

Connecting Sources and Writing

Student Essay

Watching football games, most of us have observed cornerbacks harassing wide receivers. One person wants to catch the ball thrown by the quarterback; however, an opponent is there to interfere. In this essay, Brian Landry, a former high school football player, explains that the successful cornerback is doing much more than being annoying; he is actually playing a game within a game.

Guarding a Wide Receiver
Brian Landry

Unlike golf, one of the ultimate individual sports, football is a team sport, and many people think of it as one machine facing off against another. What those people miss is that each player has a specific role, and often an individual player is engaged in a game within a game against another player who is executing his own battle plan. Few match-ups offer more challenges to individuals than the one between the cornerback and the wide receiver. As a cornerback, I finally discovered an effective process, one that begins with preparation before the game and ends with strategic action on the field during a pass play.

The most important part of winning is in the preparation. First, you need to be mentally and physically fit. Mental fitness involves studying your opposing team and its strategies, as well as knowing your own defensive schemes and having a winning attitude. Physical fitness is self-explanatory. You must have stamina, strength, and speed. Next is equipment. You must wear the appropriate gear and, especially, the shoes that suit the playing surface. With that preparation completed, you are ready for the wide receiver poised just across the line from you, his mind focused on making you look foolish on the next pass play.

Initially you must control the distance between yourself and the receiver. Before the ball is snapped, keep yourself five to ten yards from the receiver, depending on his speed. If the receiver is fast, you can either give him a couple of yards distance so it will neutralize his speed, or you can bump him at the line so he doesn't get to use his speed. When the ball is about to be hiked, if you know the receiver is slow, get close to him, about one yard away. Always keep your feet shoulder-wide apart. Crouch down slightly, bringing your weight over your toes. This should be a very balanced position. Look the receiver in the eyes and try to intimidate him.

Body contact should be just right, not too much or too little. When the ball is snapped, thrust your arms forward, striking the receiver just below his shoulder pads, making sure you are maintaining balance. If this is accomplished, then try to keep him there. Avoid grasping, because this will cause a penalty. More often than not, the receiver will move to avoid this procedure. Do not let him get inside of you. Push him towards the sidelines. Now you need to turn with him, keeping him within touching distance. You want to be between him and the quarterback. Try to remain always in contact with him. Use your outside arm for this procedure. Don't push him too much after five yards because this is another penalty.

Your eyes now become your main tools. Look into the receiver's eyes, watching his reactions. Don't get in front of him because he can then stop and turn back. Watch his moves and be his shadow. Remember to keep your balance so you can turn quickly when he does. As you are watching his eyes, you are looking for two things. If his eyes become extremely big, as if a present is coming his way, or they become fixed on an object, then you must react quickly. This means the ball is usually en route there. Turn your head away from the receiver and back toward the quarterback. Pick up the ball as quickly as possible, still keeping in touch with the receiver, with your outside arm.

At some point you may play the ball as well as the receiver. Once you see the ball, if it is off target with the receiver, run to where it is headed and catch it. If it is coming in your direction, don't let the receiver get between you and the ball. Judge the distance, and when the ball is close enough for you to jump and catch it, do so. Always catch the ball at its highest point. This technique keeps a receiver from stealing it at the last second. Remember that the receiver is trying for the ball too. You must want it more than he does. If the receiver has positioned himself in front of you, then you must react. When the ball is about to touch his hands, you must hit the ball, his hands, or both. Keep the arm that is away from the ball wrapped around his body. This way if he does catch it, you can make the tackle.

After the play is done, the key to all good cornerbacks is having a short memory. If the play went against you, forget it. There is always the next one. Remember that mental and physical preparation and the right equipment are prerequisites to the process on the field. Then you have a chance to become an effective cornerback.

Exercise 1   DISCUSSION AND CRITICAL THINKING

1. Is this essay directive or informative process analysis?

2. Although this essay explains how to do something, an interested audience might have a broader base than just football players. Who might also be interested readers?

3. Landry mentions that good cornerbacks should be both mentally and physically fit. Is one more important than the other? Discuss how the two work together.

4. On the basis of what Landry says, would you rather have a cornerback of average physical fitness and high mental ability or one with high physical fitness and average mental ability?

5. Underline the thesis for the essay and double underline the topic sentences for the support paragraphs.

Practicing Patterns of Process Analysis

A definite pattern underlies a process analysis. In some presentations, such as directions with merchandise to be assembled, the content reads as mechanically as an outline, and no reader objects. The same can be said of most recipes. In other presentations, such as your typical college assignments, the pattern is submerged in flowing discussion. The directions or information must be included, but the writing should be well-developed and interesting. Regardless of the form you use or the audience you anticipate, keep in mind that in process analysis the pattern will provide a foundation for the content.

Exercise 2

COMPLETING PATTERNS OF PROCESS ANALYSIS

Fill in the missing parts of the outline.

Thesis: As a cornerback, I finally discovered an effective process, one that begins with preparation before the game and ends with strategic action on the field during a pass play.

    I. Preparation

        A. Fitness

            1. _____

            2. _____

        B. _____

    II. Steps

        A. _____

        B. _____

        C. _____

        D. _____

Student Documented Essay

Balancing her roles as mother and wife, full-time realtor, and part-time student, Kay Eckert is a busy, energetic woman. Her assignment in a freshman composition class was to write a process analysis paper about one phase of work she is doing or has done. She was expected to give credit to any sources she used for information. Reflecting on her job as a realtor, all activities pointed to the paired objectives of customer service and sales. She decided to write about the prerequisite to company sales: obtaining a listing of property to sell.

How to Obtain a Real Estate Listing
Kay Eckert

Selling real estate is a highly competitive business. But closing a deal is often well down the line from the first essential step: getting a listing. Usually other agents are also making their pitches, and a successful person must know how to prepare for that crucial first meeting with the potential clients and then how to get the contract.

The first task in the preparation, that of evaluating a home and arriving at a potential sales price, pertains to gathering facts about the home itself and the most recent sales in the neighborhood. For my research, I use the Title Company, a business service that provides up-to-date details about recent sales. A property profile provides all important information about the subject property and the surrounding neighborhood. Whatever information the owners (assuming for this presentation that there are two) have provided me is factored in. Another tool I use is the Multiple Listing Service of the Board of Realtors. Then I make my comparison, focusing on square footage, lot size, and amenities, and do my calculations.

With that information organized, I am ready to prepare a package of information for the sellers. This package must be easy to read and understand. It should include an area map to make it easy for the homeowners to locate homes that have recently sold in the neighborhood, and a clear set of recorded sales. Now it is time to pack the briefcase. It is important to take all I am likely to need: information sheets, maps, listing forms, a calculator, magazines, newspaper ads, and letters of recommendation. It is also important not to carry in too much and intimidate the property owners. Above all, I must appear to be organized and prepared; if I am apparently not, I certainly will not get the listing. This encounter will be my one and only opportunity.

Now is the time to meet the homeowners. Both should be present. After I greet the owners with a smile, I always try to "break the ice" by making a comment about a positive feature of the property—the landscaping, structure, or interior decoration. Many times the owners are nervous and self-conscious. I know that I am the intruder, often regarded as a necessary component in this stressful operation. Therefore, I do what I can to make them feel comfortable and relaxed.

As soon as we are acquainted, I ask the owners to show me through the house. I make a few notes, but mainly I make mental notes that I will transcribe back in my car. I remind myself of a little six-word quotation from my favorite real estate textbook, by

Danielle Kennedy: "Always move and act with confidence" (197–198). Strategically, I will make sure that our tour ends in the kitchen, because most important decisions in families are made at the kitchen table. It also gives owners the feeling that they are beginning the negotiations in their territory.

After I am invited to sit down, I take out the information package and explain in detail the material to both homeowners. I ask them to interrupt me and ask questions at any time. I point out recent home sales in their neighborhood and explain how these compare with their home. If they say they have used the Internet to obtain information about comparative sales and mention a service such as Yahoo! Real Estate (Yahoo), I explain that the Internet is useful, but the Title Company that I use concentrates on regional and local property and gives me the most reliable figures. Together we review my marketing plan, the listing forms, and the financial aspects of the transaction. After all questions are answered, I ask the owners: "Are you ready to list your home with me now?" If they intend to bring in other agents, then my chances of getting the listing are greatly reduced. If the owners have no further questions, I can start to fill out the contract. All that is left is for my new clients to sign on the dotted lines. We will then talk for a few more minutes and then I will leave with the smile I came with, my hope having turned to fulfillment.

During the next days, weeks, or months I will almost certainly be returning to this location with buyers. The relationship I have established with my clients, the preparation I made, and the listing procedures all make up a foundation for a good sale and perhaps for recommendations for years to come.

Works Cited

Kennedy, Danielle. *How to List and Sell Real Estate.* New York: Prentice Hall, 1983.

Exercise 3 — DISCUSSION AND CRITICAL THINKING

1. Underline the thesis.

2. Use annotation and a vertical line in the margin to mark the preparation stage; then number the parts of the preparation.

3. Use annotation and a double vertical line in the margin to mark the steps; then number the steps in the process.

How to Paint a Fresco
Adam Goodheart

Enriching his comments with numerous references stretching back five hundred years, Adam Goodheart explains a much-admired but now seldom-used method of painting—the fresco. We learn how it was done in ancient times and, at the same time, we learn how we could do it now. This article was first published in Civilization *in 1995.*

Equipment

Lime	The bristles of a white hog
Sand	The hair of bears, sables and martens
Water	The quills of vultures, geese, hens and doves
A trowel	
Paper	Ocher, burnt grapevines, lapis lazuli
A needle	Egg yolks
A small bag of charcoal dust	Goat's milk

1   1. *Preparing the wall.* Cennino Cennini, a Tuscan master, advised pupils in 1437 to "begin by decking yourselves with this attire: Enthusiasm, Reverence, Obedience, and Constancy." You'd do better to deck yourself with some old clothes, though, since the first stage of the process is quite messy. Soak the wall thoroughly and coat it with coarse plaster, two parts sand to one part lime, leaving the surface uneven. (Andrea Pozzo, a 17th-century expert, recommended hiring a professional mason to do this, since "the lime makes a foul odor, which is injurious to the head.")

2   2. *Tracing your design.* You should already have extensive drawings for your fresco—these will be much sought by scholars and collectors in centuries to come. Make a full-size sketch, on sturdy paper, of a section of the fresco that you can paint in a day. Then go over the drawing with a needle, pricking holes along

every line. Lay a coat of fine plaster on a section of the wall corresponding to the location, size, and shape of the sketch, and press the sketch against the plaster. Fill a loosely woven bag with charcoal dust and strike it lightly all over the surface of the paper. Now peel the sketch off. Your design will be outlined in black dots on the wet plaster, giving you a guide for the day's work.

3. *Painting.* Time is of the essence: You must paint the plaster while it is wet, so that the pigments bind chemically with the lime. That gives you about six hours, although some painters had tricks to prolong drying. (Piero della Francesca packed the plaster with wet rags; problem was, this left indentations that are still visible after 500 years.) Use top-quality brushes. One 17th-century Flemish master recommended those made of "fish hair" (he probably meant seal fur), but most painters made brushes from bear, marten, or sable hairs inserted in hollow quills. Cennini suggested the bristles of a white hog for the coarser work. As for paints, every artist had his own favorite recipes, but all agreed that mineral pigments such as ocher or ground stone mixed with water were best. Avoid white lead.... A few pigments, such as dark blue azurite (often used for the Virgin Mary's mantle), must be mixed with egg yolk or goat's milk and added after the fresco is dry. Such colors will prove less durable.

Money is a consideration in choosing materials. When Michelangelo frescoed the Sistine ceiling, expenses came out of his fee, so he used cheap blue smalt for the sky. Twenty years later, when he did the *Last Judgment,* Michelangelo used semiprecious lapis lazuli for blue, since the pope was paying for the paint. (He made up for it by using burnt grapevines for black.)

4. *Casualties of style.* Realism, while a worthy goal, has its perils. Spinello Aretino, a 14th-century Tuscan, is said to have painted a fresco that depicted Lucifer with such hideous accuracy that the Evil One himself came to the artist in a dream and demanded an explanation. Spinello went half-mad with fear and died shortly thereafter. On the other hand, a Florentine woodcut from 1500 depicts a painter who has portrayed the Virgin so skillfully that when he falls off the scaffold, she reaches out of the fresco and saves him.

Warning

Frescoing ceilings can be rough on your back. While working on the Sistine Chapel, Michelangelo wrote a poem complaining: "I've already grown a goiter at this drudgery... With my beard toward heaven . . . I am bent like a bow." Don't be discouraged, though. Bad posture is a small price to pay for immortality.

Exercise 4 **DISCUSSION AND CRITICAL THINKING**

1. Is this a directive or informative process analysis?

2. What part of the essay represents the preparation stage?

3. How many steps are included in the process and what are their numbers?

4. How does Goodheart humanize his set of directions and give perspective to his subject material?

5. As the author explains steps, he refers to individuals who made contributions to the art of fresco painting. Are these references examples of formal or informal documentation?

6. What is the purpose of paragraphs 5 and 6?

7. What kind of audience does the author anticipate? How do you know?

Six Clicks from Death
Cynthia Joyce

Like so many of us, Cynthia Joyce had a health problem and turned to the Internet for answers. Unfortunately, her adventure in cyberspace was worse than her disease. Looking back with humor on her frantic search, she highlights where she went right and wrong. This article was first published in the April 1997 edition of *Salon* at http://www.salonmagazine.com.

1. I woke up one morning last fall and the entire right side of my face felt like it had been injected with Novocaine. I ran to the mirror to see what was going on and attempted a series of Jim Carrey* impersonations to work the numbness out of my face. The left side went along willingly, but the right side stared back at me, unblinking and totally expressionless.

2. By the time I made it to work, it had gotten worse. The right side of my face now looked like a fallen soufflé, and the right half of my tongue felt like rubber. I tried to downplay how scared I was, offering lame little jokes like, "Is this what they mean by 'self-effacing'?" My jokes didn't have the desired effect of putting my co-workers at ease because by now my speech was so slurred I sounded drunk. By midafternoon, the right side of my face was completely paralyzed—yet, oddly, my hearing on that side was amplified. I felt like a cross between a stroke victim and the Bionic Woman.†

3. My doctor took one look at me and, ruling out the possibility of a stroke (rare for healthy twenty-seven-year-olds), diagnosed me with Bell's palsy—a typically temporary condition resulting from damage to the seventh cranial nerve. He said no one knows what causes this damage, but most people fully recover in four to six weeks. He didn't tell me what happens to the *other* people, and I didn't ask. Although I understood that I was probably going to look like Bill the Cat‡ for at least a month, I was relieved that my doctor didn't seem overly concerned. As I went to fill his prescription for steroids, I vowed to keep busy, stay away from mirrors for a while, and learn everything I could about my syndrome.

4. As it turned out, staring at my distorted reflection would prove to be far less threatening a pastime than staring into the kaleidoscope of information on the Web.

5. The first thing I did when I returned to work the next morning was search the Web for information on Bell's palsy—beginning a series of self-misdiagnoses that did more lasting damage than the palsy itself. Because I didn't know where to find reliable health information, I started a general search on AltaVista. The first article that turned up was a *Healthgate* document from the National Library of Medicine's *Medline* database titled "Management of Bell's palsy." I read the abstract: "The natural history of Bell's palsy is favorable. Eighty-four percent show satisfactory recovery without any treatment; however, 16 percent suffer moderate to severe sequelae."

---

*Jim Carrey is a comedian and actor.
†The Bionic Woman was a character on a TV show who had superhuman abilities.
‡Bill the Cat is a comic-strip character.

6 *Sequelae?* Good God, what could that be? I'd never heard of it before. I quickly did a new search on sequelae. My heart was beating in my ears as I waited for the search results. I tried to picture what sequelae might look like. I imagined myself in scarf and gloves, trying to conceal the sequelae that covered my neck and hands. I pictured friends and co-workers recoiling in horror as sequelae spewed from my right ear. I wondered if sequelae was contagious—would I have to be quarantined?

7 The sequelae search results finally appeared, barely staving off my hysteria. I clicked on an article from the *Journal of Clinical Oncology* titled "Late Psycho-Social Sequelae in Hodgkin's Disease Survivors: A French Population-Based Case-Control Study." Of course, I'd never suffered from Hodgkin's disease, but it didn't matter. My line of reasoning went something like this: the incidence of sequelae in French populations must be pretty high to merit a control study being based on it. My mother's side of the family is French. As far as I was concerned, this constituted conclusive data. But I was forced to admit I was probably off-track when I calmed down enough to notice that the dreaded *s* word wasn't even mentioned in the conclusion.

8 I went back to the original search and followed the second entry, titled simply "Sequelae." It read: "Sequelae . . . may include persistent hypesthesia and dysesthesia, persistent motor weakness, infection, amputation, and death. These are the direct result of nerve and muscle injury." The various *-thesias* didn't mean anything to me, but seeing the words "nerve damage" and "amputation and death" so close together within the same paragraph threw me into a panic.

9 And it didn't end there. By the time I finally bothered to look up *sequelae* in Webster's and found that it means only "something that follows," I had diagnosed myself with a brain tumor, encephalitis, Lyme disease, and two different strains of the herpes virus. Whatever Web page I started from, I never seemed to be more than six clicks from a death sentence.

10 As my doctor predicted, I recovered fully within four weeks. He didn't tell me about the 16 percent who never recover or suffer the dreaded "sequelae" of recurring paralysis because he correctly assumed I'd automatically count myself among them. And since Bell's palsy may be linked to stress, he wisely decided not to give me cause for more. Nonetheless, during those four weeks, I think I found every single one of those 16 percent online.

11 Although I didn't know it at the time, it's safe to assume that because Bell's palsy usually goes away after several weeks, the people posting in online support groups like the Neurology Web

Forum represented a disproportionate segment of those Bell's palsy sufferers whose symptoms never faded. I certainly had no reason to distrust their accounts—but lots of reasons why I didn't need to hear them just then. Still, I opened every one of those links, and needless to say, with subject heads like "SCARED," "10 years later . . ." and "BELL'S STRIKES AGAIN," the stories only added to my hysteria.

12   Clearly, of course, people with serious illnesses—particularly those who have been properly diagnosed—can greatly benefit from online support groups. Dr. Allison Szapary, a resident at the University of California at San Francisco, believes that although younger residents like herself typically use medical databases like *Medline* "every day, all day," online support groups are far more useful for patients than such data-heavy sites. "I think the Web is better for offering emotional support than for actually giving good factual information," she says. "For people going through serious illnesses, it's important for them to feel connected to others going through the same thing."

13   One reason it's so useful, especially for people with chronic or degenerative illnesses, is that people can describe even their most embarrassing health problems without having to look someone in the eye—and in such situations, unlike in other kinds of Web conferences, the anonymity actually encourages more honesty.

14   As a cancer survivor, health writer, and producer for the popular *Ask Dr. Weil* alternative medicine site, Steven Petrow knows firsthand both the advantages and dangers of online medical resources.

15   "When I researched medical libraries like the University of Pennsylvania site, I wound up with more information than I knew how to interpret. When I went to my doctor I was a mess—I thought I was going to die," he says. "I've been a health writer for more than ten years, and when I read a study, I have to read all the footnotes very carefully, and sometimes I still don't understand. So you can only assume your average consumer would be confused some of the time."

16   Several sites, such as Reuters Health, offer information under two separate categories for consumers and professionals to help alleviate this problem. Patients still have access to medical research but can get it in layman's terms. Without that option, Petrow points out, having all the latest info "doesn't cure your problems—it could actually create new ones."

17   The editors of the *Journal of the American Medical Association* attempted to address some of these issues in an April 16 editorial in which they warned that "health care professionals and patients

alike should view with equal parts delight and concern the exponential growth of ... the Web as a medical information delivery tool. Delight because the Internet hosts a large number of high-quality medical resources and poses seemingly endless opportunities to inform, teach, and connect professionals and patients alike. Concern because the fulfillment of that promise remains discouragingly distant."

18   Part of the problem with the Web, they argue, is that "science and snake oil may not always look all that different on the Net." Petrow agrees that the unregulated proliferation of health information sites on the Web makes it easier for consumers to be duped, especially by sites promoting alternative medicine.

19   "I think it's easier to scam people online," he says. "Some of us are hoping there will be some kind of oversight in terms of fraud on the Web because right now there isn't. With print magazines, at least you have to have 'advertisement' written on the page if it's an ad. It's hard for someone to tell what's legitimate or not, and part of the problem is when fraud is actually being committed, you don't have an actual physical location where someone could be prosecuted. The consumer law needs to evolve to a national level that incorporates the Web."

20   The authors of the *JAMA* editorial take a different view. They argue that because the Web is a global and decentralized medium, government regulation isn't the answer. Instead, they favor a standard set of guidelines for authorship, attribution, disclosure, and currency that online resources wishing to establish their reliability would adopt. "Web publishers of all stripes—ourselves included—should be free to post whatever they like and live with the consequences. Let a thousand flowers bloom. We just want those cruising the information superhighway to be able to tell them from the weeds."

21   But as my doctor, Jesse Dohemann, points out, even by-the-book science can start to smell like snake oil* if the doctor-patient relationship is eroded. "I had a guy in here recently who had horrible hives, so I sent him to all the top allergists, and no one could figure out what it was," Dohemann recalls. "He got in touch with a doctor from New York online who prescribed him medication normally used to treat people with Parkinson's disease. The hives did get better, but the guy was now taking a combination of drugs that would have crippled him within ten years. This doctor may have been a real M.D., but he was also a ding-dong."

---

*Snake oil is a fraudulent medicine.

22   As the rise of the HMO* has put greater emphasis on primary and preventive health care, alternative medical information like that provided by *Ask Dr. Weil* has become a growth industry. And the kind of general advice to people such sites provide—watch less news, eat more broccoli—would probably keep them out of legal trouble, even without the prominently displayed liability disclaimer, a standard feature of most sites offering free health advice.

23   But the "free" part of that equation may soon come to an end for the online services of more traditional medical institutions. Because many health-related sites offer interactive elements—like the Internist's Casebook, which lets you play medical detective—their mix of straight advice and "infotainment" allows them to rely on advertising revenue. But sites that cater more to health-care professionals, like Medscape, Medline and the Mayo Clinic, may soon be forced to charge subscription fees. "I think the love affair with free information is going to be coming to an end," Petrow predicts. "And the question seems to be, you pay for this type of information now; why wouldn't you have to pay for it on the Web?"

24   Looking back on my experience with Bell's palsy, it wasn't all a nightmare—in retrospect, it even seems pretty funny. And I did, in the end, discover an entire range of health resources, as well as develop a great new pastime—albeit a rather obsessive one.

25   For a while there, I was researching my every sneeze online. I no longer needed a *Physician's Desk Reference* to tell me which drugs I couldn't take with alcohol—I could look it up at PharmInfoNet. I could find out everything I never wanted to know about the freckles on my shoulders, my receding hairline, and why I get leg cramps. I even found an interactive ovulation site—one of my personal favorites—featuring the What-If Ovulation Calendar. Believe me, figuring out the last day of your menstrual cycle has never been so much fun.

26   But as my experience showed, too much information can sometimes be a real health hazard. So do the Web a favor: if you've ever suffered a debilitating, embarrassing, or long-lasting illness and been lucky enough to live to tell about it, then please do. You may not cure anyone of whatever ails them, but you just might keep them from going crazy.

---

*HMO: health maintenance organization.

Exercise 5 — VOCABULARY HIGHLIGHTS

Write a short definition of each word as it is used in the essay. (Paragraph numbers are given in parentheses.) Be prepared to use the words in your own sentences.

kaleidoscope (4)

sequelae (5)

constituted (7)

chronic (13)

degenerative (13)

anonymity (13)

proliferation (18)

disclaimer (22)

retrospect (24)

obsessive (24)

Exercise 6 — DISCUSSION AND CRITICAL THINKING

1. In what ways can this information process analysis be thought of as having directive use?

2. Which paragraphs provide the background of this analysis?

3. What is Joyce's first step in her search?

4. Which paragraphs include the steps of the process?

5. In her quest for information about Bell's palsy, Joyce often needed to double back to reexamine what she had found and to redefine terms. Was that movement because of her ineptitude or the nature of researching information on the Web? Explain.

6. In what ways is pursuing a question on the Web similar to the writing process?

7. How do paragraphs 10 through 26 relate to paragraphs 1 through 9 (the process analysis part)?

8. What did you learn from this essay that you can apply when you need to research some medical issue?

Attitude

Garrison Keillor

Author, humorist, and storyteller, Garrison Keillor is best known as host of *A Prairie Home Companion* straight from Lake Wobegon, long featured on National Public Radio. In this essay, first published in *The New Yorker,* he tells us how to play with "attitude."

1   Long ago I passed the point in life when major-league ballplayers begin to be younger than yourself. Now all of them are, except for a few aging trigenarians and a couple of quadros who don't get around on the fastball as well as they used to and who sit out the second games of doubleheaders. However, despite my age (thirty-nine), I am still active and have a lot of interests. One of them is slow-pitch softball, a game that lets me go through the motions of baseball without getting beaned or having to run too hard. I play on a pretty casual team, one that drinks beer on the bench and substitutes freely. If a player's wife or girlfriend wants to play, we give her a glove and send her out to right field, no questions asked, and if she lets a pop fly drop six feet in front of her, nobody agonizes over it.

2   Except me. This year. For the first time in my life, just as I am entering the dark twilight of my slow-pitch career, I find myself taking the game seriously. It isn't the bonehead play that bothers me especially—the pop fly that drops untouched, the slow roller juggled and the ball then heaved ten feet over the first baseman's head and into the next diamond, the routine singles that go through outfielders' legs for doubles and triples with gloves flung after them. No, it isn't our stone-glove fielding or pussyfoot baserunning or limp-wristed hitting that gives me fits, though these have put us on the short end of some mighty ridiculous scores this summer. It's our attitude.

3   Bottom of the ninth, down 18–3, two outs, a man on first and a woman on third, and our third baseman strikes out. *Strikes out!* In slow-pitch, not even your grandmother strikes out, but this guy does, and after his third strike—a wild swing at a ball that bounces

on the plate—he topples over in the dirt and lies flat on his back, laughing. *Laughing!*

4   Same game, earlier. They have the bases loaded. A weak grounder is hit toward our second baseperson. The runners are running. She picks up the ball, and she looks at them. She looks at first, at second, at home. We yell, "Throw it! Throw it!" and she throws it, underhand, at the pitcher, who has turned and run to back up the catcher. The ball rolls across the third-base line and under the bench. Three runs score. The batter, a fatso, chugs into second. The other team hoots and hollers, and what does she do? She shrugs and smiles ("Oh, silly me"); after all, it's only a game. Like the aforementioned strikeout artist, she treats her error as a joke. They have forgiven themselves instantly, which is unforgivable. It is *we* who should forgive them, who can say, "It's all right, it's only a game." They are supposed to throw up their hands and kick the dirt and hang their heads, as if this boner, even if it is their sixteenth of the afternoon—*this* is the one that really and truly breaks their hearts.

5   That attitude sweetens the game for everyone. The sinner feels sweet remorse. The fatso feels some sense of accomplishment; this is no bunch of rumdums he forced into an error but a team with some class. We, the sinner's teammates, feel momentary anger at her—dumb! dumb play!—but then, seeing her grief, we sympathize with her in our hearts (any one of us might have made that mistake or one worse), and we yell encouragement, including the shortstop, who, moments before, dropped an easy throw for a force at second. "That's all right! Come on! We got 'em!" we yell. "Shake it off! These turkeys can't hit!" This makes us all feel good, even though the turkeys now lead us by ten runs. We're getting clobbered, but we have a winning attitude.

6   Let me say this about attitude: Each player is responsible for his or her own attitude, and to a considerable degree you can *create* a good attitude by doing certain little things on the field. These are certain little things that ballplayers do in the Bigs, and we ought to be doing them in the Slows.

7   1. When going up to bat, don't step right into the batter's box as if it were an elevator. The box is your turf, your stage. Take possession of it slowly and deliberately, starting with a lot of back-bending, knee-stretching, and torso-revolving in the on-deck circle. Then, approaching the box, stop outside it and tap the dirt off your spikes with your bat. You don't have spikes, you have sneakers, of course, but the sig-

nificance of the tapping is the same. Then, upon entering the box, spit on the ground. It's a way of saying, "This here is mine. This is where I get my hits."

2. Spit frequently. Spit at all crucial moments. Spit correctly. Spit should be *blown,* not ptuied weakly with the lips, which often results in dribble. Spitting should convey forcefulness of purpose, concentration, pride. Spit down, not in the direction of others. Spit in the glove and on the fingers, especially after making a real knucklehead play; it's a way of saying, "I dropped the ball because my glove was dry."

3. At bat and in the field, pick up dirt. Rub dirt in the fingers (especially after spitting on them). Toss dirt, as if testing the wind for velocity and direction. Smooth the dirt. Be involved with dirt. If no dirt is available (e.g., in the outfield), pluck tufts of grass. Fielders should be grooming their areas constantly between plays, flicking away tiny sticks and bits of gravel.

4. Take your time. Tie your laces. Confer with your teammates about possible situations that may arise and conceivable options in dealing with them. Extend the game. Three errors on three consecutive plays can be humiliating if the plays occur within the space of a couple of minutes, but if each error is separated from the next by extensive conferences on the mound, lace-tying, glove adjustments, and arguing close calls (if any), the effect on morale is minimized.

5. Talk. Not just an occasional "Let's get a hit now" but continuous rhythmic chatter, a flow of syllables: "Hey babe hey babe c'mon babe good stick now hey babe long tater take him downtown babe . . . hey good eye good eye."

Infield chatter is harder to maintain. Since the slow-pitch pitch is required to be a soft underhand lob, infielders hesitate to say, "Smoke him babe hey low heat hey throw it on the black babe chuck it in there back him up babe no hit no hit." Say it anyway.

6. One final rule, perhaps the most important of all: When your team is up and has made the third out, the batter and the players who were left on base do not come back to the bench for their gloves. *They remain on the field, and their teammates bring their gloves out to them.* This requires some organization and discipline, but it pays off big in morale. It says, "Although we're getting our pants knocked off, still we must conserve our energy."

14   Imagine that you have bobbled two fly balls in this rout and now you have just tried to stretch a single into a double and have been easily thrown out sliding into second base, where the base runner ahead of you had stopped. It was the third out and a dumb play, and your opponents smirk at you as they run off the field. You are the goat, a lonely and tragic figure sitting in the dirt. You curse yourself, jerking your head sharply forward. You stand up and kick the base. How miserable! How degrading! Your utter shame, though brief, bears silent testimony to the worthiness of your teammates, whom you have let down, and they appreciate it. They call out to you now as they take the field, and as the second baseman runs to his position he says, "Let's get 'em now," and tosses you your glove. Lowering your head, you trot slowly out to right. There you do some deep knee bends. You pick grass. You find a pebble and fling it into foul territory. As the first batter comes to the plate, you check the sun. You get set in your stance, poised to fly. Feet spread, hands on hips, you bend slightly at the waist and spit the expert spit of a veteran ballplayer—a player who has known the agony of defeat but who always bounces back, a player who has lost a stride on the base paths but can still make the big play.

15   This is *ball*, ladies and gentlemen. This is what it's all about.

Exercise 7 — DISCUSSION AND CRITICAL THINKING

1. Is the process analysis part of this essay informative or directive?

2. What is the source of "attitude," as Keillor would like to see it demonstrated on his slow-pitch team?

3. Why does he skip over the preparation stage?

4. Keillor provides us with six steps. Are the steps to be performed in a particular order?

5. In what other sports is attitude important? Give some examples of attitude-building rituals in other sports.

6. What attitude-building behavior is used by people outside sports: at school, at work, at worship, on the road.

7. What is the tone of this essay and what does Keillor expect readers to do?

Stars

Usha Lee McFarling

In simple, direct terms, Usha Lee McFarling, a science writer for the Boston Globe, *explains a process of enormous magnitude and complexity.*

1   A star starts out life from what seems like nothing at all. Stars are born in huge clouds of gas that are actually far less dense than the space immediately surrounding Earth.

2   "These clouds are so spread out, they make the 'vacuum' of the space around the Earth that the space shuttle flies through seem as thick as chicken soup," says Jeff Hester, an astronomer at Arizona State University in Tempe. But because the clouds are so big, they contain a lot of molecules—enough, eventually, to build massive stars.

3   How big are these clouds that serve as star nurseries? They can be a light-year across—so enormous it would take light one year to cross one. In contrast, it takes light only one-seventh of a second to travel the nearly 25,000-mile distance that equals the circumference of tiny Earth.

4   The key to star formation is gravity, says Hester. Gravity causes the multitude of spread-out molecules to move toward each other and pulls them toward the center of the cloud. "The cloud starts to collapse under the force of its own gravity," says Hester, who studies the process of star formation. This collapsing process happens relatively quickly (by cosmic standards)—only about 30 million years, or less.

5   Over time the cloud gets smaller and smaller. As the cloud contracts, it also begins to spin faster. (This is due to a little something called conservation of angular momentum—the same phenomenon that allows a figure skater like Nancy Kerrigan to speed up her spin when she pulls her arms in toward her body. As the mass of gas moves toward the center, the cloud spins faster.)

6   Next, the cloud starts to flatten. "It's just like when you make an honest pizza," says Hester. "The dough flattens as it spins."

Finally, because gravity becomes so strong in the center of the cloud, the center starts to collapse in on itself as it continues to rotate. At this point, you have a disk that's a few times the size of our solar system. (The disk would be about a couple of light-days across, if you're keeping track of the size of things.) As the disk continues to rotate, matter in the center of the disk starts to migrate further inward and a big clump forms in the middle of the disk. This clump, says Hester, is a protostar.

7   What happens to the matter that's left over further out in the disk? In our solar system, it went on to become the planets. (In essence, Earth is made up of leftovers.)

8   Protostars are very hot because so much of the gravitational energy that was once contained in the loose cloud of interstellar gas has been converted into heat. Protostars are spectacular, glowing with dull red light and infrared light. As a protostar emits this light, it continues to shrink and gets hotter and hotter. Finally, it's hot enough for real star business to begin—nuclear fusion.

9   At high enough temperatures, atoms slam together at incredibly fast speeds. When this happens, lighter atoms like hydrogen can fuse together to make heavier atoms like helium. One reaction releases massive amounts of energy; add all the reactions together, and "that's the energy that makes the stars shine," Hester says. Once nuclear fusion begins, that's truly when a star is born.

10   After a star "turns on," he says, its power can wreak havoc on the surrounding environment. A young star expands, ripping apart the cloud that formed it. In a case of stellar sibling rivalry, new stars often disrupt neighboring stars before they can form. It's hard to overstate what a powerful process star formation is. Even as they are forming, protostars eject huge amounts of material in jets and streams and create violent solar winds.

11   Astronomers have identified stellar nurseries within our galaxy—places where new stars are forming, and the Hubble telescope has taken some startling photos of the process of star formation in the Eagle nebula. Without a telescope, says Hester, you can see a stellar nursery by looking at the Milky Way in summer and looking to the south near the constellation Sagittarius. In the middle of the Milky Way, says Hester, you'll see dark splotches. These aren't areas that are free of stars, he says, "rather, they are the shadows of dense interstellar clouds that block the light from stars behind them." These clouds are the nurseries of future stars.

Exercise 8   VOCABULARY HIGHLIGHTS

Write a short definition of each word as it is used in the essay. (Paragraph numbers are given in parentheses.) Be prepared to use the words in your own sentences.

molecules (2)

angular (5)

momentum (5)

phenomenon (5)

protostar (6)

infrared (8)

fusion (8)

stellar (10)

sibling (10)

nebula (11)

Exercise 9   DISCUSSION AND CRITICAL THINKING

1. Is this essay directive or informative process analysis?

2. Annotate the essay by drawing a vertical line beside the paragraphs that present the background to this process.

3. Annotate the essay by writing numbers alongside paragraphs to show the steps by which stars are formed.

4. What is the function of paragraph 10?

5. Paragraph 11 is the conclusion. How does it relate to paragraphs 1 and 2, the introduction?

✎ Topics for Writing Process Analysis

Writing Process Worksheet

You will find a Writing Process Worksheet on page 27. It can be photocopied and enlarged, filled in, and submitted with each assignment if your instructor directs you to do so.

Source-Based Topics

Each essay developed from these suggested source-based topics should include at least one reference to the reading selection by the author's name and the title. Quotations should be enclosed in quotation marks. Follow your instructor's directions in documenting the ideas you borrow. Whether you use informal or formal documentation, the form is not complicated, and you will soon learn to use it for these essays without checking each time. See pages 73 and 74 for a discussion of MLA style and informal documentation.

Underlining and annotating reading selections will help you in finding support material. In prewriting brief essays, consider marking your outline to indicate where you will use quotations or other borrowed ideas. If the quotations or reworded statements are short and few, you could even insert them inside parentheses or circles in your outline; if you do, also include the author's last name and the page number. A sound system, consistently used, will save you time and ensure technically strong papers.

"Guarding a Wide Receiver"

1. Write about how to play another position on a football team. Use this essay as an example.

2. Write about a person playing the position of wide receiver, and refer directly to this essay in explaining techniques for outsmarting and outplaying the cornerback.

3. Write an essay about how to play any sport. Limit your topic so that you can cover it in some detail. You might write about how to shoot a free throw in basketball or how to serve in tennis. If you are writing about a team sport, concentrate on one player or on one strategy or maneuver, such as a "suicide squeeze" in baseball.

"How to Obtain a Real Estate Listing"

4. Using this essay as a model and one or more basic sources as documented aids, explain how to do something related to a job you know well through observation or practice. Consider finding information about the job in printed company guidelines, on the Web, or in library sources.

"How to Paint a Fresco"

5. Using this essay as a model, explain how to paint with oils, acrylics, or watercolors. You could strengthen your writing by including some information about artists who have excelled in the form you choose. Use your library and the Internet in your search for sources.

6. Explain how to perform in another visual art, such as sculpting or photography. Include some background information to enlighten your readers and to heighten interest.

"Six Clicks from Death"

7. Explain in detail how you have searched for information on a similar topic. Indicate what you learned in the process and discuss how your search was similar to and different from Joyce's.

8. Explain in detail how you searched for any information on the Internet: genealogy, career, consumer goods, the truth about _____.

9. Conduct a search on the Internet, keep notes of your experience, and write an informative process analysis detailing what went right and wrong. Here are some health topics: Angelman's syndrome, hepatitis C, prostatitis, carcinoma, tonsil removal, herbs as food supplements.

"Attitude"

10. Using Keillor's essay as a model of form and tone, write a process analysis about how one could master a winning attitude in other fields: a particular vocation, education (either in the role of educator or student), another sport (basketball, football, tennis, golf, skating, soccer, track and field).

11. Write about professional wrestling as a "sport" that owes much of its popularity to the bizarre exhibitions of "winning attitude." Explain exactly what steps those professional wrestlers take. Name wrestlers and describe antics.

"Stars"

12. Write an informative process analysis essay about another topic from the physical sciences: earthquake, tsunami, hurricane, tornado, volcano eruption, famous flood, mountain building, tectonic plates.

Career-Related Topics

13. Explain how to display, package, sell, or demonstrate a product.

14. Explain how to perform a service or to repair or install a product.

15. Explain the procedure for operating a machine, computer, piece of equipment, or other device.

16. Explain how to manufacture, construct, or cook something.

General Topics Most of the following topics are directive as they are phrased. However, each can be transformed into a how-it-was-done informative topic by personalizing it and explaining stage by stage how you, someone else, or a group did something. For example, you could write either a directive process analysis about how to deal with an obnoxious person or an informative process analysis about how you or someone else dealt with an obnoxious person. Keep in mind that the two types of process analysis are often blended, especially in the personal approach. Many of these topics will be more interesting to you and your readers if they are personalized.

Select one of the following topics and write a process analysis essay. Most of the topics require some narrowing to be treated in a brief essay. For example, writing about playing baseball is too broad; writing about how to throw a curve ball may be manageable.

17. How to end a relationship without hurting someone's feelings.
18. How to pass a test for a driver's license
19. How to get a job at _____
20. How to eat _____
21. How to perform a magic trick
22. How to repair _____
23. How to assemble _____
24. How to learn about another culture
25. How to approach someone you would like to know better

Writer's Guidelines: Process Analysis

1. Decide whether your process analysis is mainly directive or informative, and be appropriately consistent in using pronouns and other designations.

    - For the directive analysis, use the second person, addressing the reader as *you*. The *you* may be understood, even if it is not written.

    - For the informative analysis, use the first person, speaking as *I* or *we*, or the third person, speaking about the subject as *he, she, it,* or *they*, or by name.

2. Consider using these basic forms.

    Directive
    I. Preparation
        A.
        B.
    II. Steps
        A.
        B.
        C.

    Informative
    I. Background
        A.
        B.
    II. Sequence
        A.
        B.
        C.

3. Listing is a useful prewriting activity for this form. Begin with the Roman numeral headings indicated in guideline number 2.

4. The order of a process analysis will usually be chronological (time based) in some sense. Certain transitional words are commonly used to promote coherence: *first, second, third, then, soon, now, next, finally, at last, therefore,* and *consequently.*

10

Comparison and Contrast: Showing Similarities and Differences

Comparison and Contrast Defined, p. 250

Generating Topics and Working with the 4 *P*'s, p. 250
Purpose, p. 250
Points, p. 251
Patterns, p. 252
Presentation, p. 253

Connecting Sources and Writing, p. 255
Student Essay: "A Fast Food Face-Off," p. 255
Practicing Patterns of Comparison and Contrast, p. 258
Student Documented Essay: "Struggling Against Silence," p. 259
"The Baby Boomers and the Generation Xers," p. 261
"That Lean and Hungry Look," p. 265
"Two Ways of Viewing the River," p. 268
"Everyday Use," p. 270

Topics for Writing Comparison and Contrast, p. 279
Writing Process Worksheet, p. 279
Source-Based Topics, p. 279
Career-Related Topics, p. 281
General Topics, p. 281

Writer's Guidelines, p. 282

THE QUIGMANS by Buddy Hickerson

© Tribune Media Services, Inc. All Rights Reserved. Reprinted with permission.

Comparison and Contrast Defined

Comparison and contrast is a method of showing similarities and differences between subjects. *Comparison* is concerned with organizing and developing points of similarity; *contrast* serves the same function for differences. In some instances, a writing assignment may require that you cover only similarities or only differences. Occasionally, an instructor may ask you to separate one from the other. Usually, you will combine them within the larger design of your paragraph or essay. For convenience, the term *comparison* is often used for both comparison and contrast, because both use the same techniques and are regularly combined into one operation.

This chapter will help you deal with topics and choose strategies for developing comparison and contrast.

Generating Topics and Working with the 4 *P*'s

Comparison and contrast are basic to your thinking. In your daily activities, you consider similarities and differences between persons, things, concepts, political leaders, doctors, friends, instructors, schools, nations, classes, movies, and so on. You naturally turn to comparison and contrast to solve problems and make decisions in your life and in your writing. Because you have had so much experience with comparing, finding a topic to write about is likely to be easy and interesting. Freewriting, brainstorming, and listing will help you generate topics that are especially workable and appropriate for particular assignments.

Many college writing assignments will specify a topic or direct you to choose one from a list. Regardless of the source of your topic, the procedure for developing your ideas by comparison and contrast is the same. That procedure can appropriately be called the 4 *P*'s: purpose, points, patterns, and presentation.

Purpose

In most of your writing, the main purpose will be either to inform or to persuade.

Informative Writing

If you want to explain something about a topic by showing each subject in relationship with others, then your purpose is informative. For example, you might be comparing two composers, Beethoven and Mozart. Both were musical geniuses, so you might decide that it would be senseless to argue that one is superior to the other. Instead, you choose to reveal interesting information about both by showing them in relation to each other. The emphasis of your writing would be on insights into their characteristics, the insights heightened because the characteristics are placed alongside each other.

Persuasive Writing

If you want to show that one actor, one movie, one writer, one president, one product, or one idea is better than another, your purpose will be persuasive. Your argument will take shape as you write, beginning with emphasis in the topic sentence or thesis and reinforcement by repetition throughout your paper, in each case indicating that one side is superior.

Let's say, as an extended illustration, that you are taking a course in twentieth-century European history and you are asked to write about two leaders. You choose to write about Mussolini and Hitler as dictators. In freewriting, you discover that you know quite a bit about the two leaders. By brainstorming, you come up with some specific information.

Who?	Mussolini and Hitler
What?	fascist leaders, racists—with Hitler being more extreme
Where?	in Italy and Germany, respectively
When?	the decade before and during World War II
Why?	greed, morals, possible psychological problems, with Hitler being more extreme
How?	setting up totalitarian states

You tentatively decide that your purpose will be to persuade readers that, although both men were fascists, Hitler was more extreme in all important respects. If you need more information, you will have to consult your textbooks, your lecture notes, or sources in the library or on the Internet.

Points

The points are the ideas that will be applied somewhat equally to both sides of your comparison and contrast. They begin to emerge in freewriting, take on more precision in brainstorming, acquire a main position in listing, and assume the major part of the framework in the outline.

When writing on an assigned topic based on lectures and reading, you will probably be able to decide these points quickly. The subject material itself may dictate the points. For example, if you were comparing the governments of the United States and Great Britain, you would probably use these three points: executive, legislative, and judicial.

Using listing as a technique for finding points is simple. Follow this procedure:

1. Select one side of your two-part subject (the side you know better) and compose a list in relation to a basic treatment you expect to extend to your comparative study.

<u>Hitler</u> <u>was a fascist dictator with racist views.</u>
subject　　　　　　　　**treatment**

2. Make a list of points (about Hitler as a fascist dictator).

   commitment

   racial views

   beliefs

   fascism

   flexibility

   militaristic designs

3. Decide which points can also be applied in a useful way to the other subject, in this case, Mussolini. (You can also reverse the approach.) In this instance, all of the points can be applied in a useful way.

4. Select the points for your thesis.

   racial views

   commitment

   militaristic designs

5. Incorporate these points into a thesis. (Your final thesis need not specify the points.)

<u>Although Mussolini and Hitler were both fascist dictators,</u>
subject

<u>they were significantly different in their racial views,</u>
treatment (with points)

<u>commitment, and militaristic designs.</u>

You now have a purpose and points. An outline or outline alternative will help you select and develop a pattern for your comparison.

Patterns

Now you will choose between two basic patterns of organization: (1) subject by subject (opposing) or (2) point by point (alternating). In long papers you may mix the two patterns, but in most college assignments, you will probably select just one and make it your basic organizational plan.

Figure 10.1
Subject-by-Subject Organization

Introduction with thesis

I. Mussolini
   A. Racial views
   B. Commitment
   C. Militaristic designs

II. Hitler
   A. Racial views
   B. Commitment
   C. Militaristic designs

Conclusion

Figure 10.2
Point-by-Point Organization

Introduction with thesis

I. Racial views
   A. Mussolini
   B. Hitler

II. Commitment
   A. Mussolini
   B. Hitler

III. Militaristic designs
   A. Mussolini
   B. Hitler

Conclusion

In comparison and contrast, the outline works especially well in indicting relationships and sequence. As with most other writing forms, the sequence of a comparison-and-contrast essay can be based on time, space, or emphasis. Emphasis is the most likely order.

Figures 10.1 and 10.2 show you the two patterns as they are applied to the essay.

In the subject-by-subject approach, organize your material around the subjects—the sides of the comparative study, as shown in Figure 10.1. In the point-by-point approach, organize your paper mainly around the points that you apply to the two subjects, as shown in Figure 10.2.

Presentation

The two patterns of organization—subject by subject and point by point—are equally valid, and each has its strengths for presentation of ideas.

As shown in Figure 10.1, the subject-by-subject pattern presents material in large blocks, which means the reader can see a body of material that is complete. However, if the material is also complex, the reader has the burden of remembering ideas while going from one part to the next. Parallel development of ideas and cross-references in the second portion of the essay can often offset that problem. Transitional words and phrases also help to establish coherence.

The point-by-point pattern shown in Figure 10.2 provides an immediate and direct relationship of points to subject. Therefore, it is especially useful in arguing that one side is superior to the other, in dealing with complex topics, and in working with longer compositions. But because of its systematic nature, if development is not sufficient, it can appear mechanical and monotonous. You can avoid that appearance by developing each idea thoroughly.

Some writers believe that the subject-by-subject form works best for short (paragraph-length) assignments, and the point-by-point form works best for longer pieces (essays).

In the following example, the topic of Mussolini and Hitler is presented in the final draft stage of the essay form, using a point-by-point arrangement.

Introduction with thesis

Hitler and Mussolini have often been thought of as twin dictators, but there were considerable differences between the two men and their regimes, and Hitler was more extreme. These differences become apparent when one considers their racial views, their commitment, and their militaristic designs.

Topic sentence

(Middle paragraph)

Racism is justly associated with all fascism at that time; therefore, Mussolini, along with Hitler, is implicated. It should be pointed out, however, that the Italians' blatant racism occurred after Mussolini's deep association with Hitler. Prior to that, for many years there had been no racial doctrine in Italian fascist ideology. But Hitler held racist views from the beginning of his political movement, and it was a main motive in the Nazi movement. To resolve the "Jewish problem," he eventually slaughtered at least six million people.

Topic sentence

(Middle paragraph)

Their degree of commitment to act also varied. From a distance toward the end of the war, they may have seemed quite similar, but over the span of their reigns, they were different. Mussolini merely talked and strutted for the most part. He had few fixed doctrines and increasingly accommodated himself to circumstances. But Hitler meant every bit of his bellicosity and was willing to wage the most frightful war of all time.

Topic sentence

(Middle paragraph)

A study of their involvement in that war, however, reveals striking differences. Italian fascism was comparatively restrained and conservative until the Nazi example spurred it to new activity. Mussolini talked of a militaristic policy, but he followed a more temperate course in practice and kept the peace for thirteen years, knowing that Italy could not gain from a major war. In contrast, Hitler's radical and dynamic pace hardly flagged from January 1933 to April 1945. In the process, anti-Semitism, concentration camps, and total war produced a sadistic nightmare without any parallel in the Italian experience.

Conclusion

Thus, though both were fascist, history shows the two men to be different in both ideas and actions. Only at the end of their relationship, when Mussolini succumbed to Hitler's domination, do the two leaders appear as twin dictators, but beneath appearances it is Hitler who was the true believer, the fascist dictator.

Connecting Sources and Writing

Student Essay

Daphne Lee's assignment in her freshman composition class was to write a comparison and contrast essay of 600 to 900 words. Among her topics was one on fast food establishments, in which she would be expected to use personal experience and preferences to show that one business was superior to the other in certain respects. A bit of freewriting confirmed that this was the right topic for her.

A Fast Food Face-Off

Daphne Lee

"Burger joints are all alike. Their food is all the same—salty and greasy—so who cares which one you select!" Those were the lines I rehearsed silently while pulling my car into a Wendy's parking lot somewhere in the city of Orange, California. We were on our way to the semi-annual medical checkup for my daughter Angelina when she dramatically stated that she was so hungry she could die any second now. Pathetically, I am one of those hopelessly-in-love-with-my-child kinds of mothers, so I drove around in an unfamiliar city trying to find her a McDonald's, the only fast food restaurant she would tolerate since she was two years old. Oddly, there were no McDonald's restaurants within a five-mile radius, so I hesitantly pulled up to the nearest fast food place, which turned out to be a Wendy's. Obviously, Angelina was really hungry, for she entered with me without a protest. This was our first time at a Wendy's, and I truly expected it to probably be my last. But it was during my visit to Wendy's that I changed my opinion about fast food chains. Although McDonald's and Wendy's serve about the same clientele, the restaurants are more different than similar.

When I entered Wendy's, I immediately noticed the distinct difference between Wendy's and McDonald's in their ambiance. The interior design of Wendy's is simple and plain: a few booths, tables, and chairs. Mainly earthy tones such as natural wood and leafy green surrounded me. The design offered homely comfort. No bold decorations on walls, tables, or seats demanded my attention. Another difference was the smell. When I walked into Wendy's, no familiar scent of fried foods and hamburgers greeted me. As I looked around while standing in line, I noticed how quiet the place was. There were only subdued chatterings from diners, plus some noises from the kitchen and the cashier area, but for a fast food restaurant environment Wendy's was almost silent.

On the other hand, the McDonald's interior design, including but not limited to the booth seats, tables, chairs, décor on the walls, is all done with their color scheme of bright red and yellow. It seems to grab and captivate customers' visual sensation in an instant. In the olfactory department, McDonald's is filled with the scent of French fries and burgers and is accompanied by a hint of sweetness. These odors attack customers' olfactory receptors like a typhoon and jostle their digestive systems into overdrive. Yet the most prominent difference from Wendy's is probably the noise level. At McDonald's there are always children running up and down the aisles, jumping and going wild in the Jungle Gyms, tugging and giggling under the tables—all of this punctuated by disciplinary warnings loudly "whispered" by the parents. No doubt, McDonald's is an optimal place for sensory overload.

Studying Wendy's menu, I found that, although many of the items are similar to those of McDonald's, Wendy's provides a wider selection, including some foods that wouldn't be considered fast. Among the 99-cent mainstays are baked potatoes with sour cream and chives, chili, and stuffed pitas. There is even a well-stocked salad bar. On the minus side, for dessert Wendy's has only a few selections of milk shakes and chocolate chip cookies. Predictably, McDonald's is long on the sandwich list and short on nontraditional foods. Instead of everyday specialties, their promotional items are usually restricted to certain days. But Mac wins in the dessert lineup, with two kinds of cookies, milk shakes, apple turnovers, and soft-serve ice cream decorated by an assortment of sprinkles.

Angelina and I pondered the menu for a while before placing our order. I never hesitate in McDonald's. I get a large diet Coke, we share an extra large order of French fries, and she gets a Chicken McNuggets Happy Meal. Faced with more choices at Wendy's, we decided on a Spicy Chicken Sandwich Combo that came with a large order of French fries and a large diet Coke, an orange drink, an order of Chicken Nuggets, and a baked potato loaded with sour cream and chives. Angelina did not want a Wendy's Kid's Meal because the toy was not as "cool" as the one offered at McDonald's.

After picking up the food, we took a seat near a large window for our taste test. Examining and carefully blowing on a piece of hot chicken, Angelina dipped it into the sweet and sour sauce and then took a small bite. To my surprise, she continued to eat and even started on the French fries without complaint. I was skeptical as well; I took a breath and bit into the Spicy Chicken Sandwich. I was delighted. It has a soft bun, a crispy piece of lettuce and tomato, a hint of spices, and crunchy chicken meat, not excesively greasy tasting. In contrast, the McDonald's Spicy Chicken Sandwich, which I once considered the only palatable sandwich, usually has soggier chicken meat and greasier taste, although their buns are probably better tasting than those at Wendy's. McDonald's also supplies more lettuce than Wendy's. Next, I tried the Wendy's Chicken Nuggets, and I knew why Angelina liked them. They are meatier with thinner breading than McDonald's, so they are juicier and lighter tasting than Chicken McNuggets. When it comes to the taste of the French fries, we both agreed that McDonald's is the champion, but Wendy's is the first runner-up.

This visit to Wendy's has changed my preconception about fast food restaurants. The fast food restaurants are not all the same for me, anymore. In fact, we have been exploring other fast food establishments since that visit to Wendy's. At this point, our choice or, rather, my daughter's choice has been Wendy's more frequently than McDonald's. While we think that Wendy's surpasses McDonald's in many areas, it is difficult for us not to visit McDonald's occasionally. For Angelina, there is always a "cool" toy that McDonald's is advertising, which she must have. As for me, McDonald's brings back the memories of my little baby girl's face gleaming with smiles as she excitedly played at the Jungle Gym, or the way her eyes lit up when she tasted the French fries with ketchup for the first time. The foods served in fast food places generally are considered to be unhealthful, but for busy families fast foods are likely the next best things to home-cooked meals. Now my range of choices has widened.

Exercise 1

DISCUSSION AND CRITICAL THINKING

1. Circle the thesis.

2. Is the pattern point by point or subject by subject?

3. Is Lee's purpose to inform or to persuade?

4. Based on your experiences, are Lee's assessments of Wendy's and McDonald's sound?

5. How do the first two sentences of the essay reconcile with the next-to-the-last sentence?

Practicing Patterns of Comparison and Contrast

Understanding the two basic patterns of comparison and contrast—subject by subject and point by point—and knowing which one to use for a particular assignment will serve you well in writing for all occasions.

Exercise 2 — COMPLETING PATTERNS OF COMPARISON AND CONTRAST

Fill in the blanks to complete the comparisons and contrasts in the following skeletal outlines based on "A Fast Food Face-Off."

Point by Point

   I. Ambiance

      A. Wendy's

      B. McDonald's

  II. _____

      A. Wendy's

      B. _____

 III. _____

      A. _____

      B. McDonald's

Subject by Subject

   I. Wendy's

      A. Ambiance

      B. _____

      C. Taste test

II. _____
   A. _____
   B. Menu
   C. _____

Student Documented Essay

For her comparison and contrast assignment, Lydia Hsiao was asked to read an essay of personal experience from her textbook and to relate it point by point to her life. In her textbook, *Rereading America,* she found an excerpt from *The Woman Warrior* by Maxine Hong Kingston. The result was essentially a comparative study, one that helped Hsiao understand her own struggle and triumph. Hsiao's instructor asked her to document her essay formally. (However, essays written from single textbook sources are often presented with only informal references to indicate quoted and otherwise borrowed material.)

Struggling Against Silence
Lydia Hsiao

In "Silence," a selection from Maxine Hong Kingston's autobiographical *The Woman Warrior,* the author portrays herself as an individual with timid characteristics. I have much in common with this author. Since both of us are Chinese and learned English as a second language, our experiences in school are very similar. As I read of her struggle to communicate, her thoughts blend with my thoughts and her words become my words.

We both come from a strict Chinese background and were taught that "a ready tongue is an evil" (Kingston 252). We were also taught to keep to ourselves. We were never taught to communicate with those outside our culture. This background may have caused my self-consciousness and my paralyzing fear of being embarrassed. During my first year in the United States, I attended middle school in Riverside, California. I was constantly teased about my Chinese accent, even though initially I felt certain I did not have one, for I had attended an American school in Taiwan. Perhaps my fellow students reacted as they did because I was the only Chinese girl in school. Nevertheless, as a result of this treatment, I became silent whenever possible, and if I mispronounced a word during class, I could not help but be disgusted by my own mistake, causing me even greater embarrassment. Kingston says, "[They] scared the voice away" (254). The result was that, like Kingston, my potential was for years undiscovered.

In the same way Kingston allowed silence to "[paint] layers of black over [her life]" (254), silence continued to create a thicker darkness in *my* life. It first embarrassed me; then it soon robbed me of my self-esteem. As Kingston says, "[Talking] takes up that day's courage" (252). It was almost as if silence was more than a curtain. It seemed to grow its own body and walk beside me. That silence became my sinister friend, taking advantage of my willingness to accept this cruel school life, tricking me into believing that home was the only place I could find my voice. The monster silence kept me quiet.

As my keeper, that silence also sent a message to others. It was often a signal for people not to intrude, and, of course, it was used to prevent rejection. Like Kingston, "I enjoyed the silence" (253). It concealed words that would lead to my embarrassment, sounds that might make my already cracked confidence shatter into millions of pieces like safety glass in a car crash. Thus, in Kingston's words, soon "it did not occur to me [that] I was supposed to talk" (253). But Kingston also said that "if [she couldn't] talk, [she] couldn't have a personality" (254). Thus, silence, my wicked companion that protected me from getting hurt, now led me into retreat from life.

But both Kingston and I would achieve a breakthrough against silence. Kingston defeated her silence when she became a writer and published her writings, making her voice known. I made my voice known through my high school experience. When I moved to an area where more Asians lived, I made a supreme attempt to connect and associate with people who were willing to accept my differences in speaking. I was determined not to give in to silence. Through those interactions with new friends, silence slowly lost its hold on me. However, I still often ask people whether or not I have an accent. Interestingly enough, my Chinese friends say I do, and my Caucasian friends say I do not. I can never understand why that would be the case. Maybe a Chinese accent can be detected only by someone who knows the accent, or maybe a Chinese accent is something to be expected and, therefore, some people imagine they hear it. No matter what, I am still curious and, sometimes, feeling a bit insecure. I listen to myself. Again I am not far from Kingston, who said that even when she recited her Chinese lessons, she was two persons, "one chanting, one listening."

Now, when I begin to lose confidence and the dark curtain begins to fall or the monster begins to stir (Is it one, or both?), I remind myself that the best way to fight, as Kingston says, "is not to pause or stop to end the embarrassment, [but to keep] going until . . . the last word" (255). Like Kingston, I intend "to let people know [I] have a personality and a brain" (253).

Work Cited

Kingston, Maxine Hong. "Silence." *The Woman Warrior. Rereading America.* Ed. Gary Colombo, Robert Cullen, and Bonnie Lisle. New York: Bedford/St. Martin's, 1998. 252–255.

Exercise 3

DISCUSSION AND CRITICAL THINKING

1. Is Hsiao's purpose to inform or to persuade?

2. Circle the thesis.

3. Is Hsiao's pattern of organization point by point or subject by subject?

4. Which image, the curtain or the monster, best fits her experience with silence?

5. Can silence be caused by factors other than cultural? If so, what are they?

The Baby Boomers and the Generation Xers

Philip Kotler and Gary Armstrong

Among the many influences on generational behavior is the economic. Here, Philip Kotler and Gary Armstrong, two professors of business, discuss what two groups will represent in both the work place and the marketplace of the future. This excerpt was published in *Principles of Marketing* (2000).

1. Demographics involve people, and people make up markets. Thus, marketers track demographic trends and groups carefully. Two of today's most important demographic groups are the so-called *baby boomers* and the *generation Xers*.

The Baby Boomers

2. The postwar baby boom, which began in 1946 and ran through 1964, produced 75 million babies. Since then, the baby boomers have become one of the biggest forces shaping the marketing environment. The boomers have presented a moving target, creating new markets as they grew through infancy to preadolescent, teenage, young-adult, and now middle-age years.

3. The baby boomers account for a third of the population but make up 40 percent of the work force and earn over half of all personal income. Today, the aging boomers are moving to the suburbs, settling into home ownership, and raising families. They are also reaching their peak earning and spending years. Thus, they constitute a lucrative market for housing, furniture and appliances, children's products, low-calorie foods and beverages, physical fitness products, high-priced cars, convenience products, and financial services.

4. The older boomers are now in their fifties; the younger are in their thirties. Thus, the boomers are evolving from the "youthquake generation" to the "backache generation." They're slowing up, having children, and settling down. They're experiencing the pangs of midlife and rethinking the purpose and value of their work, responsibilities, and relationships. The maturing boomers are approaching life with a new stability and reasonableness in the way they live, think, eat, and spend. The boomers have shifted their focus from the outside world to the inside world. Community and family values have become more important, and staying home with the family has become their favorite way to spend an evening. The upscale boomers still exert their affluence, but they indulge themselves in more subtle and sensible ways.

The Generation Xers

5. Some marketers think that focusing on the boomers has caused companies to overlook other important segments, especially younger consumers. Focus has shifted in recent years to a new group, those born between 1965 and 1976. Author Douglas Coupland calls them "Generation X," because they lie in the shadow of

the boomers and lack obvious distinguishing characteristics. Others call them baby busters, or twentysomethings, or Yiffies—young, individualistic, freedom-minded, few.

6   Unlike the boomers, the Xers do not share dramatic and wrenching experiences, such as the Vietnam War and Watergate, that might have unified their subculture and lifestyle. However, they do share a different set of influences. Increasing divorce rates and higher employment for mothers have made them the first generation of latchkey kids. Whereas the boomers created a sexual revolution, the Xers have lived in the age of AIDS. Having grown up during times of recession and corporate downsizing, they have developed a pessimistic economic outlook. This outlook is aggravated by problems in finding good jobs—the management ranks already are well stocked with boomers who won't retire for another 20 years or more.

7   As a result, the Xers are a more skeptical bunch, cynical of frivolous marketing pitches that promise easy success. They know better. The Xers buy lots of products, such as sweaters, boots, cosmetics, electronics, cars, fast food, beer, computers, and mountain bikes. However, their cynicism makes them more savvy shoppers. Because they often did much of the family shopping when growing up, they are experienced shoppers. Their financial pressures make them value conscious, and they like lower prices and a more functional look. The Generation Xers respond to honesty in advertising, as exemplified by Nike ads that focus on fitness and a healthy lifestyle instead of hyping shoes. They like irreverence and sass and ads that mock the traditional advertising approach.

8   Generation Xers share new cultural concerns. They care about the environment, and respond favorably to companies such as The Body Shop and Ben & Jerry's, which have proven records of environmentally and socially responsible actions. Although they seek success, the Xers are less materialistic. They want better quality of life and are more interested in job satisfaction than in sacrificing personal happiness and growth for promotion. They prize experience, not acquisition.

9   The Generation Xers will have a big impact on the work place and marketplace of the future. There are now 40 million of them poised to displace the lifestyles, culture, and materialistic values of the baby boomers. By the year 2010, they will have overtaken the baby boomers as a primary market for almost every product category.

Exercise 4 — VOCABULARY HIGHLIGHTS

Write a short definition of each word as it is used in the essay. (Paragraph numbers are given in parentheses.) Be prepared to use the words in your own sentences.

demographics (1)

constitute (3)

lucrative (3)

evolving (4)

affluence (4)

segments (5)

wrenching (6)

aggravated (6)

skeptical (7)

cynicism (7)

Exercise 5 — DISCUSSION AND CRITICAL THINKING

1. Are Kotler and Armstrong trying to inform or to persuade?

2. What is their main focus?

3. Is the pattern point by point or subject by subject?

4. Underline the sentences in the Generation Xers section that link it to the Baby Boomers section to show contrast.

5. The authors discuss Baby Boomers and Generation Xers in considerable detail. Which characteristics do you agree with and which do you not agree with? Do you know a lot of individuals within these groups that do not fit the descriptions provided in this essay?

6. Should we expect exceptions to the descriptions given for groups such as these?

7. Have you noticed any trends that have started to develop in the time since this material was written (in 2000)? If so, describe them.

That Lean and Hungry Look

Suzanne Britt

Fat people, unite! And let this essay be your bible. Put its phrases on your bumper stickers. In a weight-conscious world, Suzanne Britt has written a revolutionary tract. Either be fat or wish you were, for the fat guys and gals are the good ones. This essay was originally published in *Newsweek*, and was later published in an anthology titled *Show and Tell*.

1 Caesar was right. Thin people need watching. I've been watching them for most of my adult life, and I don't like what I see. When these narrow fellows spring at me, I quiver to my toes. Thin people come in all personalities, most of them menacing. You've got your "together" thin person, your mechanical thin person, your condescending thin person, your tsk-tsk thin person, your efficiency-expert thin person. All of them are dangerous.

2 In the first place, thin people aren't fun. They don't know how to goof off, at least in the best, fat sense of the word. They've always got to be adoing. Give them a coffee break, and they'll jog around the block. Supply them with a quiet evening at home, and they'll fix the screen door and lick S & H green stamps.* They say things like "there aren't enough hours in the day." Fat people never say that. Fat people think the day is too damn long already.

3 Thin people make me tired. They've got speedy little metabolisms that cause them to bustle briskly. They're forever rubbing their bony hands together and eyeing new problems to "tackle." I like to surround myself with sluggish, inert, easygoing fat people, the kind who believe that if you clean it up today, it'll just get dirty again tomorrow.

4 Some people say the business about the jolly fat person is a myth, that all of us chubbies are neurotic, sick, sad people. I disagree. Fat people may not be chortling all day long, but they're a hell of a lot *nicer* than the wizened and shriveled. Thin people turn surly, mean and hard at a young age because they never learn the value of a hot-fudge sundae for easing tension. Thin people don't like gooey soft things because they themselves are neither gooey nor soft. They are crunchy and dull, like carrots. They go straight to the heart of the matter while fat people let things stay all blurry and hazy and vague, the way things actually

---

*S & H green stamps were rebate stamps that could be redeemed for merchandise.

are. Thin people want to face the truth. Fat people know there is no truth. One of my thin friends is always staring at complex, unsolvable problems and saying, "The key thing is . . ." Fat people never say that. They know there isn't any such thing as the key thing about anything.

5   Thin people believe in logic. Fat people see all sides. The sides fat people see are rounded blobs, usually gray, always nebulous and truly not worth worrying about. But the thin person persists. "If you consume more calories than you burn," says one of my thin friends, "you will gain weight. It's that simple." Fat people always grin when they hear statements like that. They know better.

6   Fat people realize that life is illogical and unfair. They know very well that God is not in his heaven and all is not right with the world. If God was up there, fat people could have two doughnuts and a big orange drink anytime they wanted it.

7   Thin people have a long list of logical things they are always spouting off to me. They hold up one finger at a time as they reel off these things, so I won't lose track. They speak slowly as if to a young child. The list is long and full of holes. It contains tidbits like "get a grip on yourself," "cigarettes kill," "cholesterol clogs," "fit as a fiddle," "ducks in a row," "organize" and "sound fiscal management." Phrases like that.

8   They think these 2,000-point plans lead to happiness. Fat people know happiness is elusive at best and even if they could get the kind thin people talk about, they wouldn't want it. Wisely, fat people see that such programs are too dull, too hard, too off the mark. They are never better than a whole cheesecake.

9   Fat people know all about the mystery of life. They are the ones acquainted with the night, with luck, with fate, with playing it by ear. One thin person I know once suggested that we arrange all the parts of a jigsaw puzzle into groups according to size, shape and color. He figured this would cut the time needed to complete the puzzle at least by 50 percent. I said I wouldn't do it. One, I like to muddle through. Two, what good would it do to finish early? Three, the jigsaw puzzle isn't the important thing. The important thing is the fun of four people (one thin person included) sitting around a card table, working a jigsaw puzzle. My thin friend had no use for my list. Instead of joining us, he went outside and mulched the boxwoods. The three remaining fat people finished the puzzle and made chocolate, double-fudged brownies to celebrate.

10   The main problem with thin people is they oppress. Their good intentions, bony torsos, tight ships, neat corners, cerebral

machinations and pat solutions loom like dark clouds over the loose, comfortable, spread-out, soft world of the fat. Long after fat people have removed their coats and shoes and put their feet up on the coffee table, thin people are still sitting on the edge of the sofa, looking neat as a pin, discussing rutabagas. Fat people are heavily into fits of laughter, slapping their thighs and whooping it up, while thin people are still politely waiting for the punch line.

11   Thin people are downers. They like math and morality and reasoned evaluation of the limitations of human beings. They have their skinny little acts together. They expound, prognose, probe and prick.

12   Fat people are convivial. They will like you even if you're irregular and have acne. They will come up with a good reason why you never wrote the great American novel. They will cry in your beer with you. They will put your name in the pot. They will let you off the hook. Fat people will gab, giggle, guffaw, gallumph, gyrate and gossip. They are generous, giving and gallant. They are gluttonous and goodly and great. What you want when you're down is soft and jiggly, not muscled and stable. Fat people know this. Fat people have plenty of room. Fat people will take you in.

Exercise 6   **DISCUSSION AND CRITICAL THINKING**

1. Is Britt trying mainly to inform or to persuade?

2. Does she use the point-by-point or subject-by-subject pattern?

3. Is Britt really serious about her characterizations of fat and thin people?

4. If you were to put the issue of weight aside, what two opposing philosophies of life would still be advanced by Britt?

5. Do your experiences confirm what Britt says?

Two Ways of Viewing the River

Mark Twain

Early in his career as a journalist, Samuel Langhorne Clemens adopted the pen name Mark Twain, which means "two fathoms deep," a phrase used in making soundings on the Mississippi River. He would go on to become one of the most respected persons in American letters in a long and celebrated career. Twain's most famous book is The Adventures of Huckleberry Finn. *This passage is taken from his autobiographical* Life on the Mississippi. *Published in 1883, it is written from the perspective of Twain as a riverboat pilot.*

1   Now when I had mastered the language of this water and had come to know every trifling feature that bordered the great river as familiarly as I knew the letters of the alphabet, I had made a valuable acquisition. But I had lost something, too. I had lost something which could never be restored to me while I lived. All the grace, the beauty, the poetry, had gone out of the majestic river! I still kept in mind a certain wonderful sunset which I witnessed when steamboating was new to me. A broad expanse of the river was turned to blood; in the middle distance the red hue brightened into gold, through which a solitary log came floating, black and conspicuous; in one place a long, slanting mark lay sparkling upon the water; in another the surface was broken by boiling, tumbling rings, that were as many-tinted as an opal; where the ruddy flush was faintest, was a smooth spot that was covered with graceful circles and radiating lines, ever so delicately traced; the shore on our left was densely wooded and the somber shadow that fell from this forest was broken in one place by a long, ruffled trail that shone like silver; and high above the forest wall a clean-stemmed dead tree waved a single leafy bough that glowed like a flame in the unobstructed splendor that was flowing from the sun. There were graceful curves, reflected images, woody heights, soft distances, and over the whole scene, far and near, the dissolving lights drifted steadily, enriching it every passing moment with new marvels of coloring.

2   I stood like one bewitched. I drank it in, in a speechless rapture. The world was new to me and I had never seen anything like this at home. But as I have said, a day came when I began to cease from noting the glories and the charms which the moon and the

sun and the twilight wrought upon the river's face; another day came when I ceased altogether to note them. Then, if that sunset scene had been repeated, I should have looked upon it without rapture, and should have commented upon it inwardly after this fashion: "This sun means that we are going to have wind tomorrow; that floating log means that the river is rising, small thanks to it; that slanting mark on the water refers to a bluff reef which is going to kill somebody's steamboat one of these nights, if it keeps on stretching out like that; those tumbling 'boils' show a dissolving bar and a changing channel there; the lines and circles in the slick water over yonder are a warning that that troublesome place is shoaling up dangerously; that silver streak in the shadow of the forest is the 'break' from a new snag and he has located himself in the very best place he could have found to fish for steamboats; that tall dead tree, with a single living branch, is not going to last long, and then how is a body ever going to get through this blind place at night without the friendly old landmark?"

3   No, the romance and beauty were all gone from the river. All the value any feature of it had for me now was the amount of usefulness it could furnish toward compassing the safe piloting of a steamboat. Since those days, I have pitied doctors from my heart. What does the lovely flush in a beauty's cheek mean to a doctor but a "break" that ripples above some deadly disease? Are not all her visible charms sown thick with what are to him the signs and symbols of hidden decay? Does he ever see her beauty at all, or doesn't he simply view her professionally and comment upon her unwholesome condition all to himself? And doesn't he sometimes wonder whether he has gained most or lost most by learning his trade?

Exercise 7   **VOCABULARY HIGHLIGHTS**

Write a short definition of each word as it is used in the essay. (Paragraph numbers are given in parentheses.) Be prepared to use the words in your own sentences.

trifling (1)	radiating (1)
acquisition (1)	somber (1)
conspicuous (1)	splendor (1)
opal (1)	wrought (2)
ruddy (1)	compassing (3)

Exercise 8 **DISCUSSION AND CRITICAL THINKING**

1. What is Twain's subject?

2. Is he trying to inform or to persuade?

3. Does he use the point-by-point or the subject-by-subject pattern?

4. What technique (conjunctive adverbs, such as *however,* or *consequently;* repeated words in the same order; italics, numbered entries) does he use in paragraph 2 to show the clear, parallel contrasts with items in paragraph 1? Give some examples.

5. Paragraph 1 deals with aesthetics, that which is beautiful, and the language is appropriate for that concern. Paragraph 2 comes with the voice of reason and knowledge and deals with more objective description. Give some examples of the evocative (emotional) language in the first paragraph and the more objective language in the second paragraph.

    Emotional word choices:

    Objective word choices:

6. How does the tone (the way the author regards his subject material and his audience) change from paragraph 1 to paragraph 2?

Everyday Use
Alice Walker

This story is concerned with differences, differences of many kinds. It begins and ends with a mother's consideration of two very different daughters, one lacking in self-esteem and the other in humility. Finally, the mother had to take sides. So will you, as a reader. In 1983, the author, Alice Walker, won the Pulitzer Prize for *The Color Purple.* Because this short story is a narrative account, you can use the basic framework presented in Chapter 5—situation, conflict, struggle, outcome, meaning—for your analysis.

1. I will wait for her in the yard that Maggie and I made so clean and wavy yesterday afternoon. A yard like this is more comfortable than most people know. It is not just a yard. It is like an extended living room. When the hard clay is swept clean as a floor and the fine sand around the edges lined with tiny, irregular grooves, anyone can come and sit and look up into the elm tree and wait for the breezes that never come inside the house.

2. Maggie will be nervous until after her sister goes: she will stand hopelessly in corners, homely and ashamed of the burn scars down her arms and legs, eyeing her sister with a mixture of envy and awe. She thinks her sister has held life always in the palm of one hand, that "no" is a word the world never learned to say to her.

3. You've no doubt seen those TV shows where the child who has "made it" is confronted, as a surprise, by her own mother and father, tottering in weakly from backstage. (A pleasant surprise, of course: What would they do if parent and child came on the show only to curse out and insult each other?) On TV mother and child embrace and smile into each other's faces. Sometimes the mother and father weep, the child wraps them in her arms and leans across the table to tell how she would not have made it without their help. I have seen these programs.

4. Sometimes I dream a dream in which Dee and I are suddenly brought together on a TV program of this sort. Out of a dark and soft-seated limousine I am ushered into a bright room filled with many people. There I meet a smiling, gray, sporty man like Johnny Carson* who shakes my hand and tells me what a fine girl I have. Then we are on the stage and Dee is embracing me with tears in her eyes. She pins on my dress a large orchid, even though she has told me once that she thinks orchids are tacky flowers.

5. In real life I am a large, big-boned woman with rough, man-working hands. In the winter I wear flannel nightgowns to bed and overalls during the day. I can kill and clean a hog as mercilessly as a man. My fat keeps me hot in zero weather. I can work outside all day, breaking ice to get water for washing; I can eat pork liver cooked over the open fire minutes after it comes steaming from the hog. One winter I knocked a bull calf straight in the brain between the eyes with a sledge hammer and had the meat hung up to chill before nightfall. But of course all this does not show on television. I am the way my daughter would want me to be: a hundred pounds lighter, my skin like an uncooked barley

---

*Johnny Carson was a late-night television personality.

pancake. My hair glistens in the hot bright lights. Johnny Carson has much to do to keep up with my quick and witty tongue.

6   But this is a mistake. I know even before I wake up. Who ever knew a Johnson with a quick tongue? Who can even imagine me looking a strange white man in the eye? It seems to me I have talked to them always with one foot raised in flight, with my head turned in whichever way is farthest from them. Dee, though. She would always look anyone in the eye. Hesitation was no part of her nature.

7   "How do I look, Mama?" Maggie says, showing just enough of her thin body enveloped in pink skirt and red blouse for me to know she's there, almost hidden by the door.

8   "Come out into the yard," I say.

9   Have you ever seen a lame animal, perhaps a dog run over by some careless person rich enough to own a car, sidle up to someone who is ignorant enough to be kind to him? That is the way my Maggie walks. She has been like this, chin on chest, eyes on ground, feet in shuffle, ever since the fire that burned the other house to the ground.

10   Dee is lighter than Maggie, with nicer hair and a fuller figure. She's a woman now, though sometimes I forget. How long ago was it that the other house burned? Ten, twelve years? Sometimes I can still hear the flames and feel Maggie's arms sticking to me, her hair smoking and her dress falling off her in little black papery flakes. Her eyes seemed stretched open, blazed open by the flames reflected in them. And Dee. I see her standing off under the sweet gum tree she used to dig gum out of; a look of concentration on her face as she watched the last dingy gray board of the house fall in toward the red-hot brick chimney. Why don't you do a dance around the ashes? I'd wanted to ask her. She had hated the house that much.

11   I used to think she hated Maggie, too. But that was before we raised the money, the church and me, to send her to Augusta to school. She used to read to us without pity; forcing words, lies, other folks' habits, whole lives upon us two, sitting trapped and ignorant underneath her voice. She washed us in a river of make-believe, burned us with a lot of knowledge we didn't necessarily need to know. Pressed us to her with the serious way she read, to shove us away at just the moment, like dimwits, we seemed about to understand.

12   Dee wanted nice things. A yellow organdy dress to wear to her graduation from high school; black pumps to match a green suit she'd made from an old suit somebody gave me. She was deter-

mined to stare down any disaster in her efforts. Her eyelids would not flicker for minutes at a time. Often I fought off the temptation to shake her. At sixteen she had a style of her own: and knew what style was.

13   I never had an education myself. After second grade the school was closed down. Don't ask me why: in 1927 colored asked fewer questions than they do now. Sometimes Maggie reads to me. She stumbles along good-naturedly but can't see well. She knows she is not bright. Like good looks and money, quickness passed her by. She will marry John Thomas (who has mossy teeth in an earnest face) and then I'll be free to sit here and I guess just sing church songs to myself. Although I never was a good singer. Never could carry a tune. I was always better at a man's job. I used to love to milk till I was hooked in the side in '49. Cows are soothing and slow and don't bother you, unless you try to milk them the wrong way.

14   I have deliberately turned my back on the house. It is three rooms, just like the one that burned, except the roof is tin; they don't make shingle roofs any more. There are no real windows, just some holes cut in the sides, like the portholes in a ship, but not round and not square, with rawhide holding the shutters up on the outside. This house is in a pasture, too, like the other one. No doubt when Dee sees it she will want to tear it down. She wrote me once that no matter where we "choose" to live, she will manage to come see us. But she will never bring her friends. Maggie and I thought about this and Maggie asked me, "Mama, when did Dee ever *have* any friends?"

15   She had a few. Furtive boys in pink shirts hanging about on washday after school. Nervous girls who never laughed. Impressed with her they worshiped the well-turned phrase, the cute shape, the scalding humor that erupted like bubbles in lye. She read to them.

16   When she was courting Jimmy T she didn't have much time to pay to us, but turned all her faultfinding power on him. He *flew* to marry a cheap city girl from a family of ignorant flashy people. She hardly had time to recompose herself.

17   When she comes I will meet—but there they are!

18   Maggie attempts to make a dash for the house, in her shuffling way, but I stay her with my hand. "Come back here," I say. And she stops and tries to dig a well in the sand with her toe.

19   It is hard to see them clearly through the strong sun. But even the first glimpse of leg out of the car tells me it is Dee. Her feet

were always neat-looking, as if God himself had shaped them with a certain style. From the other side of the car comes a short, stocky man. Hair is all over his head a foot long and hanging from his chin like a kinky mule tail. I hear Maggie suck in her breath, "Uhnnnh," is what it sounds like. Like when you see the wriggling end of a snake just in front of your foot on the road. "Uhnnnh."

20   Dee next. A dress down to the ground, in this hot weather. A dress so loud it hurts my eyes. There are yellows and oranges enough to throw back the light of the sun. I feel my whole face warming from the heat waves it throws out. Earrings gold, too, and hanging down to her shoulders. Bracelets dangling and making noises when she moves her arm up to shake the folds of the dress out of her armpits. The dress is loose and flows, and as she walks closer, I like it. I hear Maggie go "Uhnnnh" again. It is her sister's hair. It stands straight up like the wool on a sheep. It is black as night and around the edges are two long pigtails that rope about like small lizards disappearing behind her ears.

21   "Wa-su-zo-Tean-o!" she says, coming on in that gliding way the dress makes her move. The short stocky fellow with the hair to his navel is all grinning and he follows up with "Asalamalakim, my mother and sister!" He moves to hug Maggie but she falls back, right up against the back of my chair. I feel her trembling there and when I look up I see the perspiration falling off her chin.

22   "Don't get up," says Dee. Since I am stout it takes something of a push. You can see me trying to move a second or two before I make it. She turns, showing white heels through her sandals, and goes back to the car. Out she peeks next with a Polaroid. She stoops down quickly and lines up picture after picture of me sitting there in front of the house with Maggie cowering behind me. She never takes a shot without making sure the house is included. When a cow comes nibbling around the edge of the yard she snaps it and me and Maggie *and* the house. Then she puts the Polaroid in the back seat of the car, and comes up and kisses me on the forehead.

23   Meanwhile Asalamalakim is going through motions with Maggie's hand. Maggie's hand is as limp as a fish, and probably as cold, despite the sweat, and she keeps trying to pull it back. It looks like Asalamalakim wants to shake hands but wants to do it fancy. Or maybe he don't know how people shake hands. Anyhow, he soon gives up on Maggie.

24   "Well," I say. "Dee."

25   "No, Mama," she says. "Not 'Dee,' Wangero Leewanika Kemanjo!"

26   "What happened to 'Dee'?" I wanted to know.

27 "She's dead," Wangero said. "I couldn't bear it any longer, being named after the people who oppress me."

28 "You know as well as me you was named after your aunt Dicie," I said. Dicie is my sister. She named Dee. We called her "Big Dee" after Dee was born.

29 "But who was *she* named after?" asked Wangero.

30 "I guess after Grandma Dee," I said.

31 "And who was she named after?" asked Wangero.

32 "Her mother," I said, and saw Wangero was getting tired. "That's about as far back as I can trace it," I said. Though, in fact, I probably could have carried it back beyond the Civil War through the branches.

33 "Well," said Asalamalakim, "there you are."

34 "Uhnnnh," I heard Maggie say.

35 "There I was not," I said, "before 'Dicie' cropped up in our family, so why should I try to trace it that far back?"

36 He just stood there grinning, looking down on me like somebody inspecting a Model A car. Every once in a while he and Wangero sent eye signals over my head.

37 "How do you pronounce this name?" I asked.

38 "You don't have to call me by it if you don't want to," said Wangero.

39 "Why shouldn't I?" I asked. "If that's what you want us to call you, we'll call you."

40 "I know it might sound awkward at first," said Wangero.

41 "I'll get used to it," I said. "Ream it out again."

42 Well, soon we got the name out of the way. Asalamalakim had a name twice as long and three times as hard. After I tripped over it two or three times he told me to just call him Hakim-a-barber. I wanted to ask him was he a barber, but I didn't really think he was, so I didn't ask.

43 "You must belong to those beef-cattle peoples down the road," I said. They said "Asalamalakim" when they met you, too, but they didn't shake hands. Always too busy: feeding the cattle, fixing the fences, putting up salt-lick shelters, throwing down hay. When the white folks poisoned some of the herd the men stayed up all night with rifles in their hands. I walked a mile and a half just to see the sight.

44 Hakim-a-barber said, "I accept some of their doctrines, but farming and raising cattle is not my style." (They didn't tell me, and I didn't ask, whether Wangero (Dee) had really gone and married him.)

45 We sat down to eat and right away he said he didn't eat collards and pork was unclean. Wangero, though, went on through

the chitlins and corn bread, the greens and everything else. She talked a blue streak over the sweet potatoes. Everything delighted her. Even the fact that we still used the benches her daddy made for the table when we couldn't afford to buy chairs.

46 "Oh, Mama!" she cried. Then turned to Hakim-a-barber. "I never knew how lovely these benches are. You can feel the rump prints," she said, running her hands underneath her and along the bench. Then she gave a sigh and her hand closed over Grandma Dee's butter dish. "That's it!" she said, "I knew there was something I wanted to ask you if I could have." She jumped up from the table and went over in the corner where the churn stood, the milk in it clabber by now. She looked at the churn and looked at it.

47 "This churn top is what I need," she said. "Didn't Uncle Buddy whittle it out of a tree you all used to have?"

48 "Yes," I said.

49 "Uh huh," she said happily. "And I want the dasher, too."

50 "Uncle Buddy whittle that, too?" asked the barber.

51 Dee (Wangero) looked up at me.

52 "Aunt Dee's first husband whittled the dash," said Maggie so low you almost couldn't hear her. "His name was Henry, but they called him Stash."

53 Maggie's brain is like an elephant's," Wangero said, laughing. "I can use the churn top as a centerpiece for the alcove table," she said, sliding a plate over the churn, "and I'll think of something artistic to do with the dasher."

54 When she finished wrapping the dasher the handle stuck out. I took it for a moment in my hands. You didn't even have to look close to see where hands pushing the dasher up and down to make butter had left a kind of sink in the wood. In fact, there were a lot of small sinks; you could see where thumbs and fingers had sunk into the wood. It was beautiful light yellow wood, from a tree that grew in the yard where Big Dee and Stash had lived.

55 After dinner Dee (Wangero) went to the trunk at the foot of my bed and started rifling through it. Maggie hung back in the kitchen over the dishpan. Out came Wangero with two quilts. They had been pieced by Grandma Dee and then Big Dee and me had hung them on the quilt frames on the front porch and quilted them. One was in the Lone Star pattern. The other was Walk Around the Mountain. In both of them were scraps of dresses Grandma Dee had worn fifty and more years ago. Bits and pieces of Grandpa Jarrell's Paisley shirts. And one teeny faded blue piece, about the size of a penny matchbox, that was from Great Grandpa Ezra's uniform that he wore in the Civil War.

56   "Mama," Wangero said sweet as a bird. "Can I have these old quilts?"

57   I heard something fall in the kitchen, and a minute later the kitchen door slammed.

58   "Why don't you take one or two of the others?" I asked. "These old things was just done by me and Big Dee from some tops your grandma pieced before she died."

59   "No," said Wangero. "I don't want those. They are stitched around the borders by machine."

60   "That'll make them last better," I said.

61   "That's not the point," said Wangero. "These are all pieces of dresses Grandma used to wear. She did all this stitching by hand. Imagine!" She held the quilts securely in her arms, stroking them.

62   "Some of the pieces, like those lavender ones, come from old clothes her mother handed down to her," I said, moving up to touch the quilts. Dee (Wangero) moved back just enough so that I couldn't reach the quilts. They already belonged to her.

63   "Imagine!" she breathed again, clutching them closely to her bosom.

64   "The truth is," I said, "I promised to give them quilts to Maggie, for when she marries John Thomas."

65   She gasped like a bee had stung her.

66   "Maggie can't appreciate these quilts!" she said. "She'd probably be backward enough to put them to everyday use."

67   "I reckon she would," I said. "God knows I been saving 'em for long enough with nobody using 'em. I hope she will!" I didn't want to bring up how I had offered Dee (Wangero) a quilt when she went away to college. Then she had told me they were old-fashioned, out of style.

68   "But they're *priceless!*" she was saying now, furiously; for she has a temper. "Maggie would put them on the bed and in five years they'd be in rags. Less than that!"

69   "She can always make some more," I said. "Maggie knows how to quilt."

70   Dee (Wangero) looked at me with hatred. "You just will not understand. The point is these quilts, *these* quilts!"

71   "Well," I said, stumped. "What would *you* do with them?"

72   "Hang them," she said. As if that was the only thing you *could* do with quilts.

73   Maggie by now was standing in the door. I could almost hear the sound her feet made as they scraped over each other.

74   "She can have them, Mama," she said, like somebody used to never winning anything, or having anything reserved for her. "I can 'member Grandma Dee without the quilts."

75 I looked at her hard. She had filled her bottom lip with checkerberry snuff and it gave her face a kind of dopey, hangdog look. It was Grandma Dee and Big Dee who taught her how to quilt herself. She stood there with her scarred hands hidden in the folds of her skirt. She looked at her sister with something like fear but she wasn't mad at her. This was Maggie's portion. This was the way she knew God to work.

76 When I looked at her like that something hit me in the top of my head and ran down to the soles of my feet. Just like when I'm in church and the spirit of God touches me and I get happy and shout. I did something I never had done before: hugged Maggie to me, then dragged her on into the room, snatched the quilts out of Miss Wangero's hands and dumped them into Maggie's lap. Maggie just sat there on my bed with her mouth open.

77 "Take one or two of the others," I said to Dee.

78 But she turned without a word and went out to Hakim-a-barber.

79 "You just don't understand," she said, as Maggie and I came out to the car.

80 "What don't I understand?" I wanted to know.

81 "Your heritage," she said. And then she turned to Maggie, kissed her, and said, "You ought to try to make something of yourself, too, Maggie. It's really a new day for us. But from the way you and Mama still live you'd never know it."

82 She put on some sunglasses that hid everything above the tip of her nose and her chin.

83 Maggie smiled; maybe at the sunglasses. But a real smile, not scared. After we watched the car dust settle I asked Maggie to bring me a dip of snuff. And then the two of us sat there just enjoying, until it was time to go in the house and go to bed.

Exercise 9 — DISCUSSION AND CRITICAL THINKING

1. How is the narrator's life different from the television fantasy she relates?

2. How is the narrator different from each of her two children?

3. What is the significance of the characters' names and name changes?

4. What does the incident of the house burning reveal about Dee?

5. When Dee returns, in what way does she seem to regain a spontaneous connection with her family experiences?

6. What do the quilts represent?

7. How does the idea of the quilts relate to the idea of the burning home?

8. What is the significance of Dee's taking pictures of the house and her mother and sister?

9. Do you blame Dee for wanting to leave the simple, impoverished country life? Why or why not?

10. What is lacking in Dee's character?

11. In the end, does the narrator simply favor one daughter over the other or does she discover something deeper?

✎ Topics for Writing Comparison and Contrast

Writing Process Worksheet You will find a Writing Process Worksheet on page 27. It can be photocopied and enlarged, filled in, and submitted with each assignment if your instructor directs you to do so.

Source-Based Topics Each essay developed from these suggested source-based topics should include at least one reference to the reading selection by the author's name and the title. Quotations should be enclosed in quotation marks. Follow your instructor's directions in documenting the ideas you borrow. Whether you use informal or formal documentation, the form is not complicated, and you will soon learn to use it for these essays without checking each time. See pages 73 and 74 for a discussion of MLA style and informal documentation.

Underlining and annotating reading selections will help you in finding support material. In prewriting brief essays, consider marking your outline to indicate where you will use quotations or other borrowed ideas. If the quotations or reworded statements are short and few, you could even insert them inside parentheses or circles in your outline; if you do, also include the author's last name and the page number. A sound system, consistently used, will save you time and ensure technically strong papers.

"A Fast Food Face-Off"

1. Using this essay as a model, write a comparison and contrast essay about two other fast food establishments, two supermarkets, two department stores, or two products. Consider personalizing it as Lee did. You may want to find some supporting information in the library or on the Internet.

2. Write a comparative study of two fast food places, with a focus on healthfulness of their products. Most establishments have charts on fat and calorie content of their main dishes. The Internet has numerous sites devoted to health and eating out.

"Struggling Against Silence"

3. Find an essay of personal experience in this textbook (consult the table of contents) and write a comparison and contrast between your experience and views and those of the author. Use formal or informal documentation, as directed by your instructor. Use ample quotations and references.

"The Baby Boomers and the Generation Xers"

4. Using the characteristics (points) from this essay, write a well-structured statement in which you provide examples of people you know who represent the two generations. You may want to focus on one person for each generation.

5. If you disagree with the generalizations offered by the authors, use examples and reasoning to write a comparison and contrast essay of your views and those in this essay.

"That Lean and Hungry Look"

6. Using Britt's views (points) and some examples from your own experience, write an essay of comparison and contrast to argue that she is correct.

7. Using Britt's views (points) and some examples from your own experience, write an essay of comparison and contrast to argue that she is incorrect.

8. Using Britt's views in a comparison and contrast essay, argue that she is wrong about the weight aspect but right about her philosophy of life.

"Two Ways of Viewing the River"

9. Using Twain's essay as a model, write about something that you have experienced from both an emotional and a rational view or that you have encountered before and after you became knowledgeable. Examples include a piece of music before you studied music and after you studied music; a triple-cheeseburger before you studied nutrition and after you studied nutrition; birds singing before you studied ornithology and after you studied ornithology; an election before you became deeply involved in politics and after you became deeply involved in politics; a sporting event before you understood the business operations and after you understood the business operations.

"Everyday Use"

10. Write a comparison and contrast essay about the two daughters in this short story.

11. Write a comparison and contrast essay about a person you know and one character from the short story.

Career-Related Topics

12. Compare and contrast two pieces of office equipment or two services with the purpose of showing that one is better.

13. Compare and contrast two management styles or two working styles.

14. Compare and contrast two career fields to argue that one is better for you.

15. Compare and contrast a public school with a business.

16. Compare and contrast two computers or two software programs.

General Topics

Compare and contrast one or more of the following topics. After you limit your topic, personalize it or do some research so that you will have specific support.

17. Two generations of college students

18. Two automobiles, bicycles, motorcycles, snowmobiles

19. Two types of (or specific) police officers, doctors, teachers, preachers, students, athletes

20. Two famous persons—authors, generals, actors, athletes
21. Two philosophies, religions, ideologies
22. Downhill skiing and snowboarding
23. Living at college and living at home
24. A small college and a large college or a four-year college and a community college
25. Two gangs or two kinds of gangs
26. Two roommates, neighbors, friends, dates
27. Two movies, television shows, commercials, songs, singers
28. Dating and going steady, living together and being married, a specific person before and after marriage
29. Shopping malls and neighborhood stores
30. Two political candidates or office holders

Writer's Guidelines: Comparison and Contrast

1. *Purpose:* During the exploration of your topic, define your purpose clearly.
   - Decide whether you are writing a work that is primarily comparison, primarily contrast, or balanced.
   - Determine whether your main purpose is to inform or to persuade.
2. *Points*
   - Indicate your points of comparison or contrast, perhaps by listing.
   - Eliminate irrelevant points.
3. *Pattern*
   - Select the subject-by-subject or the point-by-point pattern after considering your topic and planned treatment. The point-by-point pattern is usually preferred in essays. Only in long papers is there likely to be a mixture of patterns.
   - Compose an outline reflecting the pattern you select.
   - Use this basic subject-by-subject pattern:

     I. Subject X
        A. Point 1
        B. Point 2

II. Subject Y
   A. Point 1
   B. Point 2

- Use this basic point-by-point pattern:

I. Point 1
   A. Subject X
   B. Subject Y
II. Point 2
   A. Subject X
   B. Subject Y

4. *Presentation*

- Give each point more or less equal treatment. Attention to each part of the outline will usually ensure balanced development.
- Use transitional words and phrases to indicate comparison and contrast and to establish coherence.
- Use a carefully stated topic sentence for a paragraph and a clear thesis for an essay. Each developmental paragraph should have a topic sentence broad enough to embrace its content.

Cause and Effect: Determining Reasons and Outcomes

Writing Cause and Effect, p. 285
- Exploring and Organizing, p. 285
- Composing a Thesis, p. 286
- Writing an Outline, p. 286
- Considering Kinds of Causes and Effects, p. 286
- Evaluating the Importance of Sequence, p. 287
- Introducing Ideas and Working with Patterns, p. 288

Connecting Sources and Writing, p. 289
- Student Essay: "Kick Me! Kiss Me!" p. 289
- Practicing Patterns of Cause and Effect, p. 291
- Student Documented Essay: "It's Time to KO Boxing," p. 293
- Multiple Sources on Love, Marriage, and Divorce, p. 295
  - "Why Marriages Fail," p. 296
  - "Romantic Love, Courtship, and Marriage," p. 301
  - "Female Mea Culpa," p. 305
  - "His Marriage and Hers: Childhood Roots," p. 308

Topics for Writing Cause and Effect, p. 313
- Writing Process Worksheet, p. 313
- Source-Based Topics, p. 313
- Career-Related Topics, p. 316
- General Topics, p. 316

Writer's Guidelines, p. 317

THE QUIGMANS   by Buddy Hickerson

[Cartoon: Two women facing each other. One says: "IT'S BEEN A LONG TIME, MAVIS... ARE YOU STILL THE SAME JEALOUS, INSECURE PERSON THAT BROKE UP WITH ME YEARS AGO? WHOA! CHECK OUT THE BABE IN THE RED FROCK!" The other says: "YOU THINK SHE'D LIKE ME?"]

© Tribune Media Services, Inc. All Rights Reserved. Reprinted with permission.

Writing Cause and Effect

Causes and effects deal with reasons and results; they are sometimes discussed together and sometimes separately. Like other forms of writing to explain, writing about causes and effects is based on natural thought processes. The shortest, and arguably the most provocative, poem in the English language—"I/Why?"—is posed by an anonymous author about cause. Children are preoccupied with delightful and often exasperating "why" questions. Daily we encounter all kinds of causes and effects. The same subject may raise questions of both kinds.

> The car won't start. Why? (*cause*)
> The car won't start. What now? (*effect*)

At school, from the biology lab to the political science classroom, and at work, from maintaining relationships to changing procedures, causes and effects are found everywhere.

Exploring and Organizing

One useful approach to developing a cause-or-effect analysis is listing. Write down the event, situation, or trend you are concerned about. Then on the left side, list the causes, and on the right side, list the effects. From them you will select the main causes or effects for your essay. Here is an example.

Causes	Event, Situation, or Trend	Effects
Low self-esteem	Joining a gang	Life of crime
Drugs		Drug addiction
Tradition		Surrogate family relationship
Fear		Protection
Want surrogate family		Ostracism
Need protection		Restricted vocational opportunities
Want neighborhood status		

As you use prewriting techniques to explore your ideas, you need to decide whether your topic should mainly inform or mainly persuade. If you intend to inform, your tone should be coolly objective. If you intend to persuade, your tone can be subjective. In either case, you should take into account the views of your audience as you phrase your ideas. You should also take into account how much your audience understands about your topic and develop your ideas accordingly.

Composing a Thesis

Now that you have listed your ideas under causes and effects, you are ready to focus on the causes, on the effects, or, occasionally, on both.

Your controlling idea, the thesis, might be one of the causes: "It is not just chance; people have reasons for joining gangs." Later, as you use the idea, you would rephrase it to make it less mechanical, allowing it to become part of the flow of your discussion. If you wanted to personalize the work—thereby probably making it more interesting—you could write about someone you know who joined a gang. You could use the same basic framework, the main causes, to indicate why this particular person joined a gang.

Writing an Outline

Your selection of a controlling idea takes you to the next writing phase: completing an outline or outline alternative. You need to

- consider kinds of causes and effects.
- evaluate the importance of sequence.
- introduce ideas and work with patterns.

In its most basic form, your outline, derived mainly from points in your listing, might look like one of the following:

Essay of causes

Thesis: It is not just chance; people have reasons for joining gangs.

  I. Low self-esteem (cause 1)
 II. Want surrogate family (cause 2)
III. Need protection (cause 3)

Essay of effects

Thesis: One is not a gang member without consequences.

  I. Restricted vocational opportunities (effect 1)
 II. Life of crime (effect 2)
III. Drug addiction (effect 3)
 IV. Ostracism from mainstream society (effect 4)

Considering Kinds of Causes and Effects

Causes and effects can be primary or secondary, immediate or remote.

Primary or Secondary

Primary means "major," and *secondary* means "minor." A primary cause may be sufficient to bring about the situation (subject). For example, infidelity may be a primary (and possibly sufficient by itself) cause of divorce for some people but not for others, who regard it as secondary. Or if country X is attacked by country Y, the attack itself, as a primary cause, may be sufficient to bring on a declaration of war. But a diplomatic blunder regarding visas for workers may be of secondary importance, and, though significant, it is certainly not enough to start a war.

Immediate or Remote

Causes and effects often occur at a distance in time or place from the situation. The immediate effect of sulfur in the atmosphere may be atmospheric pollution, but the long-range, or remote, effect may be acid rain and the loss of species. The immediate cause of the greenhouse effect may be the depletion of the ozone layer, whereas the long-range, or remote, cause is the use of CFCs (commonly called Freons, which are found in such items as Styrofoam cups). Even more remote, the ultimate cause may be the people who use the products containing Freons. Your purpose will determine the causes and effects appropriate for your essay.

Evaluating the Importance of Sequence

The sequence in which events occur(red) may or may not be significant. When you are dealing with several sequential events, determine whether the sequence of events has causal connections; that is, does one event bring about another?

Consider this sequence of events: Joe's parents get divorced, and Joe joins a gang. We know that one reason for joining a gang is to gain family companionship. Therefore, we may conclude that Joe joined the gang to satisfy his needs for family companionship, which he lost when his parents were divorced. But if we do so, we may have reached a wrong conclusion, because Joe's joining the gang after the family breakup does not necessarily mean that the two events are related. Maybe Joe joined the gang because of drug dependency, low self-esteem, or a need for protection.

In each case, examine the connections. To assume that one event is *caused* by another just because it *follows* the other is a logical error called a *post hoc* ("after this") fallacy. An economic depression may occur after a president takes office, but that does not necessarily mean the depression was caused by the new administration. It might have occurred anyway, perhaps in an even more severe form.

Order

The order of the causes and effects you discuss in your paper may be based on time, space, emphasis, or a combination.

- *Time:* If one stage leads to another, as in a discussion of the causes and effects of upper atmospheric pollution, your paper would be organized best by time.
- *Space:* In some instances, causes and effects are best organized by their relation in space. For example, the causes of an economic recession could be discussed in terms of local factors, regional factors, national factors, and international factors.

- *Emphasis:* Some causes and effects may be more important than others. For instance, if some causes of divorce are primary (perhaps infidelity and physical abuse) and others are secondary (such as annoying habits and laziness), a paper about divorce could present the secondary causes first, and then move on to primary causes to emphasize the latter as more important.

In some situations, two or more factors (such as time and emphasis) may be linked; in that case, select the order that best fits what you are trying to say, or combine orders.

Introducing Ideas and Working with Patterns

In presenting your controlling idea—probably near the beginning for an introductory paragraph for an essay—you will almost certainly want to perform two functions:

1. *Discuss your subject.* For example, if you are writing about the causes or effects of divorce, begin with a statement about divorce as a subject.

2. *Indicate whether you will concentrate on causes or effects or combine them.* That indication should be made clear early in the paper. Concentrating on one—causes or effects—does not mean you will not mention the other; it only means you will emphasize one of them. You can bring attention to your main concern(s)—causes, effects, or a combination—by repeating key words such as *cause, reason, effect, result, consequence,* and *outcome*.

The most likely pattern for your work is shown in Figure 11.1.

Figure 11.1
Pattern for Essay

- Subject and Thesis
- Topic sentence
  - Cause or Effect 1
- Topic sentence
  - Cause or Effect 2
- Topic sentence
  - Cause or Effect 3
- Conclusion

Exercise 1 **COMPLETING PATTERNS OF CAUSE AND EFFECT**

Complete the following cluster on teenage marriage. Then select three or more primary causes or three or more primary effects that could be used in writing an essay on this topic.

Causes   Effects

$$\text{Teenage Marriage}$$

Primary causes   Primary effects

1. _____   1. _____
2. _____   2. _____
3. _____   3. _____
4. _____   4. _____

Connecting Sources and Writing

Student Essay

Victims of abuse do not always feel sorry for themselves. They also do not always protect others who are being abused. These are the shocking conclusions reached by Shandra Morgan, a thoughtful victim.

Kick Me! Kiss Me!

Shandra Morgan (pseudonym)

I can identify with people who were physically abused as children. I am one of them, and I've got all kinds of scars. In prison, I am surrounded by people with a background similar to mine. Like me, they are trying to leave a whole pattern of thinking and behavior behind. Here in prison, a woman I know filed a grievance against a guard who, she said, had struck her numerous times. When the Watch Commander read the statement, he said, "You didn't fill in this part that says, 'Action Requested?'" Her answer was immediate. "I want people to stop beating me unless I deserve it." A former victim of child abuse, she was taking an important step. The final one would occur when she stopped believing that she should be beaten for any reason. Some people might think that point is simple, but it isn't. First, one has to understand what happens to a person who gets beat on every day.

When I was a little kid, my father used to beat me—in ways I don't want to describe just yet. Abuse was a common part of my life. He especially liked to throw things such as ashtrays, books, the TV remote control, and beer cans (usually with beer in them). Then if he missed, he'd get even madder and chase me down and pound me with his fists. Naturally I figured out it would be better to be hit with a flying object than to be pounded, so I learned to move toward whatever he threw. He never seemed to catch on. I'd lunge toward something like an ashtray, and it'd hit me—fleshy parts like my seat were the best targets—and then I'd cry, and he'd stop. Sometimes he'd say how sorry he was and how I got him all upset. It always was my fault.

Of course, I believed it was my fault. Whenever he hit me, however he did it, I knew I deserved it, if not for the immediate mischief, for something else—I was wicked. I always felt more guilt than anger. My life was full of guilt-producing incidents. I received bad grades in school. I embarrassed him in front of his friends. I got in his way around the house. The food I cooked was never as good as that cooked by my mother, who'd disappeared two years after I was born—which was another source of guilt because she probably didn't like me. There were plenty of reasons for me to feel guilty, and I didn't neglect any of them.

But I wasn't the only one around the house who felt guilty. My little brother had his share of guilt feelings. For him, it was not my father he had to watch out for. My father thought Joey could do no wrong. I was the one who beat Joey. When my father was out, I slapped Joey around and threw things—ashtrays, books, hair brushes, whatever I had. Pretty soon I had me a little whiner to pick on, so I could feel better. I even had him apologizing, acting mousier than I ever did, and even cutting on himself.

Finally, when I went to school with bruises for the hundredth time, a teacher took me to the principal, and I told all. The result was juvenile hall, followed by a half-dozen foster homes and a pattern of beating by adults in all kinds of situations—even by men I lived with.

Being abused is bad. It made me feel guilty. It made me want to be abused. And it made me want to be an abuser. Now I'm working on undoing the pattern of thinking that I've had all these years. I want to take the "Kick me" sign off my back and replace it with one that reads "Kiss me." But right now I'm all so mixed up in changing that if someone did kiss me, I don't know whether I'd kick or kiss back.

Exercise 2 — DISCUSSION AND CRITICAL THINKING

1. What is the subject (situation, circumstance, or trend) that is at the center of this discussion?

2. Circle the sentence that most clearly indicates the author's intention of writing about cause, effect, or a combination.

3. Is this passage concerned more with causes, effects, or a combination?

4. Underline the sentences that indicate the specific causes or effects.

5. In what order (time, emphasis, or a combination) are the parts presented?

6. Is the author's purpose mainly to inform or to persuade?

Practicing Patterns of Cause and Effect

A detailed outline and your subsequent writing may include a combination of causes and effects, but you almost always will emphasize one concern—either causes or effects—over the other. The emphasis will provide the main structure, reflecting your purpose. Whether you are writing a basic outline for an assignment outside class without a significant time constraint or you are writing in class under the pressure of time, you will always have time to jot down prewriting lists and create cause and effect outlines.

Exercise 3 COMPLETING PATTERNS OF CAUSE AND EFFECT

Review the following cluster on the topic of being abused, then fill in the blanks to complete the effects outline. Note how the outline headings came from the clustering strategy.

Clustering (Demonstration)

Causes

- mean crazy father
- mother had left
- might have helped me
- I felt guilty
- I didn't get early help
- school didn't act soon

My Being Abused

Effects

- I felt I deserved abuse
- he was like me
- I abused my brother
- needed scapegoat
- was abused by other men
- men I lived with
- hard to correct myself

Effects outline

<u>A person who gets beat on every day</u> <u>may feel she deserves it, but she</u>
              subject   **treatment**

<u>may still beat on others.</u>

  I. Was injured   (Effect)
    A. Physical
    B. _____
  II. Felt guilty   (Effect)

III. Became _____ (Effect)
   A. Abused _____
   B. Felt _____
IV. Found other _____ (Effect)

Student Documented Essay

Student Max Dunlop immediately thought of boxing when he received an assignment to write an essay of cause and effect that was in some way connected to entertainment. Recently, he had read a persuasive essay about boxing, "Blood on Their Hands," by Pete Hamill. It dealt mainly with the effects of boxing. Pursuing the topic, Dunlop went to the library. Using the *Reader's Guide to Periodical Literature* and the Electric Library, an electronic database, he found a few other sources. From them, he selected two he would use with the Hamill article.

It's Time to KO Boxing

Max Dunlop

We have heard the charges against boxing: The so-called sport exploits the poor, fosters crime, and destroys human bodies. The counterargument is that boxing should just be regulated more carefully. That would be fine for the first two charges. Strictly enforced rules could reduce exploitation and curtail crime, but the third charge is beyond remedy: boxing has as its objective the injury of human bodies. Unfortunately for participants, the results of body pounding take several untreatable forms.

The most untreatable of the forms is death. The *Washington Post* reported on July 4, 2001, that nationally "more than fifty professional fighters have died from boxing injuries since 1970" (D3). This figure pertains to the individuals whose deaths are clearly tied to what happened in the ring, usually with the sequence of a knockout, prolonged unconsciousness, and death. Other fatalities occur well after the brain is injured and often go unreported.

Among the long-term effects is one that can be called a slow or partial death: "dementia pugilistica." As Pete Hamill, noted sports journalist observes, this boxer is said to be punch-drunk. In the final stages, which occur between seven and sixteen years after "retirement," the boxer experiences "a decrease in general cognitive functions, memory deficits, impaired hearing, hyperreflexia, dysarthia, intention tremor, and incoordination" (93). Reporting from medical literature, Hamill continues, "This syndrome affects 9 to 25 percent of professional fighters" (94). These victims go on living but usually drift off into their separate worlds where they stumble around over invisible objects, hearing mysterious voices and dodging imaginary punches.

These shambling figures are often fortunate compared with other boxers whose injuries are thought to have been the triggers to the disabling conditions called Parkinson's disease, multiple sclerosis, and frontal-lobe tumors. All of those diseases are more common among pugilists than the general population (Hamill 94). We have all heard about links between traumas and the onset of Alzheimer's disease. We have witnessed the fate of Muhammad Ali, who suffers from Parkinson's.

Having no doubt about the effects of body pounding, the medical profession has been overwhelming in its recommendation of a ban of boxing. Amateur boxing is thought to be less dangerous, for the careers are shorter, the regulations are more strictly enforced, and the matches are shorter. But even with those factors considered, the American Academy of Pediatrics "opposes the sport of boxing for children, adolescents, and young adults. . . . Boxing [exposes] participants to potentially devastating neurologic and ocular injuries" ("Participation in Boxing" 134). The American Medical Association and the World Health Organization concur that boxing should not be legal. The medical profession has not prevailed for obvious reasons: Boxing fans look at their sport from a distance. They say things like, "That was a beautiful knockout." They never say, "That was a beautiful brain concussion."

Of course, a boxing critic should take on the popular argument of many boxing fans that no one is required to box. People volunteer to do it. A few become famous. A few are paid well. It is true that boxers do choose to participate for fame and fortune. But would we say that anyone who is willing to do anything for recognition and money should be given that choice? What if we were to place two combatants in an arena, each one armed with an AK-47, and then offer a big prize to the one who guns down the other? If the prize were large enough, some individuals would almost certainly volunteer for a shootout. If you agree that this activity should, nevertheless, not be allowed, then we both believe that in some instances people should not be permitted to do what they would willingly choose.

The final point is whether the sport of boxing should be legal. The medical community says no. Many of us join in following the evidence to its logical conclusion. This so-called sport with the primary objective of harming the opponent should be banned. It is not a split decision. Boxing should go the way of the gladiators.

Cause and Effect: Determining Reasons and Outcomes **295**

Works Cited

"Boxing-Related Deaths." *Washington Post* 4 July 2001: D3.

Hamill, Pete. "Blood on Their Hands." *Esquire* June 1996: 92–100.

"Participation in Boxing by Children, Adolescents, and Young Adults." *Pediatrics* 99 (Jan. 1997): 134–135.

Exercise 4

DISCUSSION AND CRITICAL THINKING

1. Is this essay concerned mainly with causes or effects?

2. Circle the thesis.

3. Underline each sentence that introduces a set of effects.

4. What are the main causes and the effect in the sixth paragraph?
   Causes:
   Effect:

5. Does Dunlop attempt mainly to inform or to persuade?

6. Do you agree with Dunlop's conclusion? Explain.

7. What would Dunlop say to those who say that boxing is the way for some poor kids to get out of the ghetto or barrio?

8. Does this apply equally to the growing sport of women's boxing?

Multiple Sources on Love, Marriage, and Divorce

Unfortunately for individuals and society, the title of this selection of essays, "Love, Marriage, and Divorce," defines an all-too-common sequence of events. Many of us have grown up thinking about only the first two in that continuum. Surely, love is an almost magical chemistry that is followed by marriage as a natural commitment, with divorce lurking out there somewhere—for others, not ourselves.

The four authors of the following selections represent different perspectives, and each offers a special insight. Anne Roiphe is concerned with how and why people fall in love and marry, but she focuses on psychological reasons, pointing out that our subconscious often leads us to re-create what we experienced as children in a family. Therefore, a marriage may be a satisfying fulfillment or—unless the partners work at changing negative patterns—a failure. Ian Robertson places "romantic love, courtship, and marriage" in a sociological, historical context. Taking Cupid out of the picture, he explains why the practices of loving, courting, and marrying have developed and why they have been sustained. He points out that in a different culture we might never fall in love and would not expect to do so. Moreover, he says, "A courtship system is essentially a marriage market," and people who become partners almost certainly have characteristics in common, such as age, class, and religion. In "Female Mea Culpa," Lin Rolens takes a personal look at relationships. We're all familiar with the saying, "Just what does a woman (or man) want?" Rolens has a practical suggestion. Each person in a relationship should make up a list and present that list to the significant other. For starters, Rolens offers her own preliminary list. Daniel Goleman digs deeper for the roots to the problem of love and marriage strife. There he finds the different views of men and women responsible for the divisiveness in relationships.

Why Marriages Fail

Anne Roiphe

As novelist and journalist, Anne Roiphe has been especially concerned with the topic of contemporary relationships. In this essay, first published in *Family Weekly*, she concentrates on two phenomena all too frequently linked: marriage and divorce.

1   These days so many marriages end in divorce that our most sacred vows no longer ring with truth. "Happily ever after" and "Till death do us part" are expressions that seem on the way to becoming obsolete. Why has it become so hard for couples to stay together? What goes wrong? What has happened to us that close to one-half of all marriages are destined for the divorce courts? How could we have created a society in which 42 percent of our children will grow up in single-parent homes? If statistics could only measure loneliness, regret, pain, loss of self-confidence and fear of the future, the numbers would be beyond quantifying.

2   Even though each broken marriage is unique, we can still find the common perils, the common causes for marital despair. Each

marriage has crisis points and each marriage tests endurance, the capacity for both intimacy and change. Outside pressures such as job loss, illness, infertility, trouble with a child, care of aging parents and all the other plagues of life hit marriage the way hurricanes blast our shores. Some marriages survive these storms and others don't. Marriages fail, however, not simply because of the outside weather but because the inner climate becomes too hot or too cold, too turbulent or too stupefying.

3   When we look at how we choose our partners and what expectations exist at the tender beginnings of romance, some of the reasons for disaster become quite clear. We all select with unconscious accuracy a mate who will recreate with us the emotional patterns of our first homes. Dr. Carl A. Whitaker, a marital therapist and emeritus professor of psychiatry at the University of Wisconsin, explains, "From early childhood on each of us carried models for marriage, femininity, masculinity, motherhood, fatherhood, and all the other family roles." Each of us falls in love with a mate who has qualities of our parents, who will help us rediscover both the psychological happiness and miseries of our past lives. We may think we have found a man unlike Dad, but then he turns to drink or drugs, or loses his job over and over again or sits silently in front of the TV just the way Dad did. A man may choose a woman who doesn't like kids just like his mother or who gambles away the family savings just like his mother. Or he may choose a slender wife who seems unlike his obese mother but then turns out to have other addictions that destroy their mutual happiness.

4   A man and a woman bring to their marriage bed a blended concoction of conscious and unconscious memories of their parents' lives together. The human way is to compulsively repeat and recreate the patterns of the past. Sigmund Freud* so well described the unhappy design that many of us get trapped in: the unmet needs of childhood, the angry feelings left over from frustrations of long ago, the limits of trust and the recurrence of old fears. Once an individual senses this entrapment, there may follow a yearning to escape, and the result could be a broken, splintered marriage.

5   Of course people can overcome the habits and attitudes that developed in childhood. We all have hidden strengths and amazing capacities for growth and creative change. Change, however, requires work—observing your part in a rotten pattern, bringing difficulties out into the open—and work runs counter to the basic

---

*Sigmund Freud was an Austrian neuropsychologist who founded psychoanalysis.

myth of marriage: "When I wed this person all my problems will be over. I will have achieved success and I will become the center of life for this other person and this person will be my center, and we will mean everything to each other forever." This myth, which every marriage relies on, is soon exposed. The coming of children, the pulls and tugs of their demands on affection and time, place a considerable strain on that basic myth of meaning everything to each other, of merging together and solving all of life's problems.

6   Concern and tension about money take each partner away from the other. Obligations to demanding parents or still-dependent-upon parents create further strain. Couples today must also deal with all the cultural changes brought on in recent years by the women's movement and the sexual revolution. The altering of roles and the shifting of responsibilities have been extremely trying for many marriages.

7   These and other realities of life erode the visions of marital bliss the way sandstorms eat at rock and the ocean nibbles away at the dunes. Those euphoric, grand feelings that accompany romantic love are really self-delusions, self-hypnotic dreams that enable us to forge a relationship. Real life, failure at work, disappointments, exhaustion, bad smells, bad colds and hard times all puncture the dream and leave us stranded with our mate, with our childhood patterns pushing us this way and that, with our unfulfilled expectations.

8   The struggle to survive in marriage requires adaptability, flexibility, genuine love and kindness and an imagination strong enough to feel what the other is feeling. Many marriages fall apart because either partner cannot imagine what the other wants or cannot communicate what he or she needs or feels. Anger builds until it erupts into a volcanic burst that buries the marriage in ash

9   It is not hard to see, therefore, how essential communication is for a good marriage. A man and a woman must be able to tell each other how they feel and why they feel the way they do; otherwise they will impose on each other roles and actions that lead to further unhappiness. In some cases, the communication patterns of childhood—of not talking, of talking too much, of not listening, of distrust and anger, of withdrawal—spill into the marriage and prevent a healthy exchange of thoughts and feelings. The answer is to set up new patterns of communication and intimacy.

10   At the same time, however, we must see each other as individuals. "To achieve a balance between separateness and closeness is one of the major psychological tasks of all human beings at every

stage of life," says Dr. Stuart Bartle, a psychiatrist at the New York University Medical Center.

11   If we sense from our mate a need for too much intimacy, we tend to push him or her away, fearing that we may lose our identities in the merging of marriage. One partner may suffocate the other partner in a childlike dependency.

12   A good marriage means growing as a couple but also growing as individuals. This isn't easy. Richard gives up his interest in carpentry because his wife, Helen, is jealous of the time he spends away from her. Karen quits her choir group because her husband dislikes the friends she makes there. Each pair clings to each other and is angry with each other as life closes in on them. This kind of marital balance is easily thrown as one or the other pulls away and divorce follows.

13   Sometimes people pretend that a new partner will solve the old problems. Most often extramarital sex destroys a marriage because it allows an artificial split between the good and the bad—the good is projected on the new partner and the bad is dumped on the head of the old. Dishonesty, hiding and cheating create walls between men and women. Infidelity is just a symptom of trouble. It is a symbolic complaint, a weapon of revenge, as well as an unraveler of closeness. Infidelity is often that proverbial last straw that sinks the camel to the ground.

14   All right—marriage has always been difficult. Why then are we seeing so many divorces at this time? Yes, our modern social fabric is thin, and yes the permissiveness of society has created unrealistic expectations and thrown the family into chaos. But divorce is so common because people today are unwilling to exercise the self-discipline that marriage requires. They expect easy joy, like the entertainment on TV, the thrill of a good party.

15   Marriage takes some kind of sacrifice, not dreadful self-sacrifice of the soul, but some level of compromise. Some of one's fantasies, some of one's legitimate desires have to be given up for the value of the marriage itself. "While all marital partners feel shackled at times, it is they who really choose to make the marital ties into confining chains or supporting bonds," says Dr. Whitaker. Marriage requires sexual, financial and emotional discipline. A man and a woman cannot follow every impulse, cannot allow themselves to stop growing or changing.

16   Divorce is not an evil act. Sometimes it provides salvation for people who have grown hopelessly apart or were frozen in patterns of pain or mutual unhappiness. Divorce can be, despite its

initial devastation, like the first cut of the surgeon's knife, a step toward new health and a good life. On the other hand, if the partners can stay past the breaking up of the romantic myths into the development of real love and intimacy, they have achieved a work as amazing as the greatest cathedrals of the world. Marriages that do not fail but improve, that persist despite imperfections, are not only rare these days but offer a wondrous shelter in which the face of our mutual humanity can safely show itself.

Exercise 5 — VOCABULARY HIGHLIGHTS

Write a short definition of each word as it is used in the essay. (Paragraph numbers are given in parentheses.) Be prepared to use the words in your own sentences.

obsolete (1)

perils (2)

turbulent (2)

concoction (4)

erode (7)

projected (13)

symbolic (13)

chaos (14)

myths (16)

persist (16)

Exercise 6 — DISCUSSION AND CRITICAL THINKING

1. What is the subject (a situation, circumstance, or trend) at the center of this discussion?

2. Is this essay concerned more with causes, effects, or a combination?

3. Roiphe points out that marriages fail because of both internal and external factors.
   a. What outside pressures cause stress in marriages (paragraph 2)?
   b. What pressures inside individuals cause stress in marriage (paragraphs 3, 4)?

4. If it is true that we select marriage partners with qualities that will enable us to re-create our childhood experiences, both good and bad, then are those of us who had mostly bad childhood experiences trapped into reproducing those bad patterns?

5. According to Roiphe, what specific realities puncture the dreams of romantic love (paragraph 7)?

6. What are the components (and thus the causes) of a good marriage?

Romantic Love, Courtship, and Marriage

Ian Robertson

Romantic love, courtship, and marriage are more than matters of the heart. According to Ian Robertson, they are all perfectly understandable parts of our culture, and they do not exist in the same way outside our culture. In this excerpt from his college textbook, Sociology, *Robertson explains the causes of our loving, courting, and marrying. He says that, often without thinking about what we are doing, we respond to the needs of both society and ourselves.*

Romantic Love

1. The American family is supposed to be founded on the romantic love of the marital partners. Traces of a more pragmatic attitude persist in the American upper classes, where daughters are expected to marry "well"—that is, to a male who is eligible by reason of family background and earning potential. Most Americans, however, tend to look askance at anyone who marries for money or some other practical reason in which love plays no part.

2. Happily enough, romantic love defies a clinical definition. It is a different kind of love, though, from the love you have for your parents or your dog. It involves physical symptoms, such as pounding heart and sexual desire, and psychological symptoms, such as obsessive focus on one person and a disregard for any resulting social or economic risks. Our culture encourages us to look for this love—to find that "one and only," perhaps even through "love at first sight." The phenomenon of romantic love occurs when two people meet and find one another personally and physically attractive. They become mutually absorbed, start to behave in what may appear to be a flighty, even irrational manner, decide that they are right for one another, and may then enter

a marriage whose success is expected to be guaranteed by their enduring passion. Behavior of this kind is portrayed and warmly endorsed throughout American popular culture, by books, magazines, comics, records, popular songs, movies, and TV.

Romantic love is a noble idea, and it can certainly help provide a basis for the spouses to "live happily ever after." But since marriage can equally well be founded on much more practical considerations, why is romantic love of such importance in the modern world? The reason seems to be that it has the following basic functions in maintaining the institution of the nuclear family:

1. *Transfer of loyalties.* Romantic love helps the young partners to loosen their bonds with their family of orientation, a step that is essential if a new neolocal nuclear family is to be created. Their total absorption in one another facilitates a transfer of commitment from existing family and kin to a new family of procreation, something that would be unlikely to happen under the extended family system.

2. *Emotional support.* Romantic love provides the couple with emotional support in the difficulties that they face in establishing a new life of their own. This love would not be so necessary in an extended family, where the relatives are able to confront problems cooperatively. In an extended family, in fact, romantic love might even be dysfunctional, for it could distract the couple from their wider obligations to other kin.

3. *Incentive to marriage.* Romantic love serves as a bait to lure people into marriage. In the extended family system of traditional societies, it is automatically assumed that people will marry, but in the modern world, people have considerable choice over whether they will get married or not. A contract to form a lifelong commitment to another person is not necessarily a very tempting proposition, however: to some, the prospect may look more like a noose than like a bed of roses. Without feelings of romantic love, many people might have no incentive to marry.

To most of us, particularly to those who are in love, romantic love seems to be the most natural thing in the world, but sociological analysis shows that it is a purely cultural product, arising in certain societies for specific reasons. In a different time or in a different society, you might never fall in love, nor would you expect to.

Courtship and Marriage

A courtship system is essentially a marriage market. (The metaphor of the "market" may seem a little unromantic, but in fact, the participants do attempt to "sell" their assets—physical appearance, personal charms, talents and interests, and career prospects.) In the matter of mate selection, different courtship systems vary according to how much choice they permit the individual. The United States probably allows more freedom of choice than any other society. A parent who attempts to interfere in the dating habits or marriage plans of a son or daughter is considered meddlesome and is more likely to alienate than persuade the young lover.

9   In this predominantly urban and anonymous society, young people—often with access to automobiles—have an exceptional degree of privacy in their courting. The practice of dating enables them to find out about one another, to improve their own interpersonal skills in the market, to experiment sexually if they so wish, and finally to select a marriage partner.

10   Who marries whom, then? Cupid's arrow, it turns out, does not strike at random. Despite the cultural emphasis on love as something mysterious and irrational, the selection of marital partners is more orderly and predictable than romantics might like to think. In general, the American mate-selection process produces *homogamy,* marriage between partners who share similar social characteristics. Among the characteristics that seem to attract people to one another are the following:

11   1. *Similar age.* Married partners tend to be of roughly the same age. Husbands are usually older than their wives, but this difference in age has been gradually declining throughout the century, from about 4 years in 1900 to 2.4 years today.

12   2. *Social class.* Most people marry within their own social class. The reasons are obvious: we tend to live in class-segregated neighborhoods, to meet mostly people of the same class, and to share class-specific tastes and interests. Interclass marriages are relatively more common, however, among college students. When there are class differences in a marriage, it is most often the wife who marries upward.

13   3. *Religion.* Most marriages are between people sharing the same religious faith, although Protestant interdenominational marriages are fairly common. Many people change their religion to that of their partner before marriage.

14   4. *Education.* Husbands and wives generally have a similar educational level. The college campus is, of course, a marriage market in its own right, and college-educated people are especially likely to marry people who have a similar education achievement.

15   5. *Racial and ethnic background.* Members of racial and ethnic groups are more likely to marry within their own group than outside it. In particular, interracial marriages are extremely rare.

Until the 1960s, several states had laws prohibiting interracial marriages, and such marriages still attract some social disapproval. Interracial marriages between blacks and whites are particularly unusual; in the majority of these cases, the husband is black and the wife white.

16   6. *Propinquity.* Spatial nearness is a common feature of those who marry one another, for the obvious reason that people are likely to have more social interaction and similarities with neighbors, coworkers, or fellow students than with others who are physically more distant.

Exercise 7 | **DISCUSSION AND CRITICAL THINKING**

1. What is the subject (a situation, circumstance, or trend) at the center of this discussion?

2. Is this piece concerned mainly with causes, effects, or a combination of both?

3. What are the three cultural needs or causes (also called functions) that make romantic love useful in our society?

4. How would you rank the three functions of romantic love in order of importance?

5. On the basis of what assets do individuals attempt to sell themselves on the "marriage market"?

6. What six causes (or "characteristics") does Robertson list for why people fall in love?

7. In your estimation, which of the six causes are the most important?

8. Are the assets or the characteristics more important? Should they be?

Female Mea Culpa

Lin Rolens

Freelance author Lin Rolens has a proposal to end all this animosity between the sexes. It is based on openness, and it starts and finishes with a list of needs and considerations, which are thinly veiled grievances. Ideally, this solution would be an exchange of lists. This essay was first printed in the *Santa Barbara News Press Magazine* in 1999.

1. For years now I've wanted a man who comes with a list: how he likes his coffee, what he won't eat, how he really feels about the remote control, how he likes his socks folded. I don't want the complete list, that would take volumes, but a starter list would be nice. And I don't want it presented with great ceremony; I want it slipped quietly into my pocket at just the right moment to make both our lives easier.

2. Of course, there should be a reciprocal list of all my little quirks, foibles, needs, pleasures and the like. Some of this is particular to me (I take my coffee with milk, will eat anything but okra, believe the remote should enjoy shared custody and will take my socks folded any way he cares to fold them), but certainly there are some general things about women that men would do well to know, some things that seem to escape them.

3. I offer a generalized starter list:

4. In our female hearts, we know, if there were any justice in the world, courtship would not be a phase in a relationship: It would be a way of life. Never mind dating, which is generally exhausting, but we really love, and even feel we deserve, all the little touches and enthusiasms, all those wonderful surprises and attentions that helped convince us you were the right one in the first place.

5. We love flowers: It isn't by accident that one of the features of our local farmers' market is masses of women leaving with great armfuls of flowers. We are, simply, suckers for flowers, and they often move us as words can't; men of sensibility know that women of sensibility never have too many flowers. The size of the bouquet decidedly is not the issue: We would rather receive a hand-selected nosegay than a floral display ordered through a secretary. And, this is important, flowers given for no apparent reason are flowers given for the best reason.

6. In the complicated logic of women, it is generally accepted that the only flowers not worth receiving are guilt flowers, those flowers proffered as moral groin cover or in lieu of a real apology. I

have shoved more than one rose bouquet in the trash compactor because the sender mistakenly believed I would have a total brain lapse about some recent transgression when I received them.

7   While we usually know what we want, we don't want to tell you what we want. Yes, we'll provide hints, murmured suggestions, but we don't want to have to lay it on the line. We want you to know; it's no mystery to us, and it's difficult to understand why it seems to be such a mystery to you. This goes for everything from where we want to vacation to what we would give if you just don't wear that particular pair of pants to the family reunion. Don't ask me to explain.

8   Talk is often balm, and truly being listened to is one of life's great luxuries. When the day or our lives overwhelm us, it is the wine of talk that proves settling. As we air whatever it is that disturbs us, the problem doesn't go away, but it deflates to a point where we see it in context.

9   Our rituals count; they are important and often meditative indulgences that help us center ourselves. Whether it's painting our toenails yet again in the color that horrifies you or taking long steamy baths or, as one of my friends recently did, spending an entire evening re-ironing all the cloth napkins in her linen closet, these endeavors prove healing. When we return to the fray, we will be better versions of ourselves.

10   When we buy new clothes, we want you to like them—a lot. We want to be adored, validated, or, if you can manage it, occasionally worshipped. (See "fat" for further clarification.)

11   Although it is all right, even inevitable, that we believe, whatever our current weight, that we are fat, it is never all right if you believe we are fat. We need and expect that you will find us just right, whatever our weight. While we are free to loathe extra dimples, bumps, lumps and curves, we trust that you will adore them with the same vigor that you adored our original youthful and girlish figures.

12   Food is not just food. When we cook for you, it is a way of loving you, and we'd appreciate it if you received it in the spirit in which it is given. This is particularly true when we make not only your favorite dinner or our own stellar specialty, but something, say, like your mother's secret spaghetti sauce recipe.

13   There is a widely held belief that we want to change you, that we see men as delicious raw material and that, by careful and patient encouragement or insistence, a good man can be molded into an excellent one. This is actually a problem of semantics: As we see it, we are simply providing you the opportunity to become your best self.

14   Finally, we like chick flicks, that's how they got the name. Action films are fine, but we bring hankies to the movies for a reason.

15   So that's it, a starter list. I'm sure every woman will have her own additions and variations, but it might be worth a try simply to slip this into his pocket.

Exercise 8   VOCABULARY HIGHLIGHTS

Write a short definition of each word as it is used in the essay. (Paragraph numbers are given in parentheses.) Be prepared to use the words in your own sentences.

reciprocal (2)

quirks (2)

foibles (2)

sensibility (5)

in lieu of (6)

transgression (6)

balm (8)

meditative (9)

semantics (13)

Exercise 9   DISCUSSION AND CRITICAL THINKING

1. Why does Rolens use flowers to explain "the complicated logic of women" (paragraph 6)?

2. What does she mean when she compares "talk" to "balm" (paragraph 8)?

3. What does Rolens mean when she says, "While we usually know what we want, we don't want to tell you what we want" (paragraph 7)?

4. Is Rolens really serious about making lists? After all, she did say, "We don't want to tell you what we want."

5. In making her list, is Rolens mainly concerned with herself or the man?

6. Explain what she means by referring to courtship as a "way of life" (paragraph 4).

7. Does Rolens believe that women are superior to men in showing respect and consideration? Is she right?

His Marriage and Hers: Childhood Roots

Daniel Goleman

A respected scholar, Daniel Goleman has written numerous books on psychology, including Vital Lies, Simple Truths, The Meditative Mind, *and* Working with Emotional Intelligence. *Here he discusses how conflicts within relationships are caused especially by conditioning.*

1. As I was entering a restaurant on a recent evening, a young man stalked out the door, his face set in an expression both stony and sullen. Close on his heels a young woman came running, her fists desperately pummeling his back while she yelled, "Goddamn you! Come back here and be nice to me!" That poignant, impossibly self-contradictory plea aimed at a retreating back epitomizes the pattern most commonly seen in couples whose relationship is distressed: She seeks to engage, he withdraws. Marital therapists have long noted that by the time a couple finds their way to the therapy office they are in this pattern of engage-withdraw, with his complaint about her "unreasonable" demands and outbursts, and her lamenting his indifference to what she is saying.

2. This marital endgame reflects the fact that there are, in effect, two emotional realities in a couple, his and hers. The roots of these emotional differences, while they may be partly biological, also can be traced back to childhood, and to the separate emotional worlds boys and girls inhabit while growing up. There is a vast amount of research on these separate worlds, their barriers reinforced not just by the different games boys and girls prefer, but by young children's fear of being teased for having a "girlfriend" or "boyfriend."[1] One study of children's friendships found that three-year-olds say about half their friends are of the opposite sex; for five-year-olds it's about 20 percent, and by age seven almost no boys or girls say they have a best friend of the opposite

sex.[2] These separate social universes intersect little until teenagers start dating.

3   Meanwhile, boys and girls are taught very different lessons about handling emotions. Parents, in general, discuss emotions—with the exception of anger—more with their daughters than their sons.[3] Girls are exposed to more information about emotions than are boys; when parents make up stories to tell their preschool children, they use more emotion words when talking to daughters than to sons; when mothers play with their infants, they display a wider range of emotions to daughters than to sons; when mothers talk to daughters about feelings, they discuss in more detail the emotional state itself than they do with their sons—though with the sons they go into more detail about the causes and consequences of emotions like anger (probably as a cautionary tale).

4   Leslie Brody and Judith Hall, who have summarized the research on differences in emotions between the sexes, propose that because girls develop facility with language more quickly than do boys, this leads them to be more experienced at articulating their feelings and more skilled than boys at using words to explore and substitute for emotional reactions such as physical fights; in contrast, they note, "boys, for whom the verbalization of affects is de-emphasized, may become largely unconscious of their emotional states, both in themselves and others."[4]

5   At age ten, roughly the same percent of girls as boys are overtly aggressive, given to open confrontation when angered. But by age thirteen, a telling difference between the sexes emerges: Girls become more adept than boys at artful aggressive tactics like ostracism, vicious gossip, and indirect vendettas. Boys, by and large, simply continue being confrontational when angered, oblivious to these more covert strategies.[5] This is just one of many ways that boys—and later, men—are less sophisticated than the opposite sex in the byways of emotional life.

6   When girls play together, they do so in small, intimate groups, with an emphasis on minimizing hostility and maximizing cooperation, while boys' games are in larger groups, with an emphasis on competition. One key difference can be seen in what happens when games boys or girls are playing get disrupted by someone getting hurt. If a boy who has gotten hurt gets upset, he is expected to get out of the way and stop crying so the game can go on. If the same happens among a group of girls who are playing, the *game stops* while everyone gathers around to help the girl who is crying. This difference between boys and girls at play epito-

mizes what Harvard's Carol Gilligan points to as a key disparity between the sexes: boys take pride in a lone, tough-minded independence and autonomy, while girls see themselves as part of a web of connectedness. Thus boys are threatened by anything that might challenge their independence, while girls are more threatened by a rupture in their relationships. And, as Deborah Tannen has pointed out in her book *You Just Don't Understand,* these differing perspectives mean that men and women want and expect very different things out of a conversation, with men content to talk about "things," while women seek emotional connection.

7   In short, these contrasts in schooling in the emotions foster very different skills, with girls becoming "adept at reading both verbal and nonverbal emotional signals, at expressing and communicating their feelings," and boys becoming adept at "minimizing emotions having to do with vulnerability, guilt, fear and hurt."[6] Evidence for these different stances is very strong in the scientific literature. Hundreds of studies have found, for example, that on average women are more empathic than men, at least as measured by the ability to read someone else's unstated feelings from facial expression, tone of voice, and other nonverbal cues. Likewise, it is generally easier to read feelings from a woman's face than a man's; while there is no difference in facial expressiveness among very young boys and girls, as they go through the elementary-school grades boys become less expressive, girls more so. This may partly reflect another key difference: women, on average, experience the entire range of emotions with greater intensity and more volatility than men—in this sense, women *are* more "emotional" than men.[7]

8   All of this means that, in general, women come into a marriage groomed for the role of emotional manager, while men arrive with much less appreciation of the importance of this task for helping a relationship survive. Indeed, the most important element for women—but not for men—in satisfaction with their relationship reported in a study of 264 couples was the sense that the couple has "good communication."[8] Ted Huston, a psychologist at the University of Texas who has studied couples in depth, observes, "For the wives, intimacy means talking things over, especially talking about the relationship itself. The men, by and large, don't understand what the wives want from them. They say, 'I want to do things with her, and all she wants to do is talk.'" During courtship, Huston found, men were much more willing to spend time talking in ways that suited the wish for intimacy of

their wives-to-be. But once married, as time went on the men—especially in more traditional couples—spent less and less time talking in this way with their wives, finding a sense of closeness simply in doing things like gardening together rather than talking things over.

9. This growing silence on the part of husbands may be partly due to the fact that, if anything, men are a bit Pollyannaish* about the state of their marriage, while their wives are attuned to the trouble spots: in one study of marriages, men had a rosier view than their wives of just about everything in their relationship — lovemaking, finances, ties with in-laws, how well they listened to each other, how much their flaws mattered.[9] Wives, in general, are more vocal about their complaints than are their husbands, particularly among unhappy couples. Combine men's rosy view of marriage with their aversion to emotional confrontations, and it is clear why wives so often complain that their husbands try to wiggle out of discussing the troubling things about their relationship. (Of course this gender difference is a generalization, and is not true in every case; a psychiatrist friend complained that in his marriage his wife is reluctant to discuss emotional matters between them, and he is the one who is left to bring them up.)

10. The slowness of men to bring up problems in a relationship is no doubt compounded by their relative lack of skill when it comes to reading facial expressions of emotions. Women, for example, are more sensitive to a sad expression on a man's face than are men in detecting sadness from a woman's expression.[10] Thus a woman has to be all the sadder for a man to notice her feelings in the first place, let alone for him to raise the question of what is making her so sad.

11. Consider the implications of this emotional gender gap for how couples handle the grievances and disagreements that any intimate relationship inevitably spawns. In fact, specific issues such as how often a couple has sex, how to discipline the children, or how much debt and savings a couple feels comfortable with are not what make or break a marriage. Rather, it is *how* a couple discusses such sore points that matters more for the fate of their marriage. Simply having reached an agreement about *how* to disagree is key to marital survival; men and women have to overcome the innate gender differences in approaching rocky emotions. Failing this, couples are vulnerable to emotional rifts that eventually can tear their relationship apart. . . . [T]hese rifts are

---

*Pollyanna was an extremely optimistic character in a book for children.

far more likely to develop if one or both partners have certain deficits in emotional intelligence.

Notes

1. The separate worlds of boys and girls: Eleanor Maccoby and C. N. Jacklin, "Gender Segregation in Childhood," in H. Reese, ed., *Advances in Child Development and Behavior* (New York: Academic Press, 1987).
2. Same-sex playmates: John Gottman, "Same and Cross Sex Friendship in Young Children," in J. Gottman and J. Parker, eds., *Conversation of Friends* (New York: Cambridge University Press, 1986).
3. This and the following summary of sex differences in socialization of emotions are based on the excellent review in Leslie R. Brody and Judith A. Hall, "Gender and Emotion," in Michael Lewis and Jeannette Haviland, eds., *Handbook of Emotions* (New York: Guilford Press, 1993).
4. Brody and Hall, "Gender and Emotion," p. 456.
5. Girls and the arts of aggression: Robert B. Cairns and Beverley D. Cairns, *Lifelines and Risks* (New York: Cambridge University Press, 1994).
6. Brody and Hall, "Gender and Emotion," p. 454.
7. The findings about gender differences in emotion are reviewed in Brody and Hall, "Gender and Emotion."
8. The importance of good communication for women was reported in Mark H. Davis and H. Alan Oathout, "Maintenance of Satisfaction in Romantic Relationships: Empathy and Relational Competence," *Journal of Personality and Social Psychology* 53, 2 (1987), pp. 397–410.
9. The study of husbands' and wives' complaints: Robert J. Sternberg, "Triangulating Love," in Robert Sternberg and Michael Barnes, eds., *The Psychology of Love* (New Haven: Yale University Press, 1988).
10. Reading sad faces: The research is by Dr. Ruben C. Gur at the University of Pennsylvania School of Medicine.

Exercise 10 — VOCABULARY HIGHLIGHTS

Write a short definition of each word as it is used in the essay. (Paragraph numbers are given in parentheses.) Be prepared to use the words in your own sentences.

pummeling (1)

poignant (1)

epitomizes (1)

intersect (2)

articulating (4)

ostracism (5)

vendettas (5)

disparity (6)

empathic (7)

innate (11)

Exercise 11   DISCUSSION AND CRITICAL THINKING

1. This essay uses two forms of discourse extensively: (1) contrast and (2) causes and effects. What does Goleman say is the effect of the contrasts he shows?

2. According to Goleman, what are the roots of the different ways men and women express emotions?

3. According to Goleman, are the behavioral differences between males and females mainly a result of biology or training?

4. What does Goleman say are the male and female views on communication in marriage?

5. Why don't men talk about marital problems more?

6. What is "emotional intelligence" (paragraph 11)?

✎ Topics for Writing Cause and Effect

Writing Process Worksheet

You will find a Writing Process Worksheet on page 27. It can be photocopied and enlarged, filled in, and submitted with each assignment if your instructor directs you to do so.

Source-Based Topics

Each essay developed from these suggested source-based topics should include at least one reference to the reading selection by the author's name and the title. Quotations should be enclosed in quotation marks. Follow your instructor's directions in documenting the ideas you borrow. Whether you use informal or formal documentation, the form is not complicated, and you will soon learn to use it for these essays without checking each time. See pages 73 and 74 for a discussion of MLA style and informal documentation.

Underlining and annotating reading selections will help you in finding support material. In prewriting brief essays, consider marking your outline to indicate where you will use quotations or other borrowed ideas. If the quotations or reworded statements are short and few, you could even insert them inside parentheses or circles in your outline; if you do, also include the author's last name and the page number. A sound system, consistently used, will save you time and ensure technically strong papers.

"Kick Me! Kiss Me!"

1. Write about a similar case of physical abuse (child or spousal). Concentrate on either the causes or the effects.

2. Write about the effects of verbal abuse on an individual you know.

"It's Time to KO Boxing"

3. Take the other side of the argument, that boxing is worthwhile, has many good features, and can and should be preserved. Use your own sources, and, perhaps, refer to Dunlop's argument.

4. Write a critique of Dunlop's essay in which you take issue with his points one at a time. Use your own sources for your refutation of his ideas.

5. Write about another sport, such as hockey or football, that arguably should be regulated, especially at the youth level.

"Why Marriages Fail"

6. Explain the effects of a divorce on a person you know, either the child of divorced parents or a partner in a divorce. Consider both the immediate and the long-range effects. Don't forget that Roiphe maintains that divorce is not necessarily a bad idea.

7. Roiphe says that "we all select with unconscious accuracy a mate who will recreate with us the emotional patterns of our first homes" (paragraph 3). Either agree or disagree with that statement and support your views by discussing the causal factors in a marriage you are familiar with.

8. Discuss an ideal marriage (a particular one, if possible) and explain what made it that way (causes). Consider paragraphs 8 through 13 for ideas on what Roiphe believes makes a good marriage.

9. Roiphe says, "People can overcome the habits and attitudes that developed in childhood." Write an essay in which you show that she is right, or one in which you point out the difficulties in overcoming those habits and attitudes. Use specific examples and stress the causes or effects.

"Romantic Love, Courtship, and Marriage"

10. Write a piece in which you relate all or most of the six "characteristics that seem to attract people to one another" to a marriage or a relationship you are familiar with (paragraphs 11 through 16). Your example may support Robertson's views or it may show that a marriage can be very good, even though the partners do not share several of the six characteristics.

11. Write about a marriage that failed because the partners were too different, that is, they shared few or none of the six characteristics.

12. Write an essay in which you argue that the assets that prospective mates try to "sell" each other on (appearance, charm, common interests, career prospects) either are or are not more important than the six characteristics that attract people to each other. Use references to the article and your own examples.

13. Write an essay in which you rank the six "characteristics that seem to attract people to one another" and explain the reason for your ranking.

14. Apply the six "characteristics that seem to attract people to one another" to a particular culture other than middle-class American. Which ones fit? Which ones do not? To what degree do some fit?

15. Discuss to what extent the six characteristics apply to same-sex relationships.

"Female Mea Culpa"

16. Write an essay in which you discuss why you think it would or would not be easier (stressing effects) if men and women came with a list of their likes and dislikes, perhaps exchanging lists along with wedding vows. Should there be negotiations?

17. Write a male version of this essay, or write a modification of this female version.

18. Pick several statements by Rolens and write an essay with a paragraph about each one, stressing causes, effects, or both on relationships.

    Suggestions: "Women of sensibility never have too many flowers" (paragraph 5).

    "We don't want to tell you what we want" (paragraph 7).

    "Truly being listened to is one of life's great luxuries" (paragraph 8).

    "Food is not just food" (paragraph 12).

"His Marriage and Hers: Childhood Roots"

19. Using Goleman's ideas and your own experiences, discuss the differences that exist between men's and women's ways of expressing themselves.

20. Write about a marriage you are familiar with and discuss the relationship in terms of communication and "emotional intelligence" (paragraph 11).

Multiple Sources on Love, Marriage, and Divorce

21. Consider the relationship between a couple you know or know about and write of the causes of their problems in terms of insights found in two or more of the multiple sources.

22. Consider the relationship between a couple you know or know about and write of the effects of their problems in terms of insights found in two or more of the multiple sources.

23. Consider the relationship between a couple you know or know about and write of their successful relationship in terms of insights found in two or more of the multiple sources.

Career-Related Topics

24. Discuss the effects (benefits) of a particular product or service on a business community, family life, society generally, a specific group (age, income, interest), or an individual.

25. Discuss the needs (thus the cause of development) by individuals, families, or institutions for a particular product or type of product.

26. Discuss the effects of using a certain approach or philosophy in sales, human resources management, or customer service.

General Topics

Select one of the topics below as a subject (situation, circumstance, or trend) for your essay and then determine whether you will concentrate on causes, effects, or a combination.

27. Attending or completing college
28. Having or getting a job
29. Change in policy or administration
30. Change in coaches, teachers, officeholder(s)
31. Alcoholism
32. Gambling
33. Moving to another country, state, or home
34. Exercise
35. Passing or failing a test or course

36. Popularity of a certain TV program or song
37. Early marriage

You can probably write a more interesting, well-developed, and therefore successful essay on a topic you can personalize. For example, a discussion about a specific young person who contemplated, attempted, or committed suicide is probably a better topic idea than a general discussion of suicide. If you do not personalize the topic, you will probably have to do some basic research to supply details for development.

Writer's Guidelines: Cause and Effect

1. Determine whether your topic should mainly inform or mainly persuade, and use the right tone for your purpose and audience.

2. Use listing to brainstorm cause-and-effect ideas. This is a useful form:

Causes	Event, Situation, or Trend	Effects
1.		1.
2.		2.
3.		3.
4.		4.

3. Decide whether to concentrate on causes, effects, or a combination of causes and effects. Short essays generally discuss causes and effects but will use one as the framework for the piece. A typical basic outline might look like this:

Thesis of the essay
   I. Cause or Effect 1
   II. Cause or Effect 2
   III. Cause or Effect 3

4. Do not conclude that something is an effect merely because it follows something else in time.

5. Emphasize your main concern(s)—causes, effects, or a combination—by repeating key words such as *cause, reason, effect, result, consequence,* and *outcome.*

6. Causes and effects can be primary or secondary, immediate or remote.

7. The order of causes and effects in your paper may be based on time, space, emphasis, or a combination.

12

Literary Analysis: Reacting to Stories

"I think I did pretty well, considering I started out with nothing but a bunch of blank paper." Steve Martin

Why We Read Stories 319
   Interpreting Narrative Literature 319

Writing About Literature 319
   Setting 320
   Conflict 320
   Characters 320
   Plot 320
   Theme 321
   Point of View 321
   Analysis 321

Connecting Reading and Writing 322
   Professional Writers: Reading Selections on the Theme of Love 322
      "How Do I Love Thee?" 323
      "The Girls in Their Summer Dresses" 325
      "The Story of an Hour" 331
      "Frankie and Johnny" 334
      "My Last Duchess" 337
   Student Writers 340
      "More Than Just a House Call" (demonstration with stages) 342
      "The Use of Self-Analysis" 345

Finding Topics for Literary Analysis 347

Topics for Writing About Stories 348

Writer's Guidelines 351

THE QUIGMANS by Buddy Hickerson

Date with a movie critic.

B. Hickerson, copyright Los Angeles Time Syndicate. Reprinted by permission.

Why We Read Stories

Narrative literature tells stories. Why do we read stories? Among the possible answers is one particularly intriguing theory by Robert Penn Warren. He said that we often find life disjointed and our own behavior beyond clear, reasonable explanation, but if we read stories we discover understandable patterns of human life. If the writers are good, we can see parallels with what we have experienced and causes and effects that make sense. Stories, including story poems, give us little reflective universes to ponder, to discuss with others, to marvel at, and to question.

Interpreting Narrative Literature

Because narrative literature is a representation of life, it may be discussed from many perspectives. A single short story or poem may be a study in philosophy, psychology, history, or some other field. Prepare to engage your full intellect and complete knowledge in considering the stories you read. Keep in mind that no two people will interpret them in precisely the same way, because all of us are different in our experiences, ways of thinking, and values. However, we also have much in common, and we will usually be able to agree on one or more reasonable interpretations based on the evidence we find within the narrative framework.

Writing About Literature

In previous chapters, we have discussed how to write paragraphs and essays. In this chapter, we turn our attention to the short story and the narrative poem for subject material. The change is not significant. Stories and poems contain many of the forms emphasized in this book: narration, description, exemplification, analysis by division, process analysis, cause and effect, classification, comparison and contrast, definition, and argument. Stories and poems also have raw materials that can be transformed into these patterns of writing. Therefore, learning to write about literature extends what you are learning about writing while providing a new dimension of experience. This new dimension lays the groundwork for writing in more advanced composition classes, literature classes, and other humanities classes.

The forms of narrative we work with in this chapter are not complicated. Because short stories and narrative poems both tell stories, we can use the same principles to discuss them in a broad fashion. The following discussion of setting, conflict, characters, plot, theme, point of view, and analysis will provide you with a good framework for basic reading for understanding, as well as for annotating your text, interpreting stories and poems, and even generating topics for writing.

Setting

In its simplest form, the *setting* is the environment in which the literary work takes place. It may be merely appropriate, without calling attention to itself. It may also be supportive, reinforcing the theme. For example, a story about death may occur in the winter, whereas a story about birth or rediscovery of life may occur in springtime or early summer. Edgar Allan Poe uses this reinforcing technique in "The Fall of the House of Usher," a story about a disintegrating family living in a decrepit limestone house located in the midst of a swamp stewing with decaying plants. In this instance, the setting is more than its descriptive details; certain aspects such as the house are *symbolic* (representing something in addition to itself). The house, poised precipitously above the water, is about to descend into its "grave." But in "The Lottery," an almost equally well-known story, the author, Shirley Jackson, sets her story of the barbaric execution of an innocent citizen in a bucolic village on a beautiful early summer day. The brutal act is all the more shocking because of the contrast between setting and event.

Conflict

Conflict is at the heart of every fictional work, whether it be a feature film or a prose story. In a short story, the conflict is likely to relate mostly to the main character. That main character may be at odds with forces such as another character, something in the environment, or even something within him- or herself.

Characters

The main character, the one who deals most directly and most intimately with the conflict, is often called the *protagonist*. The opposition to the protagonist in dealing with his or her problem is often called the *antagonist*. In certain stories these terms may not fit well, but the principle of the main character dealing consciously or unconsciously with conflict is basic to fiction.

In dealing with conflict, the central character or characters are likely to change, resist change, or make some self-discovery. This character or these characters will not necessarily be aware of the significance of what is occurring or even that something is occurring.

Plot

As the character or characters deal with conflict, a sequence of events will ensue. That sequence is called the *plot*. It begins with an *exposition*—an introduction to the situation and the basic conflict. Then it continues through an event or series of events to the *climax*, or highest point in the struggle. Finally, it ends with the *resolution* or a final comment on the situation.

Theme

If the plot is basically "what happens," the *theme* is the significance of what happens. The theme is what the story means in terms of human nature, the human condition, one individual, or particular institutions. The theme is sometimes called the *fictional point*. In some contemporary stories that represent a fragmented, illogical reality, the theme may not be easily stated because the depicted reality itself often defies clear comprehension.

Point of View

Each work is told from a certain perspective, or in rare instances from more than one. That perspective is called *point of view*, which in most stories is either first person or third person.

In the *first-person* story, the reader hears the story from the narrator. That narrator may be the central character in the work; for example, Holden Caulfield in *The Catcher in the Rye* is both narrator and central character. The narrator can also be a minor character or merely an observer. Regardless of the role of the narrator, we get the freshness and directness of someone who is there; the "I" person speaks.

The other common point of view is *third person*. With this perspective we have a narrator who reports from a detached view, never using "I" to refer to him- or herself but instead using third person pronouns such as "he" and "she." The author may choose to restrict him- or herself further by writing in *third person objective*. This point of view presents characters and situations as we would ordinarily perceive them. We get to know people mainly by considering (1) how they look, (2) what they say, (3) how they act, (4) how others react to them, and (5) what others say about them.

The author may claim one other prerogative and reveal what a character or characters are thinking. Thus the author seems all-knowing. This enhanced point of view can be broadly called third person omniscient (a term that may be qualified, depending on the author's self-imposed limitations or focus). The *third person omniscient* point of view (with whatever limitation) is the most common in contemporary fiction. Most thrillers, for example, are told in the third person omniscient point of view with a shifting or multiple approach to allow for a close scrutiny of several characters and their situations.

Analysis

The elements of narrative literature can be considered for emphasis in the analysis of a work, either separately or in combination. You can write a composition mainly about the use of setting in a particular work, or you can write an analysis that is equally concerned with character and theme. But regardless of the emphasis, because you are writing about a work that is made up of interdependent parts, you cannot easily write about one part and completely exclude the others. The theme of the work, the meaning of it, could scarcely be omitted when you consider the various parts, because each part is directed toward the fictional point.

Connecting Reading and Writing

Professional Writers: Reading Selections on the Theme of Love

In place of the usual brief introduction for thematically grouped reading selections, here is a well-known essay classifying eight different types of love. It will serve as a good set of criteria for evaluating the theme of love as developed in the two prose and two verse stories that follow.

The stories offer a wide spectrum of expressions of love: a man with a wandering eye in "The Girls in Their Summer Dresses"; a woman who finds brief happiness in hearing of her husband's death in "The Story of an Hour"; a loving woman and a two-timing man in "Frankie and Johnny"; and an iron-willed, autocratic, possessive husband in "My Last Duchess."

THE QUIGMANS   by Buddy Hickerson

"Your wedding announcement's in the paper, Bob. But the bride's name has been withheld, pending notification of next of kin."

How Do I Love Thee?

Robert J. Trotter

How one loves depends on many things, including who is loving and who is being loved, but each love has certain components. Robert Trotter, using the system developed by R. J. Sternberg, details the different types of love by giving explanations and providing examples.

1   Intimacy, passion, and commitment are the warm, hot, and cold vertices of Sternberg's love triangle. Alone and in combination they give rise to eight possible kinds of love relationships. The first is nonlove—the absence of all three components. This describes the large majority of our personal relationships, which are simply casual interactions.

2   The second kind of love is liking. "If you just have intimacy," Sternberg explains, "that's liking. You can talk to the person, tell about your life. And if that's all there is to it, that's what we mean by liking." It is more than nonlove. It refers to the feelings experienced in true friendships. Liking includes such things as closeness and warmth but not the intense feelings of passion or commitment.

3   If you just have passion, it's called infatuated love—the "love at first sight" that can rise almost instantaneously and dissipate just as quickly. It involves a high degree of physiological arousal but no intimacy or commitment. It's the tenth-grader who falls madly in love with the beautiful girl in his biology class but never gets up the courage to talk to her or gets to know her, Sternberg says, describing his past.

4   Empty love is commitment without intimacy or passion, the kind of love sometimes seen in a 30-year-old marriage that has become stagnant. The couple used to be intimate, but they don't talk to each other any more. They used to be passionate, but that's died out. All that remains is the commitment to stay with the other person. In societies in which marriages are arranged, Sternberg points out, empty love may precede the other kinds of love.

5   Romantic love, the Romeo and Juliet type of love, is a combination of intimacy and passion. More than infatuation, it's liking with the added excitement of physical attraction and arousal but without commitment. A summer affair can be very romantic, Sternberg explains, but you know it will end when she goes back to Hawaii and you go back to Florida, or wherever.

6   Passion plus commitment is what Sternberg calls fatuous love. It's Hollywood love: Boy meets girl, a week later they're engaged, a month later they're married. They are committed on the basis of their passion, but because intimacy takes time to develop, they don't have the emotional core necessary to sustain the commitment. This kind of love, Sternberg warns, usually doesn't work out.

7   Companionate love is intimacy with commitment but no passion. It's a long-term friendship, the kind of committed love and intimacy frequently seen in marriages in which the physical attraction has died down.

8   When all three elements of Sternberg's love triangle come together in a relationship, you get what he calls consummate love, or complete love. It's the kind of love toward which many people strive, especially in romantic relationships. Achieving consummate love, says Sternberg, is like trying to lose weight, difficult but not impossible. The really hard thing is keeping the weight off after you have lost it, or keeping the consummate love alive after you have achieved it. Consummate love is possible only in very special relationships.

(A) NONLOVE

(B) FRIENDSHIP

(C) INFATUATION

(D) EMPTY LOVE

(E) ROMANTIC LOVE

(F) FATUOUS LOVE

(G) COMPANIONATE LOVE

(H) CONSUMMATE LOVE

.... INDICATES ABSENCE   ———— INDICATES PRESENCE

Exercise 1 **DISCUSSION AND CRITICAL THINKING**

1. What are the eight different types of love described by Trotter?

2. What examples does Trotter use? Which ones are general and which are specific? What additional examples can you think of, taken from what you have read and what you have seen in movies and on television?

3. What are some specific examples of the types of love for which Trotter does not provide his own examples?

The Girls in Their Summer Dresses
Irwin Shaw

Michael looks at the girls, and his wife, Frances, becomes annoyed. Is Irwin Shaw writing only about two individuals in this short story, or do the characters represent a general, and long-standing, division between the sexes?

1   Fifth Avenue was shining in the sun when they left the Brevoort. The sun was warm, even though it was February, and everything looked like Sunday morning—the buses and the well-dressed people walking slowly in couples and the quiet buildings with the windows closed.

2   Michael held Frances' arm tightly as they walked toward Washington Square in the sunlight. They walked lightly, almost smiling, because they had slept late and had a good breakfast and it was Sunday. Michael unbuttoned his coat and let it flap around him in the mild wind.

3   "Look out," Frances said as they crossed Eighth Street. "You'll break your neck."

4   Michael laughed and Frances laughed with him.

5 "She's not so pretty," Frances said. "Anyway, not pretty enough to take a chance of breaking your neck."

6 Michael laughed again. "How did you know I was looking at her?"

7 Frances cocked her head to one side and smiled at her husband under the brim of her hat. "Mike, darling," she said.

8 "O.K.," he said. "Excuse me."

9 Frances patted his arm lightly and pulled him along a little faster toward Washington Square. "Let's not see anybody all day," she said. "Let's just hang around with each other. You and me. We're always up to our neck in people, drinking their Scotch or drinking our Scotch; we only see each other in bed. I want to go out with my husband all day long. I want him to talk only to me and listen only to me."

10 "What's to stop us?" Michael asked.

11 "The Stevensons. They want us to drop by around one o'clock and they'll drive us into the country."

12 "The cunning Stevensons," Mike said. "Transparent. They can whistle. They can go driving in the country by themselves."

13 "Is it a date?"

14 "It's a date."

15 Frances leaned over and kissed him on the tip of the ear.

16 "Darling," Michael said, "this is Fifth Avenue."

17 "Let me arrange a program," Frances said. "A planned Sunday in New York for a young couple with money to throw away."

18 "Go easy."

19 "First let's go to the Metropolitan Museum of Art," Frances suggested, because Michael had said during the week he wanted to go. "I haven't been there in three years and there're at least ten pictures I want to see again. Then we can take the bus down to Radio City and watch them skate. And later we'll go down to Cavanaugh's and get a steak as big as a blacksmith's apron, with a bottle of wine, and after that there's a French picture at the Filmarte that everybody says—say, are you listening to me?"

20 "Sure," he said. He took his eyes off the hatless girl with the dark hair, cut dancer-style like a helmet, who was walking past him.

21 "That's the program for the day," Frances said flatly. "Or maybe you'd just rather walk up and down Fifth Avenue."

22 "No," Michael said. "Not at all."

23 "You always look at other women," Frances said. "Everywhere. Every damned place we go."

24 "No, darling," Michael said, "I look at everything. God gave me eyes and I look at women and men and subway excavations and

moving pictures and the little flowers of the field. I casually inspect the universe."

25 "You ought to see the look in your eye," Frances said, "as you casually inspect the universe on Fifth Avenue."

26 "I'm a happily married man." Michael pressed her elbow tenderly. "Example for the whole twentieth century—Mr. and Mrs. Mike Loomis. Hey, let's have a drink," he said, stopping.

27 "We just had breakfast."

28 "Now listen, darling," Mike said, choosing his words with care, "it's a nice day and we both felt good and there's no reason why we have to break it up. Let's have a nice Sunday."

29 "All right. I don't know why I started this. Let's drop it. Let's have a good time."

30 They joined hands consciously and walked without talking among the baby carriages and the old Italian men in their Sunday clothes and the young women with Scotties in Washington Square Park.

31 "At least once a year everyone should go to the Metropolitan Museum of Art," Frances said after a while, her tone a good imitation of the tone she had used at breakfast and at the beginning of their walk. "And it's nice on Sunday. There're a lot of people looking at the pictures and you get the feeling maybe Art isn't on the decline in New York City, after all—"

32 "I want to tell you something," Michael said very seriously. "I have not touched another woman. Not once. In all the five years."

33 "All right," Frances said.

34 "You believe that, don't you?"

35 "All right."

36 They walked between the crowded benches, under the scrubby city-park trees.

37 "I try not to notice it," Frances said, "but I feel rotten inside, in my stomach, when we pass a woman and you look at her and I see that look in your eye and that's the way you looked at me the first time. In Alice Maxwell's house. Standing there in the living room, next to the radio, with a green hat on and all those people."

38 "I remember the hat," Michael said.

39 "The same look," Frances said. "And it makes me feel bad. It makes me feel terrible."

40 "Sh-h-h, please, darling, sh-h-h."

41 "I think I would like a drink now," Frances said.

42 They walked over to a bar on Eighth Street, not saying anything, Michael automatically helping her over curbstones and guiding her past automobiles. They sat near a window in the bar and the sun streamed in and there was a small, cheerful fire in the

fireplace. A little Japanese waiter came over and put down some pretzels and smiled happily at them.

43 "What do you order after breakfast?" Michael asked.

44 "Brandy, I suppose," Frances said.

45 "Courvoisier," Michael told the waiter. "Two Courvoisiers."

46 The waiter came with the glasses and they sat drinking the brandy in the sunlight. Michael finished half his and drank a little water.

47 "I look at women," he said. "Correct. I don't say it's wrong or right. I look at them. If I pass them on the street and I don't look at them, I'm fooling you, I'm fooling myself."

48 "You look at them as though you want them," Frances said, playing with her brandy glass. "Every one of them."

49 "In a way," Michael said, speaking softly and not to his wife, "in a way that's true. I don't do anything about it, but it's true."

50 "I know it. That's why I feel bad."

51 "Another brandy," Michael called. "Waiter, two more brandies."

52 He sighed and closed his eyes and rubbed them gently with his fingertips. "I love the way women look. One of the things I like best about New York is the battalions of women. When I first came to New York from Ohio that was the first thing I noticed, the million wonderful women, all over the city. I walked around with my heart in my throat."

53 "A kid," Frances said. "That's a kid's feeling."

54 "Guess again," Michael said. "Guess again. I'm older now. I'm a man getting near middle age, putting on a little fat and I still love to walk along Fifth Avenue at three o'clock on the east side of the street between Fiftieth and Fifty-seventh Streets. They're all out then, shopping, in their furs and their crazy hats, everything all concentrated from all over the world into seven blocks—the best furs, the best clothes, the handsomest women, out to spend money and feeling good about it."

55 The Japanese waiter put the two drinks down, smiling with great happiness.

56 "Everything is all right?" he asked.

57 "Everything is wonderful," Michael said.

58 "If it's just a couple of fur coats," Frances said, "and forty-five-dollar hats—"

59 "It's not the fur coats. Or the hats. That's just the scenery for that particular kind of woman. Understand," he said, "you don't have to listen to this."

60 "I want to listen."

61. "I like the girls in the offices. Neat, with their eyeglasses, smart, chipper, knowing what everything is about. I like the girls on Forty-fourth Street at lunchtime, the actresses, all dressed up on nothing a week. I like the salesgirls in the stores, paying attention to you first because you're a man, leaving lady customers waiting. I got all this stuff accumulated in me because I've been thinking about it for ten years and now you've asked for it and here it is."

62. "Go ahead," Frances said.

63. "When I think of New York City, I think of all the girls on parade in the city. I don't know whether it's something special with me or whether every man in the city walks around with the same feeling inside him, but I feel as though I'm at a picnic in this city. I like to sit near the women in the theatres, the famous beauties who've taken six hours to get ready and look it. And the young girls at the football games, with the red cheeks, and when the warm weather comes, the girls in their summer dresses." He finished his drink. "That's the story."

64. Frances finished her drink and swallowed two or three times extra. "You say you love me?"

65. "I love you."

66. "I'm pretty, too," Frances said. "As pretty as any of them."

67. "You're beautiful," Michael said.

68. "I'm good for you," Frances said, pleading. "I've made a good wife, a good housekeeper, a good friend. I'd do any damn thing for you."

69. "I know," Michael said. He put his hand out and grasped hers.

70. "You'd like to be free to—" Frances said.

71. "Sh-h-h."

72. "Tell the truth." She took her hand away from under his.

73. Michael flicked the edge of his glass with his finger. "O.K," he said gently. "Sometimes I feel I would like to be free."

74. "Well," Frances said, "any time you say."

75. "Don't be foolish." Michael swung his chair around to her side of the table and patted her thigh.

76. She began to cry silently into her handkerchief, bent over just enough so nobody else in the bar would notice. "Someday," she said, crying, "you're going to make a move."

77. Michael didn't say anything. He sat watching the bartender slowly peel a lemon.

78. "Aren't you?" Frances asked harshly. "Come on, tell me. Talk. Aren't you?"

79. "Maybe," Michael said. He moved his chair back again. "How the hell do I know?"

80 "You know," Frances persisted. "Don't you know?"

81 "Yes," Michael said after a while, "I know."

82 Frances stopped crying then. Two or three snuffles into the handkerchief and she put it away and her face didn't tell anything to anybody. "At least do me a favor," she said.

83 "Sure."

84 "Stop talking about how pretty this woman is or that one. Nice eyes, nice breasts, a pretty figure, good voice." She mimicked his voice. "Keep it to yourself. I'm not interested."

85 Michael waved to the waiter. "I'll keep it to myself," he said.

86 Frances flicked the corners of her eyes. "Another brandy," she told the waiter.

87 Two," Michael said.

88 "Yes, Ma'am; yes, Sir," said the waiter, backing away.

89 Frances regarded Michael coolly cross the table. "Do you want me to call the Stevensons?" she asked. "It'll be nice in the country."

90 "Sure," Michael said. "Call them."

91 She got up from the table and walked across the room toward the telephone. Michael watched her walk, thinking what a pretty girl, what nice legs.

Exercise 2 — DISCUSSION AND CRITICAL THINKING

1. Point out the significance of the setting, either stated or implied.

2. Indicate the main conflict (and any secondary conflict).

3. Name the central character(s) and his or her (their) traits.

4. State the point of view (first or third person).

5. How does the behavior of both characters change after Michael starts looking at other women?

6. Would you say one is more at fault in this argument? Explain.

7. What is the significance of Michael's last observation of Frances?

8. What do you think will happen to their marriage? Why?

9. What would be your "Dear Abby" advice to them?

10. Briefly discuss the theme (what the story means, what it says about an individual specifically or human nature generally).

The Story of an Hour

Kate Chopin

The author of this famous story on love and marriage, Kate Chopin, was left a widow with six children at age thirty-two. Turning to writing seriously, she wrote stories set mainly in the Creole bayou country around New Orleans. Her independent thinking, especially about women's emotions, attracted a firestorm of critical attention to her novel The Awakening, *and two collections of short stories,* Bayou Folk *and* A Night in Acadie, *and established her reputation as a feminist.*

1   Knowing that Mrs. Mallard was afflicted with a heart trouble, great care was taken to break to her as gently as possible the news of her husband's death.

2   It was her sister Josephine who told her, in broken sentences, veiled hints that revealed in half concealing. Her husband's friend Richards was there, too, near her. It was he who had been in the newspaper office when intelligence of the railroad disaster was received, with Brently Mallard's name leading the list of "killed." He had only taken the time to assure himself of its truth by a second telegram, and had hastened to forestall any less careful, less tender friend in bearing the sad message.

3   She did not hear the story as many women have heard the same, with a paralyzed inability to accept its significance. She wept at once, with sudden, wild abandonment, in her sister's arms. When the storm of grief had spent itself she went to her room alone. She would have no one follow her.

4   There stood, facing the open window, a comfortable, roomy armchair. Into this she sank, pressed down by a physical exhaustion that haunted her body and seemed to reach into her soul.

5   She could see in the open square before her house the tops of trees that were all aquiver with the new spring life. The delicious breath of rain was in the air. In the street below a peddler was crying his wares. The notes of a distant song which some one was singing reached her faintly, and countless sparrows were twittering in the eaves.

6   There were patches of blue sky showing here and there through the clouds that had met and piled above the other in the west facing her window.

7   She sat with her head thrown back upon the cushion of the chair quite motionless, except when a sob came up into her throat and shook her, as a child who has cried itself to sleep continues to sob in its dreams.

8   She was young, with a fair, calm face, whose lines bespoke repression and even a certain strength. But now there was a dull stare in her eyes, whose gaze was fixed away off yonder on one of those patches of blue sky. It was not a glance of reflection, but rather indicated a suspension of intelligent thought.

9   There was something coming to her and she was waiting for it, fearfully. What was it? She did not know; it was too subtle and elusive to name. But she felt it, creeping out of the sky, reaching toward her through the sounds, the scents, the color that filled the air.

10 Now her bosom rose and fell tumultuously. She was beginning to recognize this thing that was approaching to possess her, and she was striving to beat it back with her will—as powerless as her two white slender hands would have been.

11 When she abandoned herself a little whispered word escaped her slightly parted lips. She said it over and over under her breath: "Free, free, free!" The vacant stare and the look of terror that had followed it went from her eyes. They stayed keen and bright. Her pulses beat fast, and the coursing blood warmed and relaxed every inch of her body.

12 She did not stop to ask if it were not a monstrous joy that held her. A clear and exalted perception enabled her to dismiss the suggestion as trivial.

13 She knew that she would weep again when she saw the kind, tender hands folded in death; the face that had never looked save with love upon her, fixed and gray and dead. But she saw beyond that bitter moment a long procession of years to come that would belong to her absolutely. And she opened and spread her arms out to them in welcome.

14 There would be no one to live for during those coming years; she would live for herself. There would be no powerful will bend-

ing her in that blind persistence with which men and women believe they have a right to impose a private will upon a fellow-creature. A kind intention or a cruel intention made the act seem no less a crime as she looked upon it in that brief moment of illumination.

15 And yet she had loved him—sometimes. Often she had not. What did it matter! What could love, the unsolved mystery, count for in face of this possession of self-assertion which she suddenly recognized as the strongest impulse of her being!

16 "Free! Body and soul free!" she kept whispering.

17 Josephine was kneeling before the closed door with her lips to the keyhole, imploring for admission. "Louise, open the door! I beg; open the door—you will make yourself ill. What are you doing, Louise? For heaven's sake open the door."

18 "Go away. I am not making myself ill." No; she was drinking in a very elixir of life through that open window.

19 Her fancy was running riot along those days ahead of her. Spring days, and summer days, and all sorts of days that would be her own. She breathed a quick prayer that life might be long. It was only yesterday she had thought with a shudder that life might be long.

20 She arose at length and opened the door to her sister's importunities. There was a feverish triumph in her eyes, and she carried herself unwittingly like a goddess of Victory. She clasped her sister's waist, and together they descended the stairs. Richards stood waiting for them at the bottom.

21 Some one was opening the door with a latchkey. It was Brently Mallard who entered, a little travel-stained, composedly carrying his grip-sack and umbrella. He had been far from the scene of accident, and did not even know there had been one. He stood amazed at Josephine's piercing cry; at Richards's quick motion to screen him from the view of his wife.

22 But Richards was too late.

23 When the doctors came they said she had died of heart disease—of joy that kills.

Exercise 3

DISCUSSION AND CRITICAL THINKING

1. What is Mrs. Mallard's first reaction in hearing of her husband's death?

2. What is her second reaction?

3. Why hasn't she considered freedom before?

4. Did her husband love her? Did she love him?

5. Did he abuse her?

6. Is this story mainly about women's rights, freedom, or some other subject?

7. Why does Mrs. Mallard die?

Frankie and Johnny
Anonymous

Frankie really loved this guy, but he "was doing her wrong," and, well, she took action. This song narrates one of the best-known crimes of passion in folk literature.

Frank-ie and John-ny were lov-ers
Oh Lord-y how they could love. They swore to be true to each
oth-er, true as the stars a-bove, He was her
man But he was do-ing her wrong.

Frankie she was a good woman
As everybody knows,
Spent a hundred dollars
Just to buy her man some clothes.
5 He was her man, but he was doing her wrong.

Frankie went down to the corner
Just for a bucket of beer,
She said, "Mr. Bartender,
Has my loving Johnny been here?
10 He was my man, but he's a-doing me wrong."

"Now I don't want to tell you no stories
And I don't want to tell you no lies
I saw your man about an hour ago
With a gal named Nellie Bligh
15 He was your man, but he's a-doing you wrong."

Frankie went down to the hotel
Didn't go there for fun,
Underneath her kimona
She carried a forty-four gun.
20 He was her man, but he was doing her wrong.

Frankie looked over the transom
To see what she could spy,
There sat Johnny on the sofa
Just loving up Nellie Bligh.
25 He was her man, but he was doing her wrong.

Frankie got off that ladder
She didn't want to see no more;
Rooty-toot-toot three times she did shoot
Right through that hardwood door.
30 He was her man, but he was doing her wrong.

Now the first time Frankie shot Johnny
He let out an awful yell,
The second time she shot him
There was a new man's face in hell.
35 He was her man, but he was doing her wrong.

"Oh, roll me over easy
Roll me over slow
Roll me over on the right side
For the left side hurts me so."
40 He was her man, but he was doing her wrong.

Sixteen rubber-tired carriages
Sixteen rubber-tired hacks
They take poor Johnny to the graveyard
They ain't gonna bring him back.
45 He was her man, but he was doing her wrong.

Frankie looked out of the jailhouse
To see what she could see,
All she could hear was a two-string bow
Crying, "Nearer my God to thee."
50 He was her man, but he was doing her wrong.

Frankie she said to the sheriff,
"What do you reckon they'll do?"
The sheriff he said to Frankie,
"It's the electric chair for you."
55 He was her man, but he was doing her wrong.

This story has no moral
This story has no end
This story only goes to show
That there ain't no good in men!
60 He was her man, but he was doing her wrong.

Exercise 4 — DISCUSSION AND CRITICAL THINKING

1. Point out the significance of the setting, either stated or implied.

2. Indicate the main conflict (and any secondary conflicts).

3. Name the central character(s), and give his or her (their) traits.

4. State the point of view (first or third person).

5. Briefly discuss the theme (what the story means, what it says about an individual specifically or human nature generally).

My Last Duchess

Ferrara, Italy

Robert Browning

Poet Robert Browning creates a chilling character who tells about his "last duchess." Approach this poem with care. It's not easy to understand at first reading, but once you know what to look for, a person within a story will emerge, one you will not forget.

    The duke lived centuries ago in Italy. He was a proud man, powerful and self-centered. Like a king, he more or less owned the city-state of Ferrara and everything in it, even the duchess, his wife. The duchess was his duchess. He had given her his nine-hundred-year-old name. That should have been enough for her, he assumed. Naturally, he wanted her to be happy and smile—but only for him. Unfortunately, she didn't understand. Instead, she smiled frequently at things such as a bough of cherries, a local mule, a casual comment by somebody else. The duke was offended by her democratic spirit, but he didn't feel like explaining his pique. Instead he "gave commands; / Then all smiles stopped together." He did keep her portrait, where her image is "as if alive."

    In the painting, she smiles in a very fetching pose. The duke has installed a curtain in front of the picture. When he wants to see his last duchess smile, he pulls the curtain. Now she smiles only for him. He is very pleased.

    But time has passed, and at the time of this poem he is entertaining a representative of a wealthy neighbor who has a daughter eligible for marriage. She could be the next duchess. The duke pulls the curtain and tells the representative about his "last duchess," the one who had a heart "too soon made glad." It would not be good for his next duchess to be so indiscriminate. The poet does not judge the duke. He lets the duke talk. And talk he does. The duke is a gracious host. He has rare objects to point out. They are all his. If only his last duchess could have understood that! Of course, he couldn't "stoop to blame." Perhaps the next duchess will be prepared if the representative will be so kind as to carry the message. But the duke will not come right out and say that his duchess should derive pleasure only from him. It would be ill-bred and undignified for him to do so.

That's my last Duchess painted on the wall,
Looking as if she were alive. I call

That piece a wonder, now: Frà Pandolf's hands
Worked busily a day, and there she stands
Will't please you sit and look at her? I said
"Frà Pandolf" by design, for never read
Strangers like you that pictured countenance,
The depth and passion of its earnest glance,
But to myself they turned (since none puts by
The curtain I have drawn for you, but I)
And seemed as they would ask me, if they durst,
How such a glance came there; so, not the first
Are you to turn and ask thus. Sir, 'twas not
Her husband's presence only, called that spot
Of joy into the Duchess' cheek: perhaps
Frà Pandolf chanced to say "Her mantle laps
Over my lady's wrist too much," or "Paint
Must never hope to reproduce the faint
Half-flush that dies along her throat": such stuff
Was courtesy, she thought, and cause enough
For calling up that spot of joy. She had
A heart—how shall I say?—too soon made glad,
Too easily impressed; she liked whate'er
She looked on, and her looks went everywhere.
Sir, 'twas all one! My favor at her breast,
The dropping of the daylight in the West,
The bough of cherries some officious fool
Broke in the orchard for her, the white mule
She rode with round the terrace—all and each
Would draw from her alike the approving speech,
Or blush, at least. She thanked men,—good! but thanked
Somehow—I know not how—as if she ranked
My gift of a nine-hundred-years-old name
With anybody's gift. Who'd stoop to blame
This sort of trifling? Even had you skill
In speech—which I have not—to make your will
Quite clear to such an one, and say, "Just this
Or that in you disgusts me; here you miss,
Or there exceed the mark"—and if she let
Herself be lessoned so, nor plainly set
Her wits to yours, forsooth, and made excuse,
—E'en then would be some stooping; and I choose
Never to stoop. Oh, Sir, she smiled, no doubt,
Whene'er I passed her; but who passed without
Much the same smile? This grew; I gave commands;

>   Then all smiles stopped together. There she stands
>   As if alive. Will't please you rise? We'll meet
>   The company below, then. I repeat,
>   The Count your master's known munificence
> 50 Is ample warrant that no just pretense
>   Of mine for dowry will be disallowed;
>   Though his fair daughter's self, as I avowed
>   At starting, is my object. Nay, we'll go
>   Together down, Sir! Notice Neptune, tho',
> 56 Taming a sea-horse, thought a rarity,
>   Which Claus of Innsbruck cast in bronze for me!

Exercise 5 **DISCUSSION AND CRITICAL THINKING**

1. Point out the significance of the setting, either stated or implied.

2. Indicate the main conflict (and any secondary conflicts).

3. Name the central character(s) and give his or her (their) traits.

4. State the point of view (first or third person).

5. What happened to the duchess? On what evidence or reasoning do you base your answer?

6. How does the portrait covered by a curtain represent the kind of control the duke wants?

7. Briefly discuss the theme (what the story means, what it says about an individual specifically or human nature generally).

Exercise 6 — COMPARING THE SELECTIONS

1. How might each of the four couples from the four selections be classified according to the eight categories in "How Do I Love Thee?" Point out the differences between the companions. For example, Michael and Frances have different views on what a loving relationship means.

   "The Girls in Their Summer Dresses"
       Michael:
       Frances:

   "The Story of an Hour"
       Mr. Mallard:
       Mrs. Mallard:

   "Frankie and Johnny"
       Frankie:
       Johnny:

   "My Last Duchess"
       Duke:
       Duchess:

2. How is the couple in "The Girls in Their Summer Dresses" different from the couple in "Frankie and Johnny"?

3. In these four selections, which depiction of love is the most realistic? Why? Are any of them realistic?

Student Writers

Consider these key points in the following models of student writing:

- *Development:* Study these examples, especially for their clear statements of purpose. Observe also how the examples develop

the analysis through the use of references to, summaries and paraphrases of, and quotations and explanations from the story itself.
- *Verb tense:* As is customary in writing about literature, each student essay is written in the present tense. For example, the writers relate events in the story as "He goes to the farmhouse," "She eyes him with suspicion."
- *Quotations:* Quotations can effectively give the flavor of the original story while supporting the point the student writer is making. Use short quotations and blend them into your summary writing and commentary rather than quoting long passages.

Examine the following three examples for correct punctuation, and remember these main points about punctuating quotations:

- With an indirect quotation, you usually do not need commas:

    The girl looked at him "with cold steady eyes."
    He mounts the "final unreasoning assault."

- If you introduce a quotation with a statement that is grammatically complete (an independent clause), you must use a colon:

    The doctor knows why the parents are not volunteering information: "That's why they were spending three dollars on me."

- With a conversational tag such as "he said," you have a choice between a comma and a colon, but a comma is more typical:
    He said, "It is a social necessity."

The following student paragraph and essay are based on "The Use of Force," a short story by William Carlos Williams. Told from the first-person point of view, it is a fictional account of a doctor making a house call to attend to a young girl. When she refuses to allow the doctor to examine her throat (there have been cases of diphtheria, and he feels the procedure is necessary), the doctor decides to force her mouth open. During the struggle, he becomes emotionally involved until he is aware of a "fury," although only he knows he has lost sight of his original objective. However necessary, using force has made her hostile and him furious. He doesn't like what he sees of himself.

In writing about the short story "The Use of Force," Ajax Mylonas was intrigued by the way the central character struggled with two conflicts: one on the surface and one inside the mind.

Mylonas's Writing Process Worksheet shows how his writing evolved from idea to final draft. Notice how he attached short quotations to his outline and then used them in his drafts. To conserve space here, the freewriting has been omitted. The balance of his worksheet has been lengthened for you to be able to see his other work in its entirety.

You will find a full-size blank worksheet on page 27, which can be photocopied, filled in, and submitted with each assignment if your instructor directs you to do so.

Writing Process Worksheet

TITLE More Than Just a House Call

NAME Ajax Mylonas **DUE DATE** Tuesday, May 4, 9 a.m.

ASSIGNMENT In the space below, write whatever you need to know about your assignment, including information about the topic, audience, pattern of writing, length, whether to include a rough draft or revised drafts, and whether your paper must be typed.

> Write a paragraph in which you discuss how the central character deals with his or her conflict(s). Assume that your readers are at least familiar with the story "The Use of Force." Include some short quotations from the story, submit the completed worksheet, a rough draft marked for revision, and a typed final draft of about 200 to 300 words.

PREWRITING STAGE ONE

Explore Freewrite, brainstorm (list), cluster, or gather information as directed by your instructor. Use the back of this page or separate paper if you need more space.

Cluster diagram: Doctor and Two Struggles
- with girl → distrustful; she attacks; he forces → he discovers illness
- parents no help
- with self → she attacks; he's angry; he wins; he's ashamed

PREWRITING STAGE TWO

Organize Write a topic sentence or thesis; label the subject and the treatment parts.

<u>The story</u> <u>has two story lines based on two related conflicts.</u>
  subject   treatment

(For literary analysis add short quotations)

I. The surface conflict
   A. Doctor-patient relationship
   B. Physical struggle
      1. Girl won't cooperate
      2. Doctor uses force
      3. Doctor examines her throat
   C. Job done

II. The inner conflict
　　A. Doctor versus himself
　　　　1. Tries to be professional
　　　　2. Loses self-control ("attractive little thing," "damned little brat," "furious")
　　　　3. Loses sight of objective ("got beyond reason")
　　B. Emotional (brutal) side wins ("It was a pleasure to attack her," "blind fury")

WRITING STAGE THREE

Write On separate paper, write and then revise your paper as many times as necessary for coherence, language (usage, tone, and diction), unity, emphasis, support, and sentences (CLUESS). Read your paper aloud to hear and correct any grammatical errors or awkward-sounding sentences.
Edit any problems in fundamentals, such as capitalization, omissions, punctuation, and spelling (COPS).

Rough Draft with Revision and Editing

More Than Just a House Call

"The Use of Force," by William Carlos Williams, has two story lines. One appears on the surface and moves the plot along. If the author had only written about it, the ~~story~~ account would be no more than ~~journalism~~ a news story. The doctor makes a house call because a little girl is sick. Her parents are self-conscious, and the doctor is out of his comfortable environment. The girl won't open ~~up~~ her mouth for an examination. The doctor insists. After ~~and after~~ a scuffle ~~and some use of~~ he uses force, ~~and he~~ and discovers that she has an infected throat. She will be treated. The story has a happy ending. But weave it in with the other part of the story, and the ending is not happy. The surface story is all between the girl and the doctor, but the deep ~~The subterranean~~ story is between the doctor and himself. It's ~~it's~~ all about the use of force from the forcer's perspective. He's ambivalent ~~mixed-up~~ about the experience at first. The girl is an "attractive little thing," who will soon become a "damned little brat." ~~but is obviously spoiled.~~ She struggles with such vigor that he is jolted out of his easy professional manner. He struggles with her, and she is a worthwhile opponent. He ~~gets caught up in the combat.~~ becomes "furious." He doesn't like what is happening, but he has "got beyond reason." ~~He~~ Although he struggles with himself, ~~and the~~ his bad side wins. He gets what he wants, and no one else knows that he has his own ~~meanness~~ aggression inside, just below the surface. ~~He has tasted the feeling of combat to win.~~ His new role of forcing turns that aggression to even more savage feelings. He remembers that "it was a pleasure to attack her." The struggle, which had nothing to do with medicine, and everything to do with passion for triumph, took the form of a "blind fury." He won the battle ~~for~~ in the first story, but he lost the battle ~~for~~ in the second. We may forgive him for being an imperfect human being, but he won't let himself off that easily.

Final Draft

More Than Just a House Call
Ajax Mylonas

Topic sentence — <u>"The Use of Force," by William Carlos Williams, has two story lines.</u> One appears on the surface and moves the plot along. If the author had written only about it, the account would be no more than

Surface conflict — a news story. The doctor makes a house call because a little girl is sick. Her parents are self-conscious, and the doctor is out of his comfortable environment. The girl won't open her mouth for an examination.

Struggle — The doctor insists. After a scuffle he uses force and discovers that she has an infected throat. She will be treated. The story has a

Outcome — happy ending. But weave it in with the other part of the story, and the ending is not happy. The surface story is all between the girl and

Inner Conflict — the doctor, but the deep story is between the doctor and himself. It's all about the use of force from the forcer's perspective. He's ambivalent about the experience at first. The girl is an "attractive little

Struggle — thing," who will soon become a "damned little brat." She struggles with such vigor that he is jolted out of his easy professional manner. He struggles with her, and she is a worthwhile opponent. He becomes "furious." He doesn't like what is happening, but he has

Literary Analysis: Reacting to Stories   345

Outcome "got beyond reason." Although he struggles with himself, his bad side wins. He gets what he wants, and no one else knows that he has his own aggression inside, just below the surface. His new role of forcing turns that aggression to even more savage instincts. He remembers that "it was a pleasure to attack her." The struggle, which had nothing to do with medicine, and everything to do with

Meaning passion for triumph, took the form of a "blind fury." He won the battle in the first story, but he lost the battle in the second. We may forgive him for being an imperfect human being, but he won't let himself off that easily.

The Use of Self-Analysis
Gloria Mendez

This essay explains that the first-person point of view places the central character in "The Use of Force" in close focus, with all his strengths and weaknesses there on the surface for our analysis—and for his own. The underlinings and margin notes have been added to show how Mendez organized her final draft.

1   One of the main thrusts in "The Use of Force" is point of view.

Thesis The narrator, a doctor, tells his own story, a story about his encounter with an uncooperative patient but also—and mainly—a

Parts of Support story about the narrator's transformation from a mature, rational person to someone of a lower order who has lost considerable self-respect. This transformation happens in stages of attitudinal change that occur during his arrival, his early attempt at obtaining cooperation, his loss of self-control, and his reflection on his behavior.

Topic Sentence 2   When the doctor arrives at the small farmhouse, he feels like an outsider. The family is self-conscious and not sure about how to act around a doctor. They are poor, and out of concern for the daughter, are spending some of their meager funds to get a diagnosis and possible treatment. The doctor observes that they are "all very nervous, eyeing me up and down distrustfully." They tell him very little, wanting to get their money's worth.

Topic Sentence 3   The doctor initially follows standard procedure. He sees that she is feverish and panting. With concern about a local diphtheria epidemic, he asks the mother if she had looked at the girl's throat. In a foreshadowing that the doctor does not catch, the mother says, "I tried to . . . , but I couldn't see." Moving to the hands-on stage, he asks the girl to open her mouth. "Nothing doing." He tries a gentle approach, shows her he has no concealed weapons by opening his hands. But her mother mentions the word "hurt," and the doctor grinds his "teeth in disgust." He maintains his composure as he approaches her. She loses hers, as she tries to scratch his eyes out and succeeds in knocking his glasses to the floor.

Topic sentence 4 <u>Both his tact and his attitude change.</u> The parents are embarrassed; they apologize, threaten the daughter, and awkwardly try to help the doctor. He's disgusted with them, however; they've done all the wrong things. But he admires the girl, even saying he had "already fallen in love with the savage brat." He knows that her anger is caused by her fear of him. He decides to use force—for her own good. The possibility that she has diphtheria is there. The girl's resistance builds: she screams and struggles. He uses a "wooden tongue depressor," and she chews it "into splinters."

Topic sentence 5 <u>It is during this phase of the incident that the doctor joins the struggle at her level.</u> As he admits, "But now I also had grown furious—at a child. I tried to hold myself down but I couldn't." He goes for heavier equipment—a metal spoon. He convinces himself that he must get the "diagnosis now or never." Whether his rationality or truth prevailed in that decision, he does know that he "had got beyond reason. I could have torn the child apart in my fury. It was a pleasure to attack her. My face was burning with it." He has truth and reason on his side, but his emotions as "a blind fury" are in control. He mounts the "final unreasoning assault" and wins. She has an infected throat, and he has exposed it, but she still tries to attack "while tears of defeat blinded her eyes."

Topic sentence 6 <u>The final stage, the recognition, is there throughout the last part of the story.</u> If the doctor had dismissed the incident, we would have thought him insensitive. If the doctor had savored the experience, we would have called him sadistic. But the doctor, with obvious regret, has admitted that he had "grown furious," lost restraint, "got beyond reason," felt a "longing for muscular release," and gone on "to the end."

Conclusion 7 The "use of force" has two effects in this story. The girl resents the force and becomes alternately defensive and offensive. The doctor uses force and becomes so caught up in the physical and emotional conflicts that he is responding to the wrong motive for acting.

It is the point of view that highlights the doctor's feelings of guilt in retrospect. This feeling comes across much more poignantly because this story is, after all, a confessional.

Finding Topics for Literary Analysis

Analytical Writing

Any one of the aspects of a narrative can serve as a good topic for a paragraph or an essay. Here are some to stimulate your thinking:

- *Setting:* Write about the appropriateness of the setting (with or without symbols) in supporting or even in representing the theme. You might use your knowledge of the techniques of good descriptive writing by analyzing what the author has done with diction, images, and figurative language.
- *Conflict:* Discuss the extent to which the main character perceives and deals with the conflict.
- *Character:* Write about the character's changing, not changing, or gaining self-knowledge. Or write an analysis by division based on a few of the central character's traits (such as honesty, dedication, insecurity, immaturity, cleverness, or low self-esteem); use clustering or brainstorming to find these traits. You can also discuss characters in studies of comparison and contrast, definition (perhaps combined with analysis by division as in "Character X is a sexist"), or analysis of causes or effects (the whys or the results of a situation).
- *Plot:* Unless you are going to write about some idea such as irony or reversal, avoid writing about this aspect of narrative literature. The reason is that it's always a temptation to fall into the "plot summary" trap, merely telling what happens in the story rather than analyzing and interpreting.
- *Point of view:* An author selects a point of view that is advantageous to the story he or she wants to tell. Explain why a particular point of view is advantageous; for example, the first-person perspective may characterize, and the third-person objective may provide a sense of detachment or distance.
- *Theme:* Discuss how other aspects of the story (especially setting, conflict, character, and plot) support or establish the theme, the meaning of the story.

Speculative Writing

There are also more imaginative ways of writing about literature. You can personalize aspects of plot, theme, or characterization by applying them to your own life. Or you can creatively alter stories by inventing new scenes for a character, projecting a character into the future to speculate about development, moving a character from one story to another, or fabricating flashbacks that would explain behavior found in a story. You can explore these and other imaginative ways of writing about fiction by trying some of the Topics for Writing About Stories at the end of this chapter. Regardless of the type of assignment you do, you will need to support your ideas in a clear and logical manner.

Topics for Writing About Stories

Reading-Related Topics

"The Girls in Their Summer Dresses"

1. Write a comparison and contrast piece about Michael and Frances. Use particular moments in their conversation (such as at the beginning, then when she becomes annoyed, when they decide to have a drink, and when they decide to visit with friends) or character traits (such as honesty, loyalty, love, affection, lust, forgiveness) for points in your organization.

2. Write an analysis by division of Francis or Michael, using character traits such as those indicated in question 1.

3. Write about the significance of setting.

4. State the theme that you think the author implies, and then agree or disagree with it.

5. Write a piece in which you show how the characters' behavior becomes more self-conscious, mechanical, and detached as the story progresses.

6. Develop a persuasive piece in which you argue that either Michael or Frances is primarily at fault.

7. Argue that neither Michael nor Frances is at fault because men and women simply have different views toward male-female relationships.

8. Imagine the couple a year or so in the future, and write about them at that time.

"The Story of an Hour"

9. Write a diary account of some of the experiences Mrs. Mallard went through in her marriage—experiences that made her long for freedom.

10. Pose as the husband and write a eulogy that he would deliver at his wife's funeral. Include examples of the love they shared. Through his words, have him reveal what type of husband he was. For instance, he may reveal himself as a well-intentioned yet controlling person, but he will not recognize himself as such.

11. Write an essay in which you argue that Mrs. Mallard's reaction is far more likely to be experienced by a woman than by a man; or argue against that view.

12. Discuss the issue of whether, if the roles were reversed, Mr. Mallard could die of the same shock that killed Mrs. Mallard.

13. Assume that Mrs. Mallard has empty love and Mr. Mallard has companionate love, and compare and contrast these two characters in relation to the story's theme.

"Frankie and Johnny"

14. Write an essay on both the causes and effects of Frankie's shooting Johnny.

15. Write an essay in which you discuss the songwriter's techniques in using language and in developing a narrative account.

"My Last Duchess"

16. Write a character study (using analysis by division) of the duke, drawing supporting information from the poem. His traits, such as intelligence, arrogance, and pride (try brainstorming and clustering for more), could provide a framework for your statement.

17. Write a character study of the duchess, drawing supporting information from the poem. If you speculate to round out your study, label your speculation as such.

18. Write an explaination of what happened to the duchess. Use evidence from the poem.

19. Assume that you are the duchess just before the duke took whatever steps he took, and write a diary entry about your life on his estate.

20. The person listening to the duke is an envoy from the leader of another city-state. The leader's daughter is the duke's prospective bride. Write out a statement about the duke that the envoy might

deliver to the young woman. His report can either state the situation outright or be subtle and suggestive.

Reading Selections on the Theme of Love

21. Write an essay in which you classify and analyze the love in one of the four selections according to the eight types of love in "How Do I Love Thee?"

22. Compare and contrast Michael from "The Girls in Their Summer Dresses" with Johnny from "Frankie and Johnny."

23. Compare and contrast Frances from "The Girls in Their Summer Dresses" with Frankie from "Frankie and Johnny."

24. Write an essay on love in which you show that these four selections illustrate the main types of love. (References to "How Do I Love Thee?" are optional.)

25. Using the same stanzaic patterns as in "Frankie and Johnny," write a ballad about Frances and Michael from "The Girls in Their Summer Dresses."

26. Pose as the duke from "My Last Duchess" and write a statement in which he asks Frankie of "Frankie and Johnny" to be his new bride. Then write her answer to him.

27. Write a paragraph or an essay in which you argue that one of these four pieces is the most realistic view of the true nature of love. You may refer to more than one. Include insights from "How Do I Love Thee?" if you like.

28. Compare the duke from "My Last Duchess" with Brently Mallard from "The Story of an Hour."

Career-Related Topics

29. Discuss the idea of dating among employees. Is it usually a good or a bad idea? Does dating generally improve or damage workplace morale in the long run? Should there be any company guidelines? Use whatever ideas you have acquired from considering the five reading selections on the theme of love as supporting information.

General Topic

30. Write about another story from a source other than this book using the guidelines for writing about literature presented in this chapter.

Writer's Guidelines: Literary Analysis

1. In analyzing a piece of literature, consider its setting, conflict, characters, plot, point of view, and especially its theme. You would usually emphasize one of those aspects.

2. Writing about literature may be analytical (as in point 1), or it may be more speculative, personal, or comparative.

3. Develop your ideas by referring directly to the story; by explaining; and by using summaries, paraphrases, and quotations.

4. Use the present tense in relating events in the story.

5. Use quotation marks correctly around the words you borrow.

6. For organization, consider patterns of development such as analysis by division, comparison and contrast, and cause and effect.

7. Use the writing process.
   - Write and then revise your paragraph or essay as many times as necessary for coherence, language (usage, tone, and diction), unity, emphasis, support, and sentences (CLUESS).
   - Read your work aloud to hear and correct any grammatical errors or awkward-sounding sentences.
   - Edit any problems in fundamentals, such as capitalization, omissions, punctuation, and spelling (COPS).

Part III

English Usage

13

Handbook: Writing Effective Sentences

Identifying Parts of Speech, p. 355

Identifying Subjects and Verbs, p. 363

Writing Different Kinds of Sentences, p. 365

Combining Sentences, p. 368

Correcting Fragments, Comma Splices, and Run-Ons, p. 372

Working with Verb Forms, p. 375

Making Subjects and Verbs Agree, p. 381

Giving Verbs Voice, p. 385

Selecting Pronouns, p. 387

Using Adjectives and Adverbs, p. 391

Balancing Sentence Parts, p. 395

Mastering Punctuation, p. 397

Conquering Capitalization, p. 402

Improving Spelling, p. 408

Correcting ESL Problems, p. 416

THE QUIGMANS by Buddy Hickerson

[Captain! I'm in trouble up here on Hill 42! I need reinforcement!

O.K., Sarge... Well... you're a good-looking man... always well-groomed... good sense of humor...snappy dresser... is that enough?]

© Tribune Media Services, Inc. All Rights Reserved. Reprinted with permission.

This chapter presents rules and examples for grammar, usage, punctuation, and capitalization. In addition, it includes an exercise of twenty items for each unit. The answers to the first ten items within each exercise appear in the Answer Key near the end of this book. Another good way to practice basic writing skills is to write your own examples. In working with verb tense, for example, you could write sentences (perhaps similar to the model sentences) in which you apply the appropriate patterns. In working with punctuation, you could write sentences that demonstrate your ability to use different punctuation marks correctly.

Additional instruction in sentence writing can be found in Chapter 3.

Identifying Parts of Speech

To classify a word as a part of speech, we observe two simple principles:

- The word must be in the context of communication, usually in a sentence.
- We must be able to identify the word with others that have similar characteristics—the eight parts of speech: nouns, pronouns, verbs, adjectives, adverbs, prepositions, conjunctions, or interjections.

The first principle is important because some words can be any of several parts of speech. The word *round,* for example, can function as five:

- I watched the potter *round* the block of clay. (verb)
- I saw her go *round* the corner. (preposition)
- She has a *round* head. (adjective)
- The Astronauts watched the world go *round.* (adverb)
- The champ knocked him out in one *round.* (noun)

1. Nouns

a. **Nouns are naming words.** Nouns may name persons, animals, plants, places, things, substances, qualities, or ideas—for example, *Bart, armadillo, Mayberry, tree, rock, cloud, love, ghost, music, virtue.*

b. **Nouns are often pointed out by noun indicators.** These noun indicators—*the, a, an*—signal that a noun is ahead, although there may be words between the indicator and the noun itself.

    the slime   *a* werewolf   *an* aardvark
    the green slime   *a* hungry werewolf   *an* angry aardvark

2. Pronouns

A **pronoun** is a word that is used in place of a noun.

a. Some pronouns may represent specific persons or things:

I	she	they	you
me	her	them	yourself
myself	herself	themselves	yourselves
it	he	we	who
itself	him	us	whom
that	himself	ourselves	

b. Indefinite pronouns refer to nouns (persons, places, things) in a general way:

    each   everyone   nobody   somebody

c. Other pronouns point out particular things:

Singular	Plural
this, that	*these, those*
This is my treasure.	*These* are my jewels.
That is your junk.	*Those* are your trinkets.

d. Still other pronouns introduce questions:

Which is the best CD player?

What are the main ingredients of a Twinkie?

3. Verbs

Verbs show action or express being in relation to the subject of a sentence. They customarily occur in set positions in sentences.

a. **Action verbs** are usually easy to identify.

The aardvark *ate* the crisp, tasty ants. (action verb)

The aardvark *washed* them down with a snoutful of water. (action verb)

b. The **being verbs** are few in number and are also easy to identify. The most common *being* verbs are *is, was, were, are,* and *am.*

Gilligan *is* on an island in the South Pacific. (being verb)

I *am* his enthusiastic fan. (being verb)

c. The form of a verb expresses its tense, that is, the time of the action or being. The time may be in the present or the past.

Roseanne *sings* "The Star-Spangled Banner." (present)

Roseanne *sang* "The Star-Spangled Banner." (past)

d. One or more **helping verbs** may be used with the main verb to form other tenses. The combination is called a *verb phrase.*

She *had sung* the song many times in the shower. (Helping verb and main verb indicate a time in the past.)

She *will be singing* the song no more in San Diego. (Helping verbs and main verb indicate a time in the future.)

e. Some helping verbs can be used alone as main verbs: *has, have, had, is, was, were, are,* and *am.* Certain other helping verbs function only as helpers: *will, shall, should,* and *could.*

The most common position for the verb is directly after the subject or after the subject and its modifiers.

At high noon only two men [subject] *were* on Main Street.

The man with the faster draw [subject and modifiers] *walked* away alone.

4. Adjectives

Adjectives modify nouns and pronouns. Most adjectives answer the questions *What kind? Which one?* and *How many?*

a. Adjectives answering the **What kind?** question are descriptive. They tell the quality, kind, or condition of the nouns or pronouns they modify.

red convertible *dirty* fork
noisy muffler *wild* roses
The rain is *gentle.* Bob was *tired.*

b. Adjectives answering the **Which one?** question narrow or restrict the meaning of a noun. Some of these are pronouns that become adjectives by function.

my money *our* ideas the *other* house
this reason *these* apples

c. Adjectives answering the **How many?** question are, of course, numbering words.

some people *each* pet *few* goals
three dollars *one* glove

d. The words *a, an,* and *the* are adjectives called *articles.* As noun indicators, they point out persons, places, and things.

5. Adverbs

a. **Adverbs** modify verbs, adjectives, and other adverbs. Adverbs answer the questions *How? Where? When?* and *To what degree?*

    Modifying Verbs: They <u>did</u> their work <u>quickly</u>.
                                                 v   adv

    Modifying Adjectives: They were <u>somewhat</u> <u>happy</u>.
                                                         adv   adj

- Adverbs that answer the **How?** question are concerned with manner or way.

        She ate the snails *hungrily.*

        He snored *noisily.*

- Adverbs that answer the **Where?** question show location.

        They drove *downtown.*

        He stayed *behind.*

        She climbed *upstairs.*

- Adverbs that answer the **When?** question indicate time.

        The ship sailed *yesterday.*

        I expect an answer *soon.*

- Adverbs that answer the **To what degree?** question express extent.

        She is *entirely* correct.

        He was *somewhat* annoyed.

b. Most words ending in *-ly* are adverbs.

        He completed the task <u>skillfully</u>.
                                         adv

        She answered him <u>courteously</u>.
                                       adv

However, there are a few exceptions.

        The house provided a <u>lovely</u> view of the valley.
                                            adj

        Your goblin mask is <u>ugly</u>.
                                    adj

6. Prepositions

a. A **preposition** is a word or words that function as a connective. The preposition connects its object(s) to some other word(s) in the sentence. A preposition and its object(s)—usually a noun or pronoun—with modifiers make up a **prepositional phrase.**

Bart worked <u>against</u> great <u>odds.</u>
              prep   object
          prepositional phrase

Everyone <u>in</u> his <u>household</u> cheered his effort.
        prep   object
     prepositional phrase

The most common prepositions include the following:

about	before	but	into	past
above	behind	by	like	to
across	below	despite	near	toward
after	beneath	down	of	under
against	beside	for	off	until
among	between	from	on	upon
around	beyond	in	over	with

b. Some prepositions are composed of more than one word and are constructed using other parts of speech:

according to	as far as	because of	in spite of
ahead of	as well as	in back of	instead of
along with	aside from	in front of	together with

<u>According to</u> the weather <u>report</u>, a storm is forming.
     prep   object
        prepositional phrase

c. **Caution:** Do not confuse adverbs with prepositions.

I went *across* slowly. (without an object—adverb)

I went *across* the field. (with an object—preposition)

We walked *behind* silently. (without an object—adverb)

We walked *behind* the mall. (with an object—preposition)

7. Conjunctions

a. A **conjunction** connects and shows a relationship between words, phrases, or clauses. A *phrase* is two or more words acting as a part of speech. A *clause* is a group of words with a subject and a verb. An independent clause can stand by itself: *She plays bass guitar.* A dependent clause cannot stand by itself: *when she plays bass guitar.*

b. There are two kinds of conjunctions: coordinating and subordinating.

- **Coordinating conjunctions** connect words, phrases, and clauses of equal rank: noun with noun, adjective with adjective, verb with verb, phrase with phrase, main clause with main clause, and subordinate clause with subordinate clause. The seven common coordinating conjunctions are *for, and, nor, but, or, yet,* and *so.* (They form the acronym FANBOYS.)

   Two Nouns: Bring a <u>pencil</u> <u>and</u> some <u>paper</u>.
                       noun conj   noun

   Two Phrases: Did she go <u>to the store</u> <u>or</u> <u>to the game</u>?
                       prep phrase conj prep phrase

   Paired conjunctions such as *either/or, neither/nor,* or *both/and* are usually classed as coordinating conjunctions.

   <u>Neither</u> the coach <u>nor</u> the manager was at fault.
      conj   conj

- **Subordinating conjunctions** connect dependent clauses with main clauses. The most common subordinating conjunctions include the following:

after	because	provided	whenever
although	before	since	where
as	but that	so that	whereas
as if	if	till	wherever
as long as	in order that	until	
as soon as	notwithstanding	when	

   Sometimes the dependent clause comes *before* the main clause, and is set off by a comma.

   <u>Although</u> <u>she</u> <u>was</u> in pain, she stayed in the game.
      conj   sub   v
         dependent clause

   Sometimes the dependent clause comes *after* the main clause, where it usually is *not* set off by a comma.

She stayed in the game <u>because</u> <u>she</u> <u>was needed</u>.
                                                     conj   sub   v
                                                  dependent clause

c. **Caution:** Certain words can function as either conjunctions or prepositions. It is necessary to look ahead to see if the word introduces a clause with a subject and verb—conjunction function—or takes an object—preposition function. Some of the words with two functions are these: *after, for, since,* and *until.*

> *After* the concert was over, we went home. (clause follows—conjunction)
>
> *After* the concert, we went home. (object follows—preposition)

8. Interjections

a. An **interjection** conveys strong emotion or surprise. When an interjection appears alone, it is usually punctuated with an exclamation mark.

> Wow!   Curses!   Cowabunga!   Yaba dabba doo!

b. When an interjection appears as part of a sentence, it is usually followed by a comma.

> Oh, I did not consider that problem.

c. The interjection may seem exciting, but it is seldom appropriate for college writing.

Exercise 1   IDENTIFYING PARTS OF SPEECH

Identify the part of speech of each italicized word or group of words by placing the appropriate abbreviations in the blanks. (See Answer Key for answers to 1 through 10.)

n	noun	pro	pronoun
v	verb	adj	adjective
adv	adverb	prep	preposition
conj	conjunction	interj	interjection

1. You *must attend* the three sessions *or* he will dock you a day's pay.   _____

2. Roberto seemed *too tired* to answer any more questions.   _____

3. We *enjoyed* the movie *because* it was a good comedy. _____

4. *These* are very troubled times *that* require all our strength. _____

5. The *work* was progressing *according to* schedule. _____

6. Will the girls practice *later than* they did last evening? _____

7. *Among* the visitors was a *famous* novelist. _____

8. *Red* is a very *common* autumn color. _____

9. *Politics* can be a *very* divisive topic of conversation. _____

10. For the winter formal, Shadu *bought himself* a new tuxedo. _____

11. *In spite of* the weather, we *found* the hidden cave. _____

12. Charley is a *far* wiser person *since* his defeat. _____

13. *That* is an impossible *request,* which I know I cannot fulfill. _____

14. *Even though* Mitchico was *ill,* she went to her classes. _____

15. The Pacific *fleet* was *nearly* destroyed in that attack. _____

16. It was a *thrilling* novel *of* the last war. _____

17. What *kind* of individual can *he* be? _____

18. The player *who* caught the pass *is* Roy Patton. _____

19. Jonelle came to the meeting, *though* she could remain *only* a few minutes. _____

20. We *should have seen* Gordon's car approaching *earlier*.

Identifying Subjects and Verbs

The **subject** is what the sentence is about, and the **verb** indicates what the subject is doing or is being.

Subjects

You can recognize the **simple subject** by asking Who? or What? causes the action or expresses the state of being found in the verb.

1. The **simple subject** and the **simple verb** can be single or compound.

    My *friend* and *I* have much in common.

    My friend *came* and *left* a present.

2. Although the subject usually appears before the verb, it may follow the verb.

    From tiny acorns grow mighty *oaks*.

3. The command, or **imperative,** sentence has a "you" as the implied subject, and no stated subject.

    (*You* understood) Read the notes.

4. Be careful not to confuse a subject with an **object of a preposition.**

    The *leader* [subject] of the *students* [object of the preposition] is dynamic.

Verbs

Verbs show action or express being in relation to the subject.

1. **Action verbs** suggest movement or accomplishment in idea or deed.

    He *dropped* the book. (movement)

    He *read* the book. (accomplishment)

2. **Being verbs** indicate existence.

    They *were* concerned.

3. Verbs may appear as single words or phrases.

    He *led* the charge. (single word)

    She *is leading* the charge. (phrase)

4. Verbs that are joined by a coordinating conjunction such as *and* and *or* are called **compound verbs.**

   She *worked* for twenty-five years and *retired*.

5. Do not confuse verbs with **verbals;** verbals are verblike words that function as other parts of speech.

   The bird *singing* [participle acting as an adjective] in the tree is defending its territory.

   Singing [gerund acting as a noun subject] is fun.

   I want *to eat* [infinitive acting as a noun object].

6. Do not confuse **adverbs** such as *never, not,* and *hardly* with verbs; they only modify verbs.

7. Do not overlook a part of the verb that is separated from another part in a question.

   "Where *had* the defendant *gone* on that fateful night?"

Exercise 2 — IDENTIFYING SUBJECTS AND VERBS

Write the simple subject, without modifiers, in the first blank; write the verb in the second blank. Some sentences have compound subjects, compound verbs, or both. (See Answer Key for answers 1 through 10.)

1. My brother and his friend sold tickets for the field day. _____ _____

2. Can somebody in command give us permission to moor our boat? _____ _____

3. There were several excellent applicants for the position of dean of studies. _____ _____

4. Now comes the best part of the entertainment. _____ _____

5. Please read the minutes of the previous meeting. _____ _____

6. During the first ten minutes of the game, our team, with two of the players out on fouls, scored two goals. _____ _____

7. Never again will I be able to speak to Ruby about that. _____ _____

8. There will be among your visitors today two agents from the Federal Bureau of Investigation. _____

9. Both the coach and the players were angered by a series of unjust penalties. _____

10. The cast was congratulated and given bonuses by a grateful producer. _____

11. Never again will Lewan help her with the work. _____

12. A tour of the churches and castles of Denmark is a worthwhile experience. _____

13. Shut that window and take your seat. _____

14. Rodrigo wanted to dig the foundation and to erect the framework of the new building. _____

15. How many books are published each month on that particular subject? _____

16. Two important items on the agenda were salaries and a pension plan. _____

17. Anna's unassuming attitude and careful concern for details impressed her employer. _____

18. The spectators stood, cheered, and waved their pennants. _____

19. Where have we placed those new suits? _____

20. Way up the steep mountain path stood Seth. _____

Writing Different Kinds of Sentences

On the basis of number and kinds of clauses, sentences may be classified as simple, compound, complex, and compound-complex.

Clauses

1. A **clause** is a group of words with a subject and a verb that functions as a part or all of a complete sentence. There are two kinds of clauses: (1) independent (main) and (2) dependent (subordinate).

2. An **independent (main) clause** is a group of words with a subject and verb that can stand alone and make sense. An independent clause expresses a complete thought by itself and can be written as a separate sentence.

    I have the money.

3. A **dependent clause** is a group of words with a subject and verb that depends on a main clause to give it meaning. The dependent clause functions in the common sentence patterns as a noun, an adjective, or an adverb.

    When I have the money

Kinds of Sentences Defined

Kind	Definition	Example
1. Simple	One independent clause	She did the work well.
2. Compound	Two or more independent clauses	She did the work well, and she was paid well.
3. Complex	One independent clause and one or more dependent clauses	*Because she did the work well, she was paid well.*
4. Compound-Complex	Two or more independent clauses and one or more dependent clauses	*Because she did the work well, she was paid well, and she was satisfied.*

Punctuation

1. Use a comma before a coordinating conjunction (*for, and, nor, but, or, yet, so*) between two independent clauses.

    The movie was good, but the tickets were expensive.

2. Use a comma after a dependent clause (beginning with a subordinating conjunction such as *because, although, when, since,* or *before*) that occurs before the main clause.

    When the bus arrived, we quickly boarded.

3. Use a semicolon between two independent clauses if there is no coordinating conjunction.

> The bus arrived; we quickly boarded.

4. Use a semicolon before and usually a comma after a conjunctive adverb (such as *however, otherwise, therefore, on the other hand,* and *in fact*), between two independent clauses (no comma after *then, also, now, thus,* and *soon*).

> The Dodgers have not played well this year; however, the Giants have won ten games in a row.

> Spring training went well; then the regular baseball season began.

Exercise 3 — WRITING DIFFERENT KINDS OF SENTENCES

Indicate the kind of sentence by writing the appropriate abbreviations in the blanks. (See Answer Key for answers to 1 through 10.)

S	simple
CP	compound
CX	complex
CC	compound-complex

_____ 1. William and Henry James contributed much to American philosophy and literature.

_____ 2. William was the philosopher, and Henry was the novelist and short-story writer.

_____ 3. Although William revolutionized philosophy, Henry is considered the better known.

_____ 4. Henry, who lived in England, wrote fiction; William stayed home and lectured.

_____ 5. He is taller than I am.

_____ 6. Some take up bicycling; others try swimming for their exercise.

_____ 7. Those who brought equipment went skiing; others stayed in the lodge.

_____ 8. Colorful clothing styles have become popular, especially in California.

_____ 9. To avoid foolish mistakes, always read the directions carefully.

_____ 10. Any money that I receive from the trust will be invested.

_____ 11. The wait seemed endless to the lovers, but at last the wedding day came.

_____ 12. I thought that I had given the right answer; however, I was proved wrong.

_____ 13. His efforts to comfort the accident victim were endless.

_____ 14. Dropped from the fifty-story window, the flowerpot shattered on the sidewalk.

_____ 15. Because I have debts, I will have to postpone my vacation.

_____ 16. I believed that he was honest; therefore, I gave him my wallet to hold.

_____ 17. Either you pay your rent this week, or you will be asked to move out.

_____ 18. Sandy, who can pitch, and Willie, who can catch, are valuable players.

_____ 19. Sandy, who could pitch, was retained, but Willie was released from his contract.

_____ 20. In the lion's carcass was honey; Samson took some.

Combining Sentences

Coordination

If you intend to communicate two equally important and closely related ideas, you certainly will want to place them close together, probably in a **compound sentence** (two or more independent clauses).

1. When you combine two sentence by using a **coordinating conjunction,** drop the period, change the capital letter to a small letter, and insert a comma before the coordinating conjunction.

I like your home. I can visit for only three months.

I like your home, but I can visit for only three months.

2. When you combine two sentences by using a **semicolon,** replace the period with a semicolon and change the capital letter to a small letter. If you wish to use a conjunctive adverb, insert it after the semicolon and usually put a comma after it.

I like your home; I can visit for only three months.

I like your home; however, I can visit for only three months.

Subordination

If you have two ideas that are closely related, but one is secondary or dependent on the other, you may want to use a **complex sentence.**

My neighbors are considerate. They never play loud music.

Because my neighbors are considerate, they never play loud music.

1. If the dependent clause comes before the main clause, set it off with a comma.

Before you dive, be sure there is water in the pool.

2. If the dependent clause comes after the main clause, set it off with a comma only if you use the word *though* or *although,* or if the words are not necessary to convey the basic meaning in the sentence.

Be sure there is water in the pool before you dive.

Coordination and Subordination

At times you may want to show the relationship of three or more ideas within one sentence. If that relationship involves two or more main ideas and one or more supporting ideas, the combination can be stated in a **compound-complex sentence** (two or more independent clauses and one or more dependent clauses).

Before he learned how to operate a computer, he had trouble with his typewritten assignments, but now he produces clean, attractive material.

Use punctuation consistent with that of the compound and complex sentences.

Other Methods of Combining Ideas

1. Simple sentences can often be combined by using a prepositional phrase.

    Dolly Parton wrote a song about a coat. The coat had many colors.

    Dolly Parton wore a song about a coat *of many colors.*

2. To combine simple sentences, use an *appositive,* a noun phrase that immediately follows a noun or pronoun and renames it.

    Susan is the leading scorer on the team. Susan is a quick and strong player.

    Susan, *a quick and strong player,* is the leading scorer on the team.

3. Simple sentences can often be combined by dropping a repeated subject in the second sentence.

    Some items are too damaged for recycling. They must be disposed of.

    Some items are too damaged for recycling and must be disposed of.

4. Sentences can be combined by using a *participial phrase,* a group of words that includes a participle, which is a verblike word that usually ends in *-ing* or *-ed.*

    John rowed smoothly. He reached the shore.

    Rowing smoothly, John reached the shore.

Exercise 4 — COMBINING SENTENCES

Combine each group of sentences into a single sentence. Use coordination, subordination, or one of the other ways of combining ideas. (See Answer Key for answers to 1 through 10.)

1. The Joad family lived in Oklahoma.
   The time was the 1930s, during the Great Depression.

2. The dust storms hit the area.
   The Joad family headed for California.

3. In California the Joads were not welcome.
   Thousands of poor people had gone to California.

4. The poor people had heard of jobs in fruit picking.
   They discovered that California had more job seekers than jobs.

5. Some large farm owners took advantage of the workers.
   The workers banded together.

6. Jim Casey and Tom Joad became leaders.
   The people learned to help themselves.

7. Edgar Allan Poe wrote a short story titled "The Cask of Amontillado."
   In that story the narrator tells of his experience fifty years earlier.

8. He wanted revenge against an enemy.
   He walled that person up in a catacomb.

9. At first his victim said it was surely a joke.
   He begged to be freed.

10. The narrator refused.
    The narrator cannot dismiss the experience from his mind after all these years.

11. *Carrie* was Stephen King's first published novel.
    In it King used some ideas from his experience as a high school teacher.

12. Carrie is not treated well.
    She is insecure and unhappy.

13. Some of Carrie's peers try to trick her for their amusement.
    She is, at first, deceived.

14. She resorts to using a special power.
    She gets revenge.
    The town will not soon forget her.

15. Tennessee Williams wrote *The Glass Menagerie*.
    It is concerned with four people.
    Each tries to escape reality.

16. The reality is harsh.
    Life is lonely and nightmarish.

17. Laura is one of the main characters.
    She has tried to escape into the world of her glass menagerie and her music.

18. Then she meets a young man she has long admired.
    He offers kindness to her.

19. The young man dances with Laura.
    For a brief time she has confidence.

20. But then she discovers she will never see him again.
    She returns to her glass menagerie and her music.

Correcting Fragments, Comma Splices, and Run-Ons

Fragments

A correct sentence signals completeness; a **fragment** signals incompleteness—it doesn't make sense. You would expect the speaker or writer of a fragment to say or write more or to rephrase it.

1. A **dependent clause** cannot stand by itself because it begins with a subordinating word.

    Because he left.

    When she worked.

    Although they slept.

2. A **verbal phrase,** a **prepositional phrase,** and an **appositive phrase** may carry ideas, but each is incomplete because it lacks a subject and verb.

    verbal phrase: *have studied hard all evening*
    sentence: Having studied hard all evening, John decided to retire.

    prepositional phrase: *in the store*
    sentence: She worked in the store.

appositive phrase: *a successful business*
sentence: Mars Brothers, a successful business, sells clothing.

3. Each complete sentence must have an **independent clause,** meaning a word or a group of words that contains a subject and a verb that can stand alone.

He enrolled for the fall semester.

Comma Splices and Run-Ons

The **comma splice** consists of two independent clauses with only a comma between them.

The weather was disappointing, we canceled the picnic.

A comma by itself cannot join two independent clauses.

The **run-on** differs from the comma splice in only one respect: it has no comma between the independent clauses. Therefore, the run-on is two independent clauses with *nothing* between them.

The weather was disappointing we canceled the picnic.

Independent clauses must be properly connected.
Correct comma splices and run-ons:

1. Use a comma and a **coordinating conjunction** (*for, and, nor, but, or, yet, so*).

    We canceled the picnic, *for* the weather was disappointing.

2. Use a **subordinating conjunction** (such as *because, after, when, although, since, how, until, unless, before*) to make one clause dependent.

    Because the weather was disappointing, we canceled the picnic.

3. Use a **semicolon** (with or without a conjunctive adverb such as *however, otherwise, therefore, similarly, hence, on the other hand, then, consequently, also, thus*).

    The weather was disappointing; we canceled the picnic.

    The weather was disappointing; *therefore,* we canceled the picnic.

4. Make each clause a separate sentence. For a comma splice, replace the comma with a period and begin the second sentence (clause) with a capital letter. For a run-on, insert a period between the two independent clauses and begin the second sentence with a capital letter.

    The weather was disappointing. We canceled the picnic.

Exercise 5   **CORRECTING FRAGMENTS, COMMA SPLICES, AND RUN-ONS**

Write the appropriate identification in each blank and correct the errors. (See Answer Key for answers to 1 through 10.)

OK	correct
CS	comma splice
RO	run-on
FRAG	fragment

_____ 1. Don Quixote was a good man who saw evil in the world, he decided to take action.

_____ 2. He was old, nevertheless, he decided to become a knight.

_____ 3. He was old nevertheless he decided to become a knight.

_____ 4. He was old, but he decided to become a knight.

_____ 5. He was old; nevertheless, he decided to become a knight.

_____ 6. He made his armor from his materials the quality was not good.

_____ 7. He used his own horse, an old nag with a sagging back.

_____ 8. For a squire, he enlisted Sancho Panza, a peasant neighbor who would leave his family behind.

_____ 9. The reason being that he trusted and admired Don Quixote.

_____ 10. Sancho Panza riding a mule.

_____ 11. They went on many adventures together some were laughable.

_____ 12. Don Quixote and Sancho Panza were deadly serious, they had a mission.

_____ 13. Don Quixote would do what he could to rid the world of evil Sancho Panza would be rewarded with his own island kingdom.

_____ 14. Because Don Quixote often misinterpreted reality, he mistook a servant for a noble woman and devoted himself to her.

_____ 15. He usually treated people of low social status and bad behavior very well they often responded by being better persons than they ordinarily were.

_____ 16. On one occasion he attacked a windmill he thought it was an evil giant.

_____ 17. The arms of the windmill knocked him off his horse, but he had an explanation for this misfortune.

_____ 18. Evil beings will sometimes change shapes Don Quixote would not be discouraged.

_____ 19. As he became famous, some people wanted to be near him so they could laugh, however, they often went away with admiration for him.

_____ 20. He sometimes made mistakes, nevertheless, he dedicated his life to virtue, beauty, and justice.

Working with Verb Forms

The twelve verb tenses are shown in this section. The irregular verb *drive* is used as the example. (See pages 377–378 for irregular verbs.)

Simple Tenses

Present
I, we, you, they *drive*.
He, she, it *drives*.

Present, may imply a continuation from past to future

Past
I, we, you, he she, it, they *drove*.

Past

Future
I, we, you, he, she, it
they *will drive*.

Future

Pefect Tenses

Present Perfect
I, we, you, they *have driven*.
He, she, it *has driven*.

Completed recently in past, may continue in present.

Past Perfect
I, we, you, he, she, it, they *had driven*.

Prior to a specific time in the past

Future Perfect
I, we, you, he, she, it, they *will have driven*.

At a time prior to a specific time in the future

Progressive Tenses

Present Progressive
I *am driving*.
He, she, it *is driving*.
We, you, they *are driving*.

In progress now

Past Progressive
I, he, she, it *was driving*.
We, you, they *were driving*.

In progress in the past

Future Progressive
I, we, you, he she, it, they *will be driving*.

In progress in the future

Perfect Progressive Tenses

Present Perfect Progressive
I, we, you, they *have been driving*.
He, she, it *has been driving*.

In progress before now or up to now

Past Perfect Progressive
I, we, you, he, she, it, they *had been driving*.

In progress before another event in the past

Future Perfect Progressive
I, we, you, he, she, it, they *will have been driving*.

In progress before another event in the future

Past Participles

The past participle uses the helping verbs *has, have,* or *had* along with the past tense of the verb. For regular verbs, whose past tense ends in *-ed,* the past participle form of the verb is the same as the past tense.

Following is a list of some common regular verbs, showing the base form, the past tense, and the past participle. (The base form can also be used with such helping verbs as *can, could, do, does, did, may, might, must, shall, should, will,* and *would*.)

Regular Verbs

Base form (Present)	Past	Past Participle
ask	asked	asked
answer	answered	answered
cry	cried	cried
decide	decided	decided
dive	dived (dove)	dived
finish	finished	finished
happen	happened	happened
learn	learned	learned
like	liked	liked
love	loved	loved
need	needed	needed
open	opened	opened
start	started	started
suppose	supposed	supposed
walk	walked	walked
want	wanted	wanted

Whereas **regular verbs** are predictable—having an *-ed* ending for past and past-participle forms—**irregular verbs,** as the term suggests, follow no definite pattern.

Following is a list of some common irregular verbs, showing the base form (present), the past tense, and the past participle.

Irregular Verbs

Base Form (Present)	Past	Past Participle
arise	arose	arisen
awake	awoke (awaked)	awaked
be	was, were	been
become	became	become
begin	began	begun
bend	bent	bent
blow	blew	blown
break	broke	broken
bring	brought	brought
buy	bought	bought
catch	caught	caught
choose	chose	chosen
cling	clung	clung
come	came	come
creep	crept	crept
deal	dealt	dealt
do	did	done
drink	drank	drunk

Base Form (Present)	Past	Past Participle
drive	drove	driven
eat	ate	eaten
feel	felt	felt
fight	fought	fought
fling	flung	flung
fly	flew	flown
forget	forgot	forgotten
freeze	froze	frozen
get	got	got (gotten)
go	went	gone
grow	grew	grown
have	had	had
know	knew	known
lead	led	led
leave	left	left
lose	lost	lost
mean	meant	meant
read	read	read
ride	rode	ridden
ring	rang	rung
shine	shone	shone
shoot	shot	shot
sing	sang	sung
sink	sank	sunk
sleep	slept	slept
slink	slunk	slunk
speak	spoke	spoken
spend	spent	spent
steal	stole	stolen
stink	stank (stunk)	stunk
sweep	swept	swept
swim	swam	swum
swing	swung	swung
take	took	taken
teach	taught	taught
tear	tore	torn
think	thought	thought
throw	threw	thrown
wake	woke (waked)	woken (waked)
weep	wept	wept
write	wrote	written

"Problem" Verbs

The following pairs of verbs are especially troublesome and confusing: *lie* and *lay*, *sit* and *set*, and *rise* and *raise*. One way to tell them apart is to remember which word in each pair takes a direct object. A direct object answers the question *whom* or *what* in connection with a verb. The words *lay*, *raise*, and *set* take a direct object.

> He *raised* the window. (He *raised* what?)

Lie, *rise*, and *sit*, however, cannot take a direct object. We cannot, for example, say "He rose the window." In the examples, the italicized words are objects.

Present Tense	Meaning	Past Tense	Past Participle	Example
lie	to rest	lay	lain	I lay down to rest.
lay	to place something	laid	laid	We laid the *books* on the table.
rise	to go up	rose	risen	The smoke rose quickly.
raise	to lift	raised	raised	She raised the *question*.
sit	to rest	sat	sat	He sat in the chair.
set	to place something	set	set	They set the *basket* on the floor.

Verb Tense

These rules about selecting a **tense** for certain kinds of writing are flexible, but you should be consistent, changing tense only for a good reason. Usually you should select the present tense to write about literature.

> Moby Dick *is* a famous white whale.

Select the past tense to write about yourself (usually) or something historical (always).

> I *was* eighteen when I *decided* I *was* ready for independence.

Exercise 6 **WORKING WITH VERB FORMS**

Write the correct verb in the blank. (See Answer Key for answers to 1 through 10.)

_____ 1. If you (lie, lay) down, the exercise does you no good.

_____ 2. The doctor told him that his trouble was caused by the water he had (drank, drunk).

_____ 3. The game began before the bets were (lain, laid) on the table.

_____ 4. The Halloween mask and costume made the children wonder who she was (suppose, supposed) to be.

_____ 5. The audience ruined his act because it just (set, sat) there.

_____ 6. Nate wanted to do the right thing, but he didn't know what he should (had have) done.

_____ 7. The ball would not stop rolling even when she (set, sat) it between the two books.

_____ 8. In his thirties, Floyd (use, used) to rise at 8:00 and be at work by 9:00.

_____ 9. The European audiences would (rise, raise) up in a body and applaud her for several minutes.

_____ 10. The inspector accidentally (rang, rung) the bell that summoned the villagers to town meetings.

_____ 11. She lived in the old house for thirty-two years, and the shades were never (risen, raised).

_____ 12. Given her confused testimony, she must (had, have) been guilty.

_____ 13. Any good doctor would insist that a toddler (lie, lay) down every day to rest.

_____ 14. Every day for three months, they (eat, ate) the same boring meals and complained as usual.

_____ 15. Before his mother said a word, he told everyone he had been (lying, laying) down when the fire started.

_____ 16. When Gloria said her balloon (busted, burst), the other employees sympathized.

_____ 17. Rubinstein refused to start until everyone was (setting, sitting) down.

_____ 18. The last thing the board wanted was to have the president (rise, raise) from her chair and start the ticker tape.

_____ 19. The group at the church whispered that he had (drank, drunk) himself to death.

_____ 20. Four kittens (lay, laid) in the basket like balls of white yarn.

Making Subjects and Verbs Agree

This section is concerned with number agreement between subjects and verbs. The basic principle of **subject-verb agreement** is that if the subject is singular, the verb should be singular, and if the subject is plural, the verb should be plural. There are ten major guidelines. In the examples under the following guidelines, the true subjects and verbs are italicized.

1. Do not let words that come between the subject and verb affect agreement.
   a. Modifying phrases and clauses frequently come between the subject and verb:

   The various *types* of drama *were* not *discussed*.

   Angela, who is hitting third, *is* the best player.

   The *price* of those shoes *is* too high.

   b. Certain prepositions can cause trouble. The following words are prepositions, not conjunctions: *along with, as well as, besides, in addition to, including,* and *together with*. The words that function as objects of prepositions cannot also be subjects of the sentence.

   The *coach*, along with the players, *protests* the decision.

   c. In compound subjects in which one subject is positive and one subject is negative, the verb agrees with the positive subject.

   Phillip, not the other boys, *was* the culprit.

2. Do not let inversions (verb before subject, not the normal order) affect the agreement of subject and verb.
   a. Verbs and other words may come before the subject. Do not let them affect the agreement. To understand subject-verb relationships, recast the sentence in normal word order.

   Are Juan and his *sister* at home? (question form)

   Juan and his *sister are* at home. (normal order)

   b. A sentence filler is a word that is grammatically independent of other words in the sentence. The most common fillers are *there* and *here*. Even though a sentence filler precedes the verb, it should not be treated as the subject.

There *are* many *reasons* for his poor work. (The verb *are* agrees with the subject *reasons*.)

3. A singular verb agrees with a singular indefinite pronoun.
   a. Most indefinite pronouns are singular.

      Each of the women *is* ready at this time.

      Neither of the women *is* ready at this time.

      One of the children *is* not paying attention.

   b. Certain indefinite pronouns do not clearly express either a singular or plural number. Agreement, therefore, depends on the meaning of the sentence. These pronouns are *all, any, none,* and *some*.

      All of the melon *was* good.

      All of the melons *were* good.

      None of the pie *is* acceptable.

      None of the pies *are* acceptable.

4. Two or more subjects joined by *and* usually take a plural verb.

   The *captain* and the *sailors were* happy to be ashore.

   The *trees* and *shrubs need* more care.

   a. If the parts of a compound subject mean one and the same person or thing, the verb is singular; if the parts mean more than one, the verb is plural.

      The *secretary* and *treasurer is* not present (one person)

      The *secretary* and the *treasurer are* not present. (more than one person)

   b. When *each* or *every* modifies singular subjects joined by *and*, the verb is singular.

      Each *boy* and each *girl brings* a donation.

      Each *woman* and *man has asked* the same questions.

5. Alternative subjects—that is, subjects joined by *or, nor, either/or, neither/nor, not only/but also*—should be handled in the following manner:
   a. If the subjects are both singular, the verb is singular.

      Rosa or *Alicia* is responsible.

   b. If the subjects are plural, the verb is plural.

      Neither the *students* nor the *teachers were* impressed by his comments.

c. If one of the subjects is singular and the other subject is plural, the verb agrees with the nearer subject.

> Either the Garcia *boys* or their *father goes* to the hospital each day.
>
> Either their *father* or the Garcia *boys go* to the hospital each day.

6. Collective nouns—*team, family, group, crew, gang, class, faculty,* and the like—take a singular verb if the noun is considered a unit, but a plural verb if the group is considered as a number of individuals.

> The *team is playing* well tonight.
>
> The *team are getting* dressed. (Here the individuals are acting not as a unit but separately. If you don't like the way this sounds, substitute "The members of the team are getting dressed.")

7. Titles of books, essays, short stories, and plays, a word spoken of as a word, and the names of businesses take a singular verb.

> *The Canterbury Tales was written* by Geoffrey Chaucer.
>
> *Markle Brothers has* a sale this week.

8. Sums of money, distances, and measurements are followed by a singular verb when a unit is meant. They are followed by a plural verb when the individual elements are considered separately.

> *Three dollars was* the price. (unit)
>
> *Three dollars were* lying there. (individual)
>
> *Five years is* a long time. (unit)
>
> The *first five years were* difficult ones. (individual)

9. Be careful of agreement with nouns ending in *-s*. Several nouns ending in *-s* take a singular verb—for example, *aeronautics, civics, economics, ethics, measles,* and *mumps*.

> *Mumps is* an extremely unpleasant disease.
>
> *Economics is* my major field of study.

10. Some nouns have only a plural form and so take only a plural verb—for example, *clothes, fireworks, scissors,* and *trousers*.

> His *trousers are* badly wrinkled.
>
> Mary's *clothes were* stylish and expensive.

Exercise 7 — MAKING SUBJECTS AND VERBS AGREE

Write the correct verb in the blank. (See Answer Key for answers to 1 through 10.)

_____ 1. There (is, are) a number of wholesome foods on the menu.

_____ 2. After the explosion, (was were) there any people unaccounted for?

_____ 3. Not one of us (was, were) ready to promise not to fight.

_____ 4. Find out whether each of the skiers (have, has) lift tickets.

_____ 5. Most of the birds on the islands (are, is) related to the finch.

_____ 6. Only a few of the sheep (has, have) enough wool to shear.

_____ 7. Every summer night a dark sky and the evening star (appears, appear) over the western horizon.

_____ 8. The owner and manager (was, were) pleased with the team's standing.

_____ 9. Each camper and each boat (make, makes) trouble for commuters on the freeway.

_____ 10. Every glass and cup in the kitchen (has, have) lipstick on the rim.

_____ 11. Either the doctor or his lawyers (has, have) to testify.

_____ 12. Not only the oil tanks but also the office building (was, were) consumed.

_____ 13. The whole town knew he was one of those people who (spread, spreads) gossip.

_____ 14. The *Sea Gull* is one of the boats that (sail, sails) in the Honolulu race.

_____ 15. The troop, with its leaders, (assemble, assembles) in groups for contests.

_____ 16. Many helpers (become, becomes) necessary for milking the camels, tending the children, making rugs, and preparing meals.

_____ 17. *Antarctic Caves* (describe, describes) a great hole that Admiral Byrd is said to have explored.

_____ 18. The anthropologists believe semantics (is, are) within their discipline.

_____ 19. All he needs for a new watch (is, are) five dollars more.

_____ 20. The psychologist at our school believes a child's environment (is, are) more important than anything else.

Giving Verbs Voice

Which of these sentences sounds better to you?

>Ken Griffey, Jr., slammed a home run.

>A home run was slammed by Ken Griffey, Jr.

Both sentences carry the same message, but the first expresses it more effectively. The subject (*Ken Griffey, Jr.*) is the actor. The verb (*slammed*) is the action. The direct object (*home run*) is the receiver of the action. The second sentence lacks the vitality of the first because the receiver of the action is the subject; the doer is embedded in the prepositional phrase at the end of the sentence.

The first sentence demonstrates the active voice. It has an active verb (one that leads to a direct object), and the action moves from the beginning to the end of the sentence. The second exhibits the passive voice (with the action reflecting back on the subject). When given a choice, you should usually select the active voice. It promotes energy and directness.

The passive voice, though not usually the preferred form, does have its uses:

- When the doer of the action is unknown or unimportant.

>My car was stolen. (The doer, a thief, is unknown.)

- When the receiver of the action is more important than the doer

>My neighbor was permanently disabled by an irresponsible drunk driver. (The neighbor's suffering is the focus, not the drunk driver.)

As you can see, the passive construction places the doer at the end of a prepositional phrase (as in the second example) or does not include the doer in the statement at all (as in the first example). Instead, the passive voice places the receiver of the action in the subject position, and it presents the verb in its past-tense form preceded by a *to be* helper. The transformation is a simple one:

>She read the book. (active)
>
>The book was read by her. (passive)

Exercise 8   GIVING VERBS VOICE

Rewrite the following sentences, changing the passive-voice verbs to active voice.

1. The lecture was given by a famous scientist.

2. The surgery was performed by Dr. Song.

3. The opera was produced by the Vienna Boys' Choir.

4. The winning horse was ridden by Janice Baines.

5. The Wimbledon men's tennis tournament was won by Harold Stanton.

6. Lewis Carroll's *Alice's Adventures in Wonderland* was read by the class.

7. The report for the mayor was written by Jan Brown.

8. The rock star was greeted by thousands of fans.

9. The album was recorded by Elvis on June 15, 1956.

10. The gun-control legislation was passed by both houses of the state assembly.

Selecting Pronouns

A **pronoun** is a word that is used in place of a noun.

1. **Case** is the form a pronoun takes as it fills a position in a sentence.
   a. **Subjective pronouns** are *I, he,* and *she* (singular), and *we* and *they* (plural). *Who* can be either singular or plural.
   Subjective case pronouns can fill subject positions.

   > *We* dance in the park.

   > It was *she* who spoke. (referring back to and meaning the same as the subject)

   b. **Objective case pronouns** are *me, him,* and *her* (singular); and *us* and *them* (plural). *Whom* can be either singular or plural.
   Objective case pronouns fill object positions.

   > We saw *her* in the library. (object of verb)

   > They gave the results to *us*—Judy and *me*. (object of a preposition)

   c. Three techniques are useful for deciding what pronoun case to use.
   - If you have a compound element (such as a subject or object of a preposition), consider only the pronoun part.

     > They will visit Jim and (I, me). (Consider: They will visit me.)

   - If the next important word after *who* or *whom* in a statement is a noun or pronoun, the word choice will be *whom;* otherwise, it will be *who*. Disregard qualifier clauses such as *It seems* and *I feel*.

     > The person *who* works hardest will win.

     > The person *whom* judges like will win.

     > The person *who,* we think, worked hardest won. (ignoring the qualifier clause)

   - *Let's* is made up of the words *let* and *us* and means *"you let us";* therefore, when you select a pronoun to follow it, consider the two original words and select another object word—*me*.

     > Let's you and *me* go to town.

2. A pronoun agrees with its antecedent in person, number, and gender.
   a. Avoid needless shifting in **person,** which means shifting in point of view, such as from *I* to *you*.

     > *I* tried but *you* couldn't persuade her to return. (incorrect)

     > *I* tried but *I* couldn't persuade her to return. (correct)

b. Most problems with pronoun-antecedent agreement involve **number.** The principles are simple: If the antecedent (the word the pronoun refers back to) is singular, use a singular pronoun. If the antecedent is plural, use a plural pronoun.

> Jim forgot *his* notebook.
>
> Many students cast *their* votes today.
>
> Someone lost *his* or *her* [not *their*] book.

c. The pronoun should agree with its antecedent in **gender,** if the gender of the antecedent is specific. Masculine and feminine pronouns are gender-specific: *he, him, she,* and *her.* Others are neuter: *I, we, me, us, it, they, them, who, whom, that,* and *which.* The words *who* and *whom* refer to people. *That* can refer to ideas, things, and people, but usually not to people. *Which* refers to ideas and things, but never to people. In order to avoid a perceived sex bias, most writers and speakers prefer to use *he or she* or *his or her* instead of just *he* or *his;* however, many writers simply make antecedents plural.

> Everyone should work until *he* or *she* drops.
>
> People should work until *they* drop.

Exercise 9   SELECTING PRONOUNS

Write the correct pronoun in the blank. (See Answer Key for answers to 1 through 10.)

_____ 1. (Who, Whom) do you want me to call?

_____ 2. Give it to Matthew and (me, I).

_____ 3. Tony works faster than (I, me).

_____ 4. Let's you and (me, I) leave before midnight.

_____ 5. All but Maria and (he, him) left on the bus.

_____ 6. (Who, Whom) do you think is the best person for the job?

_____ 7. Nevertheless, we were just as careful as (they, them).

_____ 8. I will accept (whoever, whomever) they select.

_____ 9. We (ourself, ourselfs, ourselves) are ultimately responsible.

_____ 10. Do you expect the winner to be (he, him)?

_____ 11. I will try to help (whoever, whomever) asks.

_____ 12. Crystal was the person (who, whom) we thought would succeed.

_____ 13. (We, Us) citizens have a responsibility to be well informed.

_____ 14. They objected to (our, us) doing the work.

_____ 15. No one was more pleased than (he, him).

_____ 16. All of (we, us) residents signed the petition.

_____ 17. It will be read by (whoever, whomever) opens the mail.

_____ 18. I will ask Ruby and (he, him) to go.

_____ 19. Between you and (I, me), I am not interested in the idea.

_____ 20. The cat will not eat (its, it's) food.

Exercise 10 MATCHING PRONOUNS AND ANTECEDENTS

Write the correct pronoun in the blank. (See Answer Key for answers to 1 through 10.)

_____ 1. If anyone saw the accident, will (he or she, they) please tell me?

_____ 2. Ms. Johnson, the president and treasurer, left (their, her) home early for the meeting.

_____ 3. A person should always choose (his or her, their) friends with great care.

_____ 4. Today a nation that does not educate its citizens may find (itself, themselves) unable to compete in international markets.

_____ 5. The audience was so delighted with the performance of the soprano that (it, they) rose and applauded her loudly.

_____ 6. The group of hikers carried a two-day supply of food in (its, their) knapsacks.

_____ 7. Neither Marcalena nor her friends have ever had (their, her) ears pierced.

_____ 8. Ahmad, the former owner and manager of the store, sold (his, their) stocks in the company.

_____ 9. Someone in this class forget (his or her, their) books yesterday.

_____ 10. The jury did (its, their) best to bring in a fair but quick verdict.

_____ 11. Every student at this school must join a club of (his or her, their) choice.

_____ 12. Either Curtis or his friends lost (his, their) way to the beach.

_____ 13. What kind of man would forget (his, their) promises to Danielle?

_____ 14. No one has any knowledge of what (his or her, their) assignments will be.

_____ 15. Brown & Company is having (its, their) spring clearance sale now.

_____ 16. All the workers (which, who) were fired met at his house Tuesday.

_____ 17. Karl was one of those students who were sure of (his or her, their) answers.

_____ 18. Each boy bought a box of candy for (himself, theirselves, themselves).

_____ 19. A boxer must keep in top condition, if (you, he or she, they) expects to win consistently.

_____ 20. Leewan played tennis and basketball very well; she received letters in (it, them).

Using Adjectives and Adverbs

1. **Adjectives** modify (describe) nouns and pronouns and answer the questions *Which one? What kind?* and *How many?*

2. **Adverbs** modify verbs, adjectives, or other adverbs and answer the questions *Where? When? Why?* and *How?* Most words ending in *-ly* are adverbs.

3. If you settle for a common word such as *good* or a slang word such as *neat* to characterize something you like, you will be limiting your communication. The more precise the word, the better the communication. Keep in mind, however, that anything can be overdone; therefore, use adjectives and adverbs wisely and economically.

4. For making comparisons, most adjectives and adverbs have three different forms: the positive (one), the comparative (two), and the superlative (three or more).

   a. Adjectives

   - Add *-er* to short adjectives (one or two syllables) to rank units of two.

     Julian is *kinder* than Sam.

   - Ann *-est* to short adjectives (one or two syllables) to rank units of more than two.

     Of the fifty people I know, Julian is the *kindest*.

   - Add the word *more* before long adjectives to rank units of two.

     My hometown is *more beautiful* than yours.

   - Add the word *most* before long adjectives to rank units of three or more.

     My hometown is the *most beautiful* in all America.

   - Some adjectives are irregular in the way they change to show comparison: *good, better, best; bad, worse, worst*.

   b. Adverbs
   For most adverbs, use the word *more* to form the comparative modifier (two) and the word *most* to form the superlative modifier (three or more).

     Jim performed *skillfully*. (modifier)

     Joan performed *more skillfully* than Felix. (comparative modifier)

     But Susan performed *most skillfully* of all. (superlative modifier)

5. **Avoid double negatives.** Words such as *no, not, none, nothing, never hardly, barely,* and *scarcely* should not be combined.

> I *don't* have *no* time for recreation. (incorrect)
>
> I have no time for recreation. (correct)

6. Do not confuse adjectives with adverbs. Among the most commonly confused adjectives and adverbs are *good/well, bad/badly,* and *real/really.* The words *good, bad,* and *real* are almost always adjectives. *Well* is sometimes an adjective. The words *bad* and *really* are always adverbs. *Well* is usually an adverb.

7. Do not use an adverb such as *very, more,* or *most* before adjectives such as *perfect, round, unique, square,* and *straight.*

8. A modifier that gives information but doesn't refer to a word already in the sentence is called a **dangling modifier.**

> *Walking down the street,* a snake startled me. (dangling)
>
> Walking down the street, I was startled by a snake. (correct)

9. A modifier that is placed so that it modifies the wrong word or words is called a **misplaced modifier.**

> The sick man went to a doctor *with a high fever.* (misplaced)
>
> The sick man with a high fever went to a doctor. (correct)

Exercise 11   USING ADJECTIVES AND ADVERBS

The italicized word or words in each sentence should be omitted or corrected. Write the omission or correction in the blank. (See Answer Key for answers to 1 through 10.)

_____ 1. The father of the two boys admitted he liked the *oldest* one better.

_____ 2. After two weeks of prospecting, the old man was beginning to walk too *slow* to stay with the others.

_____ 3. *The Tempest* has *real* elaborate stage directions.

_____ 4. Clem threw the ball *more straight* than he ever had before.

_____ 5. The minister of finance felt *badly* when he discovered that the expedition had succeeded without his help.

_____ 6. I'd rather work for someone who doesn't dictate so *rapid*.

_____ 7. The king's problem was always to decide which of his valets was *honester*.

_____ 8. The early English writers *sure* borrowed a great deal from each other.

_____ 9. The wooden horse helped the Greeks win the war *easier*.

_____ 10. No one except the teacher liked those *kind* of plays.

_____ 11. Of the four years I spent in college, my sophomore year was the *harder*.

_____ 12. Gordon should have felt *real* good after recuperating in Patagonia.

_____ 13. Joan Ford and Nancy Montoya were *real* good friends.

_____ 14. The little boy *only whistled* to show them he wasn't afraid.

_____ 15. I do not have *no* time to do the assignment.

_____ 16. It was agreed that the chapel was *real* good for the meeting.

_____ 17. Washington's men got so cold that their spirits were *lowly*.

_____ 18. Lauren had the *most perfect* voice for the role of Violetta of any who tried out.

_____ 19. The doctor said, "He is doing really *good* now."

_____ 20. The stadium was the *most* round structure on campus.

Exercise 12   ELIMINATING DANGLING AND MISPLACED MODIFIERS

In the blank, write "D" for dangling modifier, "M" for misplaced modifier, and "OK" for correct sentences. Revise the incorrect sentences. (See Answer Key for answers to 1 through 10.)

_____ 1. Through hard work, writing can be learned.

_____ 2. Arriving at the airport early, no one was waiting for them.

_____ 3. They installed the carpet in the den with tough fiber.

CHAPTER 13

_____ 4. After waiting in line for three hours, our patience was lost.

_____ 5. They attempted to communicate secretly when no one was looking.

_____ 6. Being alert and well trained, the dogs found the drugs.

_____ 7. To build the house with the inspector's signature, I had to secure permits.

_____ 8. For a long time I had wanted to dance with Pravina in the worst way.

_____ 9. They only worked for three days in the mountain resort.

_____ 10. Arriving late at the box office, no tickets could be bought.

_____ 11. When people dance the twist, the music is a driving force.

_____ 12. Driving late at night in the fog, lights were very necessary.

_____ 13. We heard that the Dodgers had won on the radio.

_____ 14. Soon after I arrived, I was told on holidays that the school is always closed.

_____ 15. That kind of behavior is harmful to my way of thinking.

_____ 16. I tried to thoughtfully and carefully consider the alternatives.

_____ 17. Being well prepared, Jarrett completed the assignment in an hour.

_____ 18. A person of established reputation, Kobe was immediately recognized.

_____ 19. Irene rejected his proposal and drove away from her suitor with screeching wheels.

_____ 20. Bill watched a large crow with binoculars.

Balancing Sentence Parts

1. **Parallelism** means balancing one structure with another of the same kind—nouns with nouns, verbs with verbs, adjectives (words that can describe nouns) with adjectives, adverbs (words that can describe verbs) with adverbs, and so forth.

   Men, women, and *children* [nouns] *enjoy* the show and *return* [verbs] each year.

   She fell *in love* and *out of love* [phrases] in a few seconds.

   She fell in love with him, and *he fell in love with her* [clauses].

2. Faulty parallel structure is awkward and draws unfavorable attention to what is being said.

   To talk with his buddies and *eating* fast foods were his favorite pastimes. (The sentence should be *Talking . . . and eating* or *To talk . . . and to eat.*)

3. Some words signal parallel structure. All coordinating conjunctions (*for, and, nor, but, or, yet, so*) can give such signals.

   The weather is hot *and* humid.

   He purchased a Dodger Dog, *but* I chose Stadium Peanuts.

4. Combination words also signal the need for parallelism or balance. The most common are *either/or, neither/nor, not only/ but also, both/ and,* and *whether/or.*

   We will *either* win this game *or* go out fighting. (verb following each of the combination words)

Exercise 13 — BALANCING SENTENCE PARTS

In the blank, write "P" for parallel structure or "NP" for nonparallel structure. Correct nonparallel structures. (See Answer Key for answers to 1 through 10.)

_____ 1. Both political parties were not only sure that their platforms were needed but also happy that they were different.

_____ 2. The drivers were suspected of changing the compression of both the motor and the size of the wheels.

_____ 3. For thirty years, Senator Fogle has advocated federal work projects and urged regulative agencies to support them.

_____ 4. The newspapers are filled with stories of how deserters are working as spies and they create havoc in the provinces.

_____ 5. He believed that senior citizens make poor drivers and referred to his uncle as a good example.

_____ 6. Boxing may be a dangerous sport, but to box can also be a good discipline.

_____ 7. To increase sales, they hired a new advertising representative and held regular staff meetings.

_____ 8. Unemployment seemed to be the cause not only of the delinquency but also the reason for an increase in the number of divorces.

_____ 9. The new administration has taken over the control of food and drugs and the investigation of air and water pollution.

_____ 10. Mr. James's resignation was as much a tragedy for the company as it was victorious for him.

_____ 11. The leaders were trained in methods of organization, and the followers were coached in ways of cooperation.

_____ 12. To get an English poet for the occasion and paying the fee are two different matters.

_____ 13. Mars is about half the diameter of Earth and has only a tenth of its mass.

_____ 14. Darwin thought of his century as a "golden age," but his opponent disagreed.

_____ 15. One teacher simply ignored the cheating in his classes and rationalizing his position by saying the real students would get an education anyway.

_____ 16. There are not only thousands of cars commuting daily to the downtown hub but also vehicles of all kinds that never leave the hub.

_____ 17. In Delhi, we enjoyed both the flowers that were always in evidence and the climate made them possible.

_____ 18. She would not put up with abstract and subjective interpretations or giving credit for unsupported generalizations.

_____ 19. Madison Avenue takes people as they are and leaves them there intellectually.

_____ 20. He was an undersized man with both an enormous head and a conceited fool with delusions of grandeur.

Mastering Punctuation

1. The three marks of end punctuation are periods, question marks, and exclamation points.
   a. Periods
      Place a period after a statement.
      Place a period after common abbreviations.
   b. Question Marks
      Place a question mark at the end of a direct question.
      Use a single question mark in sentence construction that contain a double question—that is, a quoted question following a question.

> Mr. Martin said, "Did he say, 'Are we going?'"

Do *not* use a question mark after an indirect (reported) question.

> She asked me what caused the slide.

   c. Exclamation Points
Place an exclamation point after a word or group of words that expresses strong feeling.
Do not overwork the exclamation point. Do not use double exclamation points.

2. The comma is used essentially to separate and to set off sentence elements.

   a. Use a comma to separate main clauses joined by one of the coordinating conjunctions—*for, and, nor, but, or, yet, so.*

> We went to the game, *but* it was canceled.

   b. Use a comma after introductory dependent clauses and long phrases (generally, four or more words is considered long).

> *Before she and I arrived,* the meeting was called to order.

   c. Use a comma to separate words, phrases, and clauses in a series.

> He ran *down the street, across the park,* and *into the arms of his father.*

   d. Use a comma to separate coordinate adjectives not joined by *and* that modify the same noun.

> I need a *sturdy, reliable* truck.

   e. Use a comma to separate sentence elements that might be misread.

> Inside, the dog scratched his fleas.

   f. Use commas to set off nonessential (unnecessary for meaning of the sentence) words, phrases, and clauses.

> Maria, who studied hard, will pass.

   g. Use commas to set off nouns used as direct address.

> Play it again, Sam.

   h. Use commas to separate the numbers in a date.

> June 4, 1965, is a day I will remember.

   i. Use commas to separate the city from the state. No comma is used between the state and the ZIP code.

> Walnut, CA 91789

j. Use a comma following the salutation and the complementary closing in a letter (but in a business letter, use a colon after the salutation).

> Dear John,
>
> Sincerely,

k. Use a comma in numbers to set off groups of three digits. However, omit the comma in dates and in long serial numbers, page numbers, and street numbers.

> The total assets were $2,000,000.
>
> I was born in 1980.

3. The semicolon indicates a stronger division than the comma. It is used principally to separate independent clauses within a sentence.

    a. Use a semicolon to separate independent clauses not joined by a coordinating conjunction.

    > You must buy that car today; tomorrow will be too late.

    b. Use a semicolon between two independent clauses joined by a conjunctive adverb (such as *however, otherwise, therefore, similarly, hence, on the other hand, then, consequently, accordingly, thus*).

    > It was very late; therefore, I remained at the hotel.

4. Quotation marks bring special attention to words.

    a. Quotation marks are used principally to set off direct quotations. A direct quotation consists of material taken from the written work or the direct speech of others; it is set off by double quotation marks. Single quotation marks are used to set off a quotation within a quotation.

    > He said, "I don't remember if she said, 'Wait for me.'"

    b. Use double quotation marks to set off titles of shorter pieces of writing such as magazine articles, essays, short stories, short poems, one-act plays, chapters in books, songs, and separate pieces of writing published as part of a larger work.

    > The book *Literature: Structure, Sound, and Sense* contains a deeply moving poem titled "On Wenlock Edge."
    >
    > Have you read "The Use of Force," a short story by William Carlos Williams?
    >
    > My favorite Elvis song is "Don't Be Cruel."

    c. Punctuation with quotation marks follows definite rules.

    - A period or comma is always placed *inside* the quotation marks.

Our assignment for Monday was to read Poe's "The Raven."

"I will read you the story," he said. "It is a good one."

- A semicolon or colon is always placed *outside* the quotation marks.

  He read Robert Frost's poem "Design"; then he gave the examination.

- A question mark, exclamation point, or dash is placed *outside* the quotation marks when it applies to the entire sentence and *inside* the quotation marks when it applies to the material in quotation marks.

  He asked, "Am I responsible for everything?" (quoted question within a statement)

  Did you hear him say, "I have the answer"? (statement within a question)

  Did she say, "Are we ready?" (question within a question)

  She shouted, "Impossible!" (exclamation)

  "I hope—that is, I—" he began. (dash)

5. Italic print (slanting type) is used to call special attention to certain words or groups of words. In handwriting or typing, such words are underlined.

   a. Italicize (underline) foreign words and phrases that are still listed in the dictionary as foreign.

      nouveau riche   *Weltschmerz*

   b. Italicize (underline) titles of books (except the Bible), long poems, plays, magazines, motion pictures, musical compositions, newspapers, works of art, names of aircraft, ships, and letters, figures, and words referred to by their own name.

      War and Peace   *Apollo 12*   leaving *o* out of *sophomore*

6. The dash is used when a stronger break than the comma is needed. It can also be used to indicate a break in the flow of thought and to emphasize words (less formal than the colon in this situation).

   Here is the true reason—but maybe you don't care.

   English, French, history—these are subjects I like.

7. The colon is a formal mark of punctuation used chiefly to introduce something that is to follow, such as a list, a quotation, or an explanation.

> These cars are my favorites: Cadillac, Chevrolet, Buick, Oldsmobile, and Pontiac.

8. Parentheses are used to set off material that is of relatively little importance to the main thought of the sentence. Such material—numbers, parenthetical material, figures, supplementary material, and sometimes explanatory details—merely amplifies the main thought.

   > The years of the era (1961–1973) were full of action.

   > Her husband (she had been married only a year) died last week.

9. Brackets are used within a quotation to set off editorial additions or corrections made by the person who is quoting.

   > Churchill said: "It [the Yalta Agreement] contained many mistakes."

10. The apostrophe is used with nouns and indefinite pronouns to show possession, to show the omission of letters and figures in contractions, and to form the plurals of letters, figures, and words referred to as words.

    man's coat   girls' clothes   *you're* (contraction of *you are*)   five *and*'s

11. The hyphen brings two or more words together into a single compound word. Correct hyphenation, therefore, is essentially a spelling problem rather than one of punctuation. Because the hyphen is not used with any degree of consistency, consult your dictionary for current usage. Study the following as a beginning guide.

    a. Use a hyphen to separate the parts of many compound words.

       about-face   go-between

    b. Use a hyphen between prefixes and proper names.

       all-American   mid-November

    c. Use a hyphen to join two or more words used as a single adjective modifier before a noun.

       first-class service   hard-fought game   sad-looking mother

    d. Use a hyphen with spelled-out compound numbers up to ninety-nine and with fractions.

       twenty-six   two-thirds

Note: Dates, street addresses, numbers requiring more than two words, chapter and page numbers, time followed directly by A.M. or P.M., and figures after a dollar sign or before measurement abbreviations are usually written as figures, not words.

Conquering Capitalization

In English, there are many conventions concerning the use of capital letters. Here are some of them.

1. Capitalize the first word of a sentence.

2. Capitalize proper nouns and adjectives derived from proper nouns.

   - Names of persons

     Edward Jones

   - Adjectives derived from proper nouns

     a Shakespearean sonnet   a Miltonic sonnet

   - Countries, nationalities, races, and languages

     Germany   English   Spanish   Chinese

   - States, regions, localities, and other geographical divisions

     California   the Far East   the South

   - Oceans, lakes, mountains, deserts, streets, and parks

     Lake Superior   Fifth Avenue   Sahara Desert

   - Educational institutions, schools, and courses

     Santa Ana College   Spanish 3   Joe Hill School
     Rowland High School

   - Organizations and their members

     Boston Red Sox   Boy Scouts   Audubon Society

   - Corporations, governmental agencies or departments, and trade names

     U.S. Steel Corporation   Treasury Department
     White Memorial Library

   - Calendar references such as holidays, days of the week, and month

     Easter   Tuesday   January

   - Historic eras, periods, documents, and laws

     Declaration of Independence   Geneva Convention
     First Crusade   Romantic Age

3. Capitalize words denoting family relationships when they are used before a name or substituted for a name.

   He walked with his nephew and Aunt Grace.
   but
   He walked with his nephew and his aunt.

Grandmother and Mother are away on vacation.
but
My grandmother and my mother are away on vacation.

4. Capitalize abbreviations after names.

   Henry White, Jr.   William Green, M.D.

5. Capitalize titles of themes, books, plays, movies, poems, magazines, newspapers, musical compositions, songs, and works of art. Do not capitalize short conjunctions and prepositions unless they come at the beginning or the end of the title.

   Desire Under the Elms   *Terminator*

   Last of the Mohicans   *Of Mice and Men*

   "Blueberry Hill"

6. Capitalize any title preceding a name or used as a substitute for a name. Do not capitalize a title following a name.

   Judge Stone   Alfred Stone, a judge

   General Clark   Raymond Clark, a general

   Professor Fuentes   Harry Jones, the former president

Exercise 14   INSERTING COMMAS

Insert all necessary commas in the following sentences. (See Answer Key for answers to 1 through 10.)

1. John Steinbeck a great American writer was born in Salinas California.

2. Using that area for a colorful setting he wrote some of his best material.

3. In those highly descriptive works he depicts common people.

4. Many of these common people are migrants and farm workers and most are basically good.

5. His most famous novel *The Grapes of Wrath* is set in the 1930s.

6. The main group of people is the Joad family in Oklahoma a mostly rural state.

7. After the dust storms hit the Joad family loses its farm to the bank executives who are taking advantage of the poor.

8. Hearing of need for workers in California the Joads decide to leave.

9. On the trip to California these "Okies" are part of a migratory movement coming from other impoverished areas in or near Oklahoma.

10. Their trip which occupies the first part of the book is a story of suffering compassion and sacrifice.

11. They help themselves and they meet others in similar circumstances on the road.

12. Their will to survive is personified by Steinbeck's description of an ordinary determined turtle trying to cross a road.

13. Finally arriving at the California border the Joads discover that they are not welcome.

14. The large farm owners have advertised widely but they have no intention of employing all who come.

15. Instead they will cynically take advantage of the mass of poor desperate workers by paying starvation wages.

16. When the workers try to organize they are met with violence.

17. Despite the exploitation and suffering the farm workers behave with much courage and honor.

18. At the end of *The Grapes of Wrath* the workers have ennobled themselves in the struggle and have learned the importance of banding together for their human rights.

19. When the novel was published it was regarded largely as a political statement directed toward a current situation.

20. Now it has taken its place as a novel with universal appeal one that celebrates the quest of every person for human dignity.

Exercise 15   **CHOOSING THE SEMICOLON OR THE COMMA**

Insert all necessary commas or semicolons in the following sentences. (See Answer Key for answers to 1 through 10.)

1. I had real friends among my relatives and I had enemies among my former friends.

2. One mother sued the school for expelling her son the expulsion was traumatic to her.

3. She thanked Khanh Doan, the editor; Raquel Perez, the critic; Richard Varay, her secretary and Walter Ross, her agent.

4. The underdeveloped countries have about 69 percent of the world's adults however, they have about 80 percent of the world's children.

5. It was impossible to move for the crowds were overwhelming.

6. The housetops were covered with people cannons were lined up along the sidewalks, and the police officers were stationed at every corner.

7. Freud wanted to go to Rome, a city that fascinated him but his purpose was never clear to me.

8. The lexicographer wanted to put all the names under three headings—philosophers, living or dead; artists, living or dead; and scientists living or dead.

9. Albert Camus did not claim that the universe was rational however, he agreed that humans are both rational and meaningful.

10. The teacher had us reading essays for speed in fact, we were even tested for reading time and comprehension.

11. It's true that Rome fell but most Roman buildings remained standing.

12. The human mind drives us to exploration, sometimes to destruction but not all people are explorers, nor, indeed, are all people capable of real exploration.

13. The novel was exciting and it was full of colorful descriptions.

14. We like talent yet we want it to pay off.

15. He didn't take himself seriously nevertheless, he was hurt when we ignored him.

16. We need moments of privacy for self-analysis, for looking inward; for making sense of others, for looking outward for catching up with life, for looking around; and for inspiration, for looking upward.

17. The mayor regarded herself as very fortunate in winning the election for she was only thirty years old.

18. He pitted Freud against Darwin and Freud won.

19. She treats the United States as a unit her purpose is to establish its unity in the reader's mind.

20. The great artists were also philosophers and scientists indeed, their contributions range through many areas and activities.

Exercise 16 **WORKING WITH ALL MARKS OF PUNCTUATION AND CAPITALIZATION**

One punctuation mark or capital letter is omitted in each of the following sentences. Insert them as needed. (Pairs of quotation marks are considered one unit.) (See Answer Key for answers to 1 through 10.)

1. We never felt that central Park was really centrally located in New York City.

2. Father claimed him as a son, but mother didn't.

3. "Oh I can't believe it's true!" cried Francisca.

4. Tiffany tried to justify her prejudice by getting out Huxleys *Collected Essays* and quoting from them.

5. You can't understand it without the punctuation; is it two boys hats or one?

6. It could be anyones, but its color makes me think it's mine.

7. History was easy compared to any of the french courses.

8. The whale's mouth, with its hundreds of curved slats, is full of hairy fibers commonly called hog's bristles.

9. Tucker said to them, "Remember that Papa said, The good die young!"

10. Wont the question of Clint's hour of birth hold up the astrologer's predictions?

11. The 1970s were good years for us; the clerks treated us with respect and we had more leisure.

12. It was something Truman said about the kitchen—was it about too many cooks.

13. Sooner or later every tourist has to answer one question Is the adventure worth the trouble?

14. We're all two selves—one egotistic and one gregarious—and we cant separate the two.

15. Lincoln—president by mandate—was thought of as the author of the emancipation Proclamation.

16. She had two reasons for going to correct her popularity poll and to demonstrate her courage.

17. Maugham can combine (as in his short story titled On a Chinese Screen) warmth and horror in one paragraph.

18. He always said, Make your choice and take the consequences.

19. The woman was a success, but certainly there was no mystery about it—being queen was well within the scope of Elizabeths talents.

20. Two brothers, Dale and Gilbert, called him uncle Sam.

Improving Spelling

Spelling Tips

The following tips will help you become a better speller.

1. Do not omit letters.

    Many errors occur because certain letters are omitted when the word is pronounced or spelled. Observe the omissions in the following words. Then concentrate on learning the correct spellings.

Incorrect	*Correct*	*Incorrect*	*Correct*
aquaintance	acquaintance	irigation	irrigation

ajourned	a*d*journed	libary	lib*r*ary
agravate	a*g*gavate	paralell	paral*l*el
aproved	a*p*proved	parlament	parl*i*ament
artic	ar*c*tic	paticulaly	pa*r*ticula*r*ly
comodity	co*m*modity	readly	read*i*ly
efficent	effic*i*ent	sophmore	soph*o*more
envirnment	envir*o*nment	stricly	stric*t*ly
familar	famil*i*ar	unconsious	uncons*c*ious

2. Do not add letters.

Incorrect	Correct	Incorrect	Correct
ath*e*lete	athlete	om*m*ission	omission
co*m*ming	coming	pas*t*time	pastime
drown*d*ed	drowned	privile*d*ge	privilege
folk*e*s	folks	simil*i*ar	similar
occa*s*sionally	occasionally	tra*d*gedy	tragedy

3. Do not substitute incorrect letters for correct letters.

Incorrect	Correct	Incorrect	Correct
benefi*s*ial	beneficial	offen*c*e	offense
bull*i*tins	bulletins	peculi*e*r	peculiar
*s*ensus	census	re*s*itation	recitation
d*i*scription	description	scre*a*ch	screech
d*e*sease	disease	substan*s*ial	substantial
dissen*t*ion	dissension	surpr*i*ze	surprise
it*i*ms	items	techn*a*cal	technical

4. Do not transpose letters.

Incorrect	Correct	Incorrect	Correct
alu*nm*i	alumni	p*re*haps	perhaps
child*er*n	children	p*er*fer	prefer
dup*il*cate	duplicate	p*er*scription	prescription
irreve*l*ant	irrelevant	princip*el*s	principles
kind*el*	kindle	y*ei*ld	yield

Note: Whenever you notice other words that fall into any one of these categories, add them to the list.

5. Apply the spelling rules for spelling *ei* and *ie* words correctly.

Remember this poem?

> Use *i* before *e*
> Except after *c*
> Or when sounded like *a*
> As in *neighbor* and *weigh*.

i before e

achieve	chief	niece	relieve
belief	field	piece	shield
believe	grief	pierce	siege
brief	hygiene	relief	variety

Except after c

| ceiling | conceive | deceive | receipt |
| conceit | deceit | perceive | receive |

Exceptions: either, financier, height, leisure, neither, seize, species, weird

When sounded like a

deign	freight	neighbor	sleigh
eight	heinous	rein	veil
feign	heir	reign	vein
feint	neigh	skein	weigh

6. Apply the rules for dropping the final *e* or retaining the final *e* when a suffix is added.

   Words ending in a silent *e* usually drop the *e* before a suffix beginning with a vowel; for example, *accuse* + *ing* = *accusing*. Here are some common suffixes beginning with a vowel: -*able*, -*al*, -*age*, -*ary*, -*ation*, -*ence*, -*ing*, -*ion*, -*ous*, and -*ure*.

admire + -able = admirable	imagine + -ary = imaginary
arrive + -al = arrival	locate + -ion = location
come + -ing = coming	please + -ure = pleasure
explore + -ation = exploration	plume + -age = plumage
fame + -ous = famous	precede + -ence = precedence

   Exceptions: *dye* + -*ing* = *dyeing* (to distinguish it from *dying*), *acreage*, and *mileage*. Words ending in a silent *e* usually retain the *e* before a suffix beginning with a consonant; for example: *arrange* + -*ment* = *arrangement*. Here are some common suffixes beginning with a consonant: -*craft*, -*ful*, -*less*, -*ly*, -*mate*, -*ment*, -*ness*, and -*ty*.

Entire + -ty = entirety	manage + -ment = management
hate + -ful = hateful	safe + -ly = safely
hope + -less = hopeless	stale + -mate = stalemate
like + -ness = likeness	state + -craft = statecraft

Exceptions: Some words taking the *-ful* or *-ly* suffixes drop the final *e*:

awe + *-ful* = awful   true + *-ly* = truly

due + *-ly* = duly   whole + *-ly* = wholly

Some words taking the suffix *-ment* drop the final *e*; for example, *acknowledgment, argument,* and *judgment*.

Words ending in silent *e* after *c* or *g* retain the *e* when the suffix begins with the vowel *a* or *o*. The final *e* is retained to keep the *c* or *g* soft before the suffixes.

advantag*e*ous   notic*e*able
courag*e*ous   peac*e*able

7. Apply the rules for doubling a final consonant before a suffix beginning with a vowel.

Words of one syllable

blot	blotted	get	getting	rob	robbed
brag	bragging	hop	hopped	run	running
cut	cutting	hot	hottest	sit	sitting
drag	dragged	man	mannish	stop	stopped
drop	dropped	plan	planned	swim	swimming

Words accented on the last syllable

acquit	acquitted	equip	equipped
admit	admittance	occur	occurrence
allot	allotted	omit	omitting

a lot	business	divide	finally
absence	certain	dying	foreign
across	college	eighth	government
actually	coming	eligible	grammar
all right	committee	eliminate	grateful
among	competition	embarrassed	guarantee
analyze	complete	environment	guard
appearance	consider	especially	guidance
appreciate	criticism	etc.	height
argument	definitely	exaggerate	hoping
athlete	dependent	excellent	humorous
athletics	develop	exercise	immediately
awkward	development	existence	independent
becoming	difference	experience	intelligence
beginning	disastrous	explanation	interest
belief	discipline	extremely	interfere
benefit	discussed	familiar	involved
buried	disease	February	knowledge

laboratory	physically	rhythm	success
leisure	planned	ridiculous	suggest
length	pleasant	sacrifice	surprise
library	possible	safety	thoroughly
likely	practical	scene	though
lying	preferred	schedule	tragedy
marriage	prejudice	secretary	tried
mathematics	privilege	senior	tries
meant	probably	sense	truly
medicine	professor	separate	unfortunately
neither	prove	severely	unnecessary
ninety	psychology	shining	until
ninth	pursue	significant	unusual
nuclear	receipt	similar	using
occasionally	receive	sincerely	usually
opinion	recommend	sophomore	Wednesday
opportunity	reference	speech	writing
parallel	relieve	straight	written
particular	religious	studying	
persuade	repetition	succeed	

Understanding Confusing Words

The following are more words that are commonly misspelled or confused with one another. Some have similar sounds, some are often mispronounced, and some are only misunderstood.

a — An adjective (called an *article*) used before a word beginning with a consonant or a consonant sound, as in "I ate *a* donut."

an — An adjective (called an *article*) used before a word beginning with a vowel (*a, e, i, o, u*) or with a silent *h*, as in "I ate *an* artichoke."

and — A coordinating conjunction, as in "Sara *and* I like Johnny Cash."

accept — A verb meaning "to receive," as in "I *accept* your explanation."

except — A preposition meaning "to exclude," as in "I paid everyone *except* you."

advice — A noun meaning "guidance," as in "Thanks for the *advice*."

advise — A verb meaning "to give guidance," as in "Will you please *advise* me of my rights?"

all right	An adjective meaning "correct" or "acceptable," as in "It's *all right* to cry."
alright	Not used in formal writing.
all ready	An adjective that can be used interchangeably with *ready*, as in "I am *all ready* to go to town."
already	An adverb meaning "before," which cannot be used in place of *ready*, as in "I have *already* finished."
a lot	An adverb meaning "much," as in "She liked him *a lot*," or a noun meaning "several," as in "I had *a lot* of suggestions."
alot	Misspelling.
altogether	An adverb meaning "completely," as in "He is *altogether* happy."
all together	An adverb meaning "as one," which can be used interchangeably with *together*, as in "The group left *all together*."
choose	A present tense verb meaning "to select," as in "Do whatever you *choose*."
chose	The past tense form of the verb *choose*, as in "They *chose* to take action yesterday."
could of	A misspelled phrase caused by confusing *could've*, meaning *could have*, with *could of*.
could have	Correctly spelled phrase, as in "I *could have* left."
could've	Correctly spelled contraction of *could have*, as in "He *could've* succeeded."
affect	Usually a verb meaning "change," as in "Ideas *affect* me."
effect	Usually a noun meaning "result," as in "That *effect* was unexpected."
hear	A verb indicating the receiving of sound, as in "I *hear* thunder."
here	An adverb meaning "present location," as in "I live *here*."
it's	A contraction of *it is*, as in "*It's* time to dance."
its	Possessive pronoun, as in "Each dog has *its* day."

know	A verb usually meaning "to comprehend" or "to recognize," as in "I *know* the answer."
no	An adjective meaning "negative," as in "I have *no* potatoes."
lead	A present tense verb, as in "I *lead* a stable life now," or a noun referring to a substance, such as "I sharpened the *lead* in my pencil."
led	The past tense form of the verb *lead*, as in "I *led* a wild life in my youth."
loose	An adjective meaning "without restraint," as in "He is a *loose* cannon."
lose	A present tense verb from the pattern *lose, lost, lost*, as in "I thought I would *lose* my senses."
paid	The past tense form of *pay*, as in "He *paid* his dues."
payed	Misspelling.
passed	The past tense form of the verb *pass*, meaning "went by," as in "He *passed* me on the curve."
past	An adjective meaning "former," as in "That's *past* history," or a noun, as in "He lived in the *past*."
patience	A noun meaning "willingness to wait," as in "Job was a man of much *patience*."
patients	A noun meaning "people under care," as in "The doctor had fifty *patients*."
peace	A noun meaning "a quality of calmness" or "absence of strife," as in "The guru was at *peace* with the world."
piece	A noun meaning "part," as in "I gave him a *piece* of my mind."
quiet	An adjective meaning "silent," as in "She was a *quiet* child."
quit	A verb meaning "to cease" or "to withdraw," as in "I *quit* my job."
quite	An adverb meaning "very," as in "The clam is *quite* happy."
receive	A verb meaning "to accept," as in "I will *receive* visitors now."
recieve	Misspelling.
stationary	An adjective meaning "not moving," as in "Try to avoid running into *stationary* objects."

stationery	A noun meaning "paper material to write on," as in "I bought a box of *stationery* for Sue's birthday present."
than	A conjunction, as in "He is taller *than* I am."
then	An adverb, as in "She *then* left town."
their	An adjective (possessive pronoun), as in "They read *their* books."
there	An adverb, as in "He left it *there*," or a filler word, as in "*There* is no time left."
they're	A contraction of *they are*, as in "*They're* happy."
thorough	An adjective, as in "He did a *thorough* job."
through	A preposition, as in "She went *through* the yard."
to	A preposition, as in "I went *to* town."
too	An adverb meaning "exceeding or going beyond what is acceptable," as in "You are *too* late to qualify for the discount," or "also," as in "I have feelings, *too*."
two	An adjective of number, as in "I have *two* jobs."
truely	Misspelling.
truly	An adverb meaning "sincerely" or "completely," as in "He was *truly* happy."
weather	A noun meaning "condition of the atmosphere," as in "The *weather* is pleasant today."
whether	A conjunction, as in "*Whether* he would go was of no consequence."
write	A present-tense verb, as in "Watch me as I *write* this letter."
writen	Misspelling.
written	A past-participle verb, as in "I have *written* the letter."
you're	A contraction of *you are*, as in "*You're* my friend."
your	A possessive pronoun, as in "I like *your* looks."

Your Spell Checker

Your computer spell checker is an important tool with many benefits and some limitations. With about 100,000 words in a typical database, the spell checker alerts you to problem words in your text that should be verified. If you agree that the spelling of a word should be checked, you can then select from a list of words with similar spellings. A likely substitute word will be highlighted. With a keystroke, you can correct a problem, add your own word to the database, or ignore the alert. With a few more keystrokes, you can type in your own correction, and you can add an unusual spelling or word to the database. You may even be able to program your spell checker to correct automatically your most frequent spelling or typing errors. You will be amazed at how many times your computer will catch misspellings that your eye did not see.

However, the spell checker has limitations. If you intended to type *he* and instead typed *me*, the spell checker will not alert you to a possible problem because the word you typed is spelled correctly. If you use the wrong word, such as *herd* instead of *heard*, the spell checker will not detect a problem. Thus, you should always proofread your writing after you have spell checked it. Do not be lulled into a false sense of spelling security simply because you have a machine on your side. As a writer, you are the final spell checker.

Correcting ESL Problems

If you came to the United States knowing little English, you probably acquired vocabulary first. Then you began using that vocabulary within the basic patterns of your own language. If your native language had no articles, you probably used no articles; if your language had no verb tenses, you probably used no verb tenses, and so on. Using the grammar of your own language with your new vocabulary may initially have enabled you to make longer and more complex statements in English, but eventually you learned that your native grammar and your adopted grammar were different. You may even have learned that no two grammars are the same, and that English has a bewildering set of rules and an even longer set of exceptions to those rules. This chapter presents grammar (the way we put words together) and rhetoric (the way we use language effectively) that can be applied to your writing. The following are some definitions, rules, and references that are of special help to writers who are learning English as a second language (ESL).

Using Articles in Relation to Nouns

Articles

Articles are either indefinite (*an*, *a*) or definite (*the*). Because they point out nouns, they are often called *noun determiners*.

Nouns

Nouns can be either singular (*book*) or plural (*books*) and are either count nouns (things that can be counted, such as "book") or noncount nouns (things that cannot be counted, such as "homework"). If you are not certain whether a noun is a count noun or a noncount noun, try placing the word *much* before the word. You can say, "much homework," so *homework* is a noncount noun.

Rules

- Use an indefinite article (*a* or *an*) before singular count nouns and not before noncount nouns. The indefinite article means "one," so you would not use it before plural count nouns.

    Correct: I saw a book. (count noun)

    Correct: I ate an apple. (count noun)

    Incorrect: I fell in a love. (noncount noun)

    Correct: I fell in love. (noncount noun)

    Incorrect: I was in a good health. (noncount noun)

    Correct: I was in good health. (noncount noun)

- Use the definite article (*the*) before both singular and plural count nouns that have specific reference.

    Correct: I read the book. (a specific one)

    Correct: I read the books (specific ones)

    Correct: I like to read a good book. (nonspecific, therefore the indefinite article)

    Correct: A student who works hard will pass. (any student, therefore nonspecific)

    Correct: The student on my left is falling asleep. (a specific student)

- Use the definite article with noncount nouns only when they are specifically identified.

    Correct: Honesty [as an idea] is a rare commodity.

    Correct: The honesty of my friend has inspired me. (specifically identified)

    Incorrect: I was in trouble and needed the assistance. (not specifically identified)

    Correct: The assistance offered by the paramedics was appreciated. (specifically identified)

- Place the definite article before proper nouns (names) of

    oceans, rivers, and deserts (for example, *the* Pacific Ocean and *the* Red River).

countries, if the first part of the name indicates a division (*the* United States of America).

regions (*the* South).

plural islands (*the* Hawaiian Islands).

museums and libraries (*the* Los Angeles County Museum).

colleges and universities when the word *college* or *university* comes before the name (*the* University of Oklahoma).

These are the main rules. For a more detailed account of rules for articles, see a comprehensive ESL book in your library.

Sentence Patterns

The Writing Different Kinds of Sentences section (p. 365) defines and illustrates the patterns of English sentences. Some languages include patterns not used in standard English. The following principles are well worth remembering.

- The conventional English sentence is based on one or more clauses, each of which must have a subject (sometimes the implied "you") and a verb.

    Incorrect: Saw the book. (subject needed even if it is obvious)

    Correct: I saw the book.

- English does not repeat a subject, even for emphasis.

    Incorrect: The book that I read it was interesting.

    Correct: The book that I read was interesting.

Verb Endings

- English indicates time through verbs. Learn the different forms of verb tenses and the combinations of main verbs and helping verbs.

    Incorrect: He watching the game. (A verblike word ending in *-ing* cannot be a verb all by itself.)

    Correct: He is watching the game. (Note that a helping verb such as *is, has, has been, will,* or *will be* always occurs before a main verb ending in *-ing*.)

- Take special care in maintaining consistency in tense.

Incorrect: I went to the mall. I watch a movie there. (verb tenses inconsistent)

Correct: I went to the mall. I watched a movie there.

All twelve verb tenses are covered with explanations, examples, and exercises in the Working with Verb Forms section of this chapter, pages 375–385.

Idioms

Some of your initial problems with writing English are likely to arise from trying to adjust to a different and difficult grammar. If the English language used an entirely systematic grammar, your learning would be easier, but English has patterns that are both complex and irregular. Among them are idioms, word groups that often defy grammatical rules and mean something other than what they appear to mean.

The expression "He kicked the bucket" does not mean that a person struck a cylindrical container with his foot; instead, it means that someone died. That example is one kind of idiom. Because the expression suggests a certain irreverence, it would not be the choice of most people who want to make a statement about death; but if it is used, it must be used with its own precise wording, not "He struck the long cylindrical container with his foot" or "He did some bucket-kicking." Like other languages, the English language has thousands of these idioms. Expressions such as "the more the merrier" and "on the outs" are ungrammatical. They are also very informal expressions and therefore seldom used in college writing, although they are an indispensable part of a flexible, effective, all-purpose vocabulary. Because of their twisted meanings and illogic, idioms are likely to be among the last parts of language that a new speaker learns well. A speaker must know the culture thoroughly to understand when, where, and how to use slang and other idiomatic expressions.

If you listen carefully and read extensively, you will learn English idioms. Your library will have dictionaries that explain them.

More Suggestions for ESL Writers

1. Read your material aloud and try to detect inconsistencies and awkward phrasing.

2. Have others read your material aloud for the same purposes.

3. If you have severe problems with grammatical awkwardness, try composing shorter, more direct sentences until you become more proficient in phrasing.

4. On your Self-Evaluation Chart, list the problems you have (such as articles, verb endings, clause patterns), review relevant parts of Chapter 13, and concentrate on your own problem areas as you draft, revise, and edit.

Exercise 17 — EXAMINING ESL PROBLEMS

Make corrections in the use of articles, verbs, and phrasing (See Answer Key for answers.)

George Washington at Trenton

One of most famous battles during the War of Independence occur at Trenton, New Jersey, on Christmas Eve of the 1776. The colonists outmatched in supplies and finances and were outnumbered in troop strength. Most observers in other countries think rebellion would be put down soon. British overconfident and believe there would be no more battles until spring. But George Washington decide to fight one more time. That Christmas, while large army of Britishers having party and thinking about the holiday season, Americans set out for surprise raid. They loaded onto boats used for carrying ore and rowed across Delaware River. George Washington stood tall in lead boat. According to legend, drummer boy floated across river on his drum, pulled by rope tied to boat. Because British did not feel threatened by the ragtag colonist forces, they unprepared to do battle. The colonists stormed living quarters and the general assembly hall and achieved victory. It was good for the colonists' morale, something they needed, for they would endure long, hard winter before fighting again.

Answer Key: Chapter 13

Answer Key: Chapter 13

Exercise 1: Identifying Parts of Speech

1. v, conj
2. adv, adj
3. v, conj
4. pro, pro
5. n, prep
6. adv, conj
7. prep, adj
8. n, adj
9. n, adv
10. v, pro

Exercise 2: Identifying Subjects and Verbs

1. brother/friend, sold
2. somebody, can give
3. applicants, were
4. part, comes
5. (You), read
6. team, scored
7. I, will be
8. agents, will be
9. coach/players, were angered
10. cast, was congratulated/given

Exercise 3: Writing Different Kinds of Sentences

1. S
2. CP
3. CX
4. CC
5. CX

6. CP
7. CC
8. S
9. S
10. CX

Exercise 4: Combining Sentences

Answers will vary.

1. During the Great Depression of the 1930s, the Joad family lived in Oklahoma.
2. When the dust storms hit the area, the Joad family headed for California.
3. In California, the Joads were not welcome because thousands of poor people had gone to California.
4. The poor people had heard of jobs in fruit picking, but they discovered that California had more job seekers than jobs.
5. After large farm owners took advantage of the workers, the workers banded together.
6. Jim Casey and Tom Joad became leaders, and the people learned to help themselves.
7. Edgar Allan Poe wrote a short story titled "The Cask of Amontillado," in which the narrator tells of his experience fifty years earlier.
8. Because he wanted revenge against an enemy, he walled that person up in a catacomb.
9. At first his victim said it was surely a joke and begged to be freed.
10. The narrator refused; after all these years, he cannot dismiss the experience from his mind.

Exercise 5: Correcting Fragments, Comma Splices, and Run-Ons

1. CS   world;
2. CS   old;
3. RO   old; nevertheless,
4. OK
5. OK

6. RO   materials;
7. OK
8. OK
9. FRAG   was
10. FRAG   rode

Exercise 6: Working with Verb Forms

1. lie
2. drunk
3. laid
4. supposed
5. sat
6. have
7. set
8. used
9. rise
10. rang

Exercise 7: Making Subjects and Verbs Agree

1. are
2. were
3. was
4. has
5. are
6. have
7. appear
8. was
9. makes
10. has

Exercise 8: Giving Verbs Voice

1. A famous scientist gave the lecture.
2. Dr. Song performed the surgery.
3. The Vienna Boys' Choir produced the opera.
4. Janice Baines rode the winning horse.
5. Harold Stanton won the Wimbledon men's tennis tournament.
6. The class read Lewis Carroll's *Alice's Adventures in Wonderland*.
7. Jan Brown wrote the report for the mayor.
8. Thousands of fans greeted the rock star.
9. Elvis recorded the album on June 15, 1956.
10. Both houses of the state assembly passed the gun-control legislation.

Exercise 9: Selecting Pronouns

1. Whom
2. me
3. I
4. me
5. him
6. Who
7. they
8. whomever
9. ourselves
10. him

Exercise 10: Matching Pronouns and Antecedents

1. he or she
2. her
3. his or her
4. itself
5. it
6. their

7. their

8. his

9. his or her

10. its

Exercise 11: Using Adjectives and Adverbs

1. *older* replaces *oldest*
2. *slowly* replaces *slow*
3. *really* replaces *real*
4. *more nearly straight* replaces *more straight*
5. *bad* replaces *badly*
6. *rapidly* replaces *rapid*
7. *more honest* replaces *honester*
8. *surely* replaces *sure*
9. *more easily* replaces *easier*
10. *kinds* replaces *kind*

Exercise 12: Eliminating Dangling and Misplaced Modifiers

1. D   one can learn writing
2. D   when they arrived
3. M   fiber in the den
4. D   we lost our patience
5. M   when no one was looking, they
6. OK
7. M   permits with the
8. M   wanted in the
9. M   worked for only
10. D   we could not buy tickets

Exercise 13: Balancing Sentence Parts

1. P
2. NP   both of
3. P
4. NP   and how
5. P
6. NP   boxing
7. P
8. NP   not only the cause
9. P
10. NP   a victory

Exercise 14: Inserting Commas

1. Steinbeck, a great American writer, . . . Salinas,
2. setting,
3. works,
4. workers,
5. novel, *The Grapes of Wrath,*
6. Oklahoma,
7. hit, . . . executives,
8. California,
9. California,
10. trip, . . . book, . . . suffering, compassion,

Exercise 15: Choosing the Semicolon or the Comma

1. relatives,
2. son;
3. secretary;
4. adults;
5. move,
6. people,
7. him;

8. scientists,

9. rational;

10. speed;

Exercise 16: Working with All Marks of Punctuation and Capitalization

1. Central

2. Mother

3. Oh,

4. Huxley's

5. boys'

6. anyone's

7. French

8. "hog's bristles."

9. 'The . . . young'

10. Won't

Exercise 17: Examining ESL Problems

George Washington at Trenton

One of *the* most famous battles during the War of Independence ~~occur~~ *occurred* at Trenton, New Jersey, on Christmas Eve of ~~the~~ 1776. The colonists *were* outmatched in supplies and finances and ~~were~~ outnumbered in troop strength. Most observers in other countries ~~think~~ *thought the* rebellion would be put down soon. *The* British *were* overconfident and ~~believe~~ *believed* there would be no more battles until spring. But George Washington ~~decide~~ *decided* to fight one more time. That Christmas, while *a* large army of Britishers *were* having *a* party and thinking about the holiday season, *the* Americans set out for *a* surprise raid. They loaded onto boats used for carrying ore and rowed across *the* Delaware River. George Washington stood tall in *the* lead boat. According to legend,

Answer Key: Chapter 13 **429**

The drummer boy floated across the river on his drum, pulled by a rope tied to a boat. Because the British did not feel threatened by the ragtag colonist forces, they were unprepared to do battle. The colonists stormed the living quarters and the general assembly hall and achieved victory. It was good for the colonists' morale, something they needed, for they would endure a long, hard winter before fighting again.

Text Credits

American Heritage Dictionary definitions. Copyright © 2000 by Houghton Mifflin Company. Adapted and reproduced by permission from *The American Heritage Dictionary of the English Language,* Fourth Edition.

Rebecca Barry, "Lessons from a Control Freak," originally published in *Redbook,* February 1999, Vol. 192, Issue 4, p. 67. Reprinted by permission of Hearst Publications.

David Bodanis, "A Brush with Reality: Surprises in the Tube," from *The Secret House,* Simon & Schuster, 1986. Reprinted by permission of the Carol Mann Agency.

Suzanne Britt, "That Lean and Hungry Look" first published in *Newsweek* is reprinted by permission of the author.

"Frankie and Johnnie," from *American Favorite Ballads: Tunes and Songs Sung by Pete Seeger.* Edited by Irwin Silver and Ethel Raim. Copyright © 1961 (Renewed) Oak publications, a division of Misic Sales Corporation International. Copyright secured. All Rights Reserved. Reprinted by permission.

Eve Golden, "Dangerous Curves" from *Men's Health Magazine.* Reprinted by permission of *Men's Health Magazine.* Copyright 1994 Rodale, Inc. All rights reserved. For subscription info, call 1-800-666-2303.

Adam Goodheart, "How to Paint a Fresco" by Adam Goodheart from *Civilization,* July/August 1995. Copyright © 1995 by Adam Goodheart. Reprinted by permission of The Wylie Agency, Inc.

Joy Harjo, "Three Generations of Native American Women's Birth Experience," from *MS. Magazine,* 1991. Reprinted by permission of the author.

Wil Haygood, "Underground Dads," *New York Times Magazine,* November 30, 1997. Copyright © 1997 by the New York Times Co. Reprinted by permission.

William Helmreich, "Optimism, Tenacity Lead Way Back to Life," *Los Angeles Times,* 11/25/92. Reprinted by permission of the author.

Paul B. Hertneky, "You and Your Boss," *Restaurant Hospitality,* vol. 80, 8/1/96, p. 78(2). Reprinted by permission.

Richard Jerome, Ronald F. Arias, and Joanne Fowler, "Disarming the Rage," *People,* June 4, 2001. People Weekly © 2001. Time Inc. All rights reserved.

Cynthia Joyce, "Six Clicks from Death," *Salon* Magazine, April '97. Reprinted by permission of Salon Media Group.

Garrison Keillor, "Attitude" is reprinted with the permission of Scribner, an imprint of Simon & Schuster Adult Publishing Group, from HAPPY TO BE HERE by Garrison Keillor. Copyright © 1979, 1982 by Garrison Keillor.

Philip Kotler and Gary Armstrong, "The Baby Boomers and the Generation Xers," *Principles of Marketing,* Prentice Hall, 2000. From *Principles of Marketing* 10/e by Kotler/Armstrong. © 2004, p. 112-114. Reprinted by permission of Pearson Education, Inc., Upper Saddle River, NJ.

Michael D. Lemonick, "Designer Babies," *Time* special issue, "The Future of Medicine," Jan. 11, 1999. © 1999 Time Inc. Reprinted by permission.

John Leo, "Bully, Bully," *US News & World Report,* May 21, 2001, vol. 130, issue 20, p. 15. Copyright 2001 *U.S. News & World Report,* L.P. Reprinted by permission of the author.

David Levine, "I'm Outta Here!" from *Seventeen,* March 1992. Reprinted by permission of the author.

Don Mack, "Ban Cell Phones and Pagers in Classrooms" from *NEA Today*, March '01, p. 11. Reprinted by permission of the National Education Association.

Erica Manfred, "Coworkers from Hell and How to Cope," *Cosmopolitan*, February 1, 1997. Reprinted by permission of the author.

Usha Lee McFarling, "Stars" originally called "How and Why" from the *Boston Globe*. Reprinted by permission of the author.

David Orr, "Like, Whatever. . ." from *Annals of Earth* (No. 3, 1999) is reprinted by permission of the author.

Robert J. Trotter, "How Do I Love Thee?" from *The Three Faces of Love*, September 1986, p. 47. Reprinted with permission from *Psychology Today* magazine. Copyright © 1986, Sussex Publishers, Inc.

Ian Roberson, "Romantic Love, Courtship, and Marriage," from *Sociology*, by Ian Roberson © 1994, 1987, 1981 by Worth Publishers. Used with permission.

Anne Roiphe, "Why Marriages Fail," is reprinted by permission of International Creative Management, Inc. Copyright © 1993 by Anne Roiphe.

Lin Rolens, "Female Mea Culpa," *Santa Barbara News Press Magazine*, Summer '99. Reprinted by permission.

U.S. News & World Report Staff, "Why Many Good Workers Turn into Bad Bosses," *US News & World Report,* January 23, 1984, v. 96, p. 71(2). Copyright 1984 *U.S. News & World Report*, L.P. Reprinted with permission.

Glen Waggoner, "Shaking Hands," first published in *Esquire,* July 1986. Reprinted by permission of the author.

Alice Walker, "Everyday Use" from *In Love & Trouble: Stories of Black Women*, copyright © 1973 by Alice Walker, reprinted by permission of Harcourt, Inc.

Gail Washburn, "Allow Cell Phones and Pagers in Classroom" from *NEA Today*, March '01, p. 11. Reprinted by permission of the National Education Association.

Kurt Wiesenfeld, "Making the Grade." From *Newsweek*, June 17, 1996, © 1996 Newsweek, Inc. All rights reserved. Reprinted by permission of the National Education Association.

Franklin E. Zimring, "Confessions of a Former Smoker," *Newsweek*, April 20, 1987. Reprinted by permission of the author.

Author and Title Index

Alford, Jason, "Biting My Tongue—Sometimes," 103–105
"Allow Cell Phones and Pagers in the Classroom" (Washburn), 86–88
Arias, Ron, "Disarming the Rage," 137–143
Armstrong, Gary, "The Baby Boomers and the Generation Xers," 261–263
"Attitude" (Keillor), 239–242

"Baby Boomers and the Generation Xers, The," (Kotler and Armstrong), 261–253
"Ban Cell Phones and Pagers in Classrooms" (Mack), 89–90
Barry, Rebecca, "Lessons from a Control Freak," 106–109
Benedict, Ruth, *Patterns of Culture*, 125
"Biting My Tongue—Sometimes" (Alford), 103–105
Bodanis, David, "A Brush with Reality," 168–170
Boone, Mary, "Disarming the Rage," 137–143
Britt, Suzanne, "That Lean and Hungry Look," 265–267
Browning, Robert, "My Last Duchess," 337–339
"Brush with Reality, A," (Bodanis), 168–170
"Bully, Bully" (Leo), 144–146

Campos, Maria, "A Divorce with Reasons," 16
Carter, Jolene, "Types of Fly Fighters," 194–195
Catcher in the Rye, The (Salinger), 321
Chavez, Carlos, "*La Vida Loca*: Crazy Life, Crazy Death," 84
"Chinese New Year's Feast, A," (Yu), 164–165
Chopin, Kate, "The Story of an Hour," 331–333
Chow, James, "Feng Shui," 63–64
Comander, Lauren, "Disarming the Rage," 137–143
"Community College Pressures" (Follette), 197–198
"Confessions of a Former Smoker" (Zimring), 211–214
"Conserving Energy as You Ski" (Wingus), 16
Cousins, Norman, "Who Killed Benny Paret?," 16
"Coworkers from Hell and How to Cope" (Monfred), 199–204

"Dangerous Curves" (Golden), 205

Davis, Emmett, "Elvis Presley: Twentieth-Century Legend," 165–167
"Designer Babies" (Lemonich), 172–175
"Disarming the Rage" (Jerome et al.), 137–143
"Divorce with Reasons, A," (Campos), 16
Dunlop, Max, "It's Time to KO Boxing," 293–295
Dwyer, Charles, "Why Many Good Workers Turn into Bad Bosses" (interview), 151–155

Eckert, Kay, "How to Obtain a Real Estate Listing," 228–229
Elbow, Peter, 26
"Elvis Presley: Twentieth-Century Legend" (Davis), 165–167
"Everyday Use" (Walken), 270–278

"Fall of the House of Usher, The" (Poe), 320
"Fast Food Face-Off, A," (Lee), 255–257
Faulkner, William, xxv
"Female Mea Culpa" (Rolens), 305–307
"Feng Shui" (Chow), 63–64
Feshbach, Seymour, *Personality*, 21
"First Step in Improving Sex Education, The," (Hecklinger), 75
Follette, Joel, "Community College Pressures," 197–198
Fowler, Joanne, "Disarming the Rage," 137–143
Fox, Michael W., "What Is Your Pet Trying to Tell You?," 53
"Frankie and Johnny" (anonymous), 334–336

"Get Them Off the Road" (Humphries), 17
Gilbert, Holly, "Girls Form Backbone of Gangs," 84
"Girls Form Backbone of Gangs" (Gilbert), 84
Girls in Their Summer Dresses, The, (Shaw), 75, 325–330
Golden, Eve, "Dangerous Curves," 205–210
Goleman, David, "His Marriage and Hers: Childhood Roots," 308–312
Goodheart, Adam, "How to Paint a Fresco," 230–232
Griffey, Ken, Jr., 385
"Growing Up Asian in America" (Noda), 21
"Guarding a Wide Receiver" (Landry), 224–226
Harjo, Joy, "Three Generations of Native American Women's Birth Experience," 179–184
Haygood, Wil, "Underground Dads," 118–120

Hecklinger, Fred M., "The First Step in Improving Sex Education," 75
Helmreich, William, "Optimism, Tenacity Lead Way Back to Life," 176–178
Hertneky, Paul B., "You and Your Boss," 147–150
Highet, Gilbert, "Subway Station," 49
"His Marriage and Hers: Childhood Roots" (Goleman), 308–312
Horton, Sue, "Mothers, Sons, and the Gangs," 84
"How Do I Love Thee?" (Trotter), 323–324
"How to Obtain a Real Estate Listing" (Eckert), 228–229
"How to Paint a Fresco" (Goodheart), 230–232
Hsiao, Lydia, "Struggling Against Silence," 259–261
Huange, Lewan, "Using More than Laws Against Gangs," 84–86
Humphries, Daniel, "Get Them Off the Road," 17

"I'm Outta Here!" (Levine), 110–114
"It's Time to KO Boxing" (Dunlop), 293–295

Jackson, Shirley, "The Lottery," 320
Jasper, Shontel, "She Came a Long Way," 18–19
Jerome, Richard, "Disarming the Rage," 137–143
Johnson, Samuel, xxv
Joyce, Cynthia, "Six Clicks from Death," 232–237

Keillor, Garrison, "Attitude," 239–242
"Kick Me! Kiss Me!" (Morgan), 289–291
Kotler, Philip, "The Baby Boomers and the Generation Xers," 261–263

Landry, Brian, "Guarding a Wide Receiver," 224–226
La Vida Loca: Crazy Life, Crazy Death" (Chavez and Rodriguez), 84
"Leaving Los Angeles" (Maxwell), 17
Lee, Daphne, "A Fast Food Face-Off," 255–257
Lemonich, Michael D., "Designer Babies," 172–175
Leo, John, "Bully, Bully," 144–146
"Lessons from a Control Freak" (Barry), 106–108
Levine, David, "I'm Outta Here!," 110–114
"Like, Whatever . . ." (Orr), 68–71, 77–82
Lohayza, Lyvette, "Tamales, a Family Production," 4–6
"Lottery, The" (Jackson), 320

Mack, Don, "Ban Cell Phones and Pagers in Classrooms," 89–90
"Making the Grade" (Wiesenfeld), 115–117
Malone, Jackie, 75
Marrington, Maureen, "Disarming the Rage," 137–143
Maxwell, Brian, "Leaving Los Angeles," 17
Mazo, Ellen, "Disarming the Rage," 137–143
McClure, April, "Prison Tattoos," 99–101
McFarling, Usha Lee, "Stars," 243–244
Mendez, Gloria, "The Use of Self-Analysis," 345–347
Monfred, Erica, "Coworkers from Helland How to Cope," 199–204
"More Than Just a House Call" (Mylonas), 344–345
Morgan, Shandra, "Kick Me! Kiss Me!," 289–291
"Mothers, Sons, and the Gangs" (Horton), 84
"My-graines" (Sheahan), 131–133
"My Last Duchess" (Browning), 337–339
Mylonas, Ajax, "More Than Just a House Call," 344–345

Noda, Kesaya E., "Growing Up Asian in America," 21

Olvias, Lara, "Student Cheating," 98
"On Various Kinds of Thinking?" (Robinson), 125
"Optimism, Tenacity Lead Way Back to Life" (Helmreich), 176–178
Orr, David, "Like, Whatever . . .," 68–71, 77–82

Patterns of Culture (Benedict), 125
Personality (Feshbach and Weiner), 21
"Perspectives on Motivation" (Proctor), 135–136
Poe, Edgar Allan, "The Fall of the House of Usher," 320
"Prison as a Community" (Tanya), 29, 33, 36, 43–44, 57–62
"Prison Tattoos" (McClure), 99–101
Proctor, Michelle, "Perspectives on Motivation," 135–136

Reno, Jamie, "Disarming the Rage," 137–143
Robertson, Ian, "Romantic Love, Courtship, and Marriage," 301–304

Robinson, James Harvey, "On Various Kinds of Thinking?," 125
Rodriguez, Antonio H., "*La Vida Loca*: Crazy Life, Crazy Death," 84
Roiphe, Anne, "Why Marriages Fail," 296–300
Rolens, Lin, "Female Mea Culpa," 305–307
"Romantic Love, Courtship, and Marriage" (Robertson), 301–304
Salinger, J. D., *The Catcher in the Rye*, 321
"Shaking Hands" (Waggoner), 215–216
Shaw, Irwin, *The Girls in Their Summer Dresses*, 75, 325–330
Sheahan, Vincent, "My-graines," 131–133
"She Came a Long Way" (Jasper), 18–19
Sider, Don, "Disarming the Rage," 137–143
"Six Clicks from Death" (Joyce), 232–237
"Stars" (McFarling), 243–244
"Story of an Hour, The" (Chopin), 331–333
"Struggling Against Silence" (Hsiao), 259–261
"Student Cheating" (Olivas), 98
"Subway Station" (Highet), 49

"Tamales, A Family Production" (Lohayza), 4–6
Tanya, "Prison as a Community," 28, 29, 33, 36, 43–44, 57–62
"That Lean and Hungry Look" (Britt), 265–267
"Three Generations of Native American Women's Birth Experience" (Harjo), 179–184
Trotter, Robert J., "How Do I Love Thee?," 323–324
Twain, Mark, "Two Ways of Viewing the River," 268–269
"Two Ways of Viewing the River" (Twain), 268–269
"Types of Fly Fighters" (Carter), 194–195

"Underground Dads" (Haygood), 118–120
"Use of Force, The" (Williams), 341, 343–344
"Use of Self-Analysis, The" (Mendez), 345–347
"Using More than Laws Against Gangs" (Huang), 84–86

Waggoner, Glen, "Shaking Hands," 215–216
Walker, Alice, "Everyday Use," 270–278
Warren, Robert Penn, 319
Washburn, Gail, "Allow Cell Phones and Pages in the Classroom," 86–88
Weiner, Bernard, *Personality*, 21

Wescott, Gail Cameron, "Disarming the Rage," 137–143
"What Is Your Pet Trying to Tell You?" (Fox), 53
"Who Killed Benny Paret?" (Cousins), 16
"Why Many Good Workers Turn into Bad Bosses" (Dwyer interview), 151–155
"Why Marriages Fail" (Roiphe), 296–300
Wiesenfeld, Kurt, "Making the Grade," 115–117
Williams, William Carlos, "The Use of Force," 341, 343–344
Wingus, Carl, "Conserving Energy as You Ski," 16

Yegavian, Garabed, 98
"You and Your Boss" (Hertneky), 147–150
Yu, Hsiao Chin, "A Chinese New Year's Feast," 164–165

Zimring, Franklin E., "Confessions of a Former Smoker," 211–214

Subject Index

a, an, and, 358
abbreviations, punctuating, 397, 402
action verbs, 356, 363
active voice, 385–386
address, punctuation of, 398
adjectives
    adverbs versus, 392
    capitalization, 401
    comparative/superlative form, 391
    defined, 357–358, 391
    descriptive, 357
    modified by adverbs, 358
    parallelism and, 395
    selecting, 392
adverbs
    adjectives versus, 392
    comparative/superlative form, 391
    conjunctive, 55, 367, 373
    defined, 358–359, 391
    parallelism and, 395
    prepositions versus, 360
    selecting, 391–392
    verbs versus, 364
    agreement
    pronoun-antecedent, 387
    subject-verb, 381–383
alternating pattern of organization, 252–253
alternative subject and verb agreement, 382
analysis by division
    examples, 164–184
    order, 163
    organization, 163
    outline, 11
    procedure for writing, 162–163, 187
    Roman numerals in, 163
    topics for writing, 185–187
    for writing definitions, 129
    writing guidelines, 187–188
analysis. *See* process analysis
analytical approach to literary analysis, 347
analytical definition, 125–126
anecdotes in conclusion, 16
angry tone, 48
annotating, 68, 92
antagonist, 320
antecedent-pronoun agreement, 387
anthology and MLA style for citing, 75
apostrophe, 400

appositive phrase, 370, 372
articles and MLS style for citing, 74
articles (parts of speech)
    adjectives as, 358
    definite versus indefinite, 417
    in relation to nouns, 417–418
assignment, understanding, 26
attitude in skills improvement, xxvi
audience, 44, 49, 285

background in process analysis, 221–222
balance in sentences, 395
being verbs, 356, 363
book titles, punctuation for, 400, 401
brackets, 400
brainstorming, 30–32, 40; *see also* listing

capitalization
    combining sentences, 368–369
    conventions, 401–403
    in editing, 56
    skills improvement strategy, xxvi
career-related topics for literary analysis, 351
career-related writing, 398
cause and effect
    defined, 285
    examples, 289–312
    order in, 287–288, 317
    outline, 12
    outlining in, 286, 317
    patterns for, 288
    prewriting strategies, 285, 317
    thesis composition and, 286
    topics for writing, 313–317
    for writing definitions, 129
    writing guidelines, 317
characters in literature, 320, 347
circular definition, 128
citation defined, 74; *see also* documentation of sources
classification
    avoiding overlapping, 190
    in definitions, writing, 129
    establishing classes for, 191
    examples, 194–216
    procedure for writing, 190, 219
    Roman numerals in, 219

simple and complex forms, 191–193
subject selection, 190
topics for writing, 217–219
writing guidelines, 219
clauses
in compound-complex sentences, 369
conjunctions and, 360
dependent, 55, 360–361, 366, 369, 372
independent, 366, 367, 373
main, 360–361, 366
punctuation, 360–361, 397–398
as sentences, 366
clichés avoidance, 50
climax in literature, 320
CLUESS format in revision, 45, 64–65
clustering
for literary analysis, 342
outlines versus, 33
in prewriting, 33–34, 41
coherence
the revision process, 45–47
transitional terms in establishing, 222, 248, 253
unity versus, 51
collective nouns and verb agreement, 383
colon, 341, 399, 400
combination process analysis, 223
combining sentences. *See* sentence(s)
commas
for clauses, 360–361, 366, 368, 397
combining sentences, 368–370
for comma splices and run-on, 373
in complex sentences, 369
in compound-complex sentences, 369
compound sentences, 368
with conjunctive adverbs, 367
with coordinating conjunctions, 366
dependent clauses and, 366
punctuation, 397–398
in sentence combinations, 368
with subordinating conjunctions, 360
comma splice in sentences, 56, 373
comparative modifiers, 391
comparison and contrast
defined, 250
examples, 253–278
patterns of organization, 252–253, 282
points made in, 252–253, 282

presentation of ideas, 253–254, 283
procedure for writing, 250–254
purpose defined in, 250–251, 282, 317
synthesis in, 82
topics for writing, 279–282
for writing definitions, 129–130
writing guidelines, 282–283
complex classification, 191
complex sentences
defined, 366
punctuation, 369
for subordination of ideas, 369
for variety, 54
compound-complex sentences
coordination/subordination of ideas, 369
defined, 366
punctuation, 369
for variety, 54
compound sentences
coordination of ideas, 368–369
defined, 366
punctuation of, 368–369
for variety, 54
compound subject and verb agreement, 381
compound verbs, 364
compound words hyphenation, 401
computer use
skills improvement strategies, xxvi–xxvii
spell-checkers, 56, 416
time savings from, 43
concluding paragraphs, 16–17, 23
conclusion
effective versus ineffective, 17, 23
in essays, 16–18, 23
purpose, 6
conflict
in literature, 320, 347
in narratives, 11
conjunctions. *See also* coordinating conjunctions; subordinating conjunctions
capitalization, 402
defined, 360–361
paired, 360
prepositions versus, 361, 381
conjunctive adverb
punctuation with, 367, 373
for sentence variety, 55
consistency and coherence, 46–47, 387

content, skills for improving, xxvi
context
    in process analysis, 222
    tone in, 49
contractions, 387, 400
controlling idea. *See also* thesis
    cause and effect, 287
    in classification, 190
    outlining, 35
    unification with, 50–51
coordinating conjunctions. *See also* conjunctions
    combining sentences, 368–369
    comma splices and run-ons, 373
    defined, 360
    in parallel structure, 395
    punctuation, 366, 397
COPS format in editing, 56–57
count versus noncount nouns, 417–418
cross-references, parallel development of, 253

dangling modifier, 392
dash, 399, 400
definitions
    about, 125
    dictionary and, 125, 127–128
    examples, 131–156
    extended, 129–131, 159–160
    introducing, 160
    introduction and development, 131
    order in, 131, 160
    personalization, 160
    prewriting strategies, 130–131
    problems common to, 128–129
    simple, 125–126, 159
    techniques for using, 125
    topics for writing, 156–159
    writing guidelines, 159–160
dependent clause. *See also* clauses
    comma splices and run-ons, 373
    complex sentences, 369
    defined, 366
    punctuation, 366, 369, 397
    sentence fragments, 372
    for sentence variety, 55
descriptive adjectives, 357
development
    in essays, 15

    in literary analysis, 340–341
    skills improvement strategies, xxvi
    in writing definitions, 131
developmental paragraphs, 15
dialogue, quotation marks for, 399
diction. *See also* language
    adjective and adverb use, 391
    clichés versus, 50
    general versus specific, 49–50
    originality with, 50
    revision process, 49–50
    skills improvement strategies, xxvi
    usage versus, 49
dictionary usage in definition, 125, 127–128
direct explanation in definition, 125
directive process analysis, 221, 223
direct objects, 379
documentation of sources
    citation styles, 74–75
    dictionary definitions, 125
    formal, 74–75
    informal, 73
    plagiarism versus, 73
    quotation marks, 399
documented essays, xxiv, 3–4
double negatives, 392

editing. *See also* revision
    COPS format, 56–57
    guidelines for, 65
    punctuation in, 400
    spell-checkers, 416
emphasis
    idea placement for, 51
    repetition for, 51
emphasis pattern of organization
    analysis by division, 163
    cause and effect, 288, 317
    coherence and, 46
    comparison and contrast, 253
    definition, 131
    exemplification, 99
ESL (English as a second language), 416–420
essays
    components, 22–23
    concluding paragraphs, 16–17, 23
    defined, xxiv, 3, 22

440 SUBJECT INDEX

    of definitions, 129–130
    introductory paragraphs, 6, 12–14
    outlined, 4
    parts of, 6
    support paragraphs, 6, 15–16
    writing guidelines, 22–23
examples. *See also* exemplification
    definitions versus, 129
    organizing ideas with, 99
    use in exemplification, 99, 123
exclamation points as punctuation, 361, 397, 399
exemplification. *See also* examples
    characteristics of good, 97–98
    defined, 97
    number and order of examples, 99
    outline, 11
    prewriting in, 98
    topics for writing, 120–123
    for writing definitions, 129
    writing guidelines, 123
exposition, 97, 320
extended definition, 129–131, 159, 160

fictional point, 321
film/video capitalization of titles, 402
first drafts, 43–44
    examples, 343–344
first person perspective in literature, 321
foreign words italicized, 400
formal argument statements, 383
formal definition, 125–126
fragments of sentences, 55–56, 372–373
freewriting
    comparison and contrast, 251
    overview, 26
    in prewriting, 28–30, 40
future perfect progressive tense, 376
future perfect tense, 376
future progressive tense, 376
future tense, 375

gender and pronoun agreement, 387
grammar
    problem for ESL student, 416–420
    skills improvement strategies, xxvi
groups. *See* classification; clustering

helping verbs, 357
humorous tone, 48
hyphen, 401

ideas
    coordinating in sentences, 368–369
    developing for comparison, 253–255
    emphasizing, 51
    presentation patterns of organization, 253–254, 283
    repetition of, 51
idioms, 419–420
immediate causes and effects, 287
imperative sentence, 363
indefinite pronouns, 356, 382, 400
independent clause. *See also* clauses
    comma splices and run-ons, 373
    in compound sentences, 368
    defined, 366
    punctuation, 366, 367, 369, 397, 398
    sentence fragments, 373
indirect explanation in definition, 125
information gathering techniques, 41
informative process analysis, 221, 222, 223
informative purpose, 250–251
interjections, 361
introducing definitions, 131
introductory paragraphs, 6, 12–14, 23
irregular verbs, 377–378
italics, 400

job application letter, 398
journal articles. *See* articles
journal writing
    as reading-related writing, 92–93
    skills improvement strategies, xxv

language. *See also* diction
    diction, 49–50
    tone in, 48–49
    usage, 47–48
lay, lie, 379
lie, lay, 379
linking verbs in definitions, 128
listing. *See also* brainstorming
    in brainstorming, 30–32, 40
    in cause and effect analysis, 285, 317

Subject Index

points in comparison and contrast, 251–252
  in process analysis, 223
literary analysis
  analytical approach to, 347
  defined, 321–322
  development in 340–341
  elements of literature and, 319–322
  quotations in, 341
  speculative approach to, 347–348
  student writing, 340–347
  topics for writing, 348–351
  verb tense in, 341
  writing guidelines, 351
literature
  characters in, 320, 347
  conflict in, 320, 347
  importance of, 319
  interpreting, 319
  plot in, 320, 347
  point of view in, 321, 347
  professional writings, 322–339
  setting in, 320, 347
  theme in, 321, 347
  writing about, 319–322
logical sequence in cause and effect, 287

main clause, 366
meaning in narratives, 11
measurements and verb agreement, 383
misplaced modifiers, 392
MLA (Modern Language Association) style for works cited, 74–75
modifiers
  adjectives/adverbs as, 357–359
  comparative, 391
  dangling, 392
  misplaced, 392
multiple-source writing, 82–83

narrative poems, 319; *See also* literature
narratives
  outline, 11
  for writing definitions, 129
newspaper articles/editorials MLA style for citing, 75
note-taking in research, 82
noun indicators, 355
noun(s)

capitalization, 401
collective, and verb agreement, 383
count versus noncount, 417–418
defined, 355
ending in –s, 383
parallelism and, 395
possessive, 400proper, 418
in relation to articles, 417–418
verb agreement with, 383
numbers, punctuating, 398, 401

object of preposition, 363, 381
objective case pronouns, 387
objective tone, 48
omissions in editing, 56
opposing pattern of organization, 252–254
order. *See also* organization
  analysis by division, 163
  cause and effect analysis, 287–288, 317
  coherence and, 45–46
  comparison and contrast, 252–253, 282
  to convey tone, 49
  in definition, 131, 160
  in process analysis, 222, 248
organization. *See also specific patterns*
  analysis by division, 163
  basic patterns of, 252–253
  for literary analysis, 351
  outlining content, 35
  paragraphs, 19–20
  point by point/alternating pattern, 252–254, 283
  of sentences, 54–55
  skills improvement strategies, xxvi
  subject by subject/opposing pattern, 252–254, 282–283
  of supporting material, 11, 12, 23
originality
  diction and, 50
  in naming classes, 191, 219
outcome in narratives, 11
outlines
  analysis by division, 11
  cause and effect, 12
  in cause and effect analysis, 286
  clustering versus, 33
  comparison and contrast, 253
  the essay, 4

example, 35–37, 71–72
exemplification, 11
for literary analysis, 342–343
narratives, 11
in prewriting, 41
process analysis, 11
reading-related writing, 71, 92
Roman numerals in, 11
supporting forms, 11
types, 35
overbearing tone, 49

paired conjunctions, 360
paragraphs. *See also specific types*
    patterns of structure, 19–20
    types, 22
parallelism, 253, 395
paraphrase
    single-source writing, 77
    synthesis, 82
parenthesis, 400
participial phrase, 370
parts of speech, types of, 355; *See also specific types*
passive voice, 385–386
past participles, 376, 377, 379
past perfect progressive tense, 376
past perfect tense, 376
past progressive tense, 376
past tense
    confusing verb pairs, 379
    of irregular verbs, 377–378
    of regular verbs, 377
    in simple tenses, 375
patterns of organization. *See* order; organization
perfect progressive verb tenses, 376
perfect verb tenses, 375
periods, 397
personal essay, 73
personalization. *See also;* point of view
    definitions, 131
    in literary analysis, 347–348
    in process analysis, 223
perspective. *See* point of view
persuasion comparison and contrast, 251
phrases
    conjunctions and, 360

    prepositional, 55
plagiarism versus documentation, 73
plot in literature, 320, 347
poems
    narrative, 319
    punctuation for titles of, 401
point by point pattern of organization, 252–254, 283
point of view. *See also* personalization
    consistency in, 47, 387
    in literary analysis, 351
    in literature, 321, 347
    process analysis, 223
possessive nouns, 400
preparation stage in process analysis, 221–222
prepositional phrase
    defined, 359, 372
    for sentence variety, 55
    simple sentences, 370
preposition(s)
    adverbs versus, 360
    capitalization, 402
    common, 359
    conjunctions versus, 361, 381
    defined, 359–360
    object of, 363, 381
    in process analysis, 222
    subject-verb agreement, 381
    troublesome/confusing, 381
present perfect progressive tense, 376
present perfect tense, 375
present progressive tense, 376
present time
    confusing verb pairs, 379
    in simple tenses, 375
prewriting
    brainstorming/listing, 30–32
    clustering, 33–34
    comparison and contrast, 251–252
    in definition development, 130–131
    in exemplification, 98
    freewriting, 26, 28–30
    listing, 223
    outlining, 35–39, 286, 317
    process analysis, 223–224
    thesis composition, 34–35
    types, 26, 40–41
    writing guidelines, 40–41

primary causes and effects, 286
process analysis
    combination, 223
    directive and informative, 221, 223
    examples, 224–244
    forms, 222–223, 248
    order in, 222, 248
    outline, 11
    preparation/background in, 221–222
    prewriting, 223–224
    topics for writing, 245–248
    for writing definitions, 129
    writing guidelines, 248
progressive verb tenses, 376
pronoun(s)
    as adjectives, 358
    antecedent agreement, 387–388
    case, deciding form of, 387
    coherence established with, 47
    contractions and, 387
    defined, 356, 387
    indefinite, 356, 382, 400
    in process analysis, 221, 248
    and verb agreement, 382
proper nouns, 418
protagonist, 320
punctuation
    apostrophe, 400
    brackets, 400
    for clauses, 366–367
    colon, 400
    commas, 397–398
    complex sentences, 369
    compound-complex sentences, 369
    compound sentences, 368–369
    dash, 400
    in editing, 56
    exclamation points, 397
    hyphen, 401
    italics, 400
    parenthesis, 400
    periods, 397
    question marks, 397
    quotation marks, 399
    for quotations, 341
    semicolon, 369, 373, 398
    skills improvement strategies, xxvi

question marks, 397, 399
quotation marks, 399
quotations
    in conclusion, 17
    direct and indirect, 341
    in literary analysis, 341, 351
    punctuation, 341, 397, 398, 399
    supporting ideas with, 73

raise, rise, 379
reaction statement, 79, 93
reading
    skills improvement strategies, xxv
    strategies, 67
reading aloud in editing, 56
reading-related writing
    annotating, 68, 92
    documentation in, 73–75
    guidelines, 92–93
    journal writing, 91–92
    multiple-source synthesis, 82–83, 93
    outlining, 71–72, 92
    quotations and references in, 73
    reaction statement, 93
    single-source, 76–82
    summarizing, 93
    two-part response, 93
    types, 93
    underlining, 67–71, 92
recipe language, 222
recursion, 25, 44; *See also* revision
references, supporting ideas with, 73; *See also* source material
regular verbs, 377–378
remote causes and effects, 287
repetition
    cause and effect, 288, 317
    coherence established with, 46
    in conclusion, 16
    for emphasis, 51, 288, 317
    persuasive writing, 251
representative examples, 98
resolution in literature, 320
response. *See* reaction statement
revision. *See also* editing
    CLUESS format, 45
    coherence, 45–47

emphasis in, 51
evaluating support in, 52–54
first draft, 43–44
guidelines for, 64–65
language, 47–50
process examples, 343–344
sentences, 54–56
for unity, 50–51
rise, raise, 379
run-on sentences, 56, 373

sarcastic tone, 48
sat, sit, 379
secondary causes and effects, 286
Self-Evaluation Chart, xxvii
self-evaluation for skills improvement, xxv–xxvii
semicolon
    combining sentences, 369
    comma splices and run-ons, 373
    independent clauses, 367, 398
    quotation marks and, 399
sentence fillers, 381–382
sentence outline, 35
sentence(s)
    active versus passive voice, 385–386
    balance in, 395
    beginnings, varying, 55
    clauses as, 366
    combining, 368–370
    comma splice, the, 56, 373
    complete, 55, 372–373
    complex, 54, 366, 369
    compound, 54, 366, 368–369
    compound-complex, 54, 366, 369
    concluding, 16
    fragments, 55–56, 372–373
    imperative, 363
    improvement strategies, xxvi
    length of, 54
    parallelism in, 395
    patterns in, 417–418
    problems with, 55–56
    punctuation, 369
    revision process, 54–56
    run-on, 56, 373
    simple, 54, 366, 370
    types, 54–55, 366

    variety in, 54–55
servile tone, 48
setting in literature, 320, 347
short stories, 319; See also literature
simple classification, 191
simple definition, 125–126, 159
simple sentences, 54, 366, 370
simple verb tenses, 375
single-source writing
    documentation in, 73
    paraphrase, 77
    reaction, 79
    summary, 76–77
    two-part response, 80
    types, 76
sit, sat, 379
situation in narratives, 11
skills improvement strategies, xxv–xxvi
slang, 47–48, 391
source material. *See also* documentation of sources
    documenting, 74–75
    making notes of, 82
space pattern of organization
    analysis by division, 163
    causes and effects, 287
    coherence and, 46
    comparison and contrast, 253
    definition, 131
    exemplification, 99
speculative approach to literary analysis, 347–348
spelling
    computerized checking, 56
    confusing words, 411–416
    in editing, 56
    frequently misspelled words, 411
    hyphen as punctuation, 401
    skills improvement strategies, xxvi
    spell-checkers, 56, 416
    tips for, 408–412
struggle in narratives, 11
subject by subject pattern of organization, 252–254, 282–283
subjective case pronouns, 387
subject selection, 190
subjects (of sentences)
    alternative and verb agreement, 382
    compound, 381

defined, 7, 363
    objects of prepositions versus, 363, 381
    simple, 363
    verb agreement, 381–383
subject-verb agreement, 381–383
subordinate clause. *See* dependent clause
subordinating conjunctions, 360, 366, 373; *See also* conjunctions
subordinating words, 372
summary
    in conclusion, 16
    reading-related writing, 93
    single-source writing, 76–77
    synthesis as, 82
    in two-part response, 80
sums of money and verb agreement, 383
support
    conclusion as, 16
    evaluating in revision, 52–54
    patterns of organization, 11–12, 23
support paragraphs
    in essays, 15–16
    purpose, 6
symbolism in literature, 320
synonyms in definitions, 125, 127–128
synthesis of multiple-sources, 82–83, 93

technical writing. *See* process analysis
technology use in writing
    skills improvement strategies, xxvi, xxvii
    spell-checkers, 56, 416
    time savings form, 43
textbook and MLA style for citing, 75
theme in literature, 321, 347
these, those, 356
thesis. *See also* controlling idea
    in cause and effect analysis, 286
    conclusion by restatement, 16
    defined, 7
    effective versus ineffective, 7–8, 22
    example, 35
    origin of, 7, 34
    supporting forms, 11–12
third person objective perspective, 321
third person omniscient perspective, 321
third person perspective in literature, 321; *See also* point of view
this, that, 356

time pattern of organization
    analysis by division, 163
    causes and effects, 287
    coherence and, 46
    comparison and contrast, 253
    definition, 131
    exemplification, 99
    process analysis, 221, 222
titles
    capitalization, 402
    verb agreement with, 383
tone in language, 48–49, 285
topic outline, 35
topic selection, 28
topics for literary analysis, 347–350
transitional terms
    coherence established with, 46, 222, 248, 253
    in revision, 46
transition paragraphs, 6
treatment defined, 7
two-part response, 80, 93

underlining in reading, 67–71, 92
unity, elements of, 50–51
usage of language, 47–48, 49, 391–392

verbal phrase, 372
verbals versus verbs, 364
verb(s)
    action, 356, 363
    active voice, 385–386
    adverbs versus, 364
    being, 356, 363
    compound, 364
    confusing pairs, 379
    defined, 356–357, 363
    helping, 356–357
    inversions, 381
    modified by adverbs, 358
    parallelism and, 395
    passive voice, 385–386
    pronoun agreement and, 382
    subject agreement, 381–383
    verbals versus, 364
verb tense(s)
    consistency in, 379, 419

    defined, 356
    irregular verbs and, 377–378
    for literary analysis, 341
    regular verbs and, 377
    trouble spots, 418, 419
    types, 375–376
video/film and capitalization of titles, 402
viewpoint. *See* point of view
vocabulary improvement strategies, xxvi

word choice. *See* diction
word processor. *See* computer use
words
    confusing, 379, 411–416
    hyphenated, 401
    precision and communication, 391
Works Cited, 74
writing process
    audience, 44
    defined, 25
    editing, 56–57
    first draft, 43–44
    guidelines, 64–65
    prewriting strategies, 26, 28–41
    revision in, 45–56
    skills improvement strategies, xxvi
Writing Process Worksheet, xxvi, 25–26, 27
    for literary analysis, 342–345

Correction Chart

The numbers following the entries refer to the pages on which the items are discussed. See Index for more specific references. Enter different marks used by your instructor.

awk	awkward phrasing 61	org	organization 39
adj	adjective error 494	‖	parallelism 503
adv	adverb error 499	( )	parentheses 509
ˀ	apostrophe 509	pa agr	pronoun-antecedent agreement 495
b spe	be specific 54	case	pronoun case 495
cap or ≡	capitalize 510	pp sw	pronoun-person switch 495
coh	coherence 49	ref	pronoun reference 495
:	colon 508	p	punctuation 505
ˏ	comma 506	" "	quotation marks 507
cs	comma splice 60, 481	ro	run-on 60
dm	dangling modifier 494	;	semicolon 507
—	dash 508	lsv	lacking sentence variety 58, 473
⸺	delete 61	sp	spelling 516
dev	needs development 15, 56	sv agr	subject-verb agreement 489
ex	needs example(s) 166	lts	lacking topic sentence 19
frag	fragment 59, 480	∼	transpose 64
=	hyphen 509	vt	verb tense 483
∧	insert 61	t sw	verb-tense switch 487
lc or /	lowercase (no capital letters) 510	v sw	voice switch 493
mm	misplaced modifier 494	w	wordiness 61
no ¶	no paragraph 19	wc	word choice (diction) 51
nts	no thesis sentence 11, 38		
¶	new paragraph 19		